a special gift

presented to:

_____

from:

_____

date:

_____

The Women's Devotional Series

COVERED
and *Carried*

Carolyn Rathbun Sutton
EDITOR

Pacific Press®
Publishing Association
Nampa, Idaho | www.pacificpress.com

About the Editor

Carolyn Rathbun Sutton
finds great joy in being there
for other women, especially those
struggling to find renewed purpose
after a major life setback. She
particularly enjoys helping women
share their own personal stories of
God's faithfulness.

Dear Reader,

The North American Division (NAD) Women's Ministries team welcomes you to the 2022 edition of the women's devotional book. We are pleased and grateful that all proceeds from the sale of the book in the NAD will be used exclusively for scholarships in our territory.

We are praying that you will be blessed this year as you read devotionals from women like you—real women with real stories of God's love and providence in their lives. We look forward to hearing from you, and we hope that you will be inspired to submit your own stories to share with others.

Erica Jones joined the Women's Ministries Department in 2014. She didn't come far, having grown up and lived all her life just a few miles from our headquarters in Columbia, Maryland. Her background in youth ministry has given her a heart for teens and their struggles. Combined with her media experience, it was easy for her to find her ministry niche in our department—teen girls and social media. Erica lives with her four-legged children: Boots the cat, and Maisy the miniature shepherd mix.

Women Helping Women

There is an aspect of this book that is unique

None of the contributors have been paid—each has shared freely so that all profits may go to scholarships for women. Recipients of the Women's Ministries scholarships are talented women who are committed to serving the mission of the Seventh-day Adventist Church.

General Conference Women's Ministries scholarship fund in the North American Division

All profits from sales of the Women's Ministries devotional book in the North American Division support women's higher education in Seventh-day Adventist colleges and universities in the United States and Canada.

Purpose of the women's devotional book

Among Friends, published in 1992, was the first annual women's devotional book. Since then, the proceeds from these devotional books have funded scholarships for Adventist women seeking to obtain higher education. But as tuition costs have soared in North America and more women have applied for assistance, funding has not kept pace with the need. Many worthy women who apply must be turned down.

Recognizing the importance of educating women—to build stronger families, stronger communities, and a stronger church—each of us can help. Together we can change lives!

There are many ways to support our sisters

- Pray for women worldwide who are struggling to get an education.
- Tell others about the Women's Ministries scholarship program.
- Write for the women's devotional book (guidelines are available).
- Support women's education with a financial gift or a pledge.

To make a gift or receive materials, send us the following information:

Name _____

Street _____

City _____ State/Province _____

Postal Code_____ Country _____

Email_____

To contact us:

Women's Ministries Department
9705 Patuxent Woods Drive
Columbia, MD 21046

Phone: 443-391-7265
Email: ericajones@nadadventist.org
Website: https://www.nadwm.org/

The scholarship application and devotional book writers' guidelines are available at our website.

A New Heart and a New Spirit

"And I will give you a new heart, and a new spirit I will put within you. And I will remove the heart of stone from your flesh and give you a heart of flesh. And I will put my Spirit within you, and cause you to walk in my statutes and be careful to obey my rules. . . . You shall be my people, and I will be your God."
—Ezekiel 36:26–28, ESV

Recently, as I was studying Hebrews 8, I asked myself the following questions: *What does this text say about God? What does this text say about me? And what does this text say about my walk with God?* Then one sentence caught my attention: "I will put my laws into their mind, and write them in their hearts: and I will be to them a God, and they shall be to me a people" (Hebrews 8:10, KJV). I was reminded about a text that I teach regarding the gospel—today's theme text—Ezekiel 36:26–28. As I paused to comprehend the meaning of these verses, the reality of *no sin* came into focus: "I [God] will remember their [my] sins no more" (Hebrews 8:12, ESV).

The new heart and new spirit are the work of, and a gift from, the Holy Spirit when we say yes to Jesus. This newness isn't something I work for or strive to become. When I choose to believe today, God does *all* the work on my new heart and spirit that He places within me. That is the reason God can say, "I will remember [your] sins no more." Because of the shed blood of Jesus Christ, He took the sin for me, and I am without sin from the moment I believe.

But I live as a sinner, a sinful woman, because of my birth. Yet it is the blood of Jesus Christ who died on the cross that gives Him the right to gift us with the new heart and spirit that is only from the Holy Spirit (Ezekiel 36:22–28). And He promises to be our God. Oh, my dear sisters, when you and I choose Jesus, He claims us as His daughters—daughters of the King—with the new hearts and spirits He has placed within us.

As we begin this new year, may we grasp the meaning of these texts. I have chosen Him to be my God because He chose me first. Now, in newness of life, by the grace of the cross, I can live a triumphant life, daily in His presence. I challenge you to study prayerfully and meditate on these promises. In Him, we can live fuller, freer lives. Savor your relationship with Jesus Christ as you watch Him show up and show off His glory through your new heart and new spirit.

Mary H. Maxson

A Resolution Kept

Then shalt thou call, and the LORD shall answer;
thou shalt cry, and he shall say, Here I am.
—Isaiah 58:9, KJV

I understand that January comes around every year, so why does it always creep up on me? Somehow, though, I manage to make at least two New Year's resolutions, which I promptly forget. Last year I was a little more determined to do this thing right. As I packed away my Christmas decorations, I asked the Lord to give me a resolution that would bring honor to His name and make it last all year.

Through the years, my Nativity scenes have downsized from life-size figures on the lawn to small porcelain figurines on a table. Whatever their size, though, they are a reminder of the love of God and of what I want to be—someone who trusts in God and who will be the best listener, obedient to Him as He reveals Himself to me. As I carefully placed each fragile figurine back in its place in the Styrofoam liner, a thought occurred to me. *Lord, I believe it would bring honor to Your name if I, too, could "fit in" in the life You want for me this year—in my home, in the community, and in my precious church. Would You show me how and give me extra strength to do what You want?*

Being involved in our church's community services for several years has given me insight into the problems of many poverty-stricken families in our community. My steps have slowed some since I turned seventy-two a few months ago, but I stay on call for these families and distribute many articles of clothing weekly. Recently, our church started a new venture called Hope for the Hungry. Immediately, I felt the Lord urging me to volunteer. I believe this was the answer to my resolution to "fit in." I thank Him, my forever Friend, for letting me be a part of this successful ministry, "fitting in" with great workers of God. Now many starry-eyed children are not as hungry anymore. Our Hope for the Hungry has expanded to include an Angel Tree this year, providing gifts and toys for the children, new clothing, and Bibles.

No matter who you are, you can "fit in" in this world and spread joy, making an impact on children for the rest of their lives. Pray for me and my commitments this year. May we all do our part to spread the word—Jesus is coming to end hunger forever!

Jane Wiggins Moore

What God Wants for the New Year
PART 1

He has shown you, O mortal, what is good.
And what does the LORD require of you?
To act justly and to love mercy
and to walk humbly with your God.
—Micah 6:8, NIV

A question recently came to my mind: "What can I give to Jesus in this new year?" If I were going to give Jesus a gift, what could I give Him that He would appreciate? After all, He is the Creator of all things (Hebrews 1:2) and the One who holds all things together (Colossians 1:17). So what do you give Someone who not only *has* everything but actually *made* everything? That's a tough question, yet there had to be something I could give Him that would bring a smile to His face and would bring Him joy.

There *is* something! I discovered it in the little book of Micah. In his day, Micah wrote to a world facing huge problems. He not only pointed out the rampant sin and hypocrisy among God's people but also, in no uncertain terms, warned them of judgment to come.

Dropped into this severe message from God, however, Micah included a delightful passage. Although it is only three verses long (see today's theme text), it tells us exactly what God wants from you and me in this new year.

"Shall I come before him with burnt offerings, with calves a year old?" (Micah 6:6, NIV). Does God want a *quantity* of sacrifice? The answer is no!

"Will the LORD be pleased with thousands of rams, with ten thousand rivers of oil?" (verse 7, NIV). Does God want only a *quality* of sacrifice? Again, the answer is no!

"Shall I offer my firstborn for my transgression, the fruit of my body for the sin of my soul?" (verse 7, NIV). Is God asking me for the *ultimate* sacrifice? The answer is no.

What God desires to receive from us comes from a place that is very accessible yet very personal. And it has everything to do with our hearts.

Premila Pedapudi

What God Wants for the New Year
PART 2

He answered, " 'Love the LORD your God with all your heart and with all your soul and with all your strength and with all your mind'; and, 'Love your neighbor as yourself.' "
—Luke 10:27, NIV

It's so typical of us to offer big sacrifices to God: "Lord, I'll do anything You want. You name Your price. You want a missionary? I'm ready to go. You want me to be married or stay single? Just let me know. I'll be a preacher, a pastor, a deacon, or an elder. I'll pray every day and read my Bible. Whatever You want from me, that's what I'll do. I really mean it, Lord!"

Now there's nothing wrong with these sentiments. They are good and noble and proper. God is pleased when we offer ourselves to Him. So what's wrong with these offers? They deal only with things we would *do*. But, dear friend, God wants your heart. You can be a missionary and still have a hard heart. You can be married or single and still have a rebellious heart. You can be very religious yet far away from God.

So what *does* God want from us this year? The answer is found in Micah 6:8, which some consider to be the greatest verse in all the Old Testament. This verse sums up what God really wants from you and me. (This is a verse we need to commit to memory, write out on a card, and put on our mirrors so we can read it every day.)

> He has shown you, O man, what is good;
> And what does the LORD require of you
> But to do justly,
> To love mercy,
> And to walk humbly with your God? (NKJV).

What God wants from us every day is justice, mercy, and humility. These are matters of the heart. Jesus Himself came to proclaim justice to the nations (Matthew 12:18), show mercy to "them that fear him" (Luke 1:50, KJV), and humble Himself by dying on the cross (Philippians 2:8).

What He asks of us, He first gave to us by establishing justice, showing mercy, and lifting up the humble. Amen. I pray that you and I are willing to give to Jesus from the heart.

Premila Pedapudi

The Peace of Christ

*"Go in peace, and may the God of Israel
grant you what you have asked of him."*
—1 Samuel 1:17, NIV

Hannah was sad, even tormented. At a time when women were valued according to the number of children they had, she was barren. To society, Hannah was worthless. In spite of her husband's sincere love for her, she was not happy, did not feel complete, and felt almost as if she were being punished. What a heavy burden she carried! To make matters worse, her husband, Elkanah, had a second wife, Peninnah, who had given birth to several children.

Every year Elkanah took his family to Shiloh to worship the Lord and present offerings. Peninnah brought her children and repeatedly pointed out that she had many while Hannah had none. Hannah watched her sadly. Because of her anguish, Hannah did not eat and often wept. She wanted to be a mother, but being childless was a situation over which she had no control.

One year when the family was at Shiloh to worship, Hannah knelt before God. Her offering was different from what she usually presented; this time she laid her wounded heart at the feet of the Most High. She prayed as never before, feeling weak and small in the face of such trouble. There, in the silence of the house of the Lord, she sought refuge for her weary soul. Her intense demonstration of prolonged, prayerful grief caught the attention of Eli, the high priest. He assumed she was drunk and gave her a stern rebuke. When Hannah explained the reason for her sadness, Eli quickly realized he had erred. She was not a vulgar woman but rather a daughter seeking comfort in the arms of her Father. Eli pronounced a blessing of peace over her. Hannah stood up a different woman. Now she was radiant, calm, and confident.

The following year Hannah did not go on the family trip to Shiloh. Instead, she stayed home to take care of her baby—Samuel, her son, who was God's answer to her prayers. Peace reigned in her heart, filling all the broken places.

The peace that Christ gives brings forgiveness, love, and hope. It brings the assurance of His presence with us in the midst of our struggles. We remember God's mercy and grace, demonstrated by the sacrifice of Jesus on the cross to redeem us—and to be our hope in any situation. The same peace that Hannah experienced helps to make *our* burdens easier to bear.

Sueli da Silva Pereira

Facing My Fear Mountains

If any of you lacks wisdom, you should ask God,
who gives generously to all without finding fault,
and it will be given to you.
—James 1:5, NIV

Fear gripped me recently, when after a seven-year break, I was back in the workforce full time, teaching college English. But it wasn't teaching that caused me to fear; it was technology. Some of my hairiest moments of the semester came while trying to create and share a variety of resources for my students. To be embarrassingly honest, these and other seemingly simple computer tasks had me in tears. Why? Suffice it to say, for me, technology is one of those "fear mountains" we all have. Instead of asking for help or doing research, we wring our hands in despair; we weep and declare, "I can't climb that mountain!" Oh, what wasted energy!

In the past, I have wasted so much good, solid energy that I could have used to put one foot in front of the other; I have used it to complain or cry. Although sometimes the mountain really *is* a mountain, and sometimes a good cry or therapy session (or several) is called for, in general, there are better uses for our restless energy than weeping and gnashing of teeth.*

The first and most important use of our energy is prayer. When we're gripped with fear, God is always an appropriate audience, and crying out to Him is *always* a good first response. A second good use of restless energy is research. Over the past year, I've watched research transform writing students from questioningly clueless to passionately informed. Research is not just a college skill; it is a life skill. One night, as I was wondering how to get refreshed quickly on APA format, my husband suggested, "Why don't you look it up on YouTube?" Brilliant. I did.

No matter what our fear mountains may be, knowing whom to ask is half the battle. We can start by asking God for wisdom; we can also ask Him to direct us to the right people or information. The second half of the battle is putting into practice what we learn. What is the first step you can take today to start scaling your own "fear mountains"?

Lindsey Gendke

---

* Here, I would make a distinction between "big" and "little" mountains (or traumas). My history with depression and its causes was a *big* mountain, and it took years to heal. My technology mountain is considerably smaller and will be much easier to remedy.

Choosing to Be Content

*Give thanks to the L*ORD*, for He is good,*
For His lovingkindness is everlasting.
—Psalm 136:1, NASB

This past week was a rough one. My mind wanted to focus on all the things I don't have instead of focusing on how blessed I am. I decided to attend the pity party I was throwing for myself—all week. Then the Friday morning devotional I received centered on choosing to be happy with what we have instead of focusing on what others have. I guess it shouldn't have surprised me that Friday night's reading, chosen by my daughter, was titled "Gratitude." By then, my complaining spirit had somewhat subsided, but God still knew that I needed to be reminded. The thing is, I know that when I start focusing on myself instead of God, my attitude is bound to change. But I chose to allow myself to remain in a more negative mood. Conversely, I know that had I tried harder to change my focus from myself to God, it wouldn't have taken all week. I knew I needed to ask for forgiveness. I also recognized how blessed I am, and I tried to keep that in focus, but even in that, I still found things to complain about.

Friends, are you going through something that is making you feel as if you don't have enough? I had to remind myself constantly that I needed to count my blessings more than focusing on what I don't have. When we focus on the negatives, I assure you, we will find plenty of negatives. But when we focus on the positives, those multiply too.

As I was reading the "Gratitude" devotional for my daughter and myself, I was tired and decided to read just the first page of scriptures. My daughter asked whether I had read all of them, and I answered honestly that I hadn't (I was ready to go to sleep). She suggested I read all of them. I think that was my needed reminder, for one of the texts was, "In every thing give thanks: for this is the will of God in Christ Jesus concerning you" (1 Thessalonians 5:18, KJV).

Dear Lord, we thank You for the reminder that we ought to be thankful in everything, no matter what we are facing. Lord, there are times that we can't see how our present difficult paths are being used to pave the way for the future, but You can see all things from the beginning to the end. I ask that You help us learn to give thanks in all circumstances, even the hard ones, because they ultimately help to build our characters.

Kaysian C. Gordon

Who Will Go?

"Therefore go and make disciples of all nations, baptizing them in the name of the
Father and of the Son and of the Holy Spirit, and teaching them to obey everything I
have commanded you. And surely I am with you always, to the very end of the age."
—Matthew 28:19, 20, NIV

Since retirement allowed my husband and me much more flexibility, positive reports from friends inspired us to try short-term mission service. We have been active in our local church for many years, but our newly flexible time made short-term mission work appealing.

Our research revealed a building project in Modesto, California. No special skills were required, so we signed up. That experience left us with happy memories and a desire for more involvement. We were hooked! This became the first of many fulfilling projects, both in the United States of America and abroad, including building churches, schools, and an evangelism center. Despite my lack of building skills, joining the food preparation and cleanup crew, helping keep the work area free of potential hazards, aiding the electrician in stringing wire, and assisting with concrete work kept me involved.

Our mission service took us to several states in the United States, Norway, and Jamaica. After my husband's death, I accompanied my grandchildren on mission trips to Honduras and Venezuela and my sister-in-law to Peru, adding to my happy memories. Just the gratitude of the people for each project was pay enough.

When I remarried, my husband and I continued short-term mission service, which included a new experience for me. Off to Bolivia we went to do evangelism by *preaching* a series of sermons through an interpreter in Santa Cruz. What a privilege to be part of this outreach and see souls give their hearts to Jesus! My latest thrill was being part of two volunteer teams that built the church where I am a member. Finding no one else to cook meals for the second small team of fifteen, I volunteered to be responsible for three meals daily for fourteen days—something I had never done before. What a challenge, but by God's grace and the help of three of the volunteers, we met the need.

Every child of God needs to be a missionary one way or another. Age or lack of skills doesn't need to stop you because missionary work includes many kinds of outreach. God has a plan for each of us, so prayerfully seek His plan for you. When open to His leading, you may be amazed at what you find yourself doing and where He may lead you.

Marian M. Hart-Gay

Let's Keep Our Eyes on Jesus!

Do you not know that in a race all the runners run, but only one receives the prize?
So run that you may obtain it. Every athlete exercises self-control in all things.
They do it to receive a perishable wreath, but we an imperishable.
—1 Corinthians 9:24, 25, ESV

Recently, my husband and I had the opportunity to watch our grandson, Nikolas, compete in a track and field championship in California. It was an exciting and memorable experience. We traveled a long distance to attend this event as well as his graduation from high school. Nikolas practiced hard daily because he wanted to win. On the day of the competition, we arrived early to secure seats that would give us a good view. We wanted to position ourselves to see him and cheer him on. Twenty-three high schools competed that day, so the stadium was packed with spectators.

Before it was time for Nikolas's group to compete, we watched many of the races and witnessed the exuberance of victory and the agony of defeat. As athletes walked by to position themselves for some of the races, spectators called out their names and cheered them on. Surprisingly, the competitors kept their focus straight ahead. No one turned around to wave, and no one stopped to acknowledge their family. In our heavenly race, we, too, have to stay focused, with our eyes fixed on Jesus.

In two of the three races in which Nikolas competed, he came in first. It was a thrilling moment to watch him run. We were extremely proud of him. In one of the races, a young man collapsed at the finish line. As he lay on the ground, a man walked over and extended his hand, pulled him up, then put his hand on his shoulder as they walked away. Another runner kicked over the first hurdle and fell, injuring his leg. After some time, he got up and limped away, unable to complete the race. Painful moans came from spectators.

As Christians, we, too, are in a race. Sometimes life's problems will knock us down, or we may stumble and fall, but Jesus, our loving Savior, is always waiting with outstretched arms to lift us up and give us the strength to keep on going. We must always rely on His power to help us make it to the finish line. Fellow traveler, as we continue the race of life, let's keep our eyes on Jesus as we "run with endurance the race that is set before us" (Hebrews 12:1, ESV).

Shirley C. Iheanacho

The Lockbox

And we know that all things work together for good to those who love God,
to those who are the called according to His purpose.
—Romans 8:28, NKJV

We had just purchased a new home, and I was on my way to measure the windows for drapes and curtains. My mother was with me, and I was excited to show our new home to her.

When we drove into the driveway, I noticed there was a lockbox on the front door and furniture in the living room!

There must be some mistake, I thought. A call was made to my real estate agent, who discovered that he had shown us a rental house that never had been for sale. In addition, he had processed the wrong paperwork. We were actually purchasing another house at a different address—one that we had never viewed!

The real estate agent did everything in his power to make things right for us. He tried to show us the other house. Just by a simple glance, we knew that it was definitely not our style nor would it be our choice. Our earnest money was forfeited. Our previous home had been sold weeks earlier and would be occupied within eight days.

Where do we go from here?

The Bible tells us that "all things work together for good to those who love God, to those who are the called according to His purpose."

Needless to say, we were in a panic and wondered how to proceed. As we prayed, we were impressed to drive a few miles farther down the street to a separate subdivision. There we saw several houses for sale. One of them caught our eye.

You see, the previous home had a lovely park behind it, and so did this one! The park was right out the back door, and our kids would love to have such easy access to it. We contacted the agent selling the home and were able to purchase it. The buyers of our previous home were willing to extend their move to accommodate our needs. We love our new home!

Even though unforeseen circumstances occur in our lives, we can be assured that the Lord is right there with us. He cares about the things that are important to us. He will never leave us stranded (or "homeless").

Karen M. Phillips

Deferred Hope

Hope deferred makes the heart sick,
but a longing fulfilled is a tree of life.
—Proverbs 13:12, NIV

For many of us, the youthful years of life are years filled with vibrance, vitality, and big dreams. We hope to be healthy, financially stable, and happy adults who have great careers and travel the world. To sum it all up, we have big dreams that we hope one day will come to fruition. And then life happens. Perhaps we hit roadblocks that send us hurtling into ditches of dismay and depression. We might become discouraged, deflated, and sometimes, even dejected as a result of our unfulfilled dreams. Our hearts wonder whether the day will come when we can finally celebrate the fulfillment of our dreams.

The answer to our wondering hearts can be found in the book of Proverbs. Solomon tells us that we sometimes experience pain and discomfort when we have unfulfilled desires. But when our dreams are fulfilled, our lives become renewed, and springs of life well up within us.

What have you been hoping for? Do you still hope to finish that college degree or find a good husband? Have you hoped to find a new ministry or add children to your home? Are you longing to go on a mission trip or serve as a full-time missionary overseas? Whatever your hopes and dreams may have been, do not let them die. Unearth them, dust them off, nurture them, pray over them, and then kindle a fire of faith beneath them. Weeks, months, or even years might have passed without a flicker of fulfillment in sight. But maybe God has been testing your faith or reliance on Him to fulfill that dream. Remember, God's time for delivering us from a situation may not be the time when we expect the deliverance.

Luke 1:37 reminds us that nothing is impossible for God to do. Your aspirations may seem like high, insurmountable mountains, but our God can move mountains. They might seem like Goliath-size giants, but God has the perfect size stones to slay those giants. So run the race of perseverance, seek God's face, ask Him to direct your path, and then watch Him fulfill your dreams in a far greater way than you imagined.

Taniesha K. Robertson-Brown

God Is Listening

For where two or three are gathered together in my name,
there am I in the midst of them.
—Matthew 18:20, KJV

My prayer partner, Angella, and I were finishing a call on a Tuesday when she asked whether Dale, an old friend we'd lost touch with, still lived nearby. I replied that I didn't know, as I had not seen her for years. Angella commented that she and Dale were close, but they had lost touch.

On Thursday, as I was leaving the gym, my daughter texted, asking me to pick up some storage baskets for her. First, I ran a few errands and found everything else I needed except for an eyebrow pencil, which was not in stock. I decided to go to Walmart because we had gotten baskets there before. My search was successful. With baskets in hand, I headed to the cash register. Suddenly, I recalled that I needed an eyebrow pencil, so I made a beeline to the cosmetics section.

As I approached the area, I noticed a woman stooped down low, looking at something on the bottom shelf. I said to the woman, "It looks like you could use a hand getting up." At that moment, she stood up and gave me a big grin and a hug. You guessed it: it was Dale. In my excitement, I shared the conversation I'd had with Angella two days prior. I immediately retrieved my cell phone from my purse and called Angella.

When she answered, I handed the phone to Dale. I could hear Angella screaming with excitement over the phone. They talked for a few minutes and exchanged phone numbers. I stood in awe of God.

It occurred to me that we had not prayed for Angella to find Dale. It was merely a comment in passing, or so I thought. The Bible tells us that God does not sleep nor slumber and that He is ever present, willing to grant us the desires of our hearts (Psalms 141:4; 46:1; 37:4). At the end of our daily prayer session, we usually ask God to "help us be a blessing to someone today," and we go through the day not knowing who, what, when, or how He will answer.

That day Angella was blessed to be reunited with Dale, and I was overjoyed that God used me to make it happen. Had I gone straight to the cash register, I would not have encountered Dale. I was reminded again that when we are impressed by the Holy Spirit to do something, we must follow through. God is waiting to bless us.

Sharon Long

If the Glass Seems Half Empty

And now, dear brothers and sisters, one final thing.
Fix your thoughts on what is true, and honorable,
and right, and pure, and lovely, and admirable.
Think about things that are excellent and worthy of praise.
—Philippians 4:8, NLT

If the glass seems half empty, remember that it is also half full.

Several years ago, while I was in the seminary, my roommate, Michaela, and I took our regular trip to the grocery store. Being a "self-supporting" grad school student, I knew that money was, well, tight. As such, nothing was ever wasted, especially food!

One day, as we loaded the car with our treasures, I accidentally dropped a carton of blueberries. All I could see was my tasty blueberries all over the parking lot.

There goes my serving of fresh fruit! I thought. I felt completely deflated. I could not afford to buy more. But then my roommate said something that would forever change the way I looked at life: "Tricia, look! You've still got a container full of blueberries left!"

For me, what Michaela said was revolutionary. I could choose how I perceived a situation. I could focus either on what's wrong—or on what's right. I could mourn over what's lost or be thankful for what's saved. I could lament a mistake or rejoice over an accomplishment. I choose how I see the world and my circumstances. What I choose to focus on will either help propel me forward or keep me locked up in despair.

During the course of my recovery from a recent medical issue, this lesson stuck with me. Yes, there were moments when my husband, Shawn, would have to gently pry me away from a frozen stare in the mirror as I unsuccessfully tried to dress my wounds, but a brief reminder—"my cup" was half full—always helped me to keep pushing forward.

I have been learning that what we think about or how we view a situation or circumstance truly impacts not only recovery but life. How crucial it is then to guard our thoughts. We ought to be selective about what we allow our minds to dwell on and be intentional about *how* we think about our circumstances.

So how have you been perceiving your situation lately? No matter what it is, God is *bigger*!

Tricia (Wynn) Payne

Crossing the Wawa Boom
PART 1

*"When you reach the edge of the Jordan's waters,
go and stand in the river."*
—Joshua 3:8, NIV

B eing a missionary had never crossed my mind while I was growing up. It is something I just kind of fell into. Now more than twenty years into mission service, this work has changed how I look at life. It has changed my heart! I have seen, firsthand, how God reaches down into remote areas that are forgotten by most of the world—areas that are filled with poverty, hunger, and disease. I am so thankful that He has allowed me to be involved in this precious work of His!

My husband and I work in the jungles of Nicaragua, helping to set up radio stations that broadcast the love, truth, and hope of Jesus into villages that are held captive by witchcraft and the practices of voodoo, which is a polytheistic religion that includes ancestor worship.

Recently, my husband and I traveled from Puerto Cabezas to Rosita. Two other mission team members were accompanying us on this trip, which is eighty-four miles (135 kilometers) one way, on unpaved roads. The purpose of our travels that day was to transport some radio equipment to a small church that had been working hard to start its own radio station. How excited the members were about being able to share Jesus across the airwaves—both with their own community and in the surrounding areas farther out! We traveled the first hour of our day's jaunt before arriving at the Wawa Boom River. The only way to cross this river is by ferry. The ferryboat operators provide this service from sunrise to nine o'clock at night. When dusk begins to fall before the nine o'clock–closing time, the operators have bright lights in place to help guide the boat across the river. But one never wants to arrive at the river *after* nine o'clock because this ferry crossing is in the middle of nowhere. Crossing on the ferry that day, we finally made it to Rosita and delivered the equipment. Immediately, the radio station went on the air. What an exciting day! How we rejoiced—until we arrived back at the now-deserted ferry landing at twenty-four minutes past nine o'clock. We were too late! The ferry was nowhere in sight, and we were on our own.

Today, if you are feeling alone on the banks of some wide, problem-filled river with no way, humanly speaking, to cross, then remember God's children at the Red Sea and the Jordan River. Remember that when they trusted Him, He made a way. He will for you too.

Diana Halverson

Crossing the Wawa Boom
PART 2

They saw Jesus approaching the boat, walking on the water; and they were frightened.
But he said to them, "It is I; don't be afraid." Then they were willing to take him into the
boat, and immediately the boat reached the shore where they were heading.
—John 6:19–21, NIV

There, at the closed ferry landing, we found ourselves in the dark Nicaraguan night. No lights. No hotel. Not even a person in sight. The ferry was somewhere on the other side of the Wawa Boom River. The shuttered windows of the small ferry office affirmed we were on our own for the night. "We may as well try to get as comfortable as possible," our driver said as he pulled up to the edge of the river and put our vehicle into park. "We're here until dawn. Or maybe later," he added ruefully. "It just started raining. That may swell the river, so it won't be safe to cross until later tomorrow." We didn't want to spend the night in the vehicle. We couldn't sleep with the windows down because of the mosquitoes. They carry dengue fever and malaria—from which I've suffered twice. We prayed together, asking God to help us get home. With the assurance that God was in control, we made ourselves as comfortable as possible in that closed, humidity-filled vehicle and fell asleep.

"Look!" The driver's excited exclamation suddenly awakened us. We'd been asleep for forty-five minutes. Blinking, I strained to see through the rain. Something loomed in front of our vehicle. It looked like a huge ghost ship but was, in actuality, the ferryboat! But it had no lights. No crew. No sound. One solitary man untied the rope at the top of the boat's ramp and motioned for us to drive onto the ferry. We advanced onto the dark vessel—the only vehicle aboard. From a distance, the man (or angel?) waved away our offer to pay him, keeping his hoodie over his eyes in the rain. We never did see his face. So, in silence, we crossed the Wawa Boom to the other side. Though I had two cameras beside me, in my amazement and wonder, I never thought to pick one up as we glided across the water. Looking back, I saw that the little office by which we'd parked earlier was still dark and shuttered. God (whom I know was with us on that ferry!) took us all the way home that night, and I slept in safety under my own mosquito net.

God cares so much for us. He wants us to trust that He is with us in our "boats," in our trials, even in the middle of nowhere! Tough times *with* Him always build our faith *in* Him!

Diana Halverson

Granny's Habit

The LORD is nigh unto all them that call upon him,
to all that call upon him in truth.
—Psalm 145:18, KJV

I always loved Granny's house. For many summers, my two little sisters and I spent a week at her house. We got to sleep in one old-fashioned double bed upstairs in the "middle room."

My mother's mother was a passionate gardener and kept colorful flowers in her front yard and backyard gardens. Downstairs, I enjoyed peeping through the glass panes of the double French doors into her dining room from the living room. Everything was neat and clean, replete with dishes and centerpieces, testifying to her competence as a former housekeeper. Granny had also been a professional hairdresser and sometimes treated my sisters and me to a press and curl.

Granny loved baseball. Her radio radiated the excitement of the sportscasters, whose voices were sometimes drowned out by her cheers for such baseball heroes as Jackie Robinson, Hank Aaron, or Willie Mays when any of their teams were playing. But her life had not always been happy. She had fled to Detroit, Michigan, from Georgia during the time social scientists now call the Great Migration of African Americans from the South, following the heartbreaking lynching of one of her male relatives.

Younger people have asked how these migrants survived the traumas they experienced. I know that one—Mattie Mae Peoples—had a habit that I must admit I have adopted now that I am in my seventies. Each morning the first thing I would hear from her bedroom was her cry, "Lord Jesus!" or "Lord, have mercy!" as she woke up. Now I, too, find I cannot get the strength I need to arise or collect my thoughts until I verbally greet my Savior.

I value Granny's connection with the real and living God. Everyone should have such a role model. *Thank You, Lord, for mine.*

Elinor Harvin Burks

Why the Caged Bird Sings

You are my strength, I sing praise to you;
you, God, are my fortress, my God on whom I can rely.
—Psalm 59:17, NIV

Two eminent African American poets of the twentieth century, Paul Laurence Dunbar and Maya Angelou, both explored the metaphor of why the caged bird sings. They have some interesting things to say, certainly worth reading. But I'm going to share what my time in the crux of life's dark crucibles has taught me about why the caged bird sings.

First, singing is in its nature. A bird was made to sing, but in the cage, it faces a choice: to surrender to circumstances or embrace life. The caged bird that sings does so despite its circumstances—or maybe even more so because of them. The song emanates from a refusal to die.

Second, the bird knows its voice is heard. No matter how dark the situation, Someone hears. A heart of love receives the notes. Why wouldn't the caged bird sing when the song connects it to the Source by which it is sustained?

Third, the sound may fall on other ears that need to hear its voice, singing into and against the darkness.

There seem to be plenty of reasons not to sing nowadays, with the stakes growing higher each day. Our little planet is being rocked with major changes and challenges regarding weather, war, natural disasters, crime, and terrorism. Our global community is struggling with responding to displaced people. Human trafficking is at an all-time high. Our national politics are becoming increasingly polarized; rhetoric is filled with vitriol and hate. Even so, this is not the time for silence. It also is not the time for clamoring voices, rattling emotive reactions, and airing personal opinions. If you speak up, use your voice to make a difference, shed light in the darkness, and anchor those tossed and confused in the storm. Or listen to those who can do these things and work to understand the issues so you can speak intelligently and effectively when you are called upon. Let's not panic or stick our heads in the sand. Now is the time to buckle down, ground ourselves on a firm foundation, and develop our own authentic voices. It may be dark in this cage of a world, but I still have a song to sing, and I'm going to sing it. I just hope that it inspires you either to find your song or to set it free.

Rachel Williams-Smith

A Woman of Distinction

But a woman who fears the LORD, she shall be praised.
—Proverbs 31:30, NASB

She steps elegantly into the room, wearing the latest designer dress out of Paris—or is it New York? I'm not certain. Her hair is immaculately coiffed, and her diamonds sparkle under the glittering chandelier. Her perfume wafts through the air as she glides by. Surely this must be the most expensive perfume a woman could possibly wear! And look at her perfectly manicured nails and carefully applied makeup. Indeed, she stands out distinctly from the other women gathered in the room. She clearly presents herself as wealthy, beautiful, and unique—a cut above the rest! "Is she of nobility?" someone asks. "She's definitely not one of us!"

Someone else quietly whispers, "She certainly appears to be a woman of distinction."

When you think of a woman of distinction, what image is conjured up in your head? It wouldn't be a woman carrying a mop and pail. It wouldn't be a woman with three or four children tugging at her. It wouldn't be a woman toiling in a factory on a production line, a personal caregiver, a nurse, or even a doctor, necessarily. Would it be an office worker, nanny, teacher, or lawyer? No, it probably wouldn't be any of these. In our collective experience, the image of a woman of distinction would probably be someone who lives outside our own reality.

But real women of distinction are often overlooked by society. They often remain in the background, not seeking to attract attention to themselves or the work that they do. Often, they underestimate their impact on the lives of others and the members of their communities.

Many of you may be familiar with a program on a major television network that highlights, honors, and awards large sums of money to the charities and causes of individuals who are considered heroic. They are nominated for recognition by the national media. Tell me, who among us would not wish to be recognized and honored?

As Christian women, however, we are blessed and honored by our Creator, Lord, and Savior—Jesus Christ. In Proverbs 31, He shares His criteria for how He values our contributions to our families, churches, and communities. Why not take a few moments to reread and meditate on these words as a reminder of how valued we are in the sight of God?

Dear sisters, note the many ways God sees *you* as a woman of distinction!

Avis Mae Rodney

Just in Case . . .

Therefore be ye also ready:
for in such an hour as ye think not the Son of man cometh.
—Matthew 24:44, KJV

As I write this devotional, the world is in the midst of a pandemic that has affected more than 150 nations and caused the deaths of tens of thousands worldwide. Scores more are hospitalized and on ventilators—if they are available. In some areas, the sick are lying on mats in corridors in world-class hospitals because the beds are all full. Makeshift morgues are being erected to take the overflow of the dead, which are stacked up outside these morgues. World leaders, church leaders, physicians, nurses, and other health professionals are also succumbing to this pandemic caused by a coronavirus. This disease has crippled the global economy, grounded airplanes, stopped cruise ships, and canceled major events, such as the Olympic Games and even my denomination's global quinquennial conference session. It feels like the end of the world as millions are self-quarantining at home with shuttered playgrounds, beaches, parks, schools, and universities. In some places, curfews and armed guards enforce these mandates. As I write, feeling perfectly healthy, I realize that thousands of others who are dead or sick felt just as I did only one week ago.

So now, I have extra food and water in the house, just in case. I am keeping socially and physically distant, just in case. I have an arsenal of disinfectants and wipes at the entrance to my home, just in case. And I am building up my immune system, just in case.

This experience has made me wonder how ready I am for Christ's second coming. Am I as prepared for that event as I am for COVID-19? As I examine my life, I ask myself, *Have my sins been washed in the blood of the Lamb? Am I full of the fruit of the Spirit? Am I demonstrating love, joy, peace, long-suffering, goodness, meekness, and temperance? What have I done to lead others to Christ? Am I looking and longing for His return?*

I want to confidently declare that I am forgiven and clothed in the robe of Christ's righteousness, just in case. I have, by my life and influence, pointed out the way of salvation to others, just in case. Unworthy though I am, I pray that Christ will help me to be ready and stay ready to go home with Him, just in case.

Annette Walwyn Michael

The Missing Wallet

"Is anything too hard for the LORD?"
—Genesis 18:14, NKJV

Our worldwide church's sixtieth General Conference Session, held in San Antonio, Texas, United States of America, had drawn to a close. All who came from different countries and cities prepared to return home. We planned to drive from San Antonio early Sunday morning to reach Phoenix, Arizona, by that night and continue to California the next day so that we could be home by Monday evening.

Like everyone else, my husband, Abel, and I began packing our belongings. While Abel was loading the car, I looked for my wallet in my handbag. When I couldn't find it, I became anxious. *Why is it not in my handbag?* I wondered. *Did I use it during this past week?* I couldn't remember. My thoughts went elsewhere. Perhaps my husband had put it in his briefcase. Yet it wasn't there either. I looked again, but my wallet simply was not there. Then I remembered my stay in the hospital.

I called to Abel. "Where did you put my wallet when you went with me the night I was transported to the hospital by ambulance?"

"I put it in your handbag and slept over it in the hospital the night you were admitted."

I looked in my handbag again while he searched in his briefcase one more time. We looked everywhere, rechecking everything, but my wallet was nowhere to be found. I was alarmed because my bank cards, driver's license, Social Security card, and some cash were all in it. Worst-case scenarios were running through my mind. We bid farewell to our gracious host and hostess and left San Antonio, hoping that whoever had found my wallet would return it to me.

I prayed that when we arrived home, my wallet would have already been returned to me in a package when we picked up our mail at the post office. When we picked up our mail and there was no wallet, my heart sank. *Would it have been too hard, Lord, to help me find my wallet or help someone else find it and send it to me?* Before we began the tedious task of reporting the missing identity and bank cards, my husband looked once more through his briefcase. "Honey, it's here!" he said with a shaky voice. Five times we had looked through his briefcase. Two pairs of eyes and hands had carefully searched, finding nothing. Now God had answered our prayers. No, He had not answered immediately but rather at the right time—in His time. Nothing is too hard for the Lord.

Ofelia A. Pangan

A Flower in God's Garden

The grass withereth, the flower fadeth:
but the word of our God shall stand for ever.
—Isaiah 40:8, KJV

In Australia's capital city of Canberra, two magnificent flower shows are exhibited annually—one called Tulip Tops and the other, Floriade. I have had the privilege of visiting both displays, which left me marveling at the kaleidoscope of color and fragrance across such great expanses of acreage. Thousands upon thousands of seeds and bulbs were planted in such a way as to create designs with intertwined patterns of color and symmetry. Some flowers were tall, which stood out at a distance, but as I came closer, I could see the smaller varieties of flowers and ground cover popping up between the taller stems. Little pansies and daisies had their faces looking to the sun, showing how efficiently they, too, were doing their part to share in God's glory.

I imagine tending these plants is a full-time job for many people. There is not only the growing process but also the removal of all the dead growth when the plants have finished flowering. Then, I assume, the cycle starts all over again with the careful planning and preparation for the next colorful display.

A garden is a place where each plant is set in a location where it can thrive. Gardeners prepare the soil, protect each plant from pests, and make sure it receives the food, water, and sunlight it needs. The result is a beautiful, colorful, and fragrant place for people to enjoy.

I believe a garden is rich with symbols for how the church is intended to operate. Like a garden, a church is meant to be a place where everyone works together for the glory of God and the good of all—a place where everyone can grow because they are living in a safe environment of care and nurture. Each of us can take part in work that benefits others (Colossians 3:16, 17). Like well-tended plants, people growing in healthy environs have a sweet fragrance that draws others to God by displaying the beauty of His love.

God created a beautiful and perfect garden as Adam and Eve's home. It must have been so lovely, but sin destroyed it. In His love, God has left remnants of His creation for us to enjoy; they remind us of His great creative power. We know that God will renew this earth, and a beautiful garden will once again be a home for us, forever.

Lyn Welk-Sandy

"Send Me"

*Then I heard the voice of the L*ORD *saying,*
"Whom shall I send? And who will go for us?"
And I said, "Here am I. Send me!"
—Isaiah 6:8, NIV

How many times do we feel impure? Do we recognize that we are sinners? How often do we believe that what we have done is unforgivable?

The prophet Isaiah recounted a vision in which he saw the Lord lifted up high on a throne and surrounded by angels as His train filled the temple. The sound of His voice shook the foundations of the building. Before this spectacle, Isaiah was afraid because, in his words, "I am a man of unclean lips, and I live among a people of unclean lips, and my eyes have seen the King, the LORD Almighty" (Isaiah 6:5, NIV). Isaiah recognized that in his impurity, he was not adequate to stand before his Creator. But because of God's mercy, an angel took a live coal with tongs and approached the prophet.

I want to dwell on this detail. Why didn't the angel take up the live coal in his hand? Maybe for the simple, logical reason that the ember would burn. Yet the angel did touch the live coal to the lips of Isaiah. If someone is burned, it hurts. We all know that. That is why I find it striking that in verse 7, the angel says, "See, this has touched your lips; your guilt is taken away and your sin atoned for" (NIV). This makes me think of those painful situations in life that we do not understand—those times that "burn" yet help to purify and improve our characters, just as gold is refined when passing through fire. We see God's mercy toward us in allowing difficult times to help us grow in Him.

When we are purified through God's mercy and forgiveness, as was Isaiah, we can have certainty in accepting the call of God when He asks, "Whom shall I send? And who will go for us?" We can answer with total security, "Here am I. Send me!"

Cecilia Nanni

The Planner

Now to him who is able to do immeasurably more than all we ask or imagine,
according to his power that is at work within us.
—Ephesians 3:19, 20, NIV

The thing I found hard in the 2020 COVID-19 pandemic was the inability to plan ahead. I'm a planner! I plan how and when to do things so that I know what is going to happen next. But in this situation, it has often been hard to know what is going to happen the next day or even the next moment. This is difficult for me. I like to have some control. I just want a plan!

This morning I was reading in the book of Ephesians, which was written by Paul while he was a prisoner in Rome. Paul was a planner, used to working as his own boss, traveling, and doing as he felt led by the Lord, but now he was confined in prison. I'm guessing that at some point, he wondered what went wrong with his plan. But Paul learned the plan belongs to the Lord and revealed Him as the Planner: "In him [God] we were also chosen, having been predestined according to the plan of him who works out everything in conformity with the purpose of his will" (Ephesians 1:11, NIV). Did you catch that? God works out *everything* in conformity with His purpose according to His plan!

This reminds me of a favorite portion of Jeremiah 29: " 'For I know the plans I have for you,' declares the LORD, 'plans to prosper you and not to harm you, plans to give you hope and a future' " (verse 11, NIV). King David knew the Lord is a planner and wrote, "The Lord will work out his plans for my life" (Psalm 138:8, TLB). Notice the way the King James Version of the Bible puts it: "The LORD will perfect that which concerneth me."

Wherever you are right now, it may be hard to plan that which concerns you. It might be even harder to discern God's plan and purpose, but rest assured, He has a plan that concerns you, and He is working out everything according to His will. You can trust that God is "able to do immeasurably more than all we ask or imagine" (Ephesians 3:20, NIV).

Peter wrote, "Cast all your anxiety on him because he cares for you" (1 Peter 5:7, NIV). J. B. Phillips beautifully translates this verse: "For you are his personal concern." Don't hesitate to cast all your fears, anxieties, and worries on God. He is personally concerned about you.

Myrna L. Hanna

Choosing the Abundant Life

"I have come that they may have life,
and that they may have it more abundantly."
—John 10:10, NKJV

As an educator, I am always amazed at how students learn life lessons. I have been a teacher for almost fifteen years, and without fail, there is always that one student who makes a decision that is not in his or her best interest.

A few years ago, while working at a middle school, we had a student with behavior problems. No matter how many times he got into trouble, he just couldn't seem to learn his lesson. If he wasn't skipping class or smoking behind the school, he was fighting his classmates.

For a while, the student would get suspended at least once a week. After he was suspended for several weeks for a host of things, his mother accused the school of picking on her son. When the student got his tenth suspension, one of our male teachers decided to go to his home to talk to him. The teacher hoped to establish a relationship with the student and make a difference in this young man's life. But the young man refused to talk to the teacher, and his mother asked him to leave. The teacher was disappointed and hurt.

We often do the same thing to God. He continuously offers us salvation, yet we refuse to talk to Him. We run all day, and not once do we thank Him for our lives. We make decisions without asking for guidance. We refuse to accept His grace and mercy. We remain this way until something bad happens. Yet God says, "All who follow my ways are joyful" (Proverbs 8:32, NLT).

If we choose not to follow God's ways, we are choosing to live a life without joy.

During spring break, that same young man picked up a loaded gun to play with. Sadly, he accidentally shot himself in front of all his friends. While his life ended tragically, the young men who witnessed the accident were forever changed. I was changed. I remember going to his funeral and hearing his mother's words: "No one could save my son."

My prayer today is that we will not need a tragedy to learn that God wants to give us joy. I hope we learn to seek His face and trust His Word. He offers us life more abundantly, if we will simply ask. He loves us with an everlasting love. I pray each day that we choose life with God.

Paula Sanders Blackwell

Stuck in the Muck

You make springs gush forth in the valleys.
—Psalm 104:10, ESV

One of my summertime getaways is a tubing trip down a river with some lovely ladies from church. We find a house to rent for a few days, plan our meals, and pack our tubes. Then it's fun in the sun on the river. The current in this river will mostly carry us along. But sometimes we have to paddle to keep away from sticks and brush jutting out of the water. Other times, the wind is strong.

I discovered one year that getting out of my tube and walking with it was much easier than negotiating the sticks and brush. From then on, I have walked the river in those challenging places. I'll grab someone occasionally and tow them along with me. Sometimes we'll form a train and move swiftly down the river. I will stumble on a log or cluster of rocks on occasion, but all in all, I don't have trouble with walking—and it's great exercise!

Yet there are potential "traps" that go with walking the river. I have come across thick, mucky grasses and slimy weeds that tend to entangle my feet and ensnare me. This muck pulls me, and I can feel my water shoes slipping off as I sink into the squishy mud beneath the weeds. This muck tugs at me, though the current wants to carry me.

This makes me think of how the enemy of our souls also wants to ensnare us, pulling us down with him where he can drown us in temptation and sin. He wants us to lose our footing in Jesus and get stuck in the sludge. But there is something stronger than his mucky temptations! The powerful living water of the indwelling Christ will lift us above the enemy's temptations and carry us on clear, clean currents of truth and strength that are found in God's Word.

River springs bubble, gush, cleanse, and carry away impurity. Pure spring water quenches the thirst of the weary and tempted. God sets spiritual rivers and springs in the right places and seasons of our lives for the right reasons. Jesus said that those who believe in and rely on Him will experience—flowing from their *own* hearts—"rivers of living water" (John 7:38, ESV)!

When your life starts feeling like nothing but dusty hills, reflect on the refreshing springs that run between them. Then drink deeply of the living water found in the truth, comfort, and promises of God's Word. Let the currents carry you, and keep you from getting stuck in the muck.

Cyndi Woods

"How Near Is the End?"

"Blessed is the man who trusts in the LORD,
And whose hope is the LORD."
—Jeremiah 17:7, NKJV

My friend, Deborah, was involved with many activities, and one included attending some meetings about Bible prophecy that my husband was conducting in Texas. Her neighbor, a friend, was not pleased that they had not been able to get together. So Deborah invited Kathy to come with her to the meetings. The subject of the fourth meeting was "How Near Is the End?" At the conclusion of the meeting, attendees were asked to raise their hands if they wanted to accept Jesus and be ready for His return. Kathy, as well as many others, accepted the invitation.

On the way back to her apartment complex, Kathy was joyful that she had come with Deb and renewed her commitment to Christ. "I want to go back again tomorrow night," she told Deb. The next day Deborah called Kathy. No answer. Nor did Kathy come to the door when Deb stopped by to give her a ride to the meeting. On Friday evening, Deborah saw police cars at Kathy's building. Soon she learned that her friend had apparently died in her sleep sometime during the night following the meeting where she had just renewed her commitment to Christ.

At the memorial service, Deb shared with Kathy's family about her last few hours. She encouraged them to be ready to spend eternity with Jesus. After the service, a family member shared with me how much the family needed to hear about Kathy's final hours and decision.

We never know when our last breath will be taken, but Kathy's next view will be the face of Jesus! First Thessalonians 4:16, 17 reminds us that "the Lord himself shall descend from heaven with a shout, with the voice of the archangel, and with the trump of God: and the dead in Christ shall rise first: Then we which are alive and remain shall be caught up together with them in the clouds, to meet the Lord in the air: and so shall we ever be with the Lord" (KJV). May we take the opportunity each day to recommit our lives to Jesus.

No one knows the exact answer to the question of how near the end is. Yet David, speaking of God, left us with this reassurance and comfort: "You are my refuge and my shield; I have put my hope in your word" (Psalm 119:114, NIV).

Rita Kay Stevens

A Disciple of Jesus

Then spake Jesus again unto them, saying,
I am the light of the world.
—John 8:12, KJV

Levi Matthew was already feeling low most mornings, knowing that many people didn't have the tax money he needed to collect. It was that way every day. He didn't mind that they skulked around, trying to avoid him, or even that they called him despicable names, but when they truly couldn't pay, he felt a bit sorry for them. Maybe he should get into another line of work.

Then one day, Jesus came along. Matthew had heard of Him and His ministry. He knew of His interaction with the lower classes, but he never thought Jesus would actually enter his little world of tax collecting. He watched as Jesus came along the shoreline and drew closer. He stopped here and there along the path, tending to an animal or a child or just smiling at a passerby. Matthew turned away in shame. *Maybe Jesus knows how I make a living. Maybe He has seen or heard me cheating these poor people. Is that why He would come to see me, the hated tax collector? Maybe a reprimand? Maybe a new guy in town wanting my position?*

Then Matthew noticed that several men were walking in step with Jesus. *Now I remember! Jesus is making up His group of helpers, and maybe He wants me to join Him. Could it be? Is it really something I want to do? Is it something I can do?*

Jesus stopped beside Matthew and, looking straight into his eyes, said graciously, "Follow Me." Matthew, the greedy, dishonest tax collector, stepped out of the booth and joined Jesus, never once looking back or questioning. Now he was a disciple—a follower of his Friend Jesus! Never again would Matthew be ridiculed, falsely accused, or hated because of his work as a tax collector. And never again would he have to wonder what kind of Man this Jesus was. He was the Light of the world, and that meant Matthew would never again know darkness in his life.

Friend, isn't that the kind of experience you would like to have? Jesus calls you, and you answer, "Yes, Lord." You need Him; you need the love, the discipline, and the guidance He offers. You need the Light. And He promised, "He that followeth me shall not walk in darkness, but shall have the light of life" (John 8:12, KJV). Matthew made his decision, but what will *we* do when Jesus touches our hearts with love and compassion and says, "Follow Me"?

Carol Wiggins Gigante

Here Comes the Bride

The bride, a princess, looks glorious in her golden gown.
—Psalm 45:13, NLT

S ometimes when I have mindless work to do, such as ironing, I like to watch television. One of the shows I sometimes watch is *Say Yes to the Dress*. This program has brides in an upscale bridal salon select the dress of their dreams. They usually bring their mothers; bridesmaids; friends; fathers; occasionally their future mother-in-law; and, amazingly, even the groom. Not only does the bride have to love the dress, but it seems, so does her entourage. What amazes me is the money these brides are willing to spend—many thousands of dollars. I am told the most expensive dress was eighty thousand US dollars. And then sometimes they want a second dress for the reception! There seems to be no limit. There have been brides who need a special dress for a wedding underwater, on the beach, in a cathedral, or jumping from an airplane.

All this makes me so appreciate my daughter and daughter-in-law. I don't know what Gelerie's dress cost, as I was not involved in that, but I know she and my son are very money sensible. Our daughter, Rikki, picked out the fabric she wanted and had her dress made for much, much less than a thousand dollars. Her wedding was on New Year's Day, so she was able to use the church's Christmas tree lights for decorations. Since she doesn't like cake, they served cinnamon rolls and hot chocolate for their reception, and everyone loved it.

The Bible has several wedding stories, but the most important one is that which is coming soon. I have read that in the culture of Bible times, the bridegroom and bride are betrothed (engaged to be married), but then he leaves to build a home. The bride stays home with her mom and dad. When the home is ready, he comes to get her, and the wedding takes place. You see this happening in the story of the ten virgins (Matthew 25:1–13).

Our Bridegroom has gone to prepare a home for us and is coming soon to collect His bride—us! "Let us rejoice and be glad. . . . For the time has come for the wedding of the Lamb, and his bride has prepared herself for it" (Revelation 19:7, GNT).

Our dress for that wedding costs us nothing; Jesus, the Bridegroom Himself, paid it all. "God saved you by his grace when you believed. And you can't take credit for this; it is a gift from God" (Ephesians 2:8, NLT).

Ardis Dick Stenbakken

January 29

Making It Plain

And we know that in all things God works for the good of those
who love him, who have been called according to his purpose.
—Romans 8:28, NIV

Our daughter Lisa was excitedly expecting her first baby, but when the pregnancy ended in a miscarriage, she was very disappointed. The doctor caring for her noticed her thyroid seemed enlarged and suggested she get it checked. She did. The enlargement was due to cancer and had even spread to some lymph nodes. Had she not seen the doctor who treated her for the miscarriage and discovered the enlarged thyroid, things might have turned out very differently. That was a number of years ago. Now, with her good health and four children, she can look back and see that the bad miscarriage worked for her good by allowing the cancer to be found.

My pastor husband had received a call to pastor a district in southern Louisiana. Being very busily involved with all that goes into making a long-distance move, we had paid little attention to the news. So we drove to Slidell, Louisiana, one Sunday to house hunt and arrived just in time to watch the town prepare for Hurricane Andrew. At first, we were upset at the delay, but while the town prepared for the hurricane, we had time to drive the streets of Slidell. We found a house for sale at a slightly higher elevation, away from streams, and close to the church.

After the hurricane passed, we bought the house. Several years later, Slidell received nearly thirty inches (seventy-six centimeters) of rain in two days. The majority of Slidell was flooded, and even though we were surrounded by water, our home remained dry. Had it not been for Hurricane Andrew giving us time to drive the streets of Slidell and discover higher ground, we might have been flooded too. We still look back on that time when God took something bad and turned it into a blessing for us.

My favorite Bible story is the story of Joseph in the Old Testament. In spite of suffering great sorrow and hardships because of what his brothers did (Genesis 37–45), Joseph was able to say to his brothers, "It was God who sent me here ahead of you to preserve your lives" (Genesis 45:5, NLT). We may never understand the reasons for many things that happen in this life, but as the old song says, "Someday He'll make it plain to me."* I look forward to that day.

Sharon Oster

---

* Lida S. Leech, "Someday He'll Make It Plain," 1911.

Almost Missed Out

And that, knowing the time, that now it is high time to awake out of sleep: for now is our salvation nearer than when we believed. The night is far spent, the day is at hand: let us therefore cast off the works of darkness, and let us put on the armour of light.
—Romans 13:11, 12, KJV

My daughter, Keziah, and I were going to Margarita Island, which is northeast of Venezuela. We would be part of a school trip for the Form 5 Spanish students. Having not been overseas in a while, I really wanted to go. I had known for some time that my passport had expired. I would not only need to renew it but also get a new machine-readable passport. Yet I had put off doing so. *I'm not going anywhere*, I had thought. *I have time*. But now it had to be done, so I gathered all my documents and filled out the forms. We made our way to the passport office, thinking the process would be a breeze. Unfortunately, it wasn't. I had to present my copy of my divorce decree. I could not find it, so I had to get a copy from my ex-husband. Then I had to get an affidavit stating that my name always had a hyphen. Then I had to get a second affidavit because the first one was worded incorrectly.

Three affidavits, two weeks, and nine hundred dollars later, I was told to come back on Monday morning to collect the passport. Yet Monday was the date of our departure! I felt very anxious. Though we arrived at the passport office at six o'clock in the morning, we still had a long wait. I watched the hours, minutes, and seconds tick away, wondering whether we would get through in time. Many prayers went up to join the ones that had been offered since this ordeal had started. Finally, around ten o'clock, my name was called, and I received my passport. We walked briskly to the car and then drove to the airport, arriving just as the other trip members were checking in. We boarded the plane and were able to enjoy our week in Margarita with the others.

Throughout this experience, I was reminded of the times in which we live. Right now, we are preparing for our heavenly journey. It may seem as though we have all the time in the world to get that spiritual passport, but the truth is, we don't. The only time we have is now. Today. I almost missed out on the opportunity to fly with my daughter because I had procrastinated. What if my delay had concerned my salvation?

Will I be ready for the close of my probation? Will you be ready for yours?

Greta Michelle Joachim-Fox-Dyett

The Sad Verse!

The LORD God made clothes from animal skins
for the man and his wife and dressed them.
—Genesis 3:21, GW

Genesis 3:21 is one of the saddest verses in the Bible. Can you imagine how God must have felt when He killed innocent creatures in order to clothe His human children? He had created all these beautiful, gentle creatures and now ends their lives because of Adam and Eve's sin. That must have hurt.

I know it hurts us when we must put a beloved pet to sleep because of illness or old age that would continue to make the pet's life miserable. Yet God was willing to suffer hurt in His own heart to help Adam and Eve be clothed after they sinned.

So what were they wearing before sin? Genesis 2:25 says, "The man and his wife were both naked, but they weren't ashamed of it" (GW).

One author shares that "the sinless pair wore no artificial garments; they were clothed with a covering of light and glory, such as the angels wear. So long as they lived in obedience to God, this robe of light continued to enshroud them."[*]

In another book, the same author elaborates: "A beautiful soft light, the light of God, enshrouded the holy pair. This robe of light was a symbol of their spiritual garments of heavenly innocence. Had they remained true to God it would ever have continued to enshroud them. But when sin entered, they severed their connection with God, and the light that had encircled them departed. Naked and ashamed, they tried to supply the place of the heavenly garments by sewing together fig leaves for a covering."[†]

We begin to see the pain that our sins have caused God. How grateful are we that He cares so much for each one of us? Here we are, about six thousand years since Creation and the entrance of sin, and so much of God's creation has been used to clothe and sustain us. We look forward to the day Jesus returns when we will have that beautiful robe of light to wear, and eternal life will be given to us. No more animals will be sacrificed to clothe us. No more flora will die because of sin. No more "sad verses" will have to be written. Now *that* will be a time to celebrate!

Peggy Curtice Harris

---

[*] Ellen G. White, *Patriarchs and Prophets* (Nampa, ID: Pacific Press®, 2005), 45.
[†] Ellen G. White, *Christ's Object Lessons* (Battle Creek, MI: Review and Herald®, 1900), 310, 311.

Anxious for Nothing

*Be anxious for nothing, but in everything by prayer and supplication, with
thanksgiving, let your requests be made known to God; and the peace of God, which
surpasses all understanding, will guard your hearts and minds through Christ Jesus.*
—Philippians 4:6, 7, NKJV

Be anxious for nothing—not your kids, your marriage, your job, your weight, your finances, or your friendships. A pretty tough challenge from Paul, isn't it? Especially in a world where anxiety, fear, and worry are on the rise. We pray about the things or people that we're worried about but still walk away feeling anxious. Where's that promised, unsurpassed peace?

First, Paul wrote, "Be anxious for nothing" in the present active tense. He wasn't telling us, "Don't worry, be happy." His challenge isn't to *never* be anxious but not to *live* in a state of anxiousness. Next, note the words Paul uses regarding how to achieve this: *prayer, supplication, thanksgiving,* and *requests.* Paul was telling us to do more than just take our requests to God. He's outlined a way to pray that will bring the peace that passes understanding.

Prayer. The word *prayer* evokes a sense of coming before God in reverence—worship. Begin your prayer time by just worshiping God, remembering who He is and what He has promised: He is God the Father, Ruler of the universe, and the Creator. He has a good plan, loves us with an everlasting love, and will never leave nor forsake us.

Supplication. *Supplication* is coming to God for our own hearts. Submitting ourselves to His will, not ours. It implies surrender and asking for His Spirit to fill us.

With thanksgiving. Before we even ask, we thank. God is not expecting us to be thankful *for* everything but *in* everything. Look for things for which you can be thankful. He loves your kids more than you do. He promises to never leave nor forsake us. He wants more for us than we can dream or imagine.

Requests. After remembering who God is through worship, submitting your heart, and thanking Him for His promises and faithfulness, then bring your requests to God. When we pray as Paul challenged us, our perspectives will change. We will be reminded that God is bigger than the battle. He is in control. God can handle it. He's not surprised or caught off guard. God can take the worst moments of our lives and turn them around, redeem them into something beautiful. And then the peace of God that passes all understanding will guard our hearts (our feelings) and our minds (our thinking) through Christ Jesus.

Tamyra Horst

"You Knew, and You Didn't Tell Me?"

How, then, can they call on the one they have not believed in?
And how can they believe in the one of whom they have not heard?
And how can they hear without someone preaching to them?
—Romans 10:14, NIV

There's nothing like betrayal to cause you to discard all trust you had in someone.

"You knew, and you didn't tell me?" I managed to battle the emotion that was surmounting like a tsunami flood. At this moment, I didn't care that "Felicity" and "Anita" were friends before I even came along. It was the fact that everything I thought I knew about my friendships was crumbling right before my eyes, and there was nothing I could do to stop it.

I'm sure it was difficult for Felicity because she was a friend to both of us, but I was hurting at this moment. I hurt because it felt like everyone kept secrets from me about Anita, who I thought was also close to me, and the person who once vowed before God that he would cherish me forever yet willfully abdicated that role. They were now engaged. But the hurt wasn't just because the couple got engaged; it was because they didn't see me as significant enough to inform—the friend code was broken.

It was much easier to forgive the couple for their seeming deception, but I thought that at least Felicity and I were closer than that. She had information she kept from me because she thought it wasn't her place to share it. Felicity thought that getting the information from the source was a better option for me. She thought that if she just stayed out of things, it wouldn't be a problem for her.

But it was.

Considering all those intense emotions got me thinking about our witness every day. If we keep our mouths shut about our Savior Jesus who will return someday, and a friend of ours recognizes that we knew He was returning but we didn't tell him or her, how awful would that be? How cruel would it be to have information that could prepare someone for a big change yet not share it? What if God said to someone, "I never knew you," all because we chose to let someone else be a mouthpiece for God instead of us?

Rachel Privette Jennings

Real Prayer

One . . . said to him,
"Lord, teach us to pray, just as John taught his disciples."
—Luke 11:1, NIV

I often ponder this question: What is real prayer? Is it praying for things, and when you get them, or not, you stop praying? The Bible tells me that Jacob wrestled with God and said, "I won't let go until you bless me" (see Genesis 32:26). Remember, Jacob was a sinner like we are; he cheated his brother out of his birthright. Yet when we, like Jacob, meet God, our lives will never be the same. We need to wrestle with God in prayer and never let go until He blesses us.

Prayer is not a strategy to get things from God or obtain blessings. Rather, it is the means of deepening an intimate relationship with our Creator. We speak to Him as a Friend, opening our hearts to Him and engaging in conversation with Him. We give Him praise and share with Him our fears and secret desires as well as our successes.

How many of us, when faced with a challenge, quickly run to friends (who don't always have our best interest at heart) to share with them our fears or dreams? God should be the first with whom we share what is in our hearts.

We need to pray continuously. Let us never forget that prayer does not bring God down to us but brings us up to Him. Prayer is also the key to the strengthening of our faith. Life without prayer is empty. No, prayers are not always answered as we wish, but God has our best interest at heart. God does not give us everything we ask for, but He blesses us with things we need. So if His answer is no or wait, don't worry, for the best is yet to come. My prayer, as we walk through life with all the challenges we face in this world, is that we will draw closer to Him than ever before.

We live in a generation of corruption, violence, disrespect, and injustice. It appears the world is facing calamity. So what greater need could we have for staying in prayer before it's too late?

My prayer is, *Lord, teach us to pray, and let us find favor in Your sight. We have sinned and come short of the glory of Your kingdom. Please have mercy upon us, Lord. Amen.*

Deborah Matshaya

Reminders From Israel

But God demonstrates His own love toward us,
in that while we were still sinners, Christ died for us.
—Romans 5:8, NKJV

Having the privilege to travel the world as I minister to my sisters in various countries has also helped me live my dream. When I was in high school, sitting in geography or history class, I dreamed of visiting such countries as China, Russia, Italy, Israel, Switzerland, and more. But as time went by, I knew that dream would stay a dream. *Traveling the world*, I would think, *is for the rich who can afford to live their dreams.* Then one day in 2001, God called me to work in Women's Ministries at our church's international headquarters. Accepting that position called for many sacrifices and opened the door to new trials, but the blessings outweighed all the challenges. One such blessing was being able to visit the countries of my dreams.

One of my favorite countries is Israel, mostly because it is the country where Bible history took place. When I visit Israel, I think of all the stories in the Bible that I learned as a child. And then to have the opportunity to walk in places that Abraham, Ruth, Jesus, and the apostles walked makes their stories come to life more than ever before.

I especially love to visit the place many scholars believe was the location of Peter's house. There is a church built over the house, and one cannot walk into the house. Yet a person can stand outside a protective wall and look inside. In the church above the house is a glass floor through which one can see the inside of the house. I remember the story of Jesus healing Peter's mother-in-law and staying there when He was in Capernaum. I love this place because of Peter—imperfect, impulsive, emotionally charged Peter—the disciple to whom I feel most connected. He failed often, and some were public failures. Yet he never lost his faith through those failures because Jesus was there to forgive, heal, and help him become whole again. That's what Jesus does for me too. I fail and falter each day, and sometimes others see my failures. But Jesus is always there, waiting to forgive me, forgetting my missteps, and loving me through whatever situation I am in.

God answered my unspoken prayer to travel the world! What an amazing God we serve! But even more, He answers my spoken prayer for forgiveness each day and grants me the joy of heaven to come.

Heather-Dawn Small

Pray Anyway

Come unto me, all ye that labour and are heavy laden, and I will give you rest.
—Matthew 11:28, KJV

Prayer is an essential weapon used by spiritual warriors. I frequently seek others to pray with me. Sometimes when searching for someone to join me in prayer, all I get are answering machines. There have been times no one answered because they were at the mall, weeding the garden, preparing dinner, or preoccupied elsewhere. They promise to call me later, and most of them do; however, it seems I get no responses when desiring someone to pray with me at the time I need it.

Our heavenly Father never said that we must have someone to pray with. He knows the desires of our heart before we call on Him. We have a direct line to Heaven. He has given us instructions on how to pray individually, and He has provided a model prayer for us as well (Matthew 6:6, 9–13).

First Samuel 1 tells a beautiful story about Hannah, whose desire was to conceive and bear a child. God answered her prayer and granted her petition. First Kings 17:21–24 reveals the story of how Elijah prayed as an individual. As a result of his prayer, he was granted divine intervention. Acts 12:12–17 is another example, but it is a little different, for it describes a group of people praying, on behalf of Peter who was in prison. Their prayers were answered, and God granted them favor as well, miraculously releasing Peter from prison.

Whether we pray with or without others, we aren't always granted the desires of our hearts. One thing we must remember is that God knows what is best for us. He knows the end from the beginning. He is always available to us. We can pray kneeling, standing, sitting, or lying down. We can pray audibly or silently; it doesn't matter. As long as we exercise our faith and pray sincerely, God will answer our prayers. Hymn writer Joseph Scriven wrote that we often forfeit peace and bear needless pain, "all because we do not carry everything to God in prayer."*

If no one is available to pray with you today, pray anyway. God hears your prayer.

Cora A. Walker

* Joseph Medlicott Scriven, "What a Friend We Have in Jesus," 1855.

Against All Odds

"The God of my strength, in whom I will trust."
—2 Samuel 22:3, NKJV

After looking over my sightless husband's medical chart, the doctor entered the room and introduced himself. He looked closely at my husband and, with a puzzled look, said, "You don't look like a person who's ready for hospice." That shocked me. The physician proceeded to ask my husband a series of questions. Then he said he would take a few CT scans of my husband's brain to see whether there was something he could do.

You see, my husband had been rushed by ambulance to the surgical intensive care unit (SICU). The neurosurgeon on duty came into the room and said to my husband, "I have looked over your x-rays. There is no way I can operate on you because of your age and other medical issues." The doctor showed no empathy. I left the room crying, wondering what we were going to do. I told my son that, going forward, his father couldn't live this way!

My son, comforting me, said, "It'll be OK. We just have to trust God." My husband stayed in SICU for three days, then was transferred to the neuro floor. I was anxious, tired, and confused. Yet all along, God had a plan.

An "angel" neurosurgeon then came into our midst. He said, "I just can't leave your husband like this when I believe I can help him." After he looked at the CT scans, he showed them to me on his cell phone, explaining what he saw and what he could do. I asked if he would explain this to our children. He talked to our sons. They understood and agreed to surgery.

As the surgeon started preparation for the surgery, he kept telling me, "You've got to have faith." *Who was this man? Where did he come from?* The surgeon and I exchanged several scripture references and talked about the love of God. He was constantly encouraging my faith.

The surgery went well. The neurosurgeon was pleased with my husband's recovery; however, he had to spend two weeks in rehab before being able to return home. We spent a total of twenty-five days in the hospital. When we left the hospital, we had an assortment of medical equipment that was used for just a few days.

With a thankful heart, I'm looking at my husband of fifty-three years, smiling, basking in his remarkable recovery against all odds. God has been our Rock, our Healer, and our Doctor. God knows what we need and when we need it, even before we ask or think it.

Elaine J. Johnson

"Just a Matter of Time"

And it shall come to pass, that before they call, I will answer;
and while they are yet speaking, I will hear.
—Isaiah 65:24, KJV

In the middle of a cold snap that had temperatures dropping to -25°F (-31.6°C), the heater's blower fan in my pickup started screeching loudly. This went on for a few days until I finally called an auto parts store and bought a new fan. That same day I called a friend from church, asking permission to park my truck inside his shop to replace the part.

"Sure! Come on over!" he responded. I drove to his shop after work and pulled inside. As soon as I parked and got out, he said, "Your truck's leakin' oil." I looked under the cab, and sure enough, oil was steadily dripping. My other vehicle was already in the shop for major repairs, so the last thing I needed was more vehicle issues. My friend got started on replacing the heater fan while I lay down on a creeper (a low-wheeled support used when working under a vehicle) and rolled underneath my truck. Looking up from the creeper, I saw oil spattered over other parts of, well, *everything* under there. But the engine itself was dry. I looked at the oil filter and saw oil around the bottom third of it. Everything else around the filter was dry. I removed the brush guard on the bottom of the truck to reach the filter. When I did, the filter was so loose I could turn it by hand. I used one of the shop owner's filter wrenches to tighten the filter and then cleaned up the oil mess as best I could without having any degreaser spray. There is *no* way I could have done that repair job in the dark—especially in -25°F temperatures!

My friend told me that if that filter had come off, it would have dropped by the side of the road. Not only that, if I had lost the vehicle's oil, the engine may have seized up. Without my spare vehicle being available, I would have been in bad shape: -25°F temperatures and no transportation except for my four-wheeler. Not very practical for an Alaskan winter!

I am *so* glad I didn't wait for the heater fan to quit completely. The oil filter would have dropped off somewhere. It was "just a matter of time," said my friend at the shop. God knew all about that loose filter and the other vehicle issues I'd been having. In the subsequent words of a friend from work when I told her, "Oh, my! That was a tender mercy from God!"

What has God done for you lately that you can share with others about His goodness?

Sonia Brock

Hold Your Breath

"Are not two sparrows sold for a copper coin? And not one of them falls to the ground apart from your Father's will. But the very hairs of your head are all numbered. Do not fear therefore; you are of more value than many sparrows."
—Matthew 10:29–31, NKJV

When I was on a recent field trip with my students, the Lord taught me a valuable lesson. As a third-grade teacher, I love field trips and so do my students! I mean, what child doesn't?

On this particular day, we had gone on a field trip to an aquarium as part of our study of a unit on habitats. The aquarium presenter referred to different kinds of animals and how they adapt to their environment. One of the animals she told us about was an elephant seal. An elephant seal can hold its breath for up to two hours, often diving deep to forage.

Wow! I thought when I heard this. *What an amazing God!* God has given each animal what it needs to survive in its unique environment. The elephant seal doesn't worry about how much air it needs to forage. It senses that it has been given up to two hours to hunt for food and that the food is there, waiting for it deep in the ocean.

If God has done amazing things for the preservation of animals, how much more will He provide for our needs? Although we know He cares, we sometimes doubt: "I don't have food to cook for supper." "I don't have money for tuition." "I need a job." "I need to be free of this relationship." "I want a husband." "I want to be healed."

Take a breath. Then slowly exhale.

Sisters, trust God. Be confident. Know that He is providing just what you need.

Dana M. Bean

Repent

"I tell you, no; but unless you repent you will all likewise perish."
—Luke 13:5, NKJV

One morning while I was having my worship and devotional time, a childhood memory flashed before me. I recalled an incident that had happened years before while I was living in the Caribbean and was still a teenager, maybe even younger.

A certain man—I cannot remember his name, so I'll refer to him as Mr. B— was a self-made pastor. He would take the passenger bus each day from the town where he was living and travel to another part of the country. His one message was always the same: "If you don't repent, you must burn!" Only he would say it in the Jamaican way: "Burn, you must burn if you don't repent!" This individual would repeat his message several times as people entered and exited the bus.

As teenagers, we thought his behavior was really funny, if not annoying. We would laugh and jeer, but Mr. B was dead serious. Sometimes he held up his Bible in his hand as he shouted out that message—the same message—every single day. In fact, I never heard him say anything else. Mr. B wasn't a trained pastor, so he didn't know how to convey the message of salvation in a manner that was more polished.

When I study the Word of God, I believe each book is conveying the same message but in its own unique and positive way. "Believe on the Lord Jesus Christ, and you will be saved" (Acts 16:31, NKJV). The Lord is calling us to faith, repentance, and obedience: "Whoever walks blamelessly will be saved" (Proverbs 28:18, NKJV). Many of us are ignoring the promises and the warnings and living as if we had another thousand years on this earth before Jesus comes.

Folks, are we ready for Jesus to come? He is pleading with us to be ready. Let us not be like the five foolish virgins who were not prepared to meet the bridegroom. Let us be ready.

Jesus, in Matthew 25:13, admonishes us to "watch therefore, for you know neither the day nor the hour in which the Son of Man is coming" (NKJV). He counsels us in Matthew 24:44: "Therefore you also be ready, for the Son of Man is coming at an hour you do not expect" (NKJV). Are you ready for Jesus to come?

Patricia Hines

The *Titanic*

"And God will wipe away every tear from their eyes; there shall be no more death, nor sorrow, nor crying. There shall be no more pain, for the former things have passed away."
—Revelation 21:4, NKJV

After the movie *Titanic* was released in December 1997, it received great ratings because the love story between a young couple of different social classes played out against the backdrop of the actual, ill-fated maiden voyage of the *Titanic* in April 1912. Most people who see the movie probably mourn the loss of the fictional hero more than the fifteen hundred actual souls that perished in the cold Atlantic Ocean when the ship hit an iceberg.

Recently, I had the opportunity to visit the large *Titanic* Museum while vacationing in Branson, Missouri, United States of America. My husband and I walked through the museum, reading about the various people on that ship, watching video presentations, and viewing the wall that displayed the names of every person on board—first, second, and third class passengers and crew. Suddenly, everything that had been just entertainment in the movie came to life for me.

That evening we watched the movie again. Even though it is three hours and fifteen minutes long, I desired to see it one more time in light of my museum experience that day.

Throughout the movie, I was fact-checking against all that I had seen, read, heard, and experienced earlier in the day. I now was able to look for certain things and understand other details as I watched the movie through the lens of the immense human tragedy—not just from the viewpoint of the love story. I was able to see the story as if for the first time, not just as entertainment but rather as the great tragedy it was that left many families in pain. When the movie ended, I grieved, weeping as I felt the pain and horror of the event.

From my experience that day, I realized even more deeply two other things. First, the love of Jesus has no boundaries. His love overcame all obstacles that would have kept Him from dying on the cross on our behalf. Second, when you have experienced Christ on a personal level, as I experienced the *Titanic* Museum that day when history came to life, it changes everything. It changes how you view, interact, and experience life because God and His love have truly become much more real to you!

Nadine A. Joseph-Collins

Forgiveness That Binds

I will go before thee, and make the crooked places straight.
—Isaiah 45:2, KJV

I was not impressed with the new teacher at all. I'd had such great hopes, but she was falling short—at least according to my self-constructed expectations. I was very busy with preparing for a new position. It had been a period of great changes emotionally, physically, and professionally. One day this teacher sat in my office with a barrage of questions—some of which I had no direct knowledge of or interest to discuss. Visibly annoyed, I answered grumpily. She escaped my office quickly, and I seethed the rest of the school day. Later, as I reviewed my day with my husband, I grumbled about the teacher. Still upset, I shared the details of our interactions, seeking reasons for my resentment. Against my will, the Holy Spirit moved me to the truth. I shared all the good qualities that had prompted me to seek out this teacher in the first place. I had been excited and grateful to work with such a bright, devoted, and delightful educator. When I was promoted to a new job, I asked for a few months of transition so that when I left, she would be certain of her responsibilities in the new position.

I talked on as my husband listened to me, conceding that she asked questions because she wanted to succeed in teaching a program that I had created. I was her point of reference, and now, I confessed, I was mistreating her. This revelation startled me! The Holy Spirit is more interested in how I treat others than how I feel. No matter the reasons, the Lord is steadfast in His call for me to value people. For in harming others, I distort the image of Christ so that hostility replaces holiness and conflict chases away cooperation—and the enemy of the soul takes credit. I had to choose a different path, so I prayed and planned with God that night.

The next day, when that precious teacher phoned, I responded with kindness and smiled as we planned. I asked for forgiveness with an admission that I had treated her poorly and a promise that she would see that behavior no more. She extended pardon freely and thanked me for apologizing. Forgiveness cleared the way for us to continue. God's goodness had been our guide before this unfortunate patch, and it will be after it. By the Spirit's power, our work will reveal Christ, and God's name will be glorified. We had needed the Holy Spirit to mend what the enemy tried to destroy: unity among God's people and the forgiveness that binds them together.

Rose Joseph Thomas

Breaking News

Jesus reached out his hand and touched the man. "I am willing," he said.
"Be clean!" Immediately he was cleansed of his leprosy.
—Matthew 8:3, NIV

When I was growing up, we read the newspaper, watched the *Huntley-Brinkley Report* on television, and listened to the radio. That is how we got the news. With today's social media, cell phones, and the internet, we have constant, instantaneous news. How different things are now!

Can you imagine what it would have been like during Christ's ministry if, while He was performing one of His many miracles, there had been breaking-news alerts about it on television or cell phones? While Lazarus was being brought back to life, we could have seen it live! Or we could have seen the joy in the face of the woman with the flow of blood who was healed when she, in faith, touched the hem of Jesus' garment! Jesus' disciples did see those miracles, experienced those miracles in their own lives, and watched others' lives change when they met Jesus. When we pick up our Bibles and read God's Word, we also "see" those same miracles unfold as we experience the One who changes lives. We then can experience the miracle of Jesus changing our own lives.

The disciples' excitement about Christ, and that of the many people the Bible tells us about, has continued through thousands of years. After Christ's death and resurrection, the disciples spent the rest of their lives sharing the good news about Jesus with others. These, in turn, shared with many more. That is why that same excitement, awe, inspiration, and pure joy are apparent in our own lives today when we come to Him and then share Him. For some people traveling to other countries, sharing Jesus may come at a cost as it did for the long-ago disciples, who were persecuted for speaking His name. Yet tribulation didn't deter them from telling people about the One who loves you and me so much that He came from heaven to show us the face of God.

The next time you hear another breaking news story, which, unfortunately, will probably not be good news, remember that one day, that kind of news will be replaced with these words: " 'He will wipe every tear from their eyes. There will be no more death' or mourning or crying or pain, for the old order of things has passed away" (Revelation 21:4, NIV).

Then I can respond with love and gratefulness: "Thank You, my Lord."

Jean Dozier Davey

Plain and Simple

Come unto me, all ye that labour and are heavy laden, and I will give you rest.
Take my yoke upon you, and learn of me; for I am meek and lowly in heart:
and ye shall find rest unto your souls. For my yoke is easy, and my burden is light.
—Matthew 11:28–30, KJV

In the village where I was born in Guyana, there were a few scholars (mostly self-taught) who, I believe, had better educational opportunities been available to them, would have contributed significantly to academia.

There was one such fellow known as Prophet Willis. I never could figure out whether *Prophet* was his given name or his nickname because of his many quotations. A person needed a dictionary to understand responses to simple questions, such as, "How are you doing today?"

One such response was recorded when Prophet Willis had tried to buy some fish. He inquired about the price of the fish. Upon receiving a reply from the fishmonger, Prophet Willis offered this rebuke: "Oh, thou mean and perverse vendor! Dost thou think it wise in bestowing unto me such an impecunious amount of these aquatic creatures for such an exorbitant dowry?"

"Did you hear what he said?" people asked one another. Needless to say, this particular quote went around the village like wildfire, being repeated many times. We children even memorized it word for word.

The children of God do not have to be confused as to what He is saying to us.

"Come unto me, all ye that labour and are heavy laden, and I will give you rest. Take my yoke upon you, and learn of me; for I am meek and lowly in heart: and ye shall find rest unto your souls. For my yoke is easy, and my burden is light" (Matthew 11:28–30, KJV).

In Jeremiah 31:3, God declares, "Yea, I have loved thee with an everlasting love" (KJV).

In 1 Peter 5:7, God entreats us to cast all our cares upon Him because He cares for us. In Philippians 4:19, He promises to supply all our needs, and in 1 John 5:3, He assures us that "his commandments are not grievous" (KJV).

Finally, He invites us to open the door of our heart so that He can come in to stay with us. His words to us are plain and simple.

If you haven't done so yet, won't you give the uncomplicated Jesus a try?

Vashti Hinds-Vanier

Love Grows Under the Surface

All the special gifts and powers from God will someday come to an end, but love
goes on forever. Someday prophecy and speaking in unknown languages and special
knowledge—these gifts will disappear. Now we know so little. . . . But when we have
been made perfect and complete, then the need for these inadequate special gifts will
come to an end, and they will disappear.
It's like this: when I was a child I spoke and thought and reasoned as a child does. . . .
Now I have put away the childish things. In the same way, we can see and understand
only a little about God now, as if we were peering at his reflection in a poor mirror;
but someday we are going to see him in his completeness, face-to-face. Now all that I
know is hazy and blurred, but then I will see everything clearly, just as clearly as God
sees into my heart right now. There are three things that remain—faith, hope, and
love—and the greatest of these is love.
—1 Corinthians 13:8–13, TLB

At a recent health-related church mission conference, author David Brooks, who wrote *The Road to Character*, shared the story of a widower who told his daughter about the love he had shared with his wife (her mother). Remembering his wife, the widower described their love as being like two trees with roots growing deep and branches flowering profusely. And one day they realized they were not two trees but one.

Dig deeply into love, and see roots growing down and becoming entwined. Botanists tell us that trees with shallow roots cannot withstand the windstorms above the surface. Love thrives, and connections strengthen. Love, well-grounded, withstands all.

Three virtues remain: faith, hope, and love. And the greatest of the three is love. Mutual love, rooted and grounded in selflessness and other-centeredness, thrives, becoming one. Two trunks, visible to all. Exuberant and extravagant are the flowers. Roots, entwined, nourish each other.

Love so glorious, for all to see.

Two trunks; one tree. This is love.

Bless my home with love that flows from You.

Prudence LaBeach Pollard

TNTC

The faithful love of the LORD never ends!
His mercies never cease.
Great is his faithfulness;
his mercies begin afresh each morning.
—Lamentations 3:22, 23, NLT

TNTC: too numerous to count, which is a common abbreviation in lab parlance. TNTC refers to the appearance of so many bacteria in the field being viewed under a microscope that they can't be counted individually. And that's how I think of God's blessings. There are so *many* of them! Some we're fully aware of, but I believe that we're completely clueless about so many others. Why, some of them even masquerade as catastrophes!

Many of my greatest blessings have been achieved in painful circumstances that I'd rather have skipped if I could have. But God works in *every* situation for our highest good, allowing and, alternately, preventing certain things in view of our best interests.

I was let go from a job once—fired, actually—early in my career. It was an awful shock and a terrible time. I was embarrassed and demoralized and ashamed. But the Lord provided an opportunity to work in a setting that I never would have thought of if this incident hadn't occurred. In my new setting, I received specialized training that changed the entire trajectory of my career and in a most positive way. I wonder over it yet.

Obvious blessings—sunshine, a comfortable home, reliable transportation, friends, pets, a breathtaking sunrise or sunset, food—these we are effortlessly thankful for. We have no trouble at all recognizing and acknowledging them as blessings.

But let us also be grateful for those things that cause us pain through which the Lord can bless us in ways we can't imagine: illness, marital difficulties, concerns over children, a job loss, a difficult move, or separation from loved ones by death.

God is certainly faithful. His love truly never ends. His mercies will not cease. He *always* means us well. We can trust Him to make blessings out of both the obvious positives and all the rest.

And His mercies start all over again every single morning. Excellent!

Carolyn K. Karlstrom

Reframe

So we fix our eyes not on what is seen, but on what is unseen,
since what is seen is temporary, but what is unseen is eternal.
—2 Corinthians 4:18, NIV

Even as I write this morning, I feel overwhelmed with an endless to-do list. *When and how will I finish all these projects?* I am sure you are facing something similar today and can understand the way I feel. Life's many obligations always come with emotions. That's why the Bible gives us the antidote against desperation: Don't panic. Look at things in a different way. Reframe what you see in front of you. To *reframe* is simply to look at a situation from a different perspective. Or, put another way, it is placing the "picture" of what you need to do or how you feel within a new frame. I love that!

Paul was an expert on reframing—enduring all kinds of hardships yet being content in every situation. He reframed his troubles this way: "For our present troubles are small and won't last very long. Yet they produce for us a glory that vastly outweighs them and will last forever! So we don't look at the troubles we can see now; rather, we fix our gaze on things that cannot be seen. For the things we see now will soon be gone, but the things we cannot see will last forever" (2 Corinthians 4:17, 18, NLT). This is what I mean by *reframing*: experiencing—by God's help—events, ideas, concepts, and emotions within more positive alternatives.

I am looking at my list again as an email arrives. It's from my friend who is dying of cancer. As I pause to read her message, one sentence touches me deeply: "I am blessed," she says. "It is almost twelve years since my original tumor burst, and I could have died then, but God has blessed me with this extra time. Then I had one granddaughter, and now I have nine grandchildren, and I've enjoyed them all. Whatever happens, God has been good to me." What an authentic example of reframing one's life! As I pray for her, I ask God to fix my eyes not on what is seen (the temporary) but on what is unseen (the eternal). And what about my day's to-do list? I look at it again and tell myself, *You can reframe this. Start with all the things that will impact your eternal life, and everything else will fall into place.*

Today, if you are feeling overwhelmed, stop, reframe, and pray. God's Word affirms that our present troubles are small and fleeting. So place them in God's unseen, eternal frame.

Raquel Queiroz da Costa Arrais

Divine Intervention

Yea, though I walk through the valley of the shadow of death, I will fear no evil:
for thou art with me; thy rod and thy staff they comfort me.
—Psalm 23:4, KJV

Part of the requirements for the fulfillment of our studies at the College of Education was to complete a project. My group was to interview the aged, chiefs, and titled men on the origins of a particular tribe. To my dismay, the lecturer insisted that I travel alone for my part of the project. *Can ambitious lecturers place students in harm's way for their own selfish goals?* I wondered. I pleaded to go with another student but to no avail, so I left it in God's hands.

Arriving in an unfamiliar city, I visited a church of my denomination, and the pastor prayed for me. I sought directions to my destination from the city's residents. Fortunately, it was a sunny day. A taxi dropped me off in an unfamiliar environment. I met a man who told me that students visited him on a regular basis for their projects. He asked me, "Are you a Christian?"

"Yes," I answered. "Are you?" He did not respond. Then he asked me to look at holes in the office wall, which I did. He asked me whether I knew where I was. I showed him the door through which I had entered, yet I noticed that his office was filled with undesirable objects. I prayed in my heart and wished I had been allowed to come with my student team.

The chief sent me to a second chief but not before demanding that I return to his office.

By the time I arrived to interview the second chief, God had sent a male student with whom I could conduct the interview. Then we returned to the first chief. At the end of our interview, the chief stood at the door of his office. First, he permitted the male student to pass through the doorway. Then with a quick movement, he blocked my way to keep me in the room. With a rush of energy, I pushed him aside and ran out. Something said to me, "Do not conduct any more interviews. Return to your family—*now!*"

The next day in class, I related my ordeal to the lecturer as the students listened. "You were in the devil's den," the students said. "The chief thought his demon had snatched your mind." Shortly after that incident, I became sick and asked God to heal me. I was reminded of what God had prevented from happening that day in the devil's den. Then I knew God heard my prayers and would heal me. I love to tell the story of how Jesus overcame for me.

Margaret Obiocha

Singing With the Angels

He has put a new song in my mouth—
Praise to our God.
—Psalm 40:3, NKJV

Have you thought about singing with the angels? I used to think of singing with the angel choir when I get to heaven but not about singing with them while still on this earth. Yet I recently read, "All the heavenly angels are at the service of the humble, believing people of God; and as the Lord's army of workers here below sing their songs of praise, the choir above join with them in ascribing praise to God and to His Son."* Wow! This is exciting!

As a choir director of both adults and children, it is awesome to think of angels singing with us. On any given Sabbath, when one of the choirs sings, people come and say, "That music was so beautiful!" Yet I used to wonder what they were hearing because sometimes it didn't sound that wonderful to me. Now I know: it was because the angels joined with the singers and made it beautiful. *Thank You, Lord!*

Music is such a wonderful gift given to us by God. Many can worship and grow spiritually simply by singing or playing His music! I love to read stories of how certain musical pieces were inspired. These background stories make the hymns more meaningful to us personally. Many of the classical composers were inspired by God in writing their music too.

I was blessed to grow up in a musical family. We sang together around the piano that our mother played. Our parents sang in the church choir, took voice lessons, gave us piano lessons, bought a flute for each of us, and gave us flute lessons as well. In church school, we grew up singing in choirs and playing in bands. We also presented special music for church, went to nursing homes, and sang at a mission in the city. We loved to share our music!

The Bible tells us to sing "for joy" (Psalm 132:9, NIV), "with gratitude" (Colossians 3:16, NIV), and to "make music from your heart" (Ephesians 5:19, NIV). We are encouraged to "sing praise to him" (Psalm 105:2, NIV) and "sing to the Lord a new song" (Psalm 98:1, NIV).

Let's sing to the Lord, and let the angels sing with us—even while still on this earth! Then when we get to heaven, we'll sing with the angels there too! How wonderful that will be!

Sharon Follett

---

* Ellen G. White, *The Acts of the Apostles* (Nampa, ID: Pacific Press®, 2005), 154.

The Sun Will Still Rise

I will lift up mine eyes unto the hills, from whence cometh my help.
My help cometh from the LORD, which made heaven and earth.
—Psalm 121:1, 2, KJV

During a recent routine morning exercise on my back porch, I had an uplifting object lesson from nature. The time had just changed to daylight saving time, so it was more than half an hour before sunrise but still dark. For the three previous mornings, I had been enjoying the company of Venus, the bright morning star. That morning it seemed to shine brighter than ever.

I lifted my hands high as I reached toward the bright morning star. Then, suddenly, the "star" disappeared from sight. Dark clouds moved across the predawn sky and temporarily hid the bright star. I kept moving, but it was not the same.

Then I thought, *How similar this is to our life's journeys! We are enjoying life's daily, taken-for-granted gifts when suddenly things change. An unexpected dark cloud—a cancer diagnosis, maiming accident, sudden loss of a loved one, unexpected unemployment, or divorce announcement—hides the stars or even the sun. The light in our life seems to be hidden by those dark clouds, so we temporarily lose sight of the light.*

It is in times like these that we must lift our eyes and look beyond the dark clouds—from whence our help comes. We must still rise. We must look to the Bright and Morning Star—the Son of Righteousness. Only then can we get the strength to resume the journey. Even if the dark clouds turn the day cloudy, the sun will rise again!

The Son will arise with healing and give us the strength to carry on. God's Son will raise you up and renew your strength. He will even carry you when you can't carry on. It is in times like these that He upholds and sustains you. You can lean on every uplifting promise. Today, look beyond the dark clouds to the Bright and Morning Star—the Son of Righteousness. He will help you to mount up as an eagle, and He will renew your strength (see Isaiah 40:31). The sun will still rise!

Claudette Garbutt-Harding

Eagles

I do not understand:
The way of an eagle in the air.
—Proverbs 30:18, 19, NKJV

I'm glad it's winter. Well, not really, because I hate cold weather. I'm glad the trees are bare. That's not really true, either, because spring is my favorite season. What I really like about having the leaves gone is that I get to watch the beautiful bald eagles that frequent the tall trees in our backyard. They seem to have a couple of favorite branches from which they have a good view of the lake. Sometimes they'll swoop down and, with their powerful talons, catch a little fish, then sit on the perch to enjoy lunch. If they have snagged a very large fish, they can only get it onto the shore, where they eat their fill and leave the remainder for other creatures to finish.

It takes four to five years before an eagle is graced by solid white head feathers and tail markings on its brown body. Without question, this glorious bird is the king of the sky, making the ducks and geese huddle when they see its shadow fly over! And no wonder, because its diving speed is 75–99 miles per hour (120–160 kilometers per hour). It is a powerful flier that soars on thermal convection currents and can glide and flap at 35–43 miles per hour (56–70 kilometers per hour).

The eagle's mature body can range from 28 to 40 inches (71–102 centimeters) in length. Now that's really a big bird! But look at its wingspan: 5 feet 11 inches to 7 feet 7 inches (1.8–2.3 meters). Wow, did God make a beauty there! Look at this special imagery: "You have seen what I did to the Egyptians, and how I bore you on eagles' wings and brought you to Myself" (Exodus 19:4, NKJV). When I see an eagle soaring higher and higher, I like to imagine God wants to get me closer to Himself! In fact, He is the One "who satisfies your mouth with good things, so that your youth is renewed like the eagle's" (Psalm 103:5, NKJV).

Now with each birthday, wouldn't it be great to feel a year younger?

Maybe it's Isaiah who really gives us the key to feeling spiritually regenerated: "But they that wait upon the Lord shall renew their strength; they shall mount up with wings as eagles; they shall run, and not be weary; and they shall walk, and not faint" (Isaiah 40:31, KJV).

For a spiritual high, as if on an eagle's wings, let's simply wait on the Lord!

Roxy Hoehn

Listening and Obeying

But whoever listens to me will dwell secure
and will be at ease, without dread of disaster.
—Proverbs 1:33, ESV

I have a fifteen-month-old female dog named Cinnamon—a beautiful Yorkie-poo with multicolored hair of black, brown, golden tan, and beige. She is a faithful dog and a sociable sweetheart. She loves to sit near my husband or me and is quick to follow when either of us moves to another room or goes to the kitchen to grab a snack. She is naughty also, stealing the TV remote, socks, or anything low enough to grab. She is more than two retirees need to deal with, but we love her and keep hoping her behavior will change. We can't imagine life now without her.

Cinnamon was recently spayed. We brought her back home after surgery with three days of pain meds and strict recuperation instructions: Do not walk her much the first ten to fourteen days, don't let her be active in her play, never let her lick her wound, and help her on any stairs. A highly active dog is always into something, so we were leery of whether we could follow the instructions.

The first two days, she lay around, not eating, drinking, or barking, so we figured it would be easy. Before long, she was up and down the stairs as often as before, jumping off the couch and running to the window to bark at passersby, and also into other activities that taxed her abdomen. We tried predicting her moves to deter her, but it didn't work. Her mind was set on what she liked to do and when. She wasn't listening or obeying or missing out on doing her favorite things—surgery or not.

During her recuperation, my husband, Will, and I learned valuable lessons about life, healing, and rules to keep us safe. We have a good life, but, at times, the Master Physician needs to perform surgery to contend with our sins. God gives us healing instructions, too, out of concern for our health, happiness, and quality of life. We soon realize that we miss our propensities to do the things we used to do, so throwing caution to the wind and disregarding the possible potential setbacks, we go back to our old ways—not aware or caring that temporary or permanent damage could occur. Even with God nearby to guard us, we still do whatever we want, disobeying the warning signs and ignoring instructions given for our benefit. *Lord, help us to know and accept Your divine instructions, follow the leading of Your hand, and be ever thankful for Your love.*

Iris L. Kitching

Words

Your eternal word, O Lord,
stands firm in heaven.
—Psalm 119:89, NLT

A note to my fellow wordies: After going to the Merriam-Webster online dictionary at Merriam-Webster.com to key in any word—say, *basket*—to discover its definition, you can scroll down to "Learn More about *basket*." Then click on "Time Traveler for *basket*" and learn the exact year *basket* came into known use in the English language.

Recently, I keyed *freeze-dried* into Merriam-Webster's search box to make sure it should be hyphenated, and I learned this adjective came into use in 1946, which is the year my brother was born. I decided to see what words made their entrance into English the year I was born. Here are a few terms that came into common usage that year: *quiz show, nose job, MIA, DNA, debrief, thrift shop, top secret, trickle-down, skimobile, gobbledygook, bungee cord, aviator glasses, dishpan hands,* and *forklift.* Reading this list made me wonder how people in the United States of America *ever* communicated before 1944! While these words are still in use today, other words from "back in the day" have fallen into disuse or lost their meanings—their power—altogether. For example, the noun *westing* emerged in 1638 and means going in a westward direction.

Yet you and I both know another ancient word that will never lose its meaning or its power. And that is the Word of God. An Old Testament writer proclaimed, "Your eternal word, O Lord, stands firm in heaven" (Psalm 119:89, NLT). To early church believers, the apostle Peter wrote, "For you have been born again. . . . Your new life will last forever because it comes from the eternal, living word of God" (1 Peter 1:23, NLT). One commentator defined this word as the "doctrine of the living God."* Many words, over time, have lost their function and power. Yet one word will outlast them all: the life-empowering, life-sustaining Word of God. As both Old and New Testament writers point out, the eternal *Word* points us to eternal *life.* "The Gentiles . . . glorified the word of the Lord. And as many as had been appointed to eternal life believed" (Acts 13:48, NKJV). Have you spent time in God's Word today?

Carolyn Rathbun Sutton

---

* Adam Clarke, "Commentary on 1 Peter 1:23," in *The Adam Clarke Commentary,* 1832, accessed May 19, 2019, https://www.studylight.org/commentaries/acc/1-peter-1.html.

Just Like That

*So he answered and said, " 'You shall love the L*ORD *your God
with all your heart, with all your soul, with all your strength,
and with all your mind,' and 'your neighbor as yourself.' "*
—Luke 10:27, NKJV

It was time to get new furniture for our new apartment after throwing out what we'd used for fifteen years. So Samuel, a fellow church member, drove me to a shop to find what we needed. Then, since Samuel had to continue on to work, I was obliged to take the city bus home. At the bus stop, I greeted an elderly man with a friendly "Hi!"

Through a broad smile, he asked, "Do you need bus 24B too?"

"Yes, sir," I replied, smiling back. When the bus came, I realized that I had no change to pay for the fare. I hardly use the bus because I usually drive every day.

The elderly man I had just met saw me searching desperately through my purse. He simply handed me his bus ticket. I felt bad to deprive him of his ticket, so I handed him a twenty-dollar bill. He refused to take it. Since other passengers could not make change for me, there was nothing I could do but accept and use the kind man's ticket. Yes, it had happened again. I had made a new friend—just like that!

This nice grandpa opened his heart to me just because I had said hi to him. He acted as Christ instructs us to in today's text—take care of our neighbors. What might have happened if I had ignored him? I tell you, friend, he loved me more than himself when he gave me his only ticket and then had to use more of his money to pay for his own ride. And he was all smiles while repeatedly saying, "Don't worry, honey; it's OK."

May you and I do the same for others!

It was a long bus ride. When I reached my destination, I said to my benefactor, "Thank you, and God bless you." He gave me a warm handshake and again said, "Don't worry, honey."

Do you and I have big hearts as this man who helped me did? I am sure that one day our Lord will bless him for his kindness as He said He would. For when we help others, we are helping Jesus (Matthew 25:40).

Friend, keep a smile on your face as this man did. And don't forget to say hi!

Mabel Kwei

Loving Animals

*For "you were like sheep going astray," but now you have
returned to the Shepherd and Overseer of your souls.*
—1 Peter 2:25, NIV

In my seventy-eight years of life, I've lived with eight dogs, five cats, four parakeets, two gerbils, one mouse, and schools of fish. Most of us who have pets love them "in sickness and in health until death do us part." Despite their problems, we wouldn't have it any other way. As animal lovers, we also enjoy wild animals in the zoo and watching YouTube videos of their antics. Many are warm and cuddly. Others are beautiful or smart. Many have desirable traits. Others don't. We all have our favorites. (My Maltipoo dog is a mix of very good and very bad.)

What is it that makes us love our pets and other animals?

I believe the answer goes back to Creation. If God had not loved animals, He wouldn't have made the wide variety that exists. His imagination, sense of humor, and love of beauty are displayed in the giraffe, kangaroo, and multicolored birds. Originally, the whole animal kingdom was friendly to human beings. When God finished creating man and animals, He said all were very good (Genesis 1:31). It sounds to me like God intended all along for people and animals to love each other. It will be that way again in the earth made new (Isaiah 11:6–9).

Jesus is known as the Good Shepherd. He loves His sheep. In the parable of the lost sheep (Luke 15:3–7), we can picture Jesus leaving the fold and going after the one that's lost. Have you wandered from His fold? We serve a forgiving God of love. The proof? God gave Jesus to die for our sins so we don't have to die. By accepting His gift, we will live with Him forever. "In the same way there will be more rejoicing in heaven over one sinner who repents than over the ninety-nine righteous persons who do not need to repent" (Luke 15:7, NIV).

The bonus? We can live and play with every animal, without fear of harm, to our heart's content. Loving animals is God's desire for us now and throughout eternity.

Donna J. Voth

Encounter With a Stranger

The gracious hand of my God was on me.
—Nehemiah 2:8, NIV

It was a beautiful autumn day in North Carolina. The leaves had turned from brilliant green to vibrant yellow, orange, and red. I went outside to spend some time with my two children. The kids immediately began playing in the fallen leaves. They gathered leaves, made piles to jump into, and climbed trees. After some time, my children and I began walking to the mailbox, which is located down the street. As we walked, the children kicked the fallen leaves. A stranger appeared on the sidewalk in front of us and yelled for us to stop and not walk closer. I had never seen this man before, and I wondered why he was yelling for us to stop.

North Carolina is known for its variety of wildlife, including venomous copperhead snakes. Their bites can do serious harm. I had never seen one in our yard, but our friend's son had been bitten by one in an adjacent neighborhood. The stranger yelled that there was a copperhead on our pathway, but he would take care of it. Moments later, the stranger walked over to us and stated that he had taken care of the snake, allowing us to proceed to the mailbox.

Absorbed in the beauty of the day and time with my children, I was not prepared to meet a copperhead snake on the path that day. We would have walked directly into the path of the snake that was sunning itself in the leaves, camouflaged from our view.

Although we have lived in our neighborhood for many years and know most of the neighbors, before that day, we had never seen the man who saved us from the snake. Nor have we seen him since that day. My children and I are thankful that God had His hand upon us and placed a stranger along our pathway to save us from a potentially dangerous encounter. The promises of Psalm 91:11–14 are for each of us today:

> For he will command his angels concerning you
>   to guard you in all your ways;
> they will lift you up in their hands. . . .
> You will tread on the lion and the cobra;
>   you will trample the great lion and the serpent.

"Because he loves me," says the LORD, "I will rescue him" (NIV).

And He does!

Beatrice Tauber Prior

Our Eyes, Our Brain, Our Temple

"The lamp of the body is the eye. If therefore your eye is good, your whole body will be full of light. But if your eye is bad, your whole body will be full of darkness. If therefore the light that is in you is darkness, how great is that darkness!"
—Matthew 6:22, 23, NKJV

Medical science documents state that we are what we eat. Author Ellen G. White wrote about the connection between our health and our food intake more than a hundred years ago. There is also a connection between our eyes and our bodies. This connection is of utmost importance because it affects our whole being: body, mind, and soul. Nowadays, there is much moral darkness surrounding us. It affects and entraps children, teenagers, adults, families, churches, and society. One of the darkest pitfalls is the phenomenon known as pornography. Many people don't want to talk about it; however, it is real. It is corroding the lives of many, so it must be addressed if we want to save our children, spouses, and homes. The internet and electronic devices provide channels for this massive, uncontrolled sin. One study revealed that "teens and young adults consider 'not recycling' more immoral than viewing pornography."* Are we weeping for our homes, families, and churches? Are we praying and fasting for healing and ways to help those enslaved by addiction? When the eyes are sin-sick from viewing images of darkness, the whole body—including the brain—becomes affected by this spiritual disease. Sin that is hidden cannot be eradicated from our lives. Sin that is unconfessed cannot be forgiven.

As Christians, let us educate ourselves about helpful resources that can provide support and assistance for the enslaved to be set free. The enslaved must know that Jesus forgives all sins when they are confessed to Him. He alone can cleanse and heal. Of course, we believe that the devil is attacking, more than ever, those who would follow God, especially in the church family. If we ask the Lord how we can become involved in raising awareness of both the dangers of and escape from darkness, Jesus will be our Guide and Captain. He is not only the Answer to our questions but also has the solutions for every crisis, problem, and temptation in any of our lives.

Lily Morales-Narváez

---

* JMM Team, "Key Findings in Landmark Pornography Study Released," Josh McDowell Ministry, January 19, 2016, https://www.josh.org/key-findings-in-landmark-pornography-study-released/.

The Barren and the Surrogate

PART 1

Now Sarai, Abram's wife, had borne him no children.
And she had an Egyptian maidservant whose name was Hagar.
—Genesis 16:1, NKJV

As a female, I'll admit my sympathies run heavily with Hagar in today's Bible story. Her lot was slavery with no rights. Though for some, slavery meant a roof over one's head and food for the stomach; regardless, it was a life of servitude. Perhaps her life as a servant wasn't too bad. Yet Hagar really had no choice but to submit to Sarah's demand that she sleep with Sarah's husband, Abraham, to become a surrogate mother by, hopefully, conceiving a male child for Abraham.

Sarah's barrenness plagued her like a cultural black eye; she felt disgraced. Certainly, she thought, *What must people think of me? I'm an embarrassment to Abraham.* She loved her husband and felt she needed to resolve the situation. Abraham had probably wrung his hands many times in her presence, pacing their fine home-tent, pleading with God, "Why, Adonai, why, no son, no heir for me?"

Sarah eventually figured she'd been patient enough with waiting on God. He certainly wouldn't open her womb in old age. She wanted a happy husband. He wasn't. As a result, she wasn't happy either.

The wealthy household included many slaves, and Sarah selected Hagar. Her Egyptian slave girl obviously showed evidence of being able to produce a worthy heir for Abraham, with good health, strength, physical appearance, intelligence, as well as admirable character attributes. Sarah knew better than to choose a lesser woman to take her place as the provider of a son. Thus, Ishmael, child of Hagar and son of Abraham, was conceived.

Abraham felt joyful, even though he doubtless wished the child were Sarah's. After all, she was the wife of his youth—the one he'd hoped would bear his children.

Unfortunately, Hagar became proud of her pregnancy; perhaps she even thought she might one day replace the aging Sarah. In return, Sarah couldn't bear Hagar's presence and treated her so unkindly that Hagar ran away. But God graciously revealed Himself to Hagar and told her to humble herself and return home to serve. Someday she would have many descendants. When we struggle with disappointments, we can still trust God and, as Hagar did, obey His biddings. He always has a plan for our highest good.

Betty Kossick

The Barren and the Surrogate
PART 2

For Sarah conceived and bore Abraham a son in his old age,
at the set time of which God had spoken to him.
—Genesis 21:2, NKJV

God's promise was fulfilled. Sarah found herself pregnant! She'd laughed when she heard that God would provide such a son when she was far past childbearing—but He did. Now she knew a reason for joyous laughter.

After Isaac's birth, jealousy festered between Sarah and Hagar over their sons fathered by the same man, Abraham. Sarah regretted her former impatience and complained to Abraham. But he left the decision to her. "She's your slave girl," he said, so Sarah decided to send Hagar and Ishmael out to live in the desert. Though Abraham ached over Sarah's decision, he sent them off with provisions. And God came to Hagar, again, and promised that He would make Ishmael a great nation, just as He promised Abraham about Isaac.

Indeed, the footprints of both Isaac and Ishmael have been left in this world. Powerful nations have arisen through their progeny; although brothers, the history of their descendants often depicts contempt and war. If only Sarah had accepted her mistake and Hagar accepted her lot. Each wanted her son to be first in Abraham's heart and be the child of promise.

Yes, I still feel for Hagar. History was impacted because she was a slave without rights. Most of us will never know what it's like to be a slave, but fortunately, we have this story to give us guidance on patience and waiting upon God's timing, making the right choices, and accepting the role of mutual servitude. Of course, God doesn't want us to be slaves in the sense that the children of Israel were in Egypt, but service to others is an important matter. Happily, as Christians, we possess the right to choose to serve.

After all, Jesus' own words in the Scriptures reveal that He came to this earth as a servant. Matthew 20:27, 28 reads, "And whoever desires to be first among you, let him be your slave—just as the Son of Man did not come to be served, but to serve, and to give His life a ransom for many" (NKJV). All that Jesus asks is our servanthood. He's our role model, and we can serve Him. Let our question of the Lord be, "Who can I serve today and in what capacity?"

Betty Kossick

As Christ Forgave You

He has not dealt with us according to our sins,
Nor punished us according to our iniquities.
For as the heavens are high above the earth,
So great is His mercy toward them who fear Him;
As far as the east is from the west,
So far has He removed our transgressions from us.
—Psalm 103:10–12, NKJV

Mrs. Brummel, if someone stole from you and then lied, would you forgive them?" I looked down at the fourth-grade girl who was asking the question. It was after school, and I was on bus duty, supervising students as they waited for their bus to take them home. This child, whom I barely knew, was asking my advice.

"Did someone steal from you and then lie about it?" I asked. She nodded her head in the affirmative and told me about a classmate who had taken a sticker from her pencil box. Then, when the teacher spoke to the other girl about it, she lied and claimed that she had already apologized for her wrongful act.

"I just don't think I should have to forgive her," my little friend persisted. My first thought was that all this was over a sticker probably worth a nickel, but I also realized that what she was confiding to me was very important to her. So I talked to her for a little while about how forgiveness could be something she would do for herself so that she wouldn't continue feeling angry. I reminded her that she could control only her own behavior—no one else's—and told her that I hoped she would always choose to be kind and compassionate.

After the bus had come and all the children had left for the day, I pondered the conversation I'd had. Was there a grudge *I* was holding—someone whom I needed to forgive? I knew that there was. I realized that my hurt and awkward feelings were over things that were probably somewhat trivial to God, just as that sticker had been to me. I reminded myself of all the things I had said to that little girl and realized that perhaps I should focus on them myself.

When I struggle to forgive, I must also remember how kind and compassionate my Lord is and how His merciful forgiveness is extended to me over and over again. It is that inspiring, divine forgiveness that gives me the capability to let go of the grudges and hurt feelings that life brings my way.

Marsha Hammond-Brummel

A Reflection of God's Love

Beloved, if God so loved us, we also ought to love one other.
—1 John 4:11, NKJV

As I have said on a number of occasions, the biblical book of Ruth and the main characters in the story help us to understand that kind treatment, respect, and consideration are basic components for both personal and couple's relationships.

When we consider what and how Boaz (Naomi's distant, wealthy relative) spoke to Ruth (Naomi's widowed daughter-in-law), especially in an era when women often did not experience respectful treatment from men, we have a wonderful glimpse into this man's noble character through his exquisite words.

I do not know in depth all the customs of that time in Bethlehem—especially the details regarding how one relative could redeem another. I only know that this Bible story implies that Boaz could have acted in many different ways. For example, he could have taken advantage of Ruth's impoverished situation and her ignorance of the local customs. He could have abused her, especially since she was a woman and a foreigner. Instead, we see in the following verses that Boaz treated Ruth with respect and affection: "And now, my daughter, don't be afraid. I will do for you all you ask. All the people of my town know that you are a woman of noble character" (Ruth 3:11, NIV). Speaking of a closer kinsman who could marry her, Boaz tells Ruth, "If he wants to do his duty as your guardian-redeemer, good; let him redeem you. But if he is not willing, as surely as the LORD lives I will do it" (verse 13, NIV). The Bible tells us that Ruth "lay at his feet until morning, but got up before anyone could be recognized; and he said, 'No one must know that a woman came to the threshing floor' " (verse 14, NIV). Boaz even protected Ruth's reputation.

Today, when we see how abuse and violence are increasing everywhere, reading the story of a man who treated Ruth with respect, value, and care for her person and her situation provides us with a magnificent example. It helps us to understand that we are daughters of the King of kings and Lord of lords. We all deserve to be treated with dignity and respect as persons of value—the same way Boaz treated Ruth.

Always remember how Boaz treated Ruth. Remember that believing men and women should reflect in their relationships the love God has for all His children.

Maite Lavado

Baby in Her Pocket

Can a woman forget her sucking child,
that she should not have compassion on the son of her womb?
yea, they may forget, yet will I not forget thee.
—Isaiah 49:15, KJV

Our chaplain told us a remarkable story of prayer, faith, and resilience that occurred when he was a pastor in Jamaica. It seemed that one of his parishioners went to the county hospital to have her baby boy. The birthing process was long and complicated. After the baby was delivered, the doctors feared that he would not survive for much longer or would live as a vegetable permanently. In disbelief, the mother—whom we'll call Bertha—simply wrapped her precious son in a cloth, slipped him in her pocket, and marched off. Nobody dared stop her.

At home, where her twelve other children played, Bertha dumped her soiled dress into a tub of water and started washing. When friends asked about the baby, she remembered the child still in the pocket of her dress. Praying fervently, Bertha grabbed the tiny child from the pocket, warmed and soothed him, and beseeched her Lord to preserve his life. The little fellow thrived after a few hospital trips for blood transfusions. The Master Physician knew better than the other doctors. He has healing in His wings. Bertha never stopped praying. In fact, she prayed when she accompanied that son and his siblings to elementary school. She prayed when he finished university. She was still praying when he began to pastor a church. When I retold this incredible story to my girlfriends, most of whom were mothers themselves, they were incredulous. They quoted today's text but omitted the final line: "yet will I not forget thee." Bertha, however, did not leave out that important line of love. She lived that truth.

Contemplating this story, I turned to an inspired passage I used to have my college students memorize: "Prayer is the opening of the heart to God as to a friend. . . . Prayer does not bring God down to us, but brings us up to Him."* Bertha's life exuded these inspired lines. Her very existence resounded with prayer. Prayer and faith were the anchors of her spiritual narrative, which was filled with love. Her humble, simple faith encompassed all she did.

Bertha was a prayer warrior.

How can we exemplify a similar faith?

Glenda-mae Greene

---

* Ellen G. White, *Steps to Christ* (Washington, DC: Review and Herald®, 1977), 93.

A Time to Be Inspired and a Time to Inspire!

To every thing there is a season, and a time
to every purpose under the heaven.
—Ecclesiastes 3:1, KJV

Time flies!* Challenges confront us, situations arise, and opportunities come and go. Life continues its relentless journey. Recently, I noticed a project I had put aside unfinished. What a shame! Time moves on, leaving behind every second wasted, each hour carelessly spent, every day irresponsibly lived, and each opportunity inadvertently missed. No one can bring time back. To mourn the loss of time is an even greater loss of time. Move forward!

What have you started that has been laid aside unfinished? What project or ministry have you started that is still awaiting completion? Did you start to reconcile with someone but get sidetracked along the way? Or did you put God "on hold" in your life by not following His call and guidance? Has He put a desire in your heart that would enlarge His territory, but you hesitated and stopped along the way?

I pray that my life and the work the Lord has appointed me to do will inspire others and glorify the Lord, even in ways I may not be aware of. Let us step forward with the lessons learned along the way. Let us share that our Lord has been good and blessed our efforts despite our many shortcomings! Let us praise Him, for each new day is a new opportunity to do His will. Let's give Him the opportunity to fulfill His purpose in our lives.

There's a time to pray, a time to ponder, a time to share, a time to write, and a time to be aware of the blessings withheld by not sharing God's continued care and love throughout our struggles and journeys. There is a time to be inspired and a time to inspire! There is a time to work and a time to rest. Yet now is not the time to put aside the Lord's calling or His purpose for you, whatever it entails. Now *is* the time to move forward, pressing toward the goal! Time is of the essence! The Lord is coming soon! It is time to trust Him and offer Him everything, for everything we have is His. May the Lord bless you as you take time to consider His many blessings, His steadfast promises, and His calling for you—no matter what life has challenged you with! It is a time to be inspired by His faithfulness and a time to inspire others to be faithful!

Rhodi Alers de López

---

* Concepts in this devotional were previously published on the author's blog. Rhodi Alers de López, "A Time to Be Inspired, and a Time to Inspire!" *Inkspirations . . . by Rhodi* (blog), June 28, 2015, http://inkspirationsbyrhodi .blogspot.com/2015/06/a-time-to-be-inspired-and-a-time-to.html.

My Prayer Box

And all things, whatsoever ye shall ask
in prayer, believing, ye shall receive.
—Matthew 21:22, KJV

The annual women's retreats have always blessed me. But one year, the afternoon session I chose to attend taught me a walk with Jesus that would enhance my prayer life. The topic of the session was prayer, especially how to use a prayer box. My sister in Christ who led this breakout session shared her personal experiences using a prayer box. Her prayers had resulted in miracles and many other answers to her prayer requests. I picked up my "starter pack," knowing that my new prayer box would replace my prayer poster board where I had previously pinned my requests. In my daily prayer journey, I habitually opened my poster board with the attached sticky-note sheets and added many more prayer requests over which I prayed.

The next day, after returning home from that women's retreat, I was determined to go to a large chain craft store to purchase my own fancy prayer box. As I parked my car, I wished I could bump into the seminar's prayer-box facilitator so she could lead me to the section where I could find a box. After all, we live in the same city. But we rarely run into each other.

I entered the store and tried to dismiss my wishful thinking. Yet I found myself looking at people in addition to looking for a box. At one point, I took a step backward to take a second look at someone who resembled my acquaintance. But it was not her. So, I searched for a store employee to help me find a small decorative box. As I walked an aisle to the back of the store, I suddenly turned around and glanced behind me. There, further down the aisle, I saw my sister in Christ. I called out her name. She greeted me, and I explained how God had led me to find her. He had heard my modest prayer and the desire of my heart to be able to see her so she could help me find a prayer box. Happily, she led me to the section where the boxes were located and helped me pick one out. With excitement, we took a picture of our encounter.

At home, I moved my sticky note prayers and praises to my new prayer box, where I would also date the answered prayers. This is my connection to my heavenly Father for others and myself. God knows the desires of our hearts. What a blessing to know that He answers the simplest prayers! He knows how important they are to us and, therefore, to Him.

Margo Peterson

No Changes

Trust in him at all times, you people . . . for God is our refuge.
—Psalm 62:8, NIV

Yesterday I sallied forth in cold weather—for Tennessee, that is. It was only 17°F (-8.3°C) degrees outside. But I needed a few things from the grocery store, so off I went. I have a favorite market, as most of us do. This particular store is part of the same chain I frequented when living in Florida because the produce is always fresh, the employees are always so helpful, and the atmosphere is friendly to shoppers.

Because I am old, I don't take to change easily, and the store's personnel had switched around quite a few displays and food items. I grumbled inwardly as I had to walk farther than normal to find my needed items in their new locations.

Yet as I walked from aisle to aisle within the store, it dawned on me that there is another locale I frequent. But in that place, nothing *ever* changes. That's the place where I go each day to meet the Holy Spirit through prayer and Bible reading. That's where the Holy Spirit and I study the Word together. God's Word never changes. In fact, God never changes: He is the same yesterday, today, and tomorrow. You can *depend* on Him, you can *trust* Him, and you can *know* that He is there for you every second of every day.

I was talking with a friend a day or two ago about an upcoming problem with which I will have to deal. "Just give it to God," he said. "Don't ask Him for help—just give the whole problem to Him." What wonderful advice! Straight out of Job! "You, the source of my life, showered me with kindness and watched over me" (Job 10:12, CEV).

All through the Bible, we find time-honored tools for successful living despite unexpected changes in our lives. Successful living is having an ongoing relationship with Jesus, who never changes. Life's circumstances may change, but He doesn't. In fact, He promises, "I will be with you always" (Matthew 28:20, CEV).

Whether the new year brought positive or negative changes into your life, praise the Lord! Because His strength and compassion and love for you and me will *never* change!

Grace A. Keene

Guardian Angel

For He shall give His angels charge over you,
to keep you in all your ways.
—Psalm 91:11, NKJV

Many years ago we lived out in the country on our hundred-acre ranch. Only about a dozen families lived in our area, so there was not much traffic on the narrow, winding road. This road took us into the river canyon, across a one-lane bridge, and up the other side on the half-hour drive into town. On trips into town, our five-year-old son would repeat his weekly memory verse to amuse himself. At that time, our old car didn't have any seat belts to use when he and his two-year-old sister sat in the back seat. One week, as our son was musing on his memory verse in Psalm 91 (today's theme text), he said, "I'm going to pretend I'm my sister's guardian angel!" We were thankful that he had such precious thoughts on the long ride.

As the years passed and we lived in many places, later joined by another daughter, we were often aware of our guardian angels' presence with us. Other times, we probably weren't. Our travels took us throughout the United States, Mexico, and Canada, so I'm sure our guardian angels worked overtime some days.

Today, our children are grown and have families of their own. They and their children are doing their own driving. In our senior years, we have moved back to the old ranch. Now, though, a subdivision surrounds it, and much more traffic travels on that narrow, winding road. Some of the drivers think they are driving in town and forget how to drive these rural roads. I am so thankful for seat belts and always pray for my guardian angel to go with me when I start the drive into town. I also pray for others who are driving this road with me—that they will drive carefully.

It has been more than sixty years since our son first learned that memory verse in Psalm 91. Now four generations of our family have driven on this narrow mountain road. Needless to say, we have had some close calls, but God's angels have protected us from any serious accidents or injuries.

There are so many precious promises in the Bible from which we gain encouragement.

Thank You, Father, for standing behind Your wonderful promises of protection.

Betty J. Adams

Baptism

Then Jesus came from Galilee to the Jordan to be baptized by John.
—Matthew 3:13, NIV

In the "land of the yeti," where perpetual snow covers some of the highest peaks on Earth, we had the opportunity to serve as a medical missionary family. Our mission was about twenty-four miles (thirty-nine kilometers) from Kathmandu, the capital city of the Kingdom of Nepal. There, our boys received kindergarten and first-grade instruction from Mrs. Iris Adderton, a retired teacher from Australia. With other students, they studied in a single classroom. Our boys grew up playing with the local children—running, jumping, and climbing barefoot, as did the goats and their kids along the rice and wheat terraces surrounding our house.

As Christians, we always had our family worship service each evening, followed by stories from the books of Laura Ingalls Wilder. Through them and other books, our boys learned positive values and ethics for life. Like Jesus in His boyhood, they grew in "wisdom and stature, and in favor with God and men" (Luke 2:52, NKJV). My husband and I, both musicians, organized a children's church choir, and I started giving piano lessons to my boys. Soon they were playing hymns for various services at church.

In such a lovely environment, it was not difficult for our youngest son to decide he would like to be baptized in the same fashion as was our Lord Jesus Christ. While his brother was abroad due to health reasons, we received a visit from Pastor Stefano Tsukamoto, who arrived with fifty young relief volunteers to help us at our mission station. On a sunny Sabbath afternoon by the Sunkosi River, before a small group of believers, our son was submerged into those cold, rapidly flowing waters to seal his commitment to Jesus, who was also baptized in a river—the Jordan in Palestine. When the little blond head of our son went under the water and resurfaced, tears of joy and gratitude flowed down my face. Meanwhile, my eldest son was also baptized—by his grandfather—in a beautiful church halfway around the globe.

Oh, what joy for us mothers to prepare our young ones for eternity and watch as they grow and give their little hearts to the Lord! One day, standing before our Savior, we mothers of all generations will be able to present ourselves along with our loved ones and say: "Here I am and the children You have given me." May this be our goal and desire. God bless you!

Marli Elizete Ritter-Hein

A Token of Appreciation

*"May the LORD bless you
and protect you.
May the LORD smile on you
and be gracious to you.
May the LORD show you his favor
and give you his peace."*
—Numbers 6:24–26, NLT

That's a real good story and worth sharing," said Penny Wheeler, my forever friend who has faithfully served in various women's ministries positions over the years. I highly value her opinion. Penny is also an auntie (in the family of God) to my boy, Sonny. He calls her "DeeDee" (his word for *auntie*). It is also his name for one of his favorite chauffeurs—Gerry. Most often, "Dad-Ron" is our chauffeur, but there have been numerous times he has sent his "precious cargo" off with others. In fact, Sonny and I have logged thousands of miles together, especially traveling from northern Alberta, Canada, to visit family and friends in the state of Oregon. Sonny loves going on road trips! Often during prayer and praise time at church, Sonny stands and proclaims to the congregation, "Go car, DeeDee?" He is remembering good times and desires more fun road trips! There is no need for an explanation for the church family. They know how fond Sonny is of his DeeDee. She's on his support team as a part-time respite caregiver. You see, as of this date, Sonny's greatest accomplishment was getting out of diapers around the age of twelve.

Regarding Sonny's and my travels, Dad-Ron once gave me wise advice: "Whenever there is a need to make a pit stop to use a restroom at a convenience store, please buy something. It's just polite and the right thing to do!" Since we don't need treats, we buy something inexpensive. Then Sonny hands the small purchase right back to the cashier who has just sold it to us. Sonny says, "Thank you," and then tells his life's story in his "language." It's about a two-minute speech! He is doing his best to make another friend on this side of Paradise. I then explain that the small gift is "a token of appreciation for using your restroom."

Expressing gratitude this way has become another joy in my life. I believe each small gift has been a dollar well spent to express our appreciation and make a new friend.

Deborah Sanders

God's Healing Power

O LORD my God, I cried unto thee,
and thou hast healed me.
—Psalm 30:2, KJV

Four years ago, I had dental surgery, and several teeth were extracted. A year later I realized that I had lost my smile. Several people asked whether I had suffered a stroke or was experiencing Bell's palsy. Additionally, in my water aerobics class, I discovered that I was unable to raise my right arm. I became concerned and went to see my physician. She immediately referred me to a neurologist. He ordered a CT scan and an MRI, which showed that I had suffered a mild stroke.

I was impressed to send the test results to another physician. But when he looked at them, he disagreed with the findings and stated that I had not had a stroke. I was referred to a second neurologist. After more tests, he also agreed that I hadn't had a stroke, but he wanted me to see a muscular neurologist. I became very intense with my prayers to the Lord because my health was deteriorating. Neither my movement nor my speech was the same as they'd been previously. I didn't even look the same. I was very fatigued and becoming low in spirit because I couldn't smile. Some people misjudged me because of my facial expressions, over which I had no control, yet I kept a smile in my heart.

Daily, I prayed for God to place me in the path of the right physician and to provide the wisdom to help me. Eventually, in February 2019, I was diagnosed with incurable muscular dystrophy. My youngest daughter was introduced to a natural health product to try to see whether it would help me. Praise God, it did! I began to regain my energy. I was urged to attend a health retreat in 2019 with the support of my family and friends. I believe that is when the Lord began to answer my prayers. I had an experience with God at the retreat, and He began to heal me.

The Lord impressed me to remove certain things from my diet that were detrimental to my health. I also realized I needed proper rest and exercise. I now am told that my smile is coming back. Presently, I am being treated by the fourth neurologist. By faith, I choose to believe that God is guiding and granting him wisdom. Daily, I pray for God's continual healing. I praise and thank God for healing me and giving me a new smile. Have faith in Him, for He is the great Healer and Restorer.

Janice M. Turner Carter

God's Great Idea!

I have taught thee in the way of wisdom;
I have led thee in right paths.
—Proverbs 4:11, KJV

The Lord is brilliant, absolutely brilliant—His ideas work! I was looking for a new bedspread for my queen-size bed. I had one in mind, but at the time, the store only had that one in full size. A few weeks later I looked again. We needed a darker bedspread because our cats leave little paw prints and fur behind. I went to the store, and there, among the many bedspreads on sale, was the very one that would work. One queen-size bedspread in the color maroon! *Thank You, thank You, Lord!*

Then I thought of the empty curtain rods over the two bedroom windows. They needed dressing up. I was in a different store looking at clearance items when the thought occurred to me that I could use the matching pillow shams that came with the bedspread to make curtain valances. Oh, what a thought! I went home and right to work. When I slipped the first finished valance over a rod, I felt totally thrilled with the result. The Lord gave me the idea, and the idea really worked. Then I transformed the second sham into a valance. I felt amazingly happy—like a little kid.

My next thought was to keep this a little secret and not say a word to my husband. I would let him be surprised by the new valances on his own. My husband entered the bedroom after work but made no comment. *Maybe he'll notice them in the morning*, I thought. The next day as he was getting ready for work, he was still unaware of anything different in the bedroom. I felt a bit disappointed. Later on, I asked one of my sons whether he had noticed anything new in the bedroom. He said, "Yes, the curtains are new." My son then proceeded to tell me to "chill out" after I mentioned to him that Dad hadn't seemed to notice them.

That evening my son evidently let the cat out of the bag because, when my husband walked into the bedroom this time, he looked right up at the curtains and exclaimed, "I didn't know you were such a Suzy Homemaker!" This project was special to me because the Lord and I did it together. Isn't that how God wants to work in our lives always?

Dear Lord, may I trust in Your leading and prompting and put Your ideas to work. Even when others don't notice, may the knowledge of having followed what You revealed be all the approval I really need. Amen.

Rosemarie Clardy

Heaven's Graduation

I have fought the good fight,
I have finished the race, I have kept the faith.
—2 Timothy 4:7, NKJV

Nestled between the towering Maracas Mountains in Trinidad lies my alma mater. As a member of the university's board of trustees, I was invited to participate in its ninety-first graduation exercises. The board planned for the exercises to be held in new facilities built on the site of a previous auditorium that was destroyed by fire. Many doubted the new building would be completed in time. But the university president insisted that with God, all things are possible. With prayer, perseverance, and the power of God, the building was in a state of readiness for the graduation exercises. As I witnessed and participated in the grandeur of the graduation activities, I was overcome with ecstasy. I heard stories of how graduates had endured hardships and demonstrated great faith in order to achieve their goals. I witnessed the adulation of spectators as they celebrated with the graduating class, involving such family combinations as father and daughter, aunt and niece, brothers, and a family of four that included the father and mother.

Reflecting on the seemingly impossible task of completing the auditorium and on the trials and hardships experienced by some graduates, I am reminded of heaven. The workmen worked tirelessly to complete the building, and the decorators created an incredible ambiance that reminded me that God is preparing for us a magnificent home in heaven which "eye hath not seen" (1 Corinthians 2:9, KJV). I am further reminded that the redeemed, like the class of 2018, will have endured great tribulations, but by God's grace and mercy, they will have made it to the finish line.

What a grand and glorious graduation that will be when the graduating class of Earth stands before the King of kings and Lord of lords to receive, not a diploma that will fade away, but a crown of glory that will last forever. They will not wear the corruptible graduation regalia of Earth but the robe of Christ's righteousness. Among this class will be family members, friends, loved ones, and the redeemed of all the ages who have fought the good fight and kept the faith. What a day that will be when the trials of Earth will end, and we will hear the strains of the Song of Moses and the Lamb. I can't wait for that grand graduation day! How about you?

Gerene I. Joseph

Dumb as Dirt

We all, like sheep, have gone astray.
—Isaiah 53:6, NIV

A re sheep really dumb as dirt?" asked Melissa, setting her books on the table. "A few years ago, before a trip to Iceland, I might have said that sheep were dumber than dirt," I replied. Melissa looked at me carefully; her face a question mark—a typical nonverbal gesture when waiting for a story without actually asking for it. I complied.

"My friend Unnur and I embarked on a two-day driving trip to see, among other attractions, the midnight sun, one of the largest glaciers in Europe, and the blue lagoon. Unnur was driving; I was keeping an eagle eye out for erratic sheep. Quite regularly as we moved along, a sheep or two or three would stop eating grass along the side of the road, glance toward our approaching vehicle, and suddenly bolt into the middle of the road—right in front of the car, no less! It took continual vigilance plus expert driving to miss hitting them."

Melissa laughed. "You're right. Sheep *are* dumber than dirt!"

"After brunch on the first day," I continued, "we turned onto Highway 1, or so we thought. Within minutes, however, the paved two-lane road morphed into a one-lane dirt track that wound up and down hills, around rock formations, beside rivers swollen from a myriad of waterfalls, and over mountains—with no place to turn around. Driving soon became more dangerous and frightening as clouds descended, enveloping us in thick mist barely illuminated by the car's fog lamps. Unnur drove slowly. We both prayed. Eventually, fourteen exhausting miles [twenty-three kilometers] later, we connected with the *real* Highway 1. Turned out we had gotten lost on a 'shortcut'—on a road that was more suited to four-wheel-drive vehicles than to a sedan!"

Melissa sighed with eyes like saucers. "Well, you got back safely!"

"Yes," I replied. "But since the Scriptures compare humans to sheep, I'm rather loathe to trumpet that sheep are as dumb as dirt. Especially since 'we all, like sheep, have gone astray.' "

Several moments of silence passed. A long time for Melissa. Finally, she nodded and said, "I can just picture that shortcut. This will make a great story for show-and-tell tomorrow. Good thing God cares for sheep *and* people!"

Good thing, indeed. I am most grateful to have a Shepherd (Psalm 23:1).

Arlene R. Taylor

Live What You Preach

Wherefore let him that thinketh he standeth take heed lest he fall.
—1 Corinthians 10:12, KJV

The twenty-four hours graciously given us by God were hardly enough for me on any given day. With a crowded mind, I could fall asleep while driving, regardless of the time of day. Sometimes I listened to audio sermons, hymns, or religious books to keep me alert. But one Wednesday, while returning to work after running an errand, I could hardly keep my eyes open. The night before (and almost nightly for that entire week), I had slept for barely five hours. I would go to bed late but wake up early. My life was pressed with many cares that often kept me awake till midnight and beyond. No wonder I was sleep deprived!

As I drove, I fought sleep but didn't bother to stop to call or speak with someone to help me stay awake while I was driving. About three minutes before reaching my office building, I was suddenly surrounded and blocked on all sides by an assemblage of police cars, all with flashing lights and sirens. Shocked, all I could hear was, "Stop! Put that car in park position. Stop! Open the door." Still dazed, I stopped. One of them, a female officer, quickly flung open my side door, reached toward the ignition, and grabbed the key. I was gripped with a sense of foreboding as my sleepy eyes became wide awake! I was interrogated and tested for driving under the influence. I told the police that I never drank alcohol. They checked my license and found out my office was actually next door to their headquarters around the corner. Yet, unfortunately, I was still arrested because someone driving behind me had been observing my repeated swerves and near accidents before alerting the police that I was driving dangerously. That person must have thought I needed to be apprehended. After I was set free, I realized that I *was* guilty. I had put myself and others in jeopardy.

In 1978, Candi Staton sang a song titled "Victim." I saw myself as a "victim" of the very song I used to sing. As a natural-health evangelist, I emphasize the importance of the natural law of *sleep*. I am grateful to God for sparing me from what could have been a great embarrassment at the hands of the law.

Someone is always watching you. It is your responsibility to live by example—live what you teach. Personally, walk the walk, do what is right, and don't just talk about what is right.

Ekele P. Ukegbu-Nwankwo

Nothing Is Really Lost

Casting all your care upon Him, for He cares for you.
—1 Peter 5:7, NKJV

Every Tuesday and Thursday morning, one of our daughters drops by and takes her dad to the YWCA to work out. They always enjoy their special time together, but on the morning of April 23, 2019, when they returned from the Y, our daughter was frantically searching for her cell phone. She remembered having had it in the locker room at the Y. Yet she was sure she had not left it there, but where could it be? Besides that, it was her birthday. Even though we had already celebrated with her twin sister, I was thinking it was a pretty sad way to start this important day in her life.

Our daughter decided to return to the Y to see whether her phone had been turned in. It had not. While she was gone, my husband and I prayed that the Lord would show us where the phone was. Suddenly impressed, my husband looked between the cushions on our couch where our daughter had laid her jacket. As he lifted a cushion, there was the phone! Apparently, it had slid from the jacket pocket down the side of the cushion, where it was playing hide-and-seek. We contacted our daughter at her home and told her the good news. What a birthday blessing for her!

Years ago, a dear lady reminded me that nothing is ever really lost. God knows where each thing is, and all we need to do is ask Him to show us where it is. He cares about us, and even though sometimes He doesn't show us right away, eventually He will answer our prayer.

On a recent Friday, my friend lost her wallet and had looked everywhere she had recently been. She finally remembered she had not checked back at the post office. The post office, however, was closed, and she could not check there until the following Monday. Many prayers were ascending that she would find that wallet. On Monday morning, she retrieved her wallet at the post office with everything intact that had been with it. How happy she was that she had not canceled her debit card or gone to renew her driver's license! Though my friend had to wait before finding her wallet, God knew where it was all the time. Perhaps He was just using my friend's oversight as a renewed call to prayer and deeper trust in Him.

What burden is on your heart today? Have you taken it to Jesus? Use your perplexity as an opportunity to renew your prayer life and deepen your trust in Jesus. He cares for you.

Anne May Radke Waters

Jesus at a Brazilian Soccer Match

"I will go before you
and will level the mountains;
I will break down gates of bronze
and cut through bars of iron.
I will give you hidden treasures,
riches stored in secret places,
so that you may know that I am the LORD,
the God of Israel, who summons you by name."
—Isaiah 45:2, 3, NIV

Brazil versus Argentina. MetLife Stadium. June 9, 2012. At church, we worked on all the details involved in handing out four thousand bags; each bag containing a book, a bottle of water, and a newspaper. The vehicles transporting the hundreds of bags would park outside of the stadium area to meet the other members of our New York Brazilian church who would be traveling to the New Jersey stadium by train. We would meet at a predetermined train station.

When we were already on the road, our pastor called me. He said that when buying train tickets, the agent told him they were heading to the wrong train station and informed him of the right one. So I texted all the other drivers, alerting them of the new rendezvous location. After arriving at the right station, we noticed it was in an area where we would not be allowed to give out what we'd brought to share. After prayer, we decided to stay where we were because the game was already in its final quarter. A tall security officer approached and told us to leave. One of our church elders showed him our giveaway book in Portuguese. The guard paused, pointed to the huge parking lot, and said, "I don't want to know where you are." Within half an hour, as people returned to their cars in the summer heat, we had given away four thousand bags!

When we step by faith into the water of adversity, God will open the way to pass through. He will ensure that we have what we need: the right ticket agent, the right tickets, and the right security guard to point us to be where God wants us to be. When you work for God, you can plan as thoroughly as humanly possible but allow God to perfect the plan according to His will. Do not be afraid. Just go and spread the Word, and let God be God.

Kênia Kopitar

Signs From the Savior

"And this is a sign to you from the Lord,
that the Lord will do this thing which He has spoken."
—Isaiah 38:7, NKJV

My early mornings are filled with wonderful moments that God and I spend together. I cherish spending time with just Him alone. One morning, however, my mind was crowded with many concerns: my husband's brain tumor, my son's swollen adenoids, my parent's heart blockage, and so much more. It seemed the whole family was failing in health.

I was having a heart-to-heart talk with God during my predawn prayer walk. I wanted to feel Him close and deeply longed for an assurance that He was in control amid all this chaos in my life.

The sky was still dim, with only a bare hint of the approaching dawn. How my heart longed to see something brighter, some sort of reassuring sign that God loved me!

Lord, I prayed, *if You truly love me, please show me a sign. I want to see something in the sky that will remind me of Your certain presence in my life.* As soon as I said amen, I noticed a lone star in the sky shining brightly. I became super excited and thanked God profusely. That one star gave me a ray of hope that God would lead me through the present turmoil in my life. Jesus genuinely cares enough and has the time to answer the prayer of one wretched sinner like me—out of the 7.8 billion people living in this world! I was overwhelmed by His care! What a blessing to know that we have a personal God who wants to be intimately connected to us!

Our God has always communicated to humanity through various means. In ancient Israel, the high priest wore a vest bearing two stones known as the Urim and Thummim. "When questions were brought for decision before the Lord, a halo of light encircling the precious stone at the right was a token of the divine consent or approval, while a cloud shadowing the stone at the left was an evidence of denial or disapprobation."* Divine signs, patiently given, also signaled that God had chosen both Moses and Gideon to accomplish His special purposes. What a loving God to guide us! Great is His faithfulness! *Dear Jesus, You are a God of signs and wonders. Thank You for all that You do for us every day. Help us to respond to Your love with all our hearts.*

Esther Synthia Murali

* Ellen G. White, *Patriarchs and Prophets* (Nampa, ID: Pacific Press®, 2005), 351.

Daffodils in Winter

My brethren, count it all joy when you fall into various trials,
knowing that the testing of your faith produces patience. But let patience have
its perfect work, that you may be perfect and complete, lacking nothing.
—James 1:2–4, NKJV

Unseasonably warm temperatures tempted me to think spring was just around the corner. Apparently, they did the same for plants. Green noses poked out of the ground, promising purple crocuses. Daffodil leaves and stems grew, then brightened my spirits with sunshiny golden trumpets. They silently seemed to blare, "Spring is here!" Could it be? I hoped they were right.

Four mornings ago, the temperature dove to 22°F (-5.5°C). Snow covered my cheerful daffodil blooms. Instead of standing upright, each stem leaned almost to the ground. Some blossoms touched their trumpets to the earth; others came close. The next morning more snow covered them.

As I stared at the snow-laden flowers, suddenly, I thought about other kinds of storms—health issues, the death of loved ones, relationship fractures, financial pressures, and feeling far from God. We face many and various storms that try to derail our lives. The temptation to give up threatens.

But wait! Jesus promised He would always be with us. He'll walk through the storms with us. Even if we can't see Him, He'll walk with us as He walked in the fiery furnace with Shadrach, Meshach, and Abednego.

I'm not very good at counting it joyful when trials threaten, but during one of the longest, most difficult trials of my life, I have often said, "I wouldn't want to go through it again, but I wouldn't give up what I learned for anything." God holding me up through that trial has made every subsequent trial easier. And that brings me joy!

What about my bowed-to-the-ground daffodils? The day before yesterday, the snow melted. The daffodils stood a little straighter. In spite of an overnight freeze, yesterday they stood even taller. Even though they shone as brilliant yellow in the sunshine as they had days earlier, they weren't quite as sprite as before the storm. This morning they stand tall.

Thank You, God, for reminding me that You can bring us through storms with joy!

Helen Heavirland

Unity in Diversity
PART 1

For we are His workmanship [His own master work, a work of art], created in Christ Jesus
[reborn from above—spiritually transformed, renewed, ready to be used] for good works.
—Ephesians 2:10, AMP

When you get up in the morning and look into the mirror, whom do you see? Do you realize you are looking at the reflection of one of God's unique creations—you? Think about it; there is *no one* in this whole wide world *exactly* like you! Listen to what He says about you in today's text. Think about it. *You* are God's work of art! Do you know how special that makes you?

The National Forensic Science Technology Center affirms we are each so distinct that not even identical twins have the same fingerprints. Also, it's important to keep in mind that fingerprints also vary between your own fingers. This means you have a unique print on each finger. This also shows how great God is. So He needs each one of us to show the world how great and awesome *He* is!

Sometimes Christians become confused about how we show the world we are God's. We sometimes confuse *unity* with *uniformity*. Let's look at the meaning of *unity*. Definitions for this word include terms such as *integrity, wholeness,* and *undivided or unbroken completeness.* God's varied creations still reflect unity. Consider these amazing examples.

Recent research led by the American Museum of Natural History suggests that there are about eighteen thousand bird species in the world—nearly twice as many as previously thought! The research focuses on "hidden" avian diversity— birds that look similar to one another or were thought to interbreed but are actually different species. Then there are ice crystals. Water molecules line up and form a six-sided shape called a hexagon. This is why all snowflakes are six-sided! Yet no two shapes are exactly alike. In fact, two snowflakes from the same cloud will have different sizes and shapes because of their different journeys to the ground.

If God made each bird and snowflake unique, how can we not recognize and appreciate how beautiful, special, and unique each one of us is to Him? How can we *not* recognize that He has created each one of us, just as we are, for a very special purpose (Colossians 1:16)?

Wilma Kirk Lee

Unity in Diversity
PART 2

Just as a body, though one, has many parts, but all its many parts form one body,
so it is with Christ. For we were all baptized by one Spirit so as to form one body—
whether Jews or Gentiles, slave or free—and we were all given the one Spirit to drink.
Even so the body is not made up of one part but of many.
—1 Corinthians 12:12–14, NIV

If *unity* means "undivided or unbroken completeness," what does it mean to be *uniform*? *Uniformity* means "the quality of *lacking* variety or diversity." That doesn't sound like God's creation, does it, with its variations in animals, snowflakes, and people? The apostle Paul pointed out that the human body, though composed of many different parts, is still one body—all those parts are needed and must work together. So it is with the body of Christ. Some of us are tall; some short. We are all different colors, but we all still make up the body of Christ, which is the church.

So what does it mean to have unity in diversity? Unity in diversity has been described as unity *without uniformity* and diversity *without fragmentation*. This concept shifts our focus from unity—based on a mere tolerance of physical, cultural, linguistic, social, religious, political, ideological, and/or psychological differences—toward a more complex unity, based on the understanding that differences *enrich* human interactions! Unity in diversity deliberately combines "oneness" with "variety."

God wants His church to appreciate the uniqueness of each individual and celebrate the gifts he or she brings to the body of Christ. Since He created us to be unique, we can't point fingers at people who do things differently. After all, "GOD judges persons differently than humans do. . . . GOD looks into the heart" (1 Samuel 16:7, *The Message*). Furthermore, God "brings us into harmony. This goes for all the churches—no exceptions" (1 Corinthians 14:33, *The Message*).

Why not start today? Look around at all the people you meet. Smile at someone you might not even make eye contact with if you're locked into uniformity. We can make a change if we collaborate, not compete or compare! May God help us to *be* the change we want to see! In Christ, let us embrace the uniqueness of others in His body. "Love each other. Love is what holds you all together in perfect unity. Let the peace that Christ gives control your thinking. You were all called together in one body to have peace. . . . Be thankful" (Colossians 3:14, 15, ICB).

Wilma Kirk Lee

Keeping the Pace

So we don't look at the troubles we can see now; rather, we fix
our gaze on things that cannot be seen. For the things we see now
will soon be gone, but the things we cannot see will last forever.
—2 Corinthians 4:18, NLT

This morning I went jogging. Actually, I went limping, with my new case of plantar fasciitis torturing me at every step. I looked like a wounded water buffalo, behind the herd, stumbling in a losing battle across a vast savanna.

On the horizon, I spotted a man walking his dog with ease. I immediately felt self-conscious about my struggling pace. I stumbled closer—and into his dog, who greeted me with the enthusiasm only a wagging tail can convey. In my embarrassment, I managed a polite head nod, avoiding eye contact in shame, and tried to pick up my feet again.

Around the back side of the pond, the man and his pooch were also doing a second lap. As I prepared to pass again on my walk of shame, he addressed me cheerily. "You're making good time!" I hate "pity encouragement." In the past, I've done much better than this poor representation of my endurance. I used to run races, hike mountains, and bike hundreds of miles. Before I could explain why his pity wasn't deserved, I took a good look at this self-appointed coach before me. He was missing part of his face. His nose was completely sunken and bore proof that he had experienced recovery and more than his fair share of pity encouragement. I didn't look away, yet the scars and distortion faded instantly as I recognized what he was trying to convey to me.

It was a truly beautiful moment in which two people looked deeply into each other's eyes and really saw one another. In a single second, we shared a lesson of how silly we are about the perceptions of others, shook our heads, and audibly chuckled. While I have since forgotten the details of his face, I will not forget the message in his words.

We all carry scars. We all have had better days, but there is beauty beneath. We have only to exercise it, and that beauty will cover all the deformities of these outward blemishes. So, whatever you are doing to improve your physical and mental strength today, don't become discouraged. You're making great time!

Wendy Williams

Real Happiness = Serving God and Others

"And the King will say, 'I tell you the truth, when you did it to one of the least of these my brothers and sisters, you were doing it to me!'"
—Matthew 25:40, NLT

For years, my husband and I have been involved in ministry in the Philippines. I started in ministry upon my arrival in Germany while I was still single. God put a burden and love in my heart for this ministry. We help by sending money for the support of laypeople and radio and jail ministry, feeding homeless street people, and providing a home for the aged. The Lord has richly rewarded our efforts. The jail ministry alone has resulted in the decisions of more than five hundred inmates to give their hearts to Christ and be baptized. That happened in one year's time, during 2014 and 2015. To God be the glory for that amazing outcome!

My husband and I decided to involve ourselves personally by traveling to the Philippines for our vacation. We wanted to work among those we had been helping to support. To participate in the street ministry, we had to get up at three o'clock in the morning. After rising, we participated in a devotional time with our coworkers. Then we cooked big pots of noodle soup. With bread and blankets, we went into the streets to awaken those sleeping on the ground. As we gently spread blankets over them, we offered a warm breakfast—a warm breakfast for this underserved part of the population who had gone to sleep the night before on empty stomachs. My heart overflowed with joy as I reached out to these suffering individuals.

I especially remember one elderly woman on the street. As I covered her with a blanket and set down a container of soup beside her, I asked, "Where do you live?" She simply pointed to the tree beside us where I had just served her and gave us a beautiful smile of gratitude. I was deeply touched. Returning her smile, I said, "God loves you so much."

In tears, she responded, "Really? Thank you for coming here!" I handed her a small amount of cash, which brought another smile of surprise to her face.

Suddenly, I understood the words of Jesus, who said, "It is more blessed to give than to receive" (Acts 20:35, KJV). Today I challenge you, woman of God, to be involved in some kind of ministry. God will lead you, and your life will never be the same.

Let the personal motto of each of us be, "I am a woman God can use."

Loida Gulaja Lehmann

He Gave Us Eyes to See Them

And God saw every thing that he had made,
and, behold, it was very good.
—Genesis 1:31, KJV

We pulled out of our driveway in Alberta, heading west to our son's home in Alaska, almost two thousand miles (thirty-two hundred kilometers) away. That's a great distance to travel in just three days. But the distance and the hours would pass. My husband, Larry, would read to me; I'd quiz him on facts from travel guides; and we'd count wild animals to keep ourselves more alert and make us more aware of our marvelous world.

I took a small notebook from my purse and started looking around. In our neighborhood, we occasionally see porcupines waddling along the road. Once, we'd seen a pair of beavers crossing a highway. We knew that in nine hours, we'd see stone sheep in Stone Mountain Provincial Park, and tomorrow there would be wood bison near Liard River Hot Springs, but we hoped for a coyote or two, some deer, elk, moose, and bear—black and grizzly—before then. The miles sped by. No coyotes or deer in the fields. I asked Larry about the length of the Yukon River. No bears visible. The terrain changed, and I took over the driving. Larry read to me, and I scanned the sides of the road. "Nothing," I complained when he rested his voice. "Not a porcupine, coyote, or deer. Certainly not a bear or moose. Absolutely nothing. Nothing but those little ground squirrels. They're everywhere."

Larry replied, "I thought we were counting animals. Did we establish a size criterion? Does the animal need to be at least a meter [about a yard] long, like a porcupine? Or must it weigh nine hundred kilos [nearly two thousand pounds] like a wood bison? Of course, ground squirrels are only about twenty-five centimeters [ten inches] long and probably don't weigh even half a kilo [one pound]—but they're still animals, aren't they?"

His observations hung in the air between us for a moment.

I looked at him and realized how blind I'd been. "You'd better put that book away," I said, grinning. "You're going to be much too busy counting ground squirrels to get any more reading done!"

And so we traveled ever westward with a new, more vivid and inclusive appreciation of our wondrous world and all its creatures—both great and small.

Denise Dick Herr

The Old Sofa

"So my heavenly Father will also do to every one of you,
if you do not forgive your brother or sister from your heart."
—Matthew 18:35, NRSV

My friend, Amarilis, tells me that while she was still living in her native Cuba, she went to visit her sister in Havana. Her sister was highly skilled in upholstery and had recently come by a grand old sofa. She proudly showed it to Amarilis, declaring, "You wait and see what I'm going to do to this sofa. I'll leave it like new!"

And so it was that when Amarilis went back to visit her sister some months later, she was shocked to find what looked to her like a brand-new sofa. It even smelled new! Her sister's skillful hands had transformed the old, tattered sofa into a work of art. But during those times in Cuba, a beautiful possession like that could awaken both admiration and envy from one's neighbors, who might be inclined to report them to the authorities.

As Amarilis and her sister were admiring the renewed sofa, someone knocked at the front door. When they opened it, there stood a government inspector! As the family stood in stunned silence, waiting to see what would happen, the inspector began to walk parsimoniously around the living room. Every time he came to the sofa, he'd say, "My, what a beautiful sofa! It looks *so* new." Amarilis and her sister traded furtive glances, just waiting for the command to remove the "new" sofa and take it away.

Just then, Amarilis's seven-year-old nephew approached the inspector and said, "Sir, the sofa you see is new, but the old one is still there, underneath!" With that, the inspector sheepishly excused himself and walked out the door.

This child, in all his innocence, called out a problem that many of us adults have when it comes to forgiveness: We forgive but leave the old resentments lurking "underneath." An upholstered forgiveness, as it were. In the parable of the two debtors in Matthew 18, the first debtor was completely forgiven of everything—no strings attached. That is how God forgives. Micah 7:18 reminds us that when God forgives, He erases our sin. He doesn't forgive half-heartedly or keep recalling those mistakes of ours. No! Our heavenly Father forgives with His whole heart, including forgetting that at one time there was an old sofa under there!

Lourdes E. Morales-Gudmundsson

I Cried Out to the Lord

Hear me when I call, O God of my righteousness!
You have relieved me in my distress;
Have mercy on me, and hear my prayer.
—Psalm 4:1, NKJV

Four months ago, my husband and I planned to remove an air conditioner from a window. Alone one day in the house, I assessed the situation and decided I could remove it myself as I'd done a few years back. I removed everything that was holding the appliance in the window, and then I cautiously slid it to the edge of the window ledge. When I got it to the point of no return, however, I realized it was much too heavy for me. With no help nearby, I got the "bright" idea of letting it come down on its own. Then I could balance it on my thigh. But it came down much too quickly and turned during the descent. The hard metal corner hit the center of my kneecap because I had not had time to raise my supporting leg high enough or quickly enough.

Now I was in excruciating pain and very afraid I had fractured my kneecap. Though I do not ever remember doing so before, I cried out to the Lord: "Save my knee!" It hurt so badly I doubted I would be able to walk—and I *still* had to lower the air conditioner the rest of the way down. As I did, I continued to cry out to God in the midst of my terrible pain. When the machine was safely on the floor, I gingerly put weight on my leg. Despite terrible pain, I could walk! I praised God as I put ice packs on the injured knee. After sitting with the ice packs for a while, my leg pain slowly decreased, and I noticed a deep puncture wound.

Eventually, my knee healed completely with no residual pain or need for medical attention. God had heard my plea and miraculously saved my knee. And this was truly a miracle, for my knee should have been shattered. Yet x-rays this week, which a doctor ordered because of an old arthritis-caused knee injury for which I needed a cortisone injection, revealed *no* indication of a knee fracture having *ever* occurred! Praise God! I still have a tiny scar from the puncture wound, but I believe God left it there as a reminder for me not to be so foolish in the future. Truly He was gracious to me—as He is to all of us when we call upon Him.

Susan Anderson

Unity, Not Division

If the ax is dull,
And one does not sharpen the edge,
Then he must use more strength;
But wisdom brings success.
—Ecclesiastes 10:10, NKJV

Our church is dying; things are boring," Jessie cried.

"There is nothing for the kids!" Melvin complained.

"We need music for our youth," Virginia added.

"I want to start a new church," Benny replied.

"But remember," Janaki cautioned, "even Satan wanted to start his own church, causing heaven to lose one-third of its inhabitants." Ellen White once counseled her church to "be careful how you receive every new notion and those who claim to have great light. The character of their work seems to be to accuse and to tear down."*

Instead of letting church needs or deficiencies cause division, I suggest that whenever you notice a need, consider that perhaps God is calling you to that ministry—the youth, the elderly, young couples who need help with their children, or workshop presentations on healthful lifestyle choices or wise money management. Teach someone else how to play a musical instrument that could help to enrich the various services and programs of your church.

We should never underestimate—or overestimate—the power of evil. Yes, division is Satan's number-one strategy for destroying a church. He brought separation between God and His created beings when he made the heavenly beings, along with Adam and Eve, believe a lie. He still wants to replace love, joy, and peace in the church with hatred, discord, and rage.

More importantly, though, we should never underestimate the power of *love*! It brought our Lord and Savior to the cross to reconcile us to God, His Father. Love empowers our service to God and humankind as we work in unity with others, shunning evil and division. Love unites!

Suhana Chikatla

---

* Ellen G. White, *Selected Messages*, book 2 (Washington, DC: Review and Herald®, 1958), 69.

Heaven

We speak the wisdom of God in a mystery, even the hidden wisdom,
which God ordained before the world unto our glory. . . . But as it is written,
Eye hath not seen, nor ear heard, neither have entered into the heart of man,
the things which God hath prepared for them that love him.
—1 Corinthians 2:7–9, KJV

It is now summer and very hot in my part of the world. I recently gave up the hair extensions that I wore as braids and cut my hair so that I could be cooler in the heat that I was expecting. I mused, *I wonder what temperature we will have in heaven. Low seventies, maybe?*

This is not a busy time where I work, so I decided to search online for the people from where I grew up. I was able to locate Aunt Florence, who still lives in the same house (for sixty-plus years) and is now ninety-six years old! Her voice, however, is that of a fifty-year-old, and so is her memory! She remembered me, even though I have not been home for at least sixteen years. She proceeded to tell me of everyone we know who has passed away. *So many people to look for when we get to heaven!*

Our neighbor gave us a wonderful California king–size bed with a fantastic mattress. We moved to a new apartment, and the bedroom can barely contain the bed. My husband tells me that the next time we move, we can buy a different bed and also get a larger bedroom. *What will we lie on in heaven if there is no night* (Revelation 21:25, KJV)? *Will we ever lie down, or will we stand up all day?*

I recently confessed to a close friend that I am obsessed with shoes! I cannot stop buying shoes! In the past, I have ordered them online and picked them up when my husband is away so that he did not know that I had more shoes. *What will we wear on our feet in heaven* (Matthew 6:30, 31)? *Will anyone ever step on my toes?*

I will have so many questions, people to see, places to go, plenty of good food to eat, things to do . . .

But, according to God's Word, my questions are not all that important. "But seek first his kingdom and his righteousness, and all these things will be given to you as well" (Matthew 6:33, NIV).

I want to see Jesus, don't you?

Sylvia A. Franklin

Hinckley Yachts and Heavenly Homes

"If you then, being evil, know how to give good gifts to your children, how much more will your Father who is in heaven give good things to those who ask Him!"
—Matthew 7:11, NKJV

Once I wrote a book called *Love in Pictures*. My story's hero, Logan, is quite the character. His parents are wealthy and generous, so for his college graduation gift, they buy a Hinckley yacht for him to live on.

Hinckley is known as the best yacht company in America. Its designs are smooth, sleek, luxurious, and comfortable. If you love the water and you live on it in a Hinckley, you really have it made!

I found out about these alluring details during my story research for Logan's character. I spoke to a Hinckley representative, told him that I was writing a fictional story, and explained how Logan's parents buy a Hinckley for him. The representative asked me, "Are they adopting?" He wanted parents in real life who would give *him* extraordinarily good gifts as my fictional parents had given Logan. All this led me to consider that our heavenly Father wants to give us good gifts too—dare I say Hinckleys included? But above fancy homes to live in on the water, He wants to give us *more* than the worldly possessions that we desire; He wants to give us *eternal life*!

The Bible says that this world is not our home. As Christ's followers, we are strangers passing through a foreign land. "Friends, this world is not your home, so don't make yourselves cozy in it. Don't indulge your ego at the expense of your soul. Live an exemplary life in your neighborhood so that your actions will refute their prejudices. Then they'll be won over to God's side and be there to join in the celebration when he arrives" (1 Peter 2:11, 12, *The Message*).

The Bible also says that in Jesus Christ's Father's house are many mansions (see John 14:2, NKJV). He is preparing a place for us to live, and it is out of this world, literally, because that place is heaven.

Living on the water in a Hinckley yacht here on Earth sounds amazing, but living in heaven and being in the presence of God for eternity sounds so much better!

The Bible advises us to store our treasure in heaven, not on earth (Matthew 6:19–21). Therefore, I am setting my sights on my heavenly home. What about you?

Alexis A. Goring

Self-Sufficiency Syndrome
PART 1

I can do all things through Christ which strengtheneth me.
—Philippians 4:13, KJV

Confession time—I struggle with a disorder that I call self-sufficiency syndrome! I am a very independent person and have been since I was a child. I started walking at nine months of age, if that tells you anything. Yet relying on God for everything since I gave my life to Him many decades ago is really challenging for me at times. I tend to leave the big issues for Him and try to take care of the "smaller" details myself so as not to waste His time.

I grew up in a home where I had to take care of my siblings and myself from a very young age. I worked hard as a child, doing physical labor that grown men should have been doing. This gave me a good work ethic, which I greatly appreciate. It also gave me lifelong back pain, which I don't appreciate so much! I was taught, whether by word or example, that I had to do things myself. As I was growing up, it was easy to believe that if I wanted something done (or done right), I had to do it myself. Many of you can probably relate to that statement!

This has served me well in many ways in life. For example, I have been employed in various positions precisely because of my abilities, work ethic, and dedication. I am blessed that God has given me many talents. Please don't misunderstand me; I'm not boasting. I'm recognizing what God has done in my life. Sometimes, though, it is easier for me to function by relying on these innate and God-given abilities rather than relying upon God in the moment for ability, wisdom, strength, and knowledge, among other things.

As a young adult, I gave my life to Christ and asked Him to guide and direct my steps. Surrendering to Christ was my greatest accomplishment and is my ongoing work and desire. It's also one of my biggest challenges: not in everything, but when it comes to depending and relying on God for daily matters and tasks. It's easy for me to sit down in my office and start responding to emails, writing promotional materials, and conducting ministry business on all levels. But it's difficult to remember to ask God to be in *all* the details and help me with *each* thing before I dig in.

If you are having challenges along these lines, too, I invite you to join me in affirming this precious truth found in God's Word: I can do *all* things—but *only* in the strength of Christ!

Samantha Nelson

Self-Sufficiency Syndrome

PART 2

For the LORD giveth wisdom.
—Proverbs 2:6, KJV

One part of my self-sufficiency confusion and struggle comes from what I learned as a child. Another part comes from quotes like this one: "In order to receive God's help, man must realize his weakness and deficiency; he must apply his own mind to the great change to be wrought in himself. . . . Many never attain to the position that they might occupy, because they wait for God to do for them that which He has given them power to do for themselves."*

And when Jesus was about to raise Lazarus from the dead, didn't He say to others, "Take ye away the stone" (John 11:39, KJV), instead of doing it Himself? It seems that He didn't do for humanity what they could do for themselves.

Just reading those quotes tells me, on some level, that I need to do things myself and not depend on God to do all things for me. After all, I'm supposed to do those things for myself that God has given me the power and ability to do, right? Yes and no.

It's true that God will not exercise divine power to do something for us that we can do in our human strength by His grace. It's equally true that He wants us to rely on Him for everything; this means that daily, moment by moment, we are to continually surrender to Him and seek His will and advice about everything we do.

So how do we reconcile these seemingly opposing thoughts? It really is simple in theory, though it can be complicated when it comes to actual practice. How do we do it? We surrender each morning. We seek His wisdom and His will. We ask Him to lead and direct our paths. Then, as we commune with Him throughout the day, we can trust that He will be the One guiding us, giving us words, wisdom, and skill as He opens and closes doors accordingly.

Please join me in seeking to follow the advice in James 1:5 each day: "If any of you lack wisdom, let him ask of God, that giveth to all men liberally, and upbraideth not; and it shall be given him" (KJV).

What a wonderful promise that is!

Samantha Nelson

---

* Ellen G. White, *Conflict and Courage* (Hagerstown, MD: Review and Herald®, 2005), 86.

Why Pick on Me?

"Blessed are those who are persecuted for righteousness' sake,
For theirs is the kingdom of heaven."
—Matthew 5:10, NKJV

Recently, I was surprised while standing in an airport security line when an old friend and coworker spoke to me. It took me only a few seconds to recognize him. We were both older now with some graying hair; he looked great. He was traveling to visit one of his children in Texas. I was on my way to a women's ministries convention in Florida. He was still working for a local fire department but retiring in a few years. TSA (Transportation Security Administration) agents sent my friend and me to different lines. I was told the TSA computer had randomly picked me for patting down. I finally got through the security check and sat down on a bench to put my shoes back on. Looking up, I saw my friend being put through the wringer of a close security check, delaying him as well. I was saddened by all that he went through. This man had spent his life serving the community as a firefighter-paramedic. *Why are they picking on him?* I wondered. *Because he is black?* I noticed how he took this treatment of suspicion with grace and patience. "Does this happen to you often?" I asked when he finally approached the exit point. He simply smiled with no word of complaint.

My friend's experience and response made me think of Paul and Silas in Philippi. (You can read the story in Acts 16:16–40.) After setting a girl free from demonic possession, they were falsely accused of breaking the law, severely beaten, thrown into prison, and immobilized with their feet in stocks. And their response to mistreatment? They sang songs of praise to God! *Wow!* No words of complaint. No resisting. No self-pity! Then, when an earthquake opened a way of escape for them, they didn't take it. Because of their actions, the jailer and his entire family came to know and accept Christ. Again, *wow!* How many times have I complained about some minor mistreatment or slight I felt was unjustified? Oh, how I want to get closer to Jesus so that complaining can be eradicated from my character! I want to be like my friend, smiling with no words of complaint. I want to be like Paul and Silas, singing praises to God no matter how harshly I'm treated. I want to be an example for Jesus: "Kind to one another, tenderhearted, forgiving one another, even as God in Christ forgave you" (Ephesians 4:32, NKJV).

Mona Fellers

Do It Well!

Whatever you do, work at it with all your heart, as working for the Lord,
not for human masters, since you know that you will receive an inheritance
from the Lord as a reward. It is the Lord Christ you are serving.
—Colossians 3:23, 24, NIV

I recently had the opportunity to do something I rarely make time for: get a manicure and pedicure on the same day. I guessed at the time when the salon would be open and went around then. To my disappointment, both salons (same owners) were still closed. I knew there was another one not too far away, so I drove there.

When I arrived, it appeared the staff had just gotten in. They were busy cleaning up the store, and I was the only client there. I told them what I wanted. They assigned someone to me, while the others kept at their individual tasks. When they were done, they each sat down, and most of them got on their phones—except for one lady. She was practicing how to apply nail polish, using the cap of another nail polish bottle as her practice "nail."

As I was still the only client there, the beautician taking care of me gave me an extended amount of time, making sure all the details were taken care of. Yet I continued to watch the other cosmetologist practicing. I was fascinated with how much time she was taking to perfect her art. When she was done practicing on the bottle cap, she called over a colleague and practiced polishing her nails. As I watched her practice, Colossians 3:23, 24 came to mind: "Whatever you do, work at it with all your heart. . . . It is the Lord Christ you are serving" (NIV). Long after I left, I continued to be impressed with the amount of dedication I'd seen that beautician exercising. Was she new at the profession? I had no idea. In any case, her diligence caught and kept my attention.

I pray that whatever I choose to do or am called to do, I will persevere with a level of attention and diligence that will be pleasing to my Father.

Dear heavenly Father, sometimes You have asked simple things of us, and we think they are too simple and do not want to give them our best efforts. Help us to realize that before we are assigned the complicated and big things, we must prove ourselves capable of handling the simple instructions. Help us to be faithful and diligent in all we do.

Kaysian C. Gordon

A Forest Fire

A friend loveth at all times, and a brother is born for adversity.
—Proverbs 17:17, KJV

The news was terrible! More than two hundred forest fires were raging out of control in my province of British Columbia, Canada. The fires were just beyond the mountains of our little town of McBride. Friends of mine lived in Williams Lake. If the fire got closer, Ruth and her two adult children would have to evacuate in a hurry. I phoned Ruth. "If you and the family must evacuate, I have room for you all here." Shortly after that call, the raging fire jumped the mighty Fraser River, and there was no more time to wait. At eight o'clock that evening, Ruth and her family joined a long line of evacuees slowly driving to safety.

On Sunday morning, my phone rang before seven o'clock. "We are in McBride. How do we get to your place?" I quickly gave them directions. Shortly thereafter, Ruth, along with her adult children, Ken and Kathy, were walking into my place, bringing with them their family of two cats, Jerry and Mia. We all managed well as everyone helped with preparing meals and other needed chores. It was so good to have company because I live alone.

Every day Ken phoned their home. When the answering machine clicked on, they knew the house had not been destroyed. All was safe, and they could relax. Even when the Williams Lake evacuees were able to return to their places of residence, my friends could not. Their home was in an area close to the airport that had to be kept available for firefighting equipment and firefighters being flown in. Other provinces in Canada and even other countries made vital contributions to our fire-ravaged province. Eventually, my friends were able to return to their residence. The fires had been burning during the time of year when a large church camp meeting was scheduled to be held at Hope, British Columbia. Yet some of the highways were still closed. Many began praying that the fires would be contained in time for camp meeting to be held so that people could attend. We soon learned that church pastors and other helpers were on their way to prepare the camp meeting grounds for the annual meetings. God had answered our prayers.

Many of us have experienced times when "forest fires" in the form of obstacles and losses have burned their way into our lives. Yet, as with the continuation of camp meeting, God continues His work. Let us always be faithful in being a part of that work—no matter what.

Muriel Heppel

God's Fragrant Aroma

Therefore be imitators of God, as beloved children. And walk in love, just as Christ loved us and gave himself up for us, a fragrant offering and sacrifice to God.
—Ephesians 5:1, 2, ESV

During part of my life, my "God moments" (personal devotional time) had been boring and uninteresting. But now, as I choose to continue worshiping and praising God in the mornings, one certain discipleship idea has transformed my God-moments time. I challenge you to try it, for you may never be the same again either.

First, I take a scripture text or Bible story and read it. Then I ask myself some questions (in italics below). I journal my responses to these questions, expressing my thoughts. In so doing, God has become the passion of my heart as I continue to allow the Holy Spirit to live within me through this discipline.

Today, in my God-moments time, I read Ephesians 5:1 and then journaled.

What does this text or story say about God? "God's character is such that He wants us to love each other as He loves us. The description of that love—[portrays] a love offering and sacrifice which permeates the entire atmosphere."

What does this text or story say about me? "I am so loved and adored [through] this compassionate love from God that it is all consuming. It will transform the aroma of my life when I allow Him into my heart, soul, and mind—*but* it has to be my choice each day. I choose you, dearest Abba Father, to so envelop me in Your embrace and Your fragrant aroma that when I walk by, others will smell the Divine and not have a whiff of my odoriferous, sinful life."

What does this text or story say about my walk with God? "As I study God's Word in a prayerful state of mind, my entire attitude and presence will permeate with His 'fragrant aroma,' not mine. I will cuddle up to God, and His aroma will be much more powerful than mine."

Praise You, Jesus, for even desiring to spray Your aroma on my sinful life. The heavenly fragrance snuffs out my sinful, rancid aroma with Your sweet perfume of grace.

Mary H. Maxson

Sudden Terror

You need not be afraid of sudden disaster
or the destruction that comes upon the wicked,
for the LORD is your security.
He will keep your foot from being caught in a trap.
—Proverbs 3:25, 26, NLT

It was the end of June and time for me to commemorate another birthday. My family was away from home, and my husband planned an evening out for us to celebrate the occasion. After dinner, we decided to take a midnight stroll through Times Square in New York before heading home. Even though it was now in the wee hours of the morning, the streets were crowded with people. Adults and children traveling together in groups struggled to keep up with their respective clusters as they traversed the busy streets.

As we tried to make our way through the crowds, fear suddenly struck me. I started to feel uncomfortable as many thoughts raced through my mind. I began to think about a possible attack by some disturbed person, given the crowdedness of the area. I feared that someone moving toward me in the crowd could be up to no good. For the first time, I experienced agoraphobia (fear of crowds or open spaces). So, after a short walk and a few photographs, we decided to return home.

This experience reminded me that there are many things in this world that cause us to feel afraid. We fear sickness, destitution, failure, abandonment, insects, animals, and even people. But today's key text assures me that my heavenly Father will keep me safe whether I am at home or on the street. And even if God permits the enemy to execute his attacks on me, ultimately, God will conquer sin and evil and take me to heaven to spend eternity with Him.

We all have things that cause us to become terrified. Some common fears include agoraphobia, arachnophobia (fear of spiders), acrophobia (fear of heights), and claustrophobia (fear of small spaces). These phobias, among others, may cause us to tremble, but we must remember to put all our fears into the hands of God because He is our tower of strength.

So why not make a commitment today to hand over all your fears to God because He is more than able to help you conquer them.

Taniesha K. Robertson-Brown

Just Wait

Wait for the LORD: be strong and take heart and wait for the LORD.
—Psalm 27:14, NIV

I admit, I am a victim of this fast-paced, gotta-have-it-in-less-than-two-minutes society. Waiting for the train, sitting in traffic, or trying to find a parking spot during Christmas shopping have had a way of frustrating me. Somehow, however, my dad could just sit in his car, stake out a parking spot—even during the busiest holiday season—and just wait there. As a child, I would always ask him, "Daddy, why are you just waiting here for a spot?"

His reply: "A spot will soon become available. Just wait."

I have had to do quite a bit of waiting during my recovery from a medical procedure—waiting to feel better, waiting for my incisions to heal, and waiting to be able to do more. Somehow, over the course of my recovery, waiting has become more bearable. In fact, the unavoidable waiting has further developed my faith and inspired greater hope. Waiting seems to help me slow down long enough to enjoy the present moment. I have been learning how to appreciate the *now.*

Why are we in such a hurry? I'm not sure. After literally watching one of my wounds close further each day, I realize that processes in life take time. It takes time for the leaves to bud in the spring. It takes time for a caterpillar to become a butterfly. It takes time for one season to transition into the next. It even takes time for a baby to be formed in the womb!

My dad said it best as we staked out holiday-shopping parking spots at the mall: "Just wait." To my surprise, Dad was always right. Eventually, a parking spot became available. Whatever it is you are faced with today, know that it takes time. In the meantime, I hope you find something to enjoy in this present moment as you wait.

Patricia (Wynn) Payne

In the Hands of the Potter

Arise, and go down to the potter's house. . . . Behold, he wrought
a work on the wheels. . . . So he made it again another vessel.
—Jeremiah 18:2–4, KJV

Being a potter has given me insight into how God works in our lives. As I work, I have two options for getting my clay. I can buy it from the supplier, cleaned and ready to use. Or I can find a place that I think will have clay and dig for it. Both ways will require that I prepare the clay by wedging (rolling and kneading) it prior to throwing it on the potter's wheel. Digging for my own clay is going to be a longer process. It is this experience, especially, that has me in awe of God.

Based on the location of the clay, it may have impurities. I have to make sure that as I dig, I do so at a level where there are fewer impurities. I bring the clay home and dry it out because it must be broken down to liquid—an almost impossible task if the clay is already wet. After the sand or grit is allowed to settle, I strain it a few times through the finest mesh strainers, so I get only the slip (clay water). The clay is then allowed to dry out and await testing. I must test pieces of it before and after processing so that I can ascertain the differences. The clay must be stretched, punched, kneaded, and fired to extreme temperatures to see whether it can be used only for decorative work or can handle the rigors of functionality. Glazes must also be tested for "fit" before I make one single thing from the clay. All this, before the clay is perfect.

I look at my life's journey differently now. I know that every stretch, every proverbial kick, and every extreme fire I experience allows God to humble and perfect me, making me fit for service. Moses went through similar trials as he tended sheep in Midian. Joseph spent years in captivity as a slave and then a convict. His only crime? His brothers' hatred. Hannah endured ridicule from her cowife, Peninnah, because she was barren.

Are you going through what seems like a never-ending barrage of trials and heartache? Fear not. God is not punishing you. He is right there, aching because of your pain, but He knows that it is necessary for your eternal happiness. So give thanks through the pain, for God is always there—yes, even in the midst of the pain—and He is working.

Greta Michelle Joachim-Fox-Dyett

God Cares and Understands

"Call on me in the day of trouble;
I will deliver you, and you will honor me."
—Psalm 50:15, NIV

It was the first night of our evangelistic series in a town in the Philippines. I was scheduled to present a talk about family life and relationships. I also had the responsibility of sharing the children's story every evening.

Then something very unexpected and, frankly, worrisome happened! Just before the evangelistic meetings were to start, I felt something unusual in my mouth. It couldn't be, but it was happening: the crown on my left front tooth was loose. Back at the place where we were staying during the series, I took a closer look at my tooth. I could actually see that part of my crown was chipped! Somehow it had been damaged. *What am I going to do?* I wondered.

Quickly I prayed, *O Lord, please help me. Hold that crown in place. I'm here in a remote area with no medical office or even a nurse. Lord, You know there isn't even any public transportation for me to take to the city to find dental care.* Wrestling with God over this dilemma, I decided to trust Him to get me through my presentations each evening. Though I was a little nervous that first night, God kept my crown intact, and it stayed in my mouth. And stay it did for the duration of the evangelistic series! God understood my predicament. He cared about it and enabled me to fulfill my speaking responsibilities.

Though the enemy of our souls worked hard to discourage me during the series, he didn't succeed. God was more powerful. Not only did God hold my broken tooth in place but He also led many people to respond to His calling on their lives. What do you need to entrust to God today?

Ofelia A. Pangan

Mother's Gift to Me

*They will be like great oaks
that the LORD has planted for his own glory.*
—Isaiah 61:3, NLT

About three years before my mother's demise in 1995, she gave me a pretty little plant. I planted it opposite my front door and cared for it daily. Unfortunately, Mother did not know the name of the plant. It yielded small yellow berries as well as delicate sprays of tiny lilac flowers. It grew to about three feet (ninety centimeters) before winter came around.

The winter of 1999 was very severe. Later, on August 29, a tornado hit our area, our neighborhood, and our home. The twister caused much disaster and damage. In fact, our large hedge fell over onto the little plant Mother had given me. With so many other important matters to attend to—repairing the roof, replacing gutters, and fitting in new windowpanes—nine months passed before we were able to get around to freeing the now leafless, apparently lifeless little plant from underneath the fallen hedge.

My husband wanted to pull it out and cast it away.

I begged him, "Please give it a chance." I am so glad I pleaded on its behalf to remain and grow. Years later, my husband fell ill and died in September 2011. He was not able to see how tall and beautiful the plant has now grown.

Then in 2016–2017, we suffered a drought. The plant lost all its leaves, and the branches looked like dried sticks. I really thought it was dying and was so sad to see it in that state, but it rallied. In 2019, we experienced a severe winter with heavy rains, yet the plant has just kept growing. After all the years of trying to find its name, I learned it is a duranta plant.

Mother's gift tree reminds me of my life. My mom gave birth to me, nourished me, and helped me grow in goodness. She could not know what troubles of "drought" would come our way. We have had to weather all seasons to get through life, sorrow, sickness, and death. But looking to our Savior daily, we find courage and strength in Him to face each new day.

As I admire my duranta, I think of my mother's gift to me. Thanks be to God for giving me a mother who loved caring for plants and loved the Lord and taught me to do likewise. I thank the Master Gardener for growing that duranta as He also grows us through our trials.

Priscilla E. Adonis

Teach the Way

Train up a child in the way he should go:
and when he is old, he will not depart from it.
—Proverbs 22:6, KJV

Teaching children to take their first steps is easy and enjoyable; it is one of the most rewarding tasks there is. In 2001, soon after my little Samuel was born, we realized that he seemed to refuse to lie down. He forced his neck forward in an attempt to get up. Within a few months, he crawled and stood up. Before his first birthday, he was running all around. The victory of his first step was as much my own as his. It was thrilling to see his efforts to stay upright, holding his arms up despite an awkward gait. But he managed. But when it came to teaching him to walk through life, things got very complicated. There is inconsistency in human attitudes, and sometimes his childish mind could not discern between the right and the dangerous. It was necessary to repeat our instructions countless times until he understood right from wrong. Yet when we adults taught him what was right but *did* the opposite, he immediately questioned us.

Every child is a beautiful, colorful box on the outside and totally "empty" (unformed) on the inside. Each child has genetically inherited personalities and characteristics from their parents, but shaping a little mind is a gift, holy privilege, and responsibility that God has given us. Many, however, do little with this privilege and neglect the noblest task in the universe. Every child needs love, affection, patience, and also boundaries. Responsibility lies with the parents but extends to the whole family, church members, teachers, and community. We all have children around us. If each of us sets a good example, that thirsty little mind will become more and more directed to making the right choices. Sometimes our task may seem fruitless, but over time, we realize the value of an appropriate example, and the whole of society benefits.

Children should learn from an early age to walk in right paths. Although they do not understand the consequences of sin, they are still free to choose and will make good choices if they are taught the right course. We hope that once they understand the meaning of goodness, love, patience, forgiveness, and honesty, they will become honest, ethical, and responsible adults. Thus, we pray that they will always walk at God's side and understand His love and justice, bringing light and hope to many others, especially the little ones.

Sueli da Silva Pereira

Living the Christian Life

His compassions . . . are new every morning.
—Lamentations 3:22, 23, KJV

Living the Christian life does *not* entitle us to expect a life *without* pain, suffering, and disappointment. In fact, we all know that, often, the harder God's children try to live in accordance with Christ's teachings and example, the more difficult their tests and trials become. It is said that the devil hates to see a Christian on her knees. So be prepared: the closer you draw to the Lord, the more difficult your life may become.

We are encouraged to be *in* the world but not *of* the world. But we sometimes interpret this to mean we should live in isolation *from* the world. We know that is not possible. Not all Christians can work in a believer-friendly environment or in the church organization. Most of us are employed in secular workplaces, and we must interact with non-Christians on a daily basis—family, neighbors, friends, or coworkers. This presents us with challenges. Yet our lives and social interactions must always reflect our Christian values while not coming across as "preaching" or wearing religion on our sleeves.

Some employment situations prohibit the discussion of religious beliefs on the job. This requires us to walk a fine line and simply allow the light of Christ to shine through our words and actions. Jesus left us an example of how to interact with others. He was a frequent guest in the home of Mary, Martha, and Lazarus. At the wedding celebration in Cana, He saved the host from embarrassment when he ran out of wine to serve his guests. Jesus simply turned water into wine. Another time He invited Himself to dine with the socially unpopular tax collector Levi Matthew, who had stolen from the poor to enrich himself. As a result of this social interaction, a soul was saved, and a disciple gained. Matthew left his occupation to follow Jesus.

Living the Christian life means that we pattern our lives each day after the example Christ left us. It means we wake each morning with thanksgiving on our lips. We put a smile on our face despite the obstacles. We share a kind word with our family, friends, coworkers, and complete strangers. The joy in our lives will reflect the love of Christ in our hearts.

Let's determine that because God's love and mercies are new every day, we will live the Christian life by being a faithful testimony for Jesus in all we do and say.

Avis Mae Rodney

The Red-Onion Experiment

But unto you that fear my name shall the Sun of righteousness
arise with healing in his wings.
—Malachi 4:2, KJV

My red onions had sprouted. Two of my red onions, sitting in a plastic container above the microwave, had produced a cluster of green shoots. The plant nearer the edge of the microwave was tall and elegant. But the plant farther from the edge and in a confined space grew curled like a cocoon, so I knew that I had an experiment on my hands. Could the curled sprouts ever become straight? If so, how long would it take? I carefully moved both plants to a sunny windowsill and waited and waited.

An hour passed, and my mint-green sprouts looked the same against the white landscape of the January sky—a welcome and colorful contrast to the snow outside. One full day went by, and when there was still no change, I remembered the old adage, "A watched pot never boils." So I decided to give the experiment some time.

After ten days, the change was visible, though some shoots still remained in the curled position. To my joy, however, after two weeks of exposure to the sun, there was little difference between the two plants. Both stood tall and straight, reaching up to the sunshine outside.

My experiment had been a revelation not only about red onions but also about God's work in me. What would happen if I, too, gave my damaged, misshapen soul full exposure to the Sun of Righteousness? What if I gave Him my convoluted relationships and my issues that seemed to have no solutions? What if I sat in His presence for a moment, for a day, a month, or forever? One thing I realize is that just *visiting* His presence does not work. Like the red onion, I would need prolonged exposure. Growth would require regular devotions and a consistent prayer life. I would need to find myself in His house of worship—not just once in a while but regularly—for continued exposure, as my red onion had revealed. And I would need to *remain* in God's presence, growing and developing as a Christian.

Lord, I give my mixed-up life to You with all its defects. I know that there is healing if I remain in Your presence. Give me the strength to stretch my hands to You and wait for the healing that You alone can provide.

Annette Walwyn Michael

Blood Patch

But now in Christ Jesus you who once were far off
have been brought near by the blood of Christ.
—Ephesians 2:13, NKJV

I was in excruciating pain!

My neck and head hurt so bad I thought I had been in a car accident. I tried to endure the pain through the weekend and went to work on Monday morning. By then, I knew I needed to go to the emergency room. The pain was simply too intense.

I suspected what might be happening to me. The previous week I had spent three days in the hospital having tests run. For an entire year, I had been dealing with issues of debilitating pressure in my head and trouble with my eyes tracking properly. A lumbar puncture was done. That was the culprit causing my spinal tap (or postdural puncture) headache.

If you've never had one, you are fortunate!

As long as I was lying flat, there was no headache. My medical providers told me the only way to get rid of the headache was through a process called a blood patch. It is a surgical procedure that uses one's own blood to close the hole in the dura mater of the spinal cord, which was caused by the lumbar puncture. After inserting the blood, the resulting blood clot then patches the meningeal leak.

I felt immediate relief!

You know, sin also causes tremendous pressure and pain in our lives. Year after year, we try to live with it through denial, substance abuse, anger, or other coping mechanisms that may even bring on depression. But none of these are fixes. We end up in a spiritual emergency room with such pain that we can hardly stand it.

It is only when we turn to Jesus as our Great Physician that we can be healed. Instead of our blood, we need the blood of Jesus Christ, our Lord and Savior. His precious blood was shed on the cross at Calvary. He was the ultimate sacrifice that sealed the hole of sin deep down inside of us. And we don't have to worry about blood types. Jesus is our Creator, and His blood provides the redemption from all sin and suffering for each of us.

Aren't we blessed to have this kind of a Savior?

Karen M. Phillips

The Day Everything Stopped

But the day of the Lord will come as a thief in the night.
—2 Peter 3:10, KJV

The winter of 2016 had been unusually wet. By the end of September, weather warnings became frequent, advising that high-velocity winds could be expected. This would necessitate securing property and sandbagging homes in flood-prone areas. Despite the warnings, many did not realize the full impact and chaos the storm would bring, not just in our area but throughout the whole state of South Australia. The power went off for days and weeks in some places.

With the water rising, those caught on the roads became disorientated without street or traffic lights. Panic reigned as department stores and fuel stations closed, and electric trains and trams came to a halt. Some eighty thousand lightning strikes occurred, and twenty-two electrical pylons came down, bent like blades of grass. Highways closed, and roads washed away; creeks and rivers burst their banks, covering endless floodplains. Grain crops were destroyed. With no refrigeration for dairy farmers, cows' milk had to be disposed of. Our state fell into utter darkness as candles sold out and flashlights (torches) became scarce. Rain and wind arrived with ferocity, resulting in a greater rainfall in South Australia than had ever been recorded before.

Disasters such as these are becoming more frequent in all parts of our world, with millions suffering chaotic situations on a regular basis. Matthew 24 warns us of things we will face before Jesus comes, turning this world into chaos. Daniel 12:1 foretold that "there shall be a time of trouble, such as never was since there was a nation" (KJV). Matthew 25:1–13 relates the parable of the ten virgins awaiting the arrival of the bridegroom. Five had extra oil for their lamps, which they needed when the bridegroom was late. The other five ran out of oil. While going in search of more oil, they missed the arrival of the bridegroom. The door to the wedding feast shut on them. This parable reminded me of a man frantically trying to get home through dark, flooded streets. In relief, he arrived home only to find he could not open his garage door. Neither could he open the front door to his house because of the failure of his security system. How disappointing not to be able to enter the door into one's own home!

But we have another chance. I pray we will be ready with our lamps alight when the storms of life are over at Jesus' return.

Lyn Welk-Sandy

"Remember Me"

"This is my body which I am giving for you. Do this to remember me."
—Luke 22:19, NCV

As I write this devotional, it is Good Friday. I am in a lockdown at home due to the coronavirus pandemic. In fact, millions around the world share in this experience. The pandemic has caused people to feel distressed. Many have fallen ill or lost their lives. Millions grieve for loved ones. Economic uncertainty abounds. Some wonder, Is this the end?

As I jogged alone near the woods close by, seeking to benefit from fresh air and sunlight, I kept thinking of Jesus and the significance of that Friday when He died for us. The same problems were present then. People were feeling distressed, isolated, anxious, and uncertain of their future. Many were ill, dying, or mourning the death of loved ones. Economic chaos abounded due to the oppression of government rulers. I imagined Jerusalem filled with people coming and going during the Passover festivities. They were to remember God's deliverance in Egypt, yet some wondered whether God would still deliver them from their current problems. Then I pictured Jesus, who had made provision for a Passover celebration. Yet each disciple brought his own issues, including Judas, who was about to betray Him. Jesus welcomed each disciple equally, washing their feet, demonstrating His love in a last attempt to get Judas's attention. Then, as He passed the bread and the cup, He told them how He would be broken like that bread and poured out like the fruit of the vine. Then I could see my Jesus say with a loving gaze, "Do this to remember me" (Luke 22:19, NCV). So many years have passed, yet today millions of Christians still take time this week to remember Christ and how He set us free. As I returned from my morning jog, I was at peace, knowing that the same God who spared the life of His people in Egypt and died on a cross for me thousands of Good Fridays ago is still here today.

I don't know what problems you are facing today. What I can say is that as I spent time remembering Him, I felt assured that He, too, remembers me. He promised He would never forsake us. He is the Answer to all our problems. He is the Healer for our sin-sick souls. He is the One who is with you in your loneliness and distress. Whether through an unprecedented pandemic ravaging the world or any other crisis you or I may face today, our Lord Jesus Christ still says, "My body was broken for you. Remember Me."

Katia Garcia Reinert

Just Imagine

Many women were there, watching from a distance.
They had followed Jesus from Galilee to care for his needs.
Among them were Mary Magdalene, Mary the mother
of James and Joseph, and the mother of Zebedee's sons.
—Matthew 27:55, 56, NIV

Just imagine you are standing at the foot of the cross. Have you seen Jesus before this? Followed Him? Received His blessing? Are you weeping, or are you among the mocking crowd? Maybe you are the unnamed daughter of Jairus, and you remember being so sick, then nothing until you wake up with Jesus holding your hand and telling you to stand up. You were dead and now alive. And here you stand, watching Jesus dying on the cruel cross. Maybe your mother is standing beside you; after all, this is Passover, and everyone wants to be in Jerusalem. Or maybe you are the woman who had been bleeding for twelve years until you were able to touch the hem of Jesus' robe. Now you are well and have followed, hoping to see and listen to Jesus once more. Or maybe you and your son are standing there. Jesus raised your son from death in Nain while on the way to the graveyard. Oh, what a difference Jesus has made in your life!

Imagine that your name is Salome and you are the mother of Zebedee's sons, James and John. As you stand there, you think back to the day when your sons talked you into asking Jesus for a favor. After all, you had been following Jesus from village to village and helping to finance Jesus' ministry. "In your Kingdom, please let my two sons sit in places of honor next to you, one on your right and the other on your left" (Matthew 20:21, NLT). Now who is on Jesus' right and left? You remember Jesus asking whether your sons could drink the bitter cup He was about to drink, and they answered with certainty that they could (verse 22).

The Bible tells us that there were named and unnamed women standing there at a little distance, watching. "Near the cross of Jesus stood his mother, his mother's sister, Mary the wife of Clopas, and Mary Magdalene" (John 19:25, NIV). Matthew, in today's text, adds the names of Mary, the mother of James and Joseph, and Salome.

Image that you are there. Just imagine. The fact is that we are each there every day as we follow and respond to Jesus. What has He done for you, for me, that we want to follow Him? Don't just imagine—acknowledge and share what He has done.

Ardis Dick Stenbakken

I Watched Him Die!

And when Jesus had cried out with a loud voice,
He said, "Father, 'into Your hands I commit My spirit.' "
Having said this, He breathed His last.
—Luke 23:46, NKJV

Have you ever watched someone die? Your answer is probably yes. A deathwatch is one of the most agonizing experiences in life, but it's inescapable. In the beginning, God warned Adam, "Of the tree of the knowledge of good and evil you shall not eat, for in the day that you eat of it you shall surely die" (Genesis 2:17, NKJV). Adam ate and eventually died, and humankind continues to die. The experience is unnatural; it results in separation and all kinds of distress for the loved ones who are left behind.

My last deathwatch was on Father's Day in June 2016. On this day, we should have been celebrating together as a family as we had planned. Instead, we were waiting, and hope was waning as we watched Dad die. I was not physically alone because many family and friends were waiting and watching with me. Yet I felt an emptiness, an aloneness, and a deep sadness that I could not share with anyone. Dad had always been there for me, supportive, encouraging, guiding, and praying for all my concerns. On many occasions, he was there to share my joys. He did this for 104 years and 10 months until the day he had a massive stroke. Then I watched him die.

Some weeks after the funeral, as I reflected on those last moments, I thought of Mary, the mother of Jesus, as she watched her Son die a humiliating death. It was not a stroke, a heart attack, or an incurable disease. She watched Him be mocked, slapped, and spat upon. The crown of thorns and the old royal robe were intended to hurt and humiliate Him. But the cross, "the old rugged cross," was the worst possible horror. She saw her Son naked, bruised, and battered as He was dying. From the cross, He saw her pain, understood her grief, and made provision for her welfare. To his disciple John, he said, " 'Behold your mother!' And from that hour that disciple took her to his own home" (John 19:27, NKJV). Mary could not squeeze the hand of her Son and hug Him like I did with my father. She could not whisper words of love in His ears. But He reached out to her from the cross.

Praise God, He is risen! Now He is reaching out to each of us from the throne room of heaven. Even at a deathwatch, He is there with the promise of new life.

Sonia Kennedy-Brown

"You Will Rise"

"As for you, go your way till the end. You will rest, and then at the end of the days you will rise to receive your allotted inheritance."
—Daniel 12:13, NIV

Almost a year after my dad died, I wanted to see the gravestone we had chosen for his resting place in the cemetery. Mom and I decided to go on Memorial Day because, at this military site, flags are placed on every grave. I wasn't pining away or crying when Mom and I, awed by the sight of myriad flags, stood there in the cemetery. There are so many wonderful promises in the Bible that encourage me, such as the one found in 1 Corinthians 15:23: "But each in turn: Christ, the firstfruits; then, when he comes, those who belong to him" (NIV). And just as my dad rests in the sleep of death, so Daniel was told he would rest in the grave. The man clothed in linen, appearing in Daniel's vision, said to him, "As for you, go your way till the end. You will rest, and then at the end of the days you will rise to receive your allotted inheritance" (Daniel 12:13, NIV).

What startled me that Memorial Day was the sheer number of people there. When I looked around, I noticed many huddled by various gravesites. In a row behind us was a lady holding a younger man. I walked over, mentioned our loss, and asked about hers. We hugged and then shared our hope in Jesus. Next, I noticed a lady sitting beside a gravesite a few rows away. When I got close, she just reached up to hug me as I reached down to embrace her. Her husband had died. Mom and I came away really touched and convicted that this was a place of ministry.

The next year I wanted to see whether I could encourage anyone at the cemetery again. Driving down one hill, I gasped to see very small graves on a hillside. Out of curiosity, I pulled over, slipped out of the car, and walked closer. A lady, appearing to be tucked back in the woods, sat on a rock. Strolling closer, I asked, "Do you need a hug?" She explained her husband had died ten years ago, but the loss was still fresh. *One more person to encourage. And because Jesus rose from the grave, we do have encouragement to offer.* That evening at home, I glanced at Dad's Bible. It was a blessing to read one particular verse he had marked: "And the Lord will deliver me from every evil work and preserve me for His heavenly kingdom. To Him be glory forever and ever. Amen!" (2 Timothy 4:18, NKJV). Truly, we *shall* rise!

Diane Pestes

Specially Selected

But you are a chosen generation, a royal priesthood, a holy nation,
His own special people, that you may proclaim the praises of Him
who called you out of darkness into His marvelous light.
—1 Peter 2:9, NKJV

One day in October 2019, I was feeling both delighted and grateful. Once again I was traveling to Florida to visit my first grandchild, Ava, who was now four months old. Since I arrived at the airport earlier than expected for my departing flight, I looked forward to checking in and just relaxing in the lounge.

I was next in line at the ticket counter, but the waiting seemed forever. Since I was traveling from Bermuda, I moved on quickly to United States customs. As I approached the baggage drop-off, I heard an agent say to his colleague, "This lady is specially selected." His fellow agent happily replied, "Oh, good!"

Why is she so happy about that comment? I wondered. Immediately, I whispered a prayer, asking God to help me keep calm. The agent explained that my bags had to be opened and checked because the computer had randomly selected my name. After reviewing my luggage, the attendant stated that all was fine. As I proceeded to the security checkpoint, the attendant scanned my passport and confirmed I needed further scrutiny since I had been randomly selected for further screening. I'd already experienced random selection during my previous two departing flights. The attendant escorted me to the processing area, where I surrendered to the system, but this time I felt like a criminal.

I questioned God: *Why are these people always picking on me? Can't they see that I am a good senior citizen? Please give me strength to remain calm. Fix my attitude of frustration.* Several minutes later, the screening was over. I thanked God that the process was completed and asked Him to forgive me if I had displayed an un-Christlike character during the process.

This experience reminds me of Peter's statement that we are "a royal priesthood . . . His own special people" (1 Peter 2:9, NKJV). Therefore, we must always be ready and willing to "give account" of ourselves to God at any time (Romans 14:12, NKJV). On my next travel engagement, by God's grace, I plan to be ready to undergo any screening process if I am "specially selected."

Lynette Wilson

King Solomon and Me

My heart took delight in all my labor,
and this was the reward for all my toil.
Yet when I surveyed all that my hands had done
and what I had toiled to achieve,
everything was meaningless, a chasing after the wind;
nothing was gained under the sun.
—Ecclesiastes 2:10, 11, NIV

I currently have two doctorates, and my husband keeps predicting that I am going to end up pursuing a third. Now don't tell him, but the truth is that sometimes I find myself looking at another degree program, thinking, *This sure would be interesting*, or *I'd love to pursue this if I only had the time (and money)!* I haven't come close to yielding to those thoughts, but they are still there. That's because there is no limit to the human capacity to want to do and pursue things of personal interest or delight. This lesson struck home recently in reading the story of King Solomon.

I've read it before, but this time I was drawn in as if watching a movie. First, Solomon starts out building the temple, and you can almost feel the fervor and devotion that he has for God. But then he spends even longer building his house. When he's finally done with that, he continues to acquire and build and do so much that by the time the queen of Sheba arrives to visit him, she becomes so completely overwhelmed that she faints. After that, we find out about the many wives Solomon was also acquiring—more on record than anyone else in history.

By the time I finished reading about Solomon's life, I felt I had vicariously reexperienced something that I've known for years: *what you focus on and emphasize is always more important than what you may* say *is more important.* Much of what Solomon did and acquired was actually good. But in going after these things, Solomon's focus incrementally shifted to the things he was pursuing and to the pursuit itself. And his focus incrementally shifted away from God—it happened to him one day, one decision, and one preoccupation at a time.

So, today, no matter what interests me, I have to make sure that my focus is on God and seeking Him. That's because no matter how good something may be that captivates your attention and beckons you, it won't ultimately be good if you do not daily, consciously, make seeking God and dwelling in His presence the central pursuit of your life.

Rachel Williams-Smith

God Speaks Through a Rainbow

PART 1

"The rainbow shall be in the cloud, and I will look on it
to remember the everlasting covenant between
God and every living creature of all flesh that is on the earth."
—Genesis 9:16, NKJV

The time for the Bible class's annual community project and retreat was drawing near. But we had not yet been able to raise the necessary funds of six thousand kina (US$1,775) to help at a school in a remote area where we planned to go. The twelve-hour road trip necessitated having two twenty-five-seat trucks to transport the people, luggage, food, and project's tools. Our needs became a matter of urgent prayer. "God," I prayed, "please show me a rainbow to assure me that all will go well." But as days went by, no rainbow appeared in the sky. Nevertheless, we were encouraged by receiving strong support from our own school. The college dean, Dr. Elisapesi Manson, made sure all our needed projects would be ready to take with us from the university workshop: an iron bell, iron flagpoles, and other project items. The support service supplied needed metal pipes, cement, tools, and one of the workers to go with us. Three of my colleague lecturers helped in every way possible, including monetary donations. By now, we had three thousand kina—half of what we needed, and our departure date was approaching.

Though the high spirits of the students encouraged me, I had not yet seen a rainbow to give me peace about this trip. Then I began to hear occasional negative comments from some of the university staff: "Students should not be taken so far away to a place where spirit worship and animistic lifestyles thrive!" We continued to pray and wait on God.

Three days before our scheduled departure, I went to a farm to obtain fresh produce for our trip. Back in the house, I got out the project's money envelope. *Lord, show me what to do.* Then I stepped outside. Right there in front of me was the biggest, brightest rainbow I had ever seen! It stretched from the ground to the sky and arched over three guava trees. But it wasn't just one rainbow—three shadow rainbows glowed behind it. "Lord, I'm in awe! I praise You!"

The head teacher arrived and excitedly asked me to come to her house. She said, "The truck drivers have offered to provide free transport for one truck, and you can pay half fare for the second one. My family will cover the remainder."

God's provision was beyond our expectation. He is faithful when we trust Him and will respond in our time of need!

Fulori Sususewa Bola

God Speaks Through a Rainbow
PART 2

Delight yourself also in the LORD,
And He shall give you the desires of your heart.
—Psalm 37:4, NKJV

Our student outreach teams were preparing to visit villages in the area of Kukkia as well as the old site of a church, health clinic, workshop, and school. We gathered for prayer. This part of Papua New Guinea is known for its crocodiles, venomous snakes, and spiders, as well as poisonous plants. We would be crossing swamps and grasslands. Each of us had a flashlight, a walking stick, and some drinking water. The walk to the mountain where the church and old school were located would take four to six hours, depending on how fast we walked.

It had been raining before our arrival in Kukkia, which made every track and trail slippery and dangerous. We decided to wait for the Lord's instruction via a rainbow before entering the respective villages. We entrusted that to the Lord and began our hike.

We started off cross-country through the jungle until we came to a large swamp that we had to cross over on logs. Our sturdy sticks came in handy as we walked. Fortunately, we saw no crocodiles lurking in the waters and soon crossed in safety. Then we saw the first village. These villages consist of two large houses: one for men, the other for women. As we approached the settlement, a beautiful rainbow appeared in the sky, arching above the houses. As we prepared to enter the gate, people came out to join us. We sang praises. Some of our group performed a skit about Noah and the rainbow—underneath an actual rainbow! We prayed with each person before continuing our journey.

The rainbow above us shone as we visited three more villages before dark. When darkness fell, there was brightness along our path to the next village. People had already gathered outside with their lamps to welcome us to their village. The path was so muddy that several of us slipped and fell but that added to the fun we had. At last, we arrived at the old site of the mountain village and school. More folks came to meet us and seemed excited as we encouraged them to be faithful in the Lord. Visiting and praying for people that day was extra special because God accompanied us with His rainbow. Delight in the Lord, and He will lead you.

Fulori Sususewa Bola

Where Are You on Sabbath?

Not forsaking the assembling of ourselves together, as is the manner of some, but exhorting one another, and so much the more as you see the Day approaching.
—Hebrews 10:25, NKJV

I had a brother who said that he didn't need to go to church to have a relationship with Christ and that he could go to the woods and commune with Him. I also have a friend who steers clear of "organized religion." So why *should* we go to church?

First, I always attended church on the seventh day because I didn't know anything different. Now, as a parent who raised my children to do the same, I understand the importance of worshiping in church with others each Sabbath. I do so because God requested it in the fourth commandment, and I want to please Him. Furthermore, I need to be with like-minded people. Christian fellowship helps me be more accountable both to God and others.

The Sabbath rest and fellowship became even more precious to me when I had to return to work as a nurse because my husband, who had Parkinson's disease, wasn't able to work anymore. I worked two jobs to keep my three sons in private school. I had to work every other Sabbath as a behavioral medicine nurse. When I did have Sabbath off, it was such a blessing to go to church, relax, and attend the afternoon activities provided. A year ago I was able to retire and become more active in the church. After my husband died, I realized the blessings of a smaller church as the members gave us so much support during this difficult time.

The communion and support we enjoy in church are a foretaste of what we will experience in heaven. I believe the more one is involved at church, the more one is blessed.

Jesus understood the importance of keeping open communication with His Father. If He spent hours talking with God, how much more should we as fallen beings spend time with Him? Church fellowship encourages us to deepen our fellowship with Jesus. Jesus taught His disciples to commune with His Father by teaching them how to pray. Today we call it the Lord's Prayer. His Holy Word is the main way God communicates with us, along with the Holy Spirit, whom Jesus said He would ask His Father to send us (John 14:16, 17). Jesus is almost ready to take His bride, the church, to heaven, where we will spend eternity with Him. Imagine worshiping on the Sabbath in heaven with our Creator! I want to be there, don't you?

Gyl Moon Bateman

Listen and Obey!

He replied, "Blessed rather are those who
hear the word of God and obey it."
—Luke 11:28, NIV

I have often wondered whether I truly know when God is speaking to me. A recent experience confirmed that, yes, in my relationship with God, it is easy to know. It is more important to listen and obey when He speaks to us. God will not ask us to take a path or perform a task that will not glorify His character of love or exemplify His goodness, mercy, and grace.

One Sabbath eve, as I stood in the pantry looking for ingredients to prepare a meal, I also had an overwhelming conviction to pack a bag of groceries for Sister "X."

Sure, I can do that, I thought. As I became involved in preparing a meal, though, I forgot about my earlier impression.

The next morning, as I headed out the door, there was that overwhelming conviction again: *Pack a bag of groceries, and take it to church for Sister X.* I quickly headed to the pantry, packed a brown paper bag of assorted groceries, and rushed out the door. On arriving at church, I sought out Sister X and delivered the bag of groceries to her. She said, "Thank you," and we went about our separate Sabbath School duties.

A little later in the service, Sister X testified, giving God praise and thanks for the gift of food she had just received from a church member. She further indicated she was currently without the means to purchase groceries. Joy surged through my heart! I was quietly ecstatic as it appeared God had used me as a conduit to answer the prayers of Sister X.

But that was only a small part of the reason for my joy. This turn of events, orchestrated by God, had a profound effect on me. My omniscient God, with His awareness of the past, present, and future, saw Sister X's need and chose me to be His hands, feet, and heart, thereby meeting her need. The profoundness of this experience is that I had *listened*!

God, my all-knowing Father, had confirmed that in my continuing relationship with Him—through prayer, the reading of His Word, and an increasing understanding of His character—it can be easy to recognize His voice when He speaks to my heart and mind. I simply need to listen and obey. "For it is God who works in you, both to will and to work for his good pleasure" (Philippians 2:13, ESV).

Terry Roselmond-Moore

God Took Care of It

My son, attend to my words; incline thine ear unto my sayings.
Let them not depart from thine eyes;
keep them in the midst of thine heart.
—Proverbs 4:20, 21, KJV

I am a semiretired elementary teacher. One or two days a week, I am called to serve as a substitute. One of my recent assignments was to a rough school. As the secretary thanked me for coming, she handed me a walkie-talkie. "Take this. You will need it," she said. On the way to school that morning, I had already prayed for the students I would meet. Now here with the secretary, I knew I'd be praying a lot for God's presence throughout this day. My first class was very responsive. In the next class, I, along with two assistants, helped the students create handmade French books for first-grade students. All too soon, the forty minutes with that quiet class passed. One assistant breathed, "Good luck with the next bunch." I smiled as I exited.

A surprise waited for me. As I walked in the door, a tall girl came running toward me. "Do you remember me?" she called out. I told her I did and braced for her hug. She had been in another school the year before, where I had befriended her on the playground a few times. When other students piped up with similar remarks, I reminded them we had a big job to do: they were also making little books for the first graders.

"Let's work quietly and carefully. We want to give first graders a special treat," I urged. The class set to work, and before I knew it, my third class of the day was done.

The next assignment was supervising a class at lunchtime. This included handing out pizza and milk. The students were rushing me, and I prayed silently as I commanded in a careful voice, "Please return to your seats, and let me call you to come for your food." The class assistant raised her eyebrows, but it worked. The students sat down. The food was handed out quickly. All too soon, lunch was over, and the students were out the door for recess. I spent my lunch hour silently thanking God for His leadership during the morning. I knew He deserved credit for the morning's success. The afternoon also went smoothly, and I finally turned in my key and the walkie-talkie. The secretary asked why I had not used it. I told her the students had cooperated. "I don't know how you managed," she said.

"I didn't. God took care of it." I smiled at her surprised glance. *He always does.*

Patricia Cove

Ramon

Love is patient, love is kind. It does not envy,
it does not boast, it is not proud.
—1 Corinthians 13:4, NIV

Mrs. Cameron, the head teacher, stood in my doorway.
"Miss Watkins, I want to know what you have done to Ramon."
The government-sponsored program for preschoolers was new to our location. As a college student desperately needing a summer job, I had applied and had been hired but was the only person of my ethnicity in the program.

In the Deep South in the early sixties, racial prejudice for many ran deep. I prayed to have God's love for everyone, whoever they were.

"Mrs. Cameron," I quietly said, "I guess I don't know what you mean about Ramon."

She smiled. "You're doing mighty fine, girl," she began, "but what is your secret in dealing with Ramon? He's such a live wire! We assigned him to your room because the rest of us knew him all too well. What's your secret?"

I wanted to tell her that I prayed a lot! Instead, I teased, "Maybe it's my color—or lack of it!" and we both laughed.

Often, on the playground, I would feel a small, sweaty hand squeeze into mine. Looking down, I would see Ramon gazing up at me and grinning from ear to ear. We'd swing our arms, laughing in fun.

The last week of school came. Ramon fidgeted on his resting mat. I went over to him.

"Teacher," he said quietly, "why do you love me?"

"Ramon, you are a nice little boy. It's not hard to love you."

"I wish my mom and dad loved me like you do," he said quietly. "But they fuss and fight and even hit me sometimes." Tears filled both his eyes and mine.

I whispered into his little ear, "Ramon, there's a God in heaven who loves you very much. Let's ask Him to help your home be a happy one." Ramon appeared to relax. Hopefully, he had seen, through me, that God's love "is patient . . . is kind." Despite any differences between others and us, may Heaven's kindness characterize all our interactions with everyone.

Marybeth Gessele

"I Am Pregnant!"

A man's gift maketh room for him,
and bringeth him before great men.
—Proverbs 18:16, KJV

I took to the stage the last Sunday morning of a women's retreat in South Africa. "I am pregnant!" I shouted at the top of my voice. The two-hundred-plus attendees began to shout expressions of jubilation and joy. "Ladies, I already told you that I am not going to be a mother!" The room calmed down, and my next words took them by surprise: "You are *all* pregnant—pregnant with purpose!" I explained to the ladies that God had placed something great inside each of them, much like a pregnancy. Their job was to *push* out that "baby" so they could have a *unique* impact on the world, for one's "baby" cannot be birthed by anyone else.

Even though I have never been pregnant, I have read about what pregnant women experience: morning sickness, back pain, hot flashes, heartburn, swollen ankles, and fatigue. I am convinced that sometimes women who are "pregnant" with purpose fear that their growing "stomach" (purpose) may be offensive or unacceptable or may make others uncomfortable. They may choose to band the stomach to hide their purpose. Other pregnant-with-purpose women may be fearful about "pushing" the baby out into existence. As a result, they try to hold the baby back, fearful of the responsibilities living their purpose would bring. That day at the South African women's retreat, I shared a personal story about my sister, who, while in labor, had a very difficult time pushing out her baby. In fact, my mother recounted that the baby went back inside four times, almost leaving my sister dead. Then there may be other "pregnant" women who are fearful of judgment from others and simply feel unprepared to "mother" their purposes.

Every woman who is pregnant with purpose has to realize that she must give birth to what God has placed inside of her. She cannot push it back inside because it will make her sick. Doing so may even leave her "dead" because her unbirthed purpose weighs on her as she proceeds through life on autopilot, just going with the flow. That way of living, however, only causes her more pain. She will constantly experience feelings of disequilibrium because she is not living in her true purpose. Rarely will she experience great peace because she is not doing what she was meant to do.

The only choice that you have as a "pregnant" woman is, in God's strength, to *push*!

Nadine A. Joseph-Collins

April 27

Praying for Red Lights

Being confident of this very thing, that He who has begun a good work
in you will complete it until the day of Jesus Christ.
—Philippians 1:6, NKJV

Some days I don't even make it out of bed before I set my heart on earthly problems instead of heavenly light.* Often, I seem to be the same person, with the same un-Christian attitude, after I pray as when I awoke! *Was I really sincere? Did I really mean what I prayed? Or were those just empty words rising to the ceiling and then falling back down?*

Last week, while I was rushing around, preparing to leave the house for an appointment, I thought back to the time when someone told me that being late is a choice. I don't fully agree with that statement, but on this day, my poor choices were certainly not helping. When I finally got on the road, I seemed to be stopped by every red traffic light. Then, just before my last turn, a big tractor trailer pulling a giant piece of equipment blocked the main entrance to the parking lot! Fussing and fuming, I managed to make it in the front door for my appointment exactly on time. The receptionist and I often share work-related woes. Afterward, our conversation turns to Jesus and how He sustains us. We remind each other that He will give us strength if only we remember to ask Him. I left my appointment that day in a more God-focused frame of mind. Thinking back to the beginning of my day, I realized a poor attitude stunted the effectiveness of my prayer.

> If I regard iniquity in my heart,
> The Lord will not hear.
> But certainly God has heard me;
> He has attended to the voice of my prayer (Psalm 66:18, 19, NKJV).

On my way to work, instead of fussing at the red lights, I decided to pray for the first person who came to mind. My attitude shift did not alter my situation, but my whole outlook changed so much that I started praying *for* red lights! As Christians, we all have bad days, but true growth is evident by our determination to let Jesus help us use those red lights for the glory of God! Being on time with Heaven is of far greater importance than being late here on Earth.

Deidre A. Jones

---

* This devotional was previously published on the Highland Seventh-day Adventist Church's blog. "Praying for Red Lights," *Highland Seventh-day Adventist Church: Sabbath Thoughts* (blog), November 13, 2018, http://highlandcounty22.adventistchurchconnect.org/sabbath-thoughts-blog/praying-for-red-lights.

"No Man Is an Island"

Behold, how good and how pleasant it is
For brethren to dwell together in unity!
—Psalm 133:1, NKJV

I waited behind the cart that was parked in the middle of the grocery-store aisle. The shopper was engrossed in viewing the rotisserie chicken displayed in the heated glass warmer. Eventually sensing that someone was behind her, the smiling customer looked my way and said, "I am looking at food." The supermarket was filling up with panicked buyers (or so I thought) since we, in the United States Virgin Islands, were expecting yet another tropical storm. Winds were predicted to reach 125 miles per hour. Heavy rain was also projected, although that would be nothing compared to the two category 5 hurricanes that we had experienced two years earlier.

I, too, was looking for food but not fish, meat, or poultry. Rather, my fruit supply was exhausted, and I needed to restock. *Eating a piece of fruit is better than crunching on chips*, I reasoned while looking at the fresh produce display.

Then I saw another shopper, a man, looking at the avocados and squeezing each one before deciding which ones to take.

"I wish I were an avocado," I quipped, "because sometimes I feel as if I need a squeeze."

He smiled kindly and said, "Sometimes we all need a little squeeze."

Subsequently, I began thinking about how fearfully and wonderfully God has made each of us. He created us not only with the physical need for nutritious food but also with the need to have social, intellectual, and emotional support and fulfillment. A long-ago poet once wrote these often-quoted words: "No man is an island."* How true!

The Bible exhorts us to be our brother's keeper, for anyone who needs our help is our neighbor. What kind of neighbor are you?

Hyacinth V. Caleb

---

* John Donne, "Meditation XVII," in *Devotions Upon Emergent Occasions*, 1624.

The Blessings of Obedience
PART 1

When you eat the labor of your hands,
You shall be happy, and it shall be well with you.
—Psalm 128:2, NKJV

Career options were limited in the sixties for a female growing up in Trinidad. When I visited my grandmother in the hospital the day before she died, I decided to enter the nursing profession. When the time was right, I was accepted into a nursing program and looked forward, with my fellow nursing students, to graduating in three years as a registered nurse. As we entered the final year of the program, we were required to attend lectures on Saturday. Five of us held that day as the Sabbath, the biblical day of rest, and did not feel we could attend lectures on that day. We were then told our options were to work at the hospital but never graduate, leave the nursing program, or attend the Saturday lectures. I was the first to resign from the program, I got married, and I accompanied my husband to the United States of America to continue his education.

Giving up on becoming a registered nurse, however, was not an option for me. Arriving in the States, I immediately began looking for a program that would allow me to continue my nursing studies. Yet when my transcript was evaluated, I was told that my earlier diploma-level courses were not compatible with the bachelor's degree level, and I would have to start from the beginning. I was devastated but not discouraged. By then, my husband and I were expecting our first child. I continued the admissions process and was accepted. After four years and with two preschool-aged children, I graduated with a bachelor of science in nursing instead of with a diploma. Over the years, I have advanced to the highest educational level of nursing and have been blessed tremendously. I have also enjoyed being a nurse educator, and my life has been enriched, happy, and fruitful because of being obedient to God's Word.

God has a plan for all of us. When we honor, obey, and give our allegiance to Him, He gives us the power and strength to achieve His plans for us. Let us be willing to trust Him completely with our lives, even when we can't see the future, because He has promised never to leave us nor forsake us.

Lydia D. Andrews

The Blessings of Obedience
PART 2

"But seek first his kingdom and his righteousness,
and all these things will be given to you as well."
—Matthew 6:33, NIV

A t the beginning of my nursing career, my ultimate desire was to become a midwife. Therefore, after graduation, I found employment in a hospital labor and delivery unit. When I had finished two years of clinical experience, I was accepted into a midwifery program at a large university in the Washington, DC, area, where I received my certification. Some years later, our family relocated to Alabama so that our children could obtain a Christian education. Though working night duty in a hospital there, in addition to being a part-time clinical instructor at the university, I decided to pursue a master's degree. With only one quarter's tuition in hand, I took a leap of faith and enrolled in the program, knowing I would have to commute two hours each way. Though it took two years for my husband to sell our home in Maryland and join us, God was definitely in control. Before the first quarter ended, I found myself eligible to receive a nursing traineeship from the National Institutes of Health. What a blessing! Look at God!

This enabled me to complete two master's degrees, including one in midwifery, and also accept full-time teaching status at the university as an assistant professor of nursing.

After our three children graduated from the university, I accepted a full-scope midwifery assignment in Kentucky. When the clinic downsized, offering a severance pay incentive—and my husband accepted early retirement from his government position—we felt God was preparing the way for me to accept an invitation to join the faculty of a Christian university in Kenya as a midwifery lecturer. After prayerful consideration, we were convinced that this call to Africa was a divine appointment, so we accepted without hesitation. My husband and I spent six wonderful and happy years in the motherland. One year after returning home, we were again called to Africa; this time to establish a bachelor's degree nursing program at a Christian university in Ghana. This was the highlight of my nursing career. I give total praise to God for His leading.

Truly He is able to do for us much more than we could have imagined. Being obedient to God brings happiness and richness to life. When we put Him first, He will reward exceedingly abundantly above all we can ever ask or think (Ephesians 3:20). What a mighty God we serve!

Lydia D. Andrews

Modern Miracles

You are the God who performs miracles;
you display your power among the peoples.
With your mighty arm you redeemed your people.
—Psalm 77:14, 15, NIV

I love miracle stories, and today I want to share my own miracle story: I'm celebrating the nineteenth anniversary of my stage 4 breast cancer diagnosis. The doctors estimated that I had a five-year life expectancy—much too soon to leave my three-year-old grandson, Andrew, and six-month-old granddaughter, Micah. Why would anyone celebrate that? My family reminded the doctors that I had done everything they had recommended: surgery, radiation, and the dreaded chemotherapy. The doctors explained that cancer would probably recur because it had already metastasized to the lymph nodes. "It's in the bloodstream," one doctor stated plainly. "We must warn you that only a miracle can help now." True to their dire warnings, the cancer came back in 2006, but the same treatments have given me fourteen more cancer-free years. Today I am enjoying my grandbabies, who are all grown up.

They also have miracle stories to share. High schooler Andrew suffered a debilitating football injury that caused him to say to me, "Nana, I wish the surgeon would just go ahead and amputate this leg. It would be so much better." But with many prayers, intense therapy, and much faith, he is a survivor. He is now pursuing a college degree.

Teenage Micah was involved in a head-on car crash. The towing attendant asked, "How did anyone survive this?" The other driver was killed instantly; Micah fully recovered after having knee surgery.

Why have we survived and so many have not? I don't know. My mind and heart find it hard to comprehend, but we are grateful and know God has His reasons.

I accept these miracles as gifts from God.

Jane Wiggins Moore

What a Day!

He who testifies to these things says,
"Yes, I am coming soon." Amen. Come, Lord Jesus.
—Revelation 22:20, NIV

Last Friday night, while my family was having worship, someone asked the question, "What do you think the atmosphere in heaven will be like?" As we made the rounds with answers from each family member, I was thinking about how I would answer the question. Almost everyone's answer seemed to mirror everyone else's: heaven would be a place of peace and quiet.

Then I got it! When I think of the atmosphere in heaven, I think of a lot of people and noise. Here's why. Some years ago, on the first weekend in May, I attended my twentieth high school class reunion in Oshawa, Ontario, Canada. I still get chills when I remember that weekend, especially Sabbath. You see, Sabbath was really the highlight of the weekend. Oh, there were events planned on other days, but not everyone could make those events. But when Sabbath arrived, it seemed that everyone was there. The number of people was amazing!

I had flown to Canada from Bermuda. Another classmate had flown in from the Bahamas. Others had flown in from different parts of the United States. Then, of course, there were my Canadian classmates who were from all over Canada. Some lived in Oshawa, while others had driven to be there. Most of us didn't know who would be there until Sabbath. More classmates attended this twentieth class reunion than had attended our ten-year class reunion.

The speaker who had been a few years behind me in school was fantastic! Different and older classes were honored. I was able to sit with friends. The variety of music, as I remembered it, was heavenly. You know what? As much I want to tell you about the weekend, it is hard. I wish you could have been there to experience it with me!

This encounter with old friends reminds me of the greatest reunion of all—Jesus' second coming. There will be people from all over. The talks will be wonderful, and the music also heavenly. I will be able to sit with friends. I will be reunited with loved ones I haven't seen in a long time. I can't describe all that will happen, but you have to experience it with me. It will be a reunion to remember! Will you plan to be there?

Dana M. Bean

Invitations

"Come, all you who are thirsty,
come to the waters;
and you who have no money,
come, buy and eat! . . .
Why spend money on what is not bread,
and your labor on what does not satisfy?"
—Isaiah 55:1, 2, NIV

Many mornings I find myself waking up and immediately thinking that I am a weak Christian. I desire that the day be easy, with no complications, no heartache, nothing difficult to solve, and no excessive thinking required. I just want a peaceful day. Why is living the Christian life so hard sometimes? As I pray, I am reminded by God's Spirit and His Word that there is much I bring to this mindset. You see, I am an intense person, and I can invite worry, anxiety, and complications. I can create a difficult day with no help from anyone else. God shows me the self-fulfilling prophecy of my own thinking. Christ lovingly points out where I might invite complication and confusion; He invites me to order and clarity. Where I might invite worry, He invites me to peace. Where I invite ease and comfort, He invites trust and provision. God knows us better than we know ourselves. He is always working for our good. He does this with an invitation, not demands or control. He invites us to something better.

Oh, thank You, Father, for your blessed invitations. All I have to do is accept them and enter into that something better. From the beginning of Jesus' ministry, He extended loving invitations—from the calling of His disciples (Matthew 4) to His words in Matthew 11:28: "Come to me, all you who are weary and burdened, and I will give you rest" (NIV).

So, each morning when I wake, I have the freedom and opportunity to respond to Christ's invitation. I can keep my eyes focused on my challenges and invite all the negative responses that go with them. Or I can accept the invitation of Christ. When I choose Christ's invitation each morning, that is when the abundant life that God so generously desires to give me will be a reality. It is not a reality of circumstances that is always easy or comfortable, but that choice results in a heart that is abundant with confidence in God. He is an invitation worth accepting every day.

Lee Lee Dart

It's a Miracle

"Call upon Me in the day of trouble;
I will deliver you, and you shall glorify Me."
—Psalm 50:15, NKJV

If you are a pet lover and make pets a part of your family, you will enjoy this story!

My husband, Ron, and I were driving back up our mountain following prayer meeting on a Wednesday evening. He was driving a pickup truck filled with a barrel train (children's choo-choo train made from barrels) in preparation for a fall party the following Saturday night. Following him in our van, I noticed a yellow cat on the road. Later at home, I said to Ron, "I'm so glad you didn't hit that cat on the road."

"I didn't see any cat," he replied.

The next day Ron asked whether I'd seen our yellow cat, Cal (short for Miracle), around. As we talked together, we realized that the cat I had seen on the road was most certainly our very own Cal, who had jumped out of the pickup! Cal must have been sleeping on one of the cushions in one of the barrels. He had ridden all the way to prayer meeting and halfway back home!

Now we were sad and began to pray not only that Cal was safe but that he would also find his way back home. Several weeks passed.

Our granddaughter, Savannah, was sad too. She posted a little video of Cal on social media. The next day she received a message from a schoolmate, saying, "I think your cat is at our house." Savannah's friend lived eight miles away from us! Later that day, Ron got a call from the family of the schoolmate, and they brought Cal back home! When I came home later that evening, Cal was on Ron's lap, purring loudly. I was happily surprised and so thankful!

Cal had come to live with us five years earlier. Soon after he had arrived, he got out of the garage, and our dog caught and shook him! We were afraid he might die. We wrapped him up and put him in a box overnight. By morning, he had revived from his traumatic experience. Savannah said, "It's a miracle!" Then she asked, "Can we call him Miracle?" As we enjoy having Cal with us again, we realize we have just experienced another miracle with our cat.

In His Word, God invites us to call upon Him especially in our times of perplexity, loss, and sadness. He will lift our burdens. Praise the Lord for His goodness toward each of us!

Sharon Follett

Give Thanks

Be thankful to Him, and bless His name.
—Psalm 100:4, NKJV

Though my life has been a challenge, I also have a bucket full of blessings. When I think of them, I just smile. Since finishing my studies, I have never been unemployed or experienced sickness to the point of needing hospitalization. God blessed me with a car at the right time in my life. I have a roof over my head, go to the gym every day, experience good health, and thank God for all the small mercies as well. He has given me life and talent, family, and family support. He has also given me wonderful Christian friends—people who will encourage me but also tell me when I do wrong (even when I don't want to hear it).

All I am saying is, let's pause and appreciate the things that God has done for us. Look at the things you have and be grateful because some people don't have them. Learn to laugh at your mistakes and forgive yourself. Stop taking life so seriously. Enjoy life with all the good and bad it brings. Keep a song in your heart; encourage someone. Listen without judging, help somebody, and smile at a stranger.

A happy life also comes from forgiving one another and learning to be kind. A happy and thankful life will speak blessing to others. The essence of forgiveness is the notion of canceling a debt (Mark 11:25, 26). The question is, How do we pray when we can't forgive those who have offended us? When we fail to forgive, bitterness increases, disagreements multiply, and despair becomes deeply rooted. Forgiveness can be a painful experience, especially when the one who hurt you never apologizes. But God breaks our spirits to save our souls. God breaks our hearts to make us whole. God allows pain in our lives so that we can be stronger. Pain is a part of life on this earth, but we can still be thankful for it. God wants us to give Him thanks in all our circumstances (see 1 Thessalonians 5:18).

So let's stop complaining and live life to the fullest, becoming the best that God intended us to be. Remember, He is the Potter, and we are just clay in His hands. Let's allow Him to mold us into His image and according to His plans—for our best interest.

May we always give thanks to God for the blessings and the trials!

Deborah Matshaya

God Will Take Care of You

"Look at the birds of the air; they do not sow or reap or store away in barns, and yet your heavenly Father feeds them. Are you not much more valuable than they? . . .
". . . If that is how God clothes the grass of the field, which is here today and tomorrow is thrown into the fire, will he not much more clothe you—you of little faith?"
—Matthew 6:26, 30, NIV

Right around Thanksgiving Day (late November in the United States) each year, seed catalogs start appearing in my mailbox. They contain beautiful photographs of scrumptious-looking fruits and vegetables and colorful flowers.

The sight of them fills me with hope and longing for warmer days. As they pile up on my kitchen island, I start visualizing the garden. What will I plant where? What new crop will I try this year? The catalogs are a welcome bit of clutter in my home.

To provide some background, in 2014, two friends gave another friend and me permission to farm a portion of their four acres of property. They do not garden or plant anything. As payment for our use of their acreage, they asked only that they have the privilege of sharing in the harvest. No problem. We already shared most of the harvest from the small plots we had in a community garden. We selected a quarter acre in a sunny spot.

This year as I contemplated the photos in the catalogs and started sketching out my portion of the garden, I thought about the work that goes into the garden and the reward of eating that first ripe strawberry in early May. And how nice it is when I take a basket of produce to church and invite people to take what they want.

I carefully plan the garden to include plants that will attract pollinators—bees, birds, and butterflies. All summer long, the raspberry bushes are covered with bees; so many birds gather that onlookers comment on the large number. People take photos of the monarch and swallowtail butterflies that invade the zinnias.

As I look at all the various creatures and the gorgeous, colorful flowers, I am reminded of Jesus' words when He told His listeners to consider the lilies in the field or the birds in the air. Neither reaps or sows or labors or spins, yet God takes care of them. How much more will God take care of us? We only need to ask God to take care of our needs.

Jean Arthur

He Cares

"For with God nothing will be impossible."
—Luke 1:37, NKJV

Smokey weighs four pounds. But when wearing his tiny red puppy jacket, he weighs a few ounces more. Laurie, another friend, and Smokey were hiking a remote trail in the state of Washington. It was December and very cold; snow was falling. A party with a dog passed the trio; Smokey bolted after the group. No amount of calling would bring him back, so Laurie and her friend started down also. There was no sign of the puppy at any point. They stopped at a home near the base of the trail and asked the man at the door to watch for the little guy. "I will," he promised. "In fact, I'll have my buddy, Brian, look for Smokey too. He knows the trail like the back of his hand."

Laurie and her friend returned to the trail and headed back up, praying and calling. At ten o'clock that night, they turned back, frozen and demoralized, fearful for their own safety in the dark, slippery terrain. Laurie alerted her husband, who was traveling, and her Facebook friends of Smokey's situation. The prayers commenced. A sleepless night followed.

Early the next day, Laurie was back on the mountain. She was tired, anxious, cold, and frankly, somewhat doubtful that God actually cared about her personally, much less a little dog. Still, she plowed on, praying. At one point, when she didn't think she could hike any higher (and was already higher than where she'd been when Smokey had taken off—downhill, remember), she concluded that Smokey must be gone for good. It had been thirty-six hours since he'd been seen, and Laurie couldn't believe that he might still be alive. She returned to a slightly widened spot in the trail and stopped to rest and think. That's when she heard a sound from above her and watched, with little interest at first and through her miserable tears, a man round the corner. He was holding a tiny red bundle in his arms.

It couldn't be! But it was.

Brian said, "Is he yours?" and thrust the bundle toward Laurie. "I found him in a hole he'd dug near the trail at thirty-five hundred feet (1,067 meters) elevation. He was sleeping." Try to tell Laurie or her husband, Butch, that God doesn't care. They believe He does, as do I.

How about you?

Carolyn K. Karlstrom

Mothers

Making her the joyous mother of children.
—Psalm 113:9, NRSV

Mother's Day is celebrated every year in the United States of America. It's a day to remember the good times with your mother or make new memories. It's a day a mother shares with her children, feeling blessed that the Lord gave them to her. One woman in the Old Testament, however, had never had the blessing of being a mother. As her story begins, Hannah suffers the verbal abuse of her husband's second wife, who is a mother several times over. Though Hannah has prayed often about her infertility, motherhood has not become a reality.

Have you had friends who share their excitement over being pregnant, totally forgetting how long you have prayed to be so? Sure, you are thrilled for them, but your own pain is deep. You might have wondered: Does God hear others' prayers but not mine?

During the family's visit to the tabernacle, Hannah pleads her case to God one more time. She is so focused on her plea that she is oblivious to anyone else being there. Eli, the priest, totally misjudges her demonstration of anguish, thinking it coming from a drunk person. Poor Hannah! She explains her situation. Eli is man enough to admit he made a wrong assumption and blesses her. God answers with a yes this time. In deep appreciation for her baby boy, Samuel—the son who has made her a mother—Hannah keeps her vow to God. She gives the child to the Lord to serve in the tabernacle. Her separation anxiety has to be strong. Yet she keeps her vow to God, trusting He will be with Samuel.

We mothers try to protect our children from wrong influences. I remember how hard we looked for a house in a nice, safe neighborhood when our boys were young. We monitored who their friends were when they were young. But Samuel lived in the tabernacle with a priest who didn't discipline his own sons. Hannah's fervent prayers, however, protected her son from the evil practices around him. Likewise, we must trust God and put our children in His capable hands. And Hannah's eldest son, Samuel, became one of the greatest judges Israel ever had.

The rest of this mother's story finds Hannah being blessed with more children, and she faithfully visits Samuel each year at the tabernacle. Through one mother's faith and faithfulness, God both works a miracle in her life and blesses, through her son, an entire nation.

Louise Driver

A Beautiful Garden

In the beginning God created the heavens and the earth. . . .
. . . God called the light Day, and the darkness He called Night.
So the evening and the morning were the first day.
—Genesis 1:1, 5, NKJV

Today is a beautiful day," I said to myself. After experiencing several bitterly cold days, I was so happy to relax, open my window, and drink in some of the bright, beautiful sunshine. As I relaxed, I thought about how our heavenly Father has everything under control. He hears our prayers and cries, and He attends to every detail in our lives. My bones had started to ache, and my feet felt as if they were unable to carry on (as a result of staying in the house for so long without exercise). But that day, I was able to work outside and complete many of the chores I had been unable to do during the cold season.

Sometimes I wonder why people say there is no God when He has everything under control. He has a reason why He allows those several days of bitterly cold weather. I did some research and learned that the cold kills certain germs in the atmosphere. On the other hand, the cold weather can also destroy many beautiful plants, including mine. I had several plants that I adored, and I sadly watched their leaves turn from green to brown, and some eventually died.

Sometimes this is what Satan does: he attempts to destroy God's beautiful creation, yet God will not allow him to destroy the beautiful earth that He once created. There will be an end to sin. I think of the heavenly garden where He is waiting. He bids us come and meet Him there. We must do our part earnestly to be ready to meet Him and keep our eyes on the prize.

> There's a garden where Jesus is waiting,
> There's a place that is wondrously fair.
> For it glows with the light of His presence.
> 'Tis the beautiful garden of prayer.*

Lord, I really want to meet You in that beautiful garden where there will be no more bitterly cold days, sickness, sadness, death, or aching feet and bones. There will only be beauty and joy all around us.

Our only task is to trust Him and be faithful until He welcomes us there.

Patricia Hines

---

* Eleanor A. Schroll, "The Beautiful Garden of Prayer," 1920.

Wedding-Night Scare

"I am with you and will watch over you wherever you go."
—Genesis 28:15, NIV

As we celebrated our fortieth anniversary in 2017, I reflected on God's amazing leading over the last four decades. Then I remembered how close we had come to not celebrating our first night together. Our marriage journey almost ended before it began.

We had an unforgettable and lovely wedding ceremony and reception that beautiful summer day in Montego Bay, Jamaica. Then we packed our honeymoon bags into the car and started our journey on the scenic north coast. We were heading to Ocho Rios, which is another special spot on the island of Jamaica. We would have enjoyed the scenic journey if night had not already fallen—a moonless night. We were excited when we saw the Drax Hall sign. That meant we were only a few miles from Dunn's River Falls and Ocho Rios.

Then it happened! A black cow stepped out of the thick bushes in the dark night just as we were negotiating a corner in the cow's direction. As it stumbled into the road, it hit the car on the driver's side. I froze with fear. To the credit of the young groom, his eyes were on the road and his hands on the wheel. But we know that alone was not what saved us. God's promise to watch over us wherever we go and protect and uphold us was tested—and proven.

On that and many roads in Jamaica, others had lost their lives in similar incidents. Yet God delivered us. We rounded the corner and came to a safe spot to offer praise to God for His miraculous deliverance. It also helped to calm our nerves and prepare us to resume the journey. We had much more now to celebrate in addition to our brand-new marriage!

I encourage all my sisters who read this story to place themselves in God's care each time they get in their vehicles to go on a journey, however short it may be. God's promises are faithful. I have written "PP" (proven promise) in my Bible beside some of my favorite promises. I am sure you have many proven promises in your Bible too. Mine include Isaiah 41:10; 43:2; Psalm 91:11, 12; Matthew 28:20; and Hebrews 13:5. Let's memorize and claim these precious, proven promises. They are awesome!

Claudette Garbutt-Harding

A Most Common Sin

When pride comes, then comes disgrace,
but with humility comes wisdom.
—Proverbs 11:2, NIV

Have you ever thought about which is the worst sin? It seems that we are often most horrified by the sins that we can see. Yet what about the ones that are not so visible?

I would suggest that perhaps even if pride is not the worst sin, it is definitely one of the most common sins. Society—even the church—has experienced the pollution of pride and arrogance in the lives of many. Perhaps you have had thoughts such as these: We are better than others because we do not do this or that. We do not sin as others do. They are wrong, and we are right.

The Bible has much to say about pride and those who are proud. One such text is Isaiah 2:11. I find it interesting that Isaiah, when speaking of the coming of Jesus, says, "The lofty looks of man shall be humbled, and the haughtiness of men shall be bowed down" (KJV).

In fact, Isaiah mentions twice in that chapter (verses 11, 17) that when the arrogance and pride of humankind is humbled, "the Lord *alone* will be exalted in that day" (verse 11, NIV; emphasis added).

How do these texts on pride, especially Isaiah 2:11, apply to our lives today? Just as certain prideful behaviors were observable in Isaiah's time, this common sin can be observed today in our actions, even when people can't read our thoughts, by the way we relate to those within our sphere of influence. Let's ask God to help us pursue a humble spirit, looking at others as equal to ourselves and not "less than." Then God alone will be exalted in our lives.

Cecilia Nanni

Overweight!

Let us lay aside every weight,
and the sin which doth so easily beset us.
—Hebrews 12:1, KJV

Returning on an international flight after burying my brother, I approached the domestic airline counter to present my ticket and luggage in preparation for the final leg of my trip home. I looked forward to the two-hour flight after being in transit for the last six-plus hours. The ticketing agent verified my identity and flight information, returned my passport, and was just about to tag my luggage when he calmly stated, to my dismay: "Houston, we have a problem!"

There was no problem with the weight of my luggage on the previous flight, I thought, so I was a bit surprised.

"Your suitcase is overweight," the ticketing agent said. A quick glance at the scale confirmed that it was so by approximately ten pounds. I had to make a quick decision: pay the extra airline fee or remove some items from my suitcase. A little embarrassed, I moved away from the counter and opened the suitcase with a prayer that God would show me what I needed to remove and transfer to my carry-on bag.

Immediately, my eyes rested on a small bag that contained some clothing needing to be laundered. I quickly pulled it out, stuffed it in the carry-on, zipped up the suitcase, and again placed it on the scale. Amazingly, the scale registered fifty pounds exactly. My heart was shouting, *Thank You, Jesus!* I noticed a lady in line at the next counter who had been watching my predicament.

"Exactly fifty pounds!" she exclaimed.

I replied, "Praise the Lord!" My suitcase was tagged, placed on the conveyor belt, and sent on to the aircraft. I proceeded to the designated gate to board my flight.

As I began walking toward my gate, I reflected on my spiritual journey. I considered how I may also be guilty of carrying extra "weight" in my spiritual life. Perhaps I need to reassess and "unpack" my cares, grudges, unforgiveness, regrets, and pain. After all, the Bible says, "Cast thy burden upon the LORD, and he shall sustain thee" (Psalm 55:22, KJV). We all need to fly light, being intentional to give all our baggage to the Lord. Then we'll be heaven-bound without being overweight!

Claudine Houston

The Greatest Lifeguard

The LORD makes firm the steps
of the one who delights in him;
though he may stumble, he will not fall,
for the LORD upholds him with his hand.
—Psalm 37:23, 24, NIV

His knees trembled beneath him; his eyes were a picture of pure terror. It wasn't the first time a student refused to jump off the diving board; in fact, I was becoming accustomed to it. But jumping off the diving board into the swimming pool below wasn't a new task, for he had already done it. Maybe his terror was associated with me—an adolescent coteacher with no experience in catching him after he splashed down from the diving board. Had he seen through my mask of perfect composure?

Suppressing the panic that tightened my chest, I glanced up just in time to see his knees bend. His toes wiggled once or twice while my coteacher encouraged him softly. The entire pool seemed to quiet while my heart beat faster. Before I could perceive the boy's slight movements, he jumped. Instantly, I reached for him, pulling him onto the rescue tube. I smiled, showering him with encouragement: he had jumped, and I had caught him.

This experience of catching a kid from off the diving board, although unnerving, was rewarding. Later in the afternoon, when I was on break, I sat down and thought about the whole experience. I was ecstatic that I had caught a kid, for, in my mind, that was the same thing as saving him. I reflected on how our spiritual lives are much like that boy's diving-board experience. The problems we face, the terrifying situations we find ourselves in, are like dealing with a high diving board that we must jump from in order to reach our goals. Sometimes we can't see what's beyond the jump, for the waters are dark and their depths, unfathomable. In addition, we wonder whether we will find ourselves safe and whole on the other side of the jump. In life, however, we often must make those leaps of faith, trusting that someone will catch us.

Thankfully, there's an immense difference between my swimming-pool diving board and the leaps of faith that God encourages us to make. That difference is this: Rather than a teenager waiting to catch you after you jump, it's the Creator of heaven and Earth who catches you. He will never let you drown.

Madeleine E. Miyashiro

Will Anyone Ever Love Me Again?

And Joseph said to his brothers, "Please come near to me."
So they came near. Then he said: "I am Joseph your brother,
whom you sold into Egypt. But now, do not
therefore be grieved or angry with yourselves because you sold me here;
for God sent me before you to preserve life."
—Genesis 45:4, 5, NKJV

The early years of my education began in a one-room school in Pennsylvania. When the weather permitted, we formed teams and played softball. One of those games remains vivid in my memory. My sister and I were chosen to play on opposite teams. Maxine, who was twelve months younger than I, had brown hair with golden-red highlights, complementing her freckled cheeks and button nose. As I walked up to the plate to bat, I noticed she was the catcher. Not the best arrangement! I had a bad habit of slinging my bat the instant I heard the ball connect with the bat. Fearing for my little sister's safety, I warned her to stand back, for I was getting ready to hit the ball. Just as I expected, she did not budge! Seconds later, I hit a fly ball and ran to first base. I turned to see a crowd gathered around my sister at home plate. Running back to home plate, I found her bleeding from the mouth with two front teeth broken at the gums.

Quietly, I slipped away to dry my tears for her pain and nurse my shame while wondering whether anyone would ever love me after what I had just done! After ringing the school bell, our teacher ushered all the children inside, kindly telling my sister and me that we could sit on the school's front porch while waiting for the school bus—of which our mother was the driver. When Mother opened the bus door, I quickly slipped inside, going directly to the back. I slid down into my seat. Our teacher accompanied my sister, sharing with Mother about the accident. I wanted to disappear. Thankfully, the other children sensed my pain and gave me the space and privacy I needed. Time did its work of healing within the silence that surrounded me, and I accepted forgiveness for myself. Instead of words of anger, blame, or resentment being directed at my wounded heart, I experienced the gifts of unconditional love and forgiveness.

In Genesis 45, Joseph offered mercy to his brothers, who had intentionally brought him pain, changing his life forever. "Come near to me. . . . Do not . . . be grieved or angry with yourselves" (verses 4, 5, NKJV). God Himself speaks to each of us today through the beautiful spirit of Joseph.

Dottie Barnett

"Commit Thy Way Unto the Lord"

I shall not die, but live,
and declare the works of the LORD.
—Psalm 118:17, KJV

Jesus came to Earth as a man and lived a sinless life. His life is an example for us to follow. He taught that when we confess our sins, repent of our sins, and ask God for forgiveness, we are awarded a right to the tree of life. Satan is a liar, thief, and murderer. He constantly throws stumbling blocks in our path. He uses any means to distract us from reaching our heavenly goal, including envy, jealousy, hurt, hatred, discouragement, guilt, disappointment, and oppression, to mention a few. These are diseases that cannot be cured by a medical regimen, hydrotherapy, physical or psychological therapy, surgery, or some special diet. They originated from sin and can be cured only through the blood of Jesus.

The great controversy began in heaven and continues until this very moment. The adversary is determined to lure God's children as far away from Him as he possibly can. He enjoys playing mind games. Once he has clouded your mind with any of the diseases previously mentioned, he feels confident he has won your vote! We must remember we are wrestling not with "flesh and blood, but against principalities, against powers, against the rulers of the darkness of this world" in high places (Ephesians 6:12, KJV). We must exercise our faith and trust in God, for He is able to deliver us, and He is the only one who can. Sometimes we feel as if Satan has attacked us from every angle. We cannot allow our emotions to take control. Although we may be perplexed, we must not despair. God has promised not to leave us even when we are being persecuted. When we are cast down, remember Isaiah 41:10. The Lord promises to strengthen us, help us, and uphold us with the right hand of His righteousness. The Lord will fight for us, and we will stay in perfect peace as long as we keep our minds on Him and trust in Him (see Isaiah 26:3).

Victory is ours through Christ. All we have to do is claim it. Christ speaks to us today in John 16:33: "These things I have spoken unto you, that in me ye might have peace" (KJV). Aren't these words comforting? He continues, "In the world ye shall have tribulation: but be of good cheer; I have overcome the world." If Jesus has the whole world in His hand and He has overcome the world, why should we worry? Lean on Psalm 37:5: "Commit thy way unto the LORD; trust also in him; and he shall bring it to pass" (KJV). God is willing, and He is able.

Cora A. Walker

The Project

This is the confidence we have in approaching God: that if we ask anything according to his will, he hears us. And if we know that he hears us—whatever we ask—we know that we have what we asked of him.
—1 John 5:14, 15, NIV

God has promised that when He calls us to a certain work, He will be responsible for its outcome. He will supply the necessary support that the project requires. As we invest our time and effort into our calling, He will provide for our daily needs as well.

In January 2003, Pastor Daniel approached me about working on a ministry project with him. We prayerfully began our work on the project whenever he was available. In April, I went to the Philippines to complete a master of ministry degree, interrupting my work on the project. After my return home, Pastor Daniel and I prayerfully continued with our project. I was informed I would be given a contract for this project to continue as a researcher. In May, I began serious research in libraries, on the internet, and through surveys and interviews.

After our research was completed, we drafted our findings and computer work into the final product, which was printed in a religious publication. We also produced, under the guidance of Pastor Daniel, two different pamphlets regarding our research project. Then came the responsibility of translating all the work from English into Chinese—both traditional and simplified Chinese. Ms. Kathleen recommended Pastor Edmund of Hong Kong to help with the translation. How thankful I was to be guided by two experts in the completion of this project (including PowerPoint slides)! Praise the Lord, who provides for our needs!

The project was finished in December 2004 and put onto CDs for a well-known ministry, ending my very busy one-year, seven-month contract. Then it became necessary for me to care for my parents, especially my father, who was not in good health.

About a year or two years later, however, I was invited to attend a large church conference. While there, I had the privilege of introducing to all attendees the completed ministry project with the PowerPoint presentation. God will bless any project He gives us!

Siew Ghiang Yan

Slow

Know this, my beloved brothers: let every person be quick to hear, slow to speak,
slow to anger; for the anger of man does not produce the righteousness of God.
—James 1:19, 20, ESV

No, lady, you can't board. You don't have the requirements to enter Serbia. Please find another flight, and go back to your home country." I was speechless. Simultaneously, I felt anger rise because I did, indeed, have the necessary requirements. I caught my breath as I reminded myself to speak slowly and without anger—and presented my documents again.

Notice in the Bible verse for today that James isn't calling us to stifle our reactions; he calls us to change our reactions and be slow in our response. Although slowness is not an attractive asset in our fast-paced society, where quick opinions and responses are abundant, James tells us that being slow to speak and slow to anger is important to God. Whatever comes our way, James instructs us to be quick to hear, which frees us to listen attentively to what others say. Slowness of speech also requires us to practice self-control over our own thoughts and feelings.

The Word of truth has power. When we are quick to anger, the power of truth does not belong to us. This is why James writes that our anger "does not produce the righteousness of God." The righteousness of God is directly tied to His faithfulness and Word of truth. One of the attributes of God is being slow to anger. We misrepresent God's character when we use anger as a primary reaction toward people and circumstances. Misrepresenting God puts us in conflict with Him, which is the same as siding with unbelievers and the enemies of God.

At the airport that day, I swallowed my disappointment and anger and prayed silently, *Lord, help me to reflect who You are as I speak. Amen.* Again, I explained my situation to the man behind the counter. He looked at my papers, then said, "Thank you for your patience and kind words, but you can't board." Yet he didn't dismiss me. Immediately, he searched for a seat on the next flight home. When he found a seat, he forgave the difference in the ticket price. As I expressed my gratitude, he replied, "Thank you for speaking kindly to me. Enjoy your flight."

Are you facing a situation that needs more slow listening? Listening attentively can be therapeutic and healing. Be quick to hear because the Bible tells us a "gentle answer" can diffuse wrath, "but a harsh word stirs up anger" (Proverbs 15:1, NIV).

Raquel Quiroz da Costa Arrais

"Before They Call, I Will Answer"

"Before they call I will answer;
while they are still speaking I will hear."
—Isaiah 65:24, NIV

At the beginning of the year 2020, many of my family and friends were getting sick with the flu. Sure enough, my five-year-old grandson, Maxwell, also caught it at school. My daughter called me on Sunday evening and asked me to take care of Max, so I took off from work that Monday and Tuesday and stayed home to take care of him.

To keep from catching the flu, I started to take some natural flu and cold capsules, which an office friend had gotten for me from Australia. In one box of this medicine, there are two sheets of day capsules and one sheet of night capsules. I was happy that I had some capsules left to take. Within a week, I had used up all the day capsules. Since I used up the daytime capsules and had only three nighttime capsules left, I went ahead and took a nighttime capsule. But that made me feel a little sleepy at work. (I'm sure the nighttime capsules have some ingredients to enhance sleep at night.) I had asked my friend to get me more of these capsules, and he was kind enough to give me a supply the very next day.

On Friday morning, January 24, 2020, I opened a new box of capsules and took one. I decided to keep the rest of the sheet of capsules in the old box with the leftover night capsules. To my utter amazement, when I opened the old box to put my new sheet of capsules inside, I saw a full sheet of the day capsules. I clearly remember using up all the daytime capsules and even throwing away the used-up sheet. I was shocked to find a full sheet of day capsules. In fact, when I was opening the new box of capsules, I was thanking God for supplying me with more of those capsules. But how did a full sheet of the day capsules get inside the old box? I will never know. All I can say is that I regarded this find as a miracle. My loving God wanted to supply my needs.

Another great blessing from my wonderful heavenly Father was that I did not contract the flu from my grandson, even though I took care of him for two days! What a merciful and gracious God we have, who knows and cares for our every need in life!

I praise and thank Him for His marvelous love and grace toward each one of us!

Stella Thomas

Thoughts About Job

Job was a man who lived in Uz. He was honest inside
and out, a man of his word, who was totally devoted
to God and hated evil with a passion.
—Job 1:1, *The Message*

One night I couldn't get to sleep, so I listened to CDs from the Word of Promise audio Bible. I specifically listened to the book of Job. Job was a wealthy man who seemed to have everything going for him: family, the rest of his community, and widely spread business connections. He was also very dedicated to God and prayed every day.

Then his life started to fall apart. First, he suffered the destruction of his livestock and servants. Next, he lost his children in a storm. Finally, he lost his health. His grieving wife told him to give up on both life and God. She thought there was no hope left for him.

Job poured out his frustration, anger, pain, and anxiety to both God and his friends. He did not understand why God had allowed this to happen because he had tried to live a righteous life.

What Job didn't seem to consider was that beyond what was seen, a battle had been raging ever since sin entered the Garden of Eden—the battle between Satan and God, evil and good. We, too, have experienced the pain of being caught up in this conflict, which continues to this day. Job's cries of anguish, along with those of many others down through the ages, were joined by the cry of Jesus on the cross of Calvary: "Why, God, have You forsaken Me?"

When Satan hurls his attacks at us, we often wonder where God is. He seems so far away. In truth, though, He is close to us during our trials. When Job exhausted all his arguments with his "friends" and emptied himself, then God spoke to him. Job listened, speechless at first.

Sometimes loss renders us speechless as it initially did Job's friends. When they came to visit him, they sat with him in silence. Sometimes we don't know what to say when someone we know is suffering. Sadly, we sometimes don't even go to visit because we are afraid of saying the wrong thing. We may not understand the suffering a friend or loved one is going through, yet just being there for that person may bring comfort. The best thing to do is to ask God how we should respond. He will never fail to give us the courage to speak His words of comfort; however, listening to their pain first may be a big help. Finally, reminding the sufferer that he or she is not alone, because of God's love and presence, may be the greatest comfort we can offer.

Peggy Curtice Harris

Fear Turned to Joy

What time I am afraid, I will trust in thee.
—Psalm 56:3, KJV

Have you ever met with a situation that made your heart shiver? Have you ever been gripped with sudden fear, and it seemed as if the heavens were falling on your head? In those times, what is the best thing to do? Let me share my testimony to demonstrate the truth and power of today's text.

Fear gripped me when the treasurer of our church headquarters in our part of the world told me that I would need to budget the finances of the upcoming meeting in such a manner that no debt would be brought to his office after the program. Though this stipulation was reasonable, fear gripped me because I felt the weight of this enormous responsibility: I must not run the conference into debt. Troubling questions raced through my head: If I fall short of money, where do I go for help? If emergencies arise, who will come to my aid?

Just at that moment when those troubled thoughts were tormenting me, the words of Psalm 56:3 shone into my heart like a flash of light in the midst of thick darkness. I whispered a prayer in my heart: *Jesus, I now give You all my fears. I know that You will take care of them for me.*

As I prayed daily with my office secretary and the directors of the other participating areas about the meeting and its related budget, the Spirit of the Lord taught me strategies about the best ways to handle the finances as I worked with the treasury team assigned to me. Daily I gave my fears to God and prayed for miraculous blessings. I kept strictly to the budget, refused any extravagant spending, and bargained carefully for all transactions. I encouraged my treasury team to be faithful and trusted in the Lord to help me out.

At the end of the meeting, I was surprised at the blessings of the Lord. All that had been planned and budgeted was achieved; we had some cash left instead of debt! Praise God, my fear was turned into joy as the treasurer gave me the conference's financial report. What a God we serve! The One who is able to turn our fears into joy! I do not know your source of fear today. Is it related to finances, as was mine? Is it a health issue or a family problem? Whatever your fear and its source, carry them to Jesus. In His ways and timing, He will turn your fear into joy and give you the grace to bear the burdens. "What time I am afraid, I will trust in thee" (Psalm 56:3, KJV)!

Omobonike Adeola Sessou

He Leadeth Me

PART 1

In all things He had to be made like His brethren.
—Hebrews 2:17, NKJV

I stood at my husband's bedside with my arm across his chest. He was unconscious. He was dying. I felt the steady up and down of his breathing. Then I didn't. I knew then that our fifty-year love relationship as husband and wife on this earth had ended. *Why now, Lord? Where are You? I'm not ready for this! How can I live without him? He did everything for me.* I was numb. I couldn't cry for six months! When the tears did come, it felt like a boxing glove repeatedly knocking me down. I started to cry, often loudly, for long periods of time every day. After a while, my sons said, "Mom, Daddy wouldn't want you to do this." I heard them and thought, *No, and neither would God.* But I couldn't stop on my own. I was down and out, and I didn't think I'd be able to live my life anymore. How could I when I was so weak and helpless, alone, and brokenhearted? I turned to my Bible. God led me to Psalm 34:18: "The LORD is near to the brokenhearted and saves those who are crushed in spirit" (NIV).

In my weakened state of mind, God spoke to me. I realized that Christ subjected Himself to humanity for me and you (Hebrews 2:17). And because He did, He was actually able to feel my heavy heart, grief, and intense suffering. He knew what I was experiencing. That's why He could be so compassionate and sympathetic. He had walked this path before me. I cried out to the Lord, asking for comfort and healing. I knew He would hear my desperate plea.

My husband had once told me that I had more faith than anyone he ever knew. Now I remembered his words and reached inside to tap that faith. As I drew upon it, I felt Jesus personally with me, wiping away my tears and wrapping me securely in His arms. I knew my tears were precious to Him (Psalm 56:8). I knew He was comforting me (Isaiah 66:13). My pain eased. I wiped my tears, blew my nose, and began to function again little by little.

I am still in need of comfort—some days more than others. Yet I'm so relieved to know that our Jesus understands how difficult my walk and your walk are. I know He will help us manage the losses and perplexities of this life because of this assurance which He gives us: "I can do all things through Christ who strengthens me" (Philippians 4:13, NKJV).

Mary Lou Buoymaster

He Leadeth Me
PART 2

He makes me to lie down in green pastures;
He leads me beside the still waters.
He restores my soul;
He leads me in the paths of righteousness
For His name's sake.
—Psalm 23:2, 3, NKJV

I have a lot of fond memories with my husband; I treasure each one. I believe in the resurrection, so I know I'll see my husband again (1 Thessalonians 4:14–18). Until that day, I will walk with God and find ways to be a blessing.

Are you also grieving the loss of a loved one: a child, spouse, parent, sibling, relative, dear friend, or even a beloved furry, scaled, or winged creature? You are not alone. Someone who knows how you feel is with you. Just call on Him! Your value to Him is immeasurable. He chose to come to our world and assume our human nature so that we would know He really understands our every emotion. Through faith, we can feel His touch of love.

Some days since losing my husband are still very hard for me to get through. But I know there is never a place in my heart where God is not. My husband's arms are a cherished memory, yet in the darkness of loneliness, I know I am still loved. God states outright that we are "precious" to Him, honored, and that He loves us (Isaiah 43:4). Believe His promises! God knows your feelings of pain. Jesus was "a man of sorrows, and acquainted with grief" (Isaiah 53:3, KJV). He wept for Lazarus. He wept in the Garden of Gethsemane. Yes, Jesus grieved, but He didn't lose hope—and neither should we! Jesus can and will mend you if you ask Him. "Pour out your heart before Him" (Psalm 62:8, NKJV). Seek Him in His Word. He is "the Father of mercies and God of all comfort" (2 Corinthians 1:3, NKJV).

As you walk—or stumble—through this day, know that God is with you every single minute throughout the mundane, the joys, and the heaviest burden of grief. Because of His presence, you are making it. You are surviving it all because you are strong through Christ. So get up now. Make your bed to help organize your life and thoughts. Then say a prayer, committing yourself to embrace the many blessings of this day—starting with you!

Mary Lou Buoymaster

The Prayers We Pray

*Likewise the Spirit also helps in our weaknesses. For we do not
know what we should pray for as we ought, but the Spirit Himself
makes intercession for us with groanings which cannot be uttered. . . .
He makes intercession for the saints according to the will of God.*
—Romans 8:26, 27, NKJV

One of my grandsons' favorite Bible stories is about a young Israelite slave girl who worked for Captain and Mrs. Naaman (2 Kings 5). As the storybook tells it, she did everything Mrs. Naaman asked her to do to help around the house. But she would not pray to an idol with them. She explained to Captain and Mrs. Naaman, "I pray to the God in heaven who sees me and hears me."

One morning as our boys sat down at the table, I asked Aeden to say the blessing. He cheerfully agreed.

"O Lord!" he began without preamble. "I will not bow down to idols. I will not pray to them. I love You, Jesus, very much. And my birthday presents. And the food."

I peeked through half-closed eyes at Aeden's four-year-old head, bowed over clasped hands that barely cleared the bowl of oatmeal in front of him. As soon as the amen was said, his twin brother gave him a long, appraising look, obviously sharing my astonishment at this strange breakfast prayer. "Wow, Aeden," Trystan said. "I didn't see that coming."

Until that moment at the breakfast table, I hadn't thought Aeden had even been listening when I read the boys the story, since he seemed to be primarily employed with sticking a green rubber lizard into his brother's ear during story time.

As I thought about it, though, Aeden's prayer probably isn't so different from the ones I send up to heaven. Not speaking the language of heaven, I often have difficulty finding words that adequately convey the longings of my heart. This brings me to my knees, and I plead, "O Lord! Thank You for the gift of Your Holy Spirit, who translates the groanings of my 'oatmeal' prayers into the language of heaven, making sense of that which I haven't the words to express, so that our beautiful Savior comes down and walks with me when I 'pass through the waters' so that they shall not overflow me!" (Isaiah 43:2, NIV).

Jeannette Busby Johnson

Listening Saves Lives

A wise man will hear and increase learning.
—Proverbs 1:5, NKJV

My recent study into the fifty-one-day siege of the Branch Davidians in Waco, Texas, in 1993 has reinforced my belief in the importance of listening.* Through active listening, respect, and gentle methods, the FBI hostage negotiation team secured the release of thirty-five people—twenty-one of them children. But after the more aggressive tactical team took over, not another person was released from the compound. We know that story ended with fire and needless death.

We, too, can negotiate smaller crises through active listening. Being heard and understood soothes the soul. When someone really listens to us, we start to feel our complex emotions untangle; they are smoothed and combed out and carried away. James 1:19 counsels that we should "be quick to listen, slow to speak, and slow to get angry" (NLT). God tells us to listen before speaking, but we reverse that order. The bedrock of listening is reflection, saying back to the person in our own words what they have said to us.

One day I found crusted-over dishes in the kitchen sink. I marched into my college-aged daughter's bedroom, ready to defend my right. "You say you love me, but then you leave dishes in the sink. If you don't do them, I end up doing them and feel like your maid!"

"Mom, I hate it when you say things like that!" Her body was scrunched in defense mode; her voice ragged with hurt. I suddenly remember the little girl whose tears I'd dried so many times. There had to be a better way. Then I remembered reflective listening!

I calmly asked, "So it bothers you when I say that?" She nodded. "What about that bothers you?" I continued.

She said she didn't want me to feel like a maid or question her love for me. She admitted that though she didn't always show it, she truly did love me.

An amazing thing happened as I reflected her thoughts back to her. The red-faced girl's shoulders dropped about three inches, from being scrunched up around her neck to being relaxed.

At last, I said, "I'm sorry, baby. I need to change the way I do things. I'll do my best not to overinterpret your carelessness as not loving me. How about that?"

"Thanks, Mom. And you're right. I am careless. I'll do better." And she did. It works.

Jennifer Jill Schwirzer

---

* This devotion first appeared as a blog post. Jennifer Jill Schwirzer, "Listening Saves Lives," *Jennifer Jill Schwirzer* (blog), October 2, 2019, https://jenniferjill.org/listening-saves-lives/.

My Secrets

*You have searched me, L*ORD*,*
and you know me.
You know when I sit and when I rise;
you perceive my thoughts from afar.
You discern my going out and my lying down;
you are familiar with all my ways.
—Psalm 139:1–3, NIV

The dryer hummed its familiar rhythm as the towels tumbled around the drum. Next, I heard a loud pop, then silence. The three-year-old dryer had died. After a series of phone calls, I finally talked to someone about scheduling a service call. Of course, she would want the model and serial numbers of the dryer. And of course, those would be printed in small type and mounted in an awkward place to read. I apologized on my end of the phone for taking so long to get the numbers. The young voice on the other end sweetly and patiently responded, "Oh, you're doing very well for being ___ years old!" I was incensed! How did a dryer-repair secretary know my age? I felt violated to be reminded that in this high-tech world we don't have any secrets anymore. Of course, God knows my age, my weight, and the number of hairs on my head. That's all right; because of all the things He knows, those are inconsequential. Of real and eternal significance is the fact that God knows my heart! What secrets do I try to keep hidden there?

When God sent Samuel to anoint David to be the future king of Israel, Samuel was impressed with David's brothers' appearance and height. But God reminded him that "people look at the outward appearance [like my age on the computer!], but the LORD looks at the heart" (1 Samuel 16:7, NIV). My DNA was determined by God before the two cells from my parents were ever joined, before "I was made in the secret place" (Psalm 139:15, NIV). He knew the journey my life would take. He didn't force me into one role or another, but His foreknowledge is based on the fact that He gave me free will. And because He knows my heart, He saw ahead of time what choices I would make. Considering that God knows everything about me and knows the things I do that I don't want other people to know—including the private things I tell Him—I can trust Him because God doesn't tell my secrets!

Roxy Hoehn

A Sorrowful Beginning

Oh that thou wouldest bless me indeed.
—1 Chronicles 4:10, KJV

Into what circumstances were you born? We do not have control over who our birth parents are or where we are born. We sometimes find ourselves in situations that we have no control over or did not even seek out. Life just happens to us. As a school-based speech and language pathologist, I have had the unique privilege of reviewing the background history of the students I serve. At times, I had to close the folder as tears welled up in my eyes. I experienced the same deep empathy at a women's retreat where an elderly lady shared with the group her trauma of being raped by a family member at an early age. The experience was still fresh in her mind, and the deep wound had not yet healed. Her story left no one in the room with dry eyes.

Is it possible to receive a blessing out of the sorrowful experiences in life? I believe this question is answered by a young man with the name of Jabez. His birth name, given to him by his mother, meant "pain." She stated that she bore him in "sorrow" (1 Chronicles 4:9, KJV). Even though Jabez was "more honorable than his brethren" (verse 9, KJV), he was aware of the circumstance (sorrow) in which he was born. He knew the meaning of his name (pain). Yet he also knew about a God who can change situations. His story is contained within only two Bible verses. It was told during what seems like a pause in a long genealogy. Jabez knew there was evil all around. He did what all of us must do: reach out to the One who hears, sees, understands, delivers, and heals. Jabez prayed. This prayer has echoed hope and encouragement down the corridors of time.

"And Jabez called on the name of the God of Israel saying, Oh that thou wouldest bless me indeed, and enlarge my coast, and that thine hand might be with me, and that thou wouldest keep me from evil, that it may not grieve me! And God granted him that which he requested" (verse 10, KJV). Jabez rose above his sorrowful beginning. God heard and answered his sincere prayer that requested a blessing indeed, despite it all.

Dear reader, like Jabez, we may have a sorrowful start or sad experience in this life, but if we can fathom the power of God who is "a rewarder of them that diligently seek him" (Hebrews 11:6, KJV), we can have a fresh start.

May you find the faith to know that God can change your pain into a blessing and your sorrow into joy. Like Jabez, you, too, can become an instrument of hope and encouragement to others.

Donna J. Norman

God Will Provide

But my God shall supply all your need
according to his riches in glory by Christ Jesus.
—Philippians 4:19, KJV

Having grown up in a home with uneducated parents and six siblings, I knew what being poor was all about. However poor we may have been, our parents instilled in us, from a young age, the same morals, principles, and integrity that they allowed to govern their lives. My parents (particularly my mother) were blessed with the ability to focus on the positive and thus bring out the best in a person.

Though we were poor, dignity abounded. There were times when I was unable to participate in school functions because my parents were unable to provide whatever may have been necessary for me to participate. Still, I could always count on my heavenly Father to come through for me.

Though there were many examples of God's providence in my life, I recall one event in particular. I was one of the students chosen to travel to a state college to represent my high school on a debate team. My mom was unable to provide the necessary items for me to attend; however, my kind aunt and her youngest daughter supplied me with everything that I would need, including clothes and toiletries. I count this as one of the best experiences in my life. Yes, we as a team brought back a trophy, but a life lesson was demonstrated to me that has helped to shape my life in becoming the adult that I am today. The lesson is that kind deeds can be life changing for others.

Through the kind deeds of others on my behalf during my youth, which softened my heart, the Holy Spirit has been able to use me in compassionate ways to reach out to others and help those in need—especially children. Consequently, many years ago, I started a ministry of purchasing food and donating it to help feed the hungry. I thank God for blessing me with the means to be able to reach back and help others as I was helped.

Since retiring and relocating to the state of Georgia (United States of America), I have been blessed with the ability to continue sharing with others through the provisions God has given me. His promises are sure, and He never fails. Let's trust Him, then stand still and see how He always provides for us.

Mary Head Brooks

The Gift of Courage

Part 1

My flesh and my heart may fail,
but God is the strength of my heart
and my portion forever.
—Psalm 73:26, NIV

I am very fond of the lion character in *The Wizard of Oz*. Looking for courage is his main reason for going with Dorothy to meet the great Wizard of Oz, known throughout the fictitious region as one who gives out wise assistance. Without courage, the lion knows that he will never be able to function to his full potential. As the story line unfolds, however, we see that what the lion feels he needs most, he already has!

Fast-forward to 2000. I was invited to speak at a prayer breakfast in Soweto, South Africa. "Come and teach us" had been the request. Soweto was the seat of the 1976 political uprising and the very same place where social justice rose up in the hearts and minds of this country's fearless, courageous young people who wanted to be treated with dignity and respect. This township—with its rich mixture of past, present, and future that stares you in the face—took my breath away. After accepting the invitation, I hung up the phone and sat in silence. I would need courage. I pondered, *Could this be the answered prayer of a seventeen-year-old girl with visions of serving at a mission station in Peru? But South Africa is a very long way from Peru!* But at seventeen, I had begun to understand that I could make my request in prayer and then trust the answer and its timing to the One who made me.

A certain anticipation, which comes only from deep reflection, started welling up inside me, replacing the fear from the invitation to "come and teach" in Soweto. I probably wouldn't teach or preach but rather share my own personal experiences. I knew how it felt to be marginalized and misunderstood and second-guess myself because of someone else's misplaced perceptions. I, too, wanted to be accepted for myself—not for what I drove, where I lived, or the color of my skin. Like the women I met in Soweto, I had longed to honor an agreement with myself to let the past go—my personal past, in particular. I wanted to learn the art of forgiveness and embrace this new today with both hands so as not to lose any more tomorrows. Only God gives the courage to do that!

Gail Masondo

The Gift of Courage

PART 2

"They were swifter than eagles, they were stronger than lions."
—2 Samuel 1:23, NIV

Praying for new courage in my heart, I accepted the speaking invitation for the prayer breakfast and went to Soweto, South Africa. I would have much in common with the women I would meet. Yet having similarities should not be confused with being identical; I would find out the hard way in my American-born arrogance. While I had experienced some forms of discrimination with its painful aftermath, I really knew nothing of the extent of what my South African husband or these women had gone through or felt.

I would need to be sensitive, careful with my words, and not patronizing in any way. It's easy to shrug off someone else's experience if you have not lived it. I would not try to compare or even compete with their struggle for freedom. Yet wherever one faces adversity and setbacks, it takes courage to pick up the broken pieces and rebuild bridges torn apart by someone else's decisions. I would share my experiences of living in restoration since coming to this country of theirs, and I would listen, learn, and gain lessons from them as they shared their hopes for a new, better tomorrow.

It takes courage to stand, shoulders back and head high, while looking in the face of any foe and going after what belongs to you—no matter what!

I walked away from that September 2000 Sunday morning breakfast in Soweto more renewed and enriched than when I first walked in. I was never the same, for courage walked into the room and sat down right next to me! Courage met me through Sisi—a woman who was forced to exchange South Africa for exile at the age of fifteen. Despite the remaining scars from that season in her life, Sisi has managed to regroup and not allowed the bitterness of the past to stifle the life she has chosen to live today. I also met Cheryl, a white South African woman, whose family suffered greatly. Cheryl's main reason for gently sharing, as did Sisi, was not to incite debate or argue but rather to supply me with the facts of how ugly the previous system had been and remind us all of our duty to pray through our actions as we stand for the right with courage.

The courage-seeking lion in *The Wizard of Oz* and these Soweto mothers reminded me that every hard situation in my life calls forth what Heaven had placed in me before the foundations of the earth—the gift of courage. In this courage, we can all be stronger than lions!

Gail Masondo

A Great Army of Women

The Lord announces the word,
and the women who proclaim it are a mighty throng.
—Psalm 68:11, NIV

I find it fascinating that I can read over a section of scripture time and time again, and then suddenly, one time, the words just jump out at me. Today's text is an example. I have been reading a one-year edition of the New Living Translation that has an Old and New Testament portion, a psalm, and a verse or two from Proverbs. On March 25, I read Psalm 68, and one line read, "And a great army brings the good news." Of course, I had to look up the footnote; it said, "Or *a host of women.*"

Wow, I thought, *I don't remember reading that before. I had better check some other versions.* I found that four of the most respected translations all say "women," as do some other lesser-known versions. Yet another version has "women" in the footnote, and two others just say a "company" or "host" in the footnote.

I have been picturing what could happen if a host, a company, or an army of women went forth to tell anything but especially the Word of God.

I remember Rose Otis, the foresighted woman who started this devotional book series, telling a little joke: If you wanted news to get out, you could phone, or you could tell a woman. That is a truth that can be put to use—put to use in telling the world about Jesus.

Psalm 68 is a psalm of David, imploring God to save His people. David praises God for being a God who is the Father of the fatherless and a defender of widows. Besides that, He cares for the lonely by putting them in families, and He sets the prisoners free—free from all the things that bind, as Jesus told His audience in Nazareth (Luke 4). David then praises God for leading Israel through the desert on the way to the Promised Land. He does it with might and physical demonstrations. And then they settle in peace in the land provided for them. He gives His word, and the women go forth to proclaim it, even getting the plunder when the enemies are defeated.

So it is for us. We face an enemy, but we serve a mighty God; a God who has, does, and will win; a God who cares for His people, yes, His women. It is then up to the mighty multitude of women to go to proclaim it.

Ardis Dick Stenbakken

May 31

Ten Minutes Too Late

And while they went to buy, the bridegroom came; and they that were
ready went in with him to the marriage: and the door was shut.
—Matthew 25:10, KJV

For more than a month, I had been awaiting the arrival of a cargo vessel to ship auto parts to my brother who lived on another island in the Caribbean. Despite the holiday freight confusion, I finally found the contact information for the port authority. When I called, the attendant informed me the vessel had finally arrived, and it would depart at 5:00 P.M. that day.

I felt I had enough time to get to the dock before 5:00 P.M., so I followed my day's schedule: I taught my two classes from 9:00 to 11:00 A.M., then followed up with other previously scheduled activities that necessitated fulfilling various duties and keeping some appointments. As I moved from one activity to another, I remained very cognizant of the 5:00 P.M. departure time, believing that I had a lot of time before heading out to the dock.

I concluded my final assignment at 3:50 P.M. before driving toward the dock. I was very pleased that I had accomplished so much. I was also relieved that the package would soon be on its way. At 4:40 P.M., I stopped at the chained entrance to the port authority, and in one glance, I saw the vessel with its crew moving about, some even looking at me. I informed the guard of my mission and prepared to drive through and deliver my cargo, but that was not to be! He informed me that the boat had received its last cargo at 3:30 P.M.; it had already been checked out, and it was about to depart. My entreaties were in vain. I looked longingly at the vessel whose door was about to be shut—only one hour and ten minutes—I was too late!

In my disappointment, I thought of another scenario where ten maidens had been waiting for the bridal party at a wedding, but five of the maidens had not equipped themselves with enough oil in their lamps, which made them leave to buy more oil. When the bridegroom came, they had not returned, and the door was shut. They could not attend the wedding for which they thought they had been prepared. Sisters, I pray that we will always be prepared, being alert to the signs of the time, and have our lamps filled with oil and the wicks trimmed. I pray that our heavenly Father will keep us faithful, ever alert to the signs that point to the coming of our Lord and Savior Jesus, so that we will be ready to enter with Him.

Valerie Knowles Combie

Happy Father's Day

*"I will be a Father to you, and you will be
my sons and daughters," says the Lord Almighty.*
—2 Corinthians 6:18, NIV

Since childhood, I have memories of preparing homemade cards for Mother's Day. As I got older, I became more creative as I carefully planned and came up with ways to honor the mother figures in my life.

Father's Day was more of a problem. I was raised by a grandmother for most of my childhood because my own single mother lived far away, earning a living to support us. Father's Day rolled by year after year with no particular acknowledgment from me. Yet as I reflect, there were times (and not only on Father's Day) when that missing element in my life was palpable. I saw friends and family members interact with their fathers, and the twinge of that missing factor in my life would return. I had uncles who filled that missing role to some extent. Also, in time, I had a stepfather on whom I could lavish the cards and creativity deserving of a father.

I was brought up in a Christian home and knew many Scripture passages by heart even before I could read. I had repeated the Lord's Prayer countless times, but "our Father" was still in heaven for me. When I was a child, that was where He stayed—maybe my guardian angel would have to substitute for an earthly dad? What is my point in describing this part of my childhood? Certainly not to have you join me in a pity party. Yet as different holidays come around, let us be more conscious of those for whom these holidays trigger sad memories and lonely times and those who may not be in a celebratory mindset. Let us ask God's guidance for including them or giving them the space they need to be introspective and quiet while dealing with their emotions in their chosen ways. In our mindfulness of others, let us endeavor to respect their individuality. While offering inclusive activities, may we allow them the option of accepting or refusing our well-meaning offer—without taking it personally.

As we endeavor to forge meaningful relationships in our lives, my prayer is that "the peace of God, which transcends all understanding, will guard your hearts and your minds in Christ Jesus" (Philippians 4:7, NIV).

Doreen Evans-Yorke

Everything Has Purpose

To every thing there is a season, and a time
to every purpose under the heaven.
—Ecclesiastes 3:1, KJV

I was blessed with my dream car! My children and two of my best friends came to visit and see my dream car. But while backing up (being so excited), I backed into my daughter's vehicle! We managed to get through all the post-accident formalities. When the time came for my "dream" to go to the shop, I asked, "Who is there that can drive us back home?"

I thought of my friend Renee and called her at work. After I had quickly explained our dilemma, she said, "No problem. Just call when you're ready for me to pick you up and take you home. I don't have to go to work today until two o'clock this afternoon." That was a blessing!

My husband, Pete, had an eye appointment at eight thirty that morning. Then we stopped for breakfast, trying to allow enough time for Renee to get up before she would have to pick us up.

When we got to the automotive shop, the owner said, "Oh yeah, you'll need a ride home. Let me call this fellow that I know."

"We already have a backup plan," I said, explaining it to him.

"No, let your friend sleep," he responded. We did and rode home with the young man that had been called.

When we told him where we lived, our driver said, "I live right down the street from you!" As we drove along, we found we had quite a bit in common. As we neared home, my husband (the navigator) started giving directions to our house. "Wait a minute," interrupted the driver. "Didn't you guys have some carpet installed about two years ago?" We had. "I helped lay your carpet. I thought you folks looked familiar when I saw you."

I admitted to him, "And I thought you looked familiar too." *What next, God?*

As soon as I got home, I called Renee and shared what had happened. She said, "Well, praise God!" Then I noticed a message on my phone from a neighbor, asking whether we could pick up her heart medicine.

There is really no need to be stressed if we trust God to be in control. God is always there, working things out. He blesses us so that, through Him, we can be a blessing to others.

Elaine J. Johnson

Slicing Bread

Pleasant words are like a honeycomb,
Sweetness to the soul and health to the bones.
—Proverbs 16:24, NKJV

One Sabbath I was preparing for potluck dinner after church. A young woman approached and asked, "Is there anything I can do to help?" She was new to our congregation, having just married one of our beloved young bachelors. Not being one to turn down assistance, I asked her to slice a loaf of bread that I had brought. She smiled and agreed, so I supplied her with a knife and cutting board. After I had put food on the table, I returned to see how the young woman was doing. On the table was a beautifully sliced loaf of bread, each slice being cut perfectly uniform and straight. I exclaimed, "Wow! You are really good at slicing bread. It looks so perfect!" One of my friends came along and echoed what I had just said. I continued finishing up with the food preparation. Then out of the corner of my eye, I saw the young woman's husband had joined her in the kitchen. His arm was around her. I overheard him softly exclaim, "They like the way you slice bread!" She responded with a big smile.

It surprised me that our offhand comments about how she sliced bread had brought them such joy. It was then that I realized that I was now one of the older women in the church, and my words had the ability to affirm other women.

Growing up in the church, I had often been admonished to avoid ugly, hurtful words. The analogies of the toothpaste and the nails in the fence were ever in my mind. Toothpaste can never be put back into its tube once it's squeezed out. We can never take back words we have spoken. Nails pulled out of a fence still leave holes in the wood. Whatever words we speak always leave some type of an impression. We must be careful not to speak hurtful words.

The experience with the young woman and her sliced bread that day gave me a new revelation about being a mature Christian. My words could affirm others, not only what they do but their personal worth—who they are. I'm not talking about self-serving flattery; I'm talking about Christlike and Christ-inspired love and affirmation.

Today I pray for the Spirit of Christ to be in the words I speak to others. Let me not just refrain from derogatory words but choose to speak words of affirmation and love.

Marsha Hammond-Brummel

My "Hip" Story

"This is what the LORD, the God of your father David, says:
I have heard your prayer and seen your tears; I will heal you."
—2 Kings 20:5, NIV

It was January 19, 2019, and I was on greeter duty at my church. As I walked toward my usual post, I noticed that another greeter was already there. So I went to another post where help was needed. I greeted people as I handed out church bulletins and hugs.

Approximately half an hour later, the head greeter approached me and said she wanted me to return to my usual post in the main lobby. I said goodbye to my fellow greeter and turned around to walk with the head greeter back to the post. Instantly, I felt excruciating pain in my left hip. I was unable to move. I screamed loudly as I tightly squeezed the head greeter's arm. "What's wrong?" she asked as she looked at me with great concern.

"I can't move. I can't walk," I replied. I held on to her for some time as we stood in the hallway. Immediately, I began to pray, *Lord, please help me. I drove to church alone, and I must make it back home.* Church members stopped by to inquire as to what was wrong and whether they could help. "Pray for me," I responded.

About ten minutes passed before I was able to move. We slowly walked to the front lobby, then I sat at the back of the church. Sitting there, I continued to pray, *Lord, help me to finish my duties and make it home.* The head greeter returned to check on me and asked whether I would like to sit out or complete my duties. I chose to complete my duties and prayed that God would continue to ease the pain.

As the main worship service began, we walked to the front of the sanctuary, where I sat in the place reserved for greeters. When the time came to welcome our visitors, I could feel the pain throbbing in my hip at a moderately high level. Again, I prayed for God to help me greet our visitors with a smile. Next came the children's story, where we collected the children's offering for Christian education. I could still feel the throbbing pain, so I held on tightly to the pew and continued to pray as the children came forward. I prayed for strength not to fall. God heard my prayer and gave me strength to complete my duties and drive home safely.

Thank You, God, for Your healing touch.

Pauline A. Griffith

Give Me Your "Not Enough"

"Give me your son," Elijah replied. He took him from her arms, carried him to the upper room. . . . Then he cried out to the LORD. . . . And the boy's life returned.
—1 Kings 17:19, 20, 22, NIV

When Elijah asks the widow of Zarephath for "a morsel of bread in your hand" (1 Kings 17:11, NKJV), his request seems to imply something that's already prepared or leftover food. Today we would say, "Please, just give me a lunch box snack from your pantry; I don't need a hot, cooked meal." When Elijah understands she has no leftovers, not even a bite, he asks for all she has.

We are astonished as she goes home to scrape out her flour barrel. What's left is not enough for even one ample meal for a hungry traveler. But "not enough" continues to sustain the woman, her child, and Elijah.

Sometime later, her child dies suddenly, and the widow is bereft, holding broken bits of plans and remnant drops of hope that even in a famine she finally dares to dream for their future.

"Give me your son," Elijah commands. Can you hear her crying out as she clasps her now lifeless child to her heart, "This is all I have; there is not enough left to give"? The grieving mother is no longer able to scrape out her barrel, so Elijah takes her "not enough," this empty barrel of life, and carries the child to the upper room.

The man of God prays for resurrection power. In faith, he lies down on the child's body with arms outreached. His posture prefigures Jesus in dying for the penalty of our sins, in redeeming His children, and in giving resurrection hope to us with nothing to save ourselves.

Jesus wants to teach us a lesson through Elijah's story. He wants us to give Him our "not enough"—the unfulfilled dreams and last dregs of hope—and go to the upper room to pray. Pray more fearlessly than Elijah praying for a resurrection miracle for which there was no precedent. Pray more deeply than Elijah praying for Israel to be brought to its knees by drought. Pray more fiercely than Elijah praying for Israel to be brought to its feet by fire. Pray more earnestly than Elijah praying for the power of the (latter) rain.

In the upper room, tiny resources scraped from our barrels can be anointed with Christ's resurrection power. Gathered up by Jesus the Miracle Worker, our bits and pieces of "not enough" are infused with new life, new energy, new vision, new purpose, and new ministry.

Rebecca Turner

Twelve Golden Puppies

The Lord watches over you—
the Lord is your shade at your right hand;
the sun will not harm you by day,
nor the moon by night. . . .
The Lord will watch over your coming and going
both now and forevermore.
—Psalm 121:5, 6, 8, NIV

One of our care center's kitchen staff had a yellow Labrador retriever that birthed twelve golden puppies. When they were a month and two days old, the cook brought these cuddly creatures to our center's gazebo for Family Fun Day. Some attendants even brought their own little ones. We were all charmed. The mother dog, however, looked exhausted. For most of that morning, she rested but kept a watchful eye on her pups. When a toddler accidentally dropped a squirming pup, the mother dog was immediately at its side. What I saw that day was the quintessence of self-sacrificing love. Despite the dog's fatigue, she instinctively knew she was the guardian of her pups—a faint reflection of God's watch care of His children.

The puppies thrived. As they grew, they needed instruction modeled by their mother. God knows this about all His creatures. He knows that we need an example to follow too. Paul gives us wise counsel that is as simple as it is complex: "Follow God's example, therefore, as dearly loved children and walk in the way of love, just as Christ loved us and gave himself up for us as a fragrant offering and sacrifice to God" (Ephesians 5:1, 2, NIV). Through that mother Lab's watch care over her pups that morning, I witnessed a profound mystery.

The subsequent month's newsletter included photos of several joyful residents embracing the yellow pups. I yearn for that graceful interplay of love, watch care, comforting touch, and gentle pressure to shed light in my heart and soul. I long for the incredible beauty of heaven.

Thank You, God, for the opportunity to study more about the precious truths found in what You have created and in Your holy Word.

What can you do to help spread the truth of His Word? Which personal experience can you use to introduce your neighbor to God's love for us, His earthly children?

Glenda-mae Greene

Prayer Requests

*Now unto him that is able to do exceeding abundantly above all
that we ask or think, according to the power that worketh in us.*
—Ephesians 3:20, KJV

"Miss Goring! Teacher!" My second-grade students were calling my name and telling me their requests. They were not taking turns. Several of my sweet students were calling out to me; each had a different request or question. Frustration bubbled up within me because I felt inadequate. How could I answer each question and respond to each request when they were all coming at once? I remember thinking, *I'm only one person, and they're asking me a million questions at once! How am I supposed to meet all their needs?*

Years later, reflecting on this experience, a spiritual parallel formed in my mind. I realized that God always hears all our prayers and requests that we send to Him. He's not overwhelmed by the magnitude of millions of people presenting their prayer requests to Him, even if they're praying to Him at once.

God hears every single person. He understands every person's language. And He is completely capable of answering each prayer, catering to each request, and meeting each person's needs as if there were only one person presenting his or her prayer requests to Him.

God manages the entire universe, yet He still has time for His human creation and pays attention to each of us in a very personal and wonderful way.

Sometimes I ask my close friends, whom I confide in, whether I'm exasperating them with my issues. They always tell me that I'm not exasperating them and that they are sincerely praying for me. I am grateful for my friends here on Earth. But even more, I am grateful for my Father who lives in heaven but is also present on this earth through His Spirit.

I deeply appreciate how God never tires of hearing my issues, concerns, and dreams. I love how He listens to me as if I were the only person in the world (as He does for you too), and I deeply appreciate how He always answers my prayers beyond all I could ever ask or imagine.

God doesn't always give us the answers we want. But He always gives us the answers we need. He is a good God who loves us with all His heart. He knows what's best for us, and He never tires of meeting our needs.

Alexis A. Goring

Follow the Leader

"I am the good shepherd.
The good shepherd gives His life for the sheep."
—John 10:11, NKJV

Recently, the Lord opened an opportunity for my husband and me, along with another couple, to buy an old schoolhouse in the heart of Wyoming's ranching country. As we are getting to know some of the ranchers nearby, we have learned that ranching takes a lot of work. Ranchers must frequently move the cattle from one grazing field to another. It is fun and exciting to watch the ranchers drive the cattle down the dirt road in front of our school. Sometimes they are on horseback and sometimes on ATVs (all-terrain vehicles). The ranchers tell us the older cows that have made the move before already know what's going on, so they put them in the lead with the younger cows following them. This arrangement makes the move less stressful for them. Every now and then, one of the cows will break out of the group and go right or left, but the ranchers always guide the cow back into the group.

Another thing we've learned by living here is how these ranchers know their cows. They don't name them or make them pets, but they know each of their cows. They tend to their needs. They haul hay and water for them. No matter the weather, the ranchers are there to care for their livestock. It's a hard and difficult life, and they love it.

As I watch all those cows moving down our street, simply content to follow, I think of how Jesus is our Good Shepherd. He said His sheep know His voice and follow Him. He tends to our needs and provides for us. He gives us His Word and also people to help guide us so that our journey down the road of life will be less stressful. Our Good Shepherd knows us and calls us by name; in fact, He has engraved our names on the palms of His hands. No matter what challenges life puts in our path, we don't need to be afraid because Jesus will lead us to green pastures.

"The LORD is my shepherd; I shall not want. He maketh me to lie down in green pastures: he leadeth me beside the still waters. He restoreth my soul: he leadeth me in the paths of righteousness for his name's sake. Yea, though I walk through the valley of the shadow of death, I will fear no evil. . . . Surely goodness and mercy shall follow me all the days of my life: and I will dwell in the house of the LORD for ever" (Psalm 23:1–4, 6, KJV).

Mona Fellers

Miss Goody Two-Shoes

The LORD will guide you continually,
giving you water when you are dry
and restoring your strength.
You will be like a well-watered garden,
like an ever-flowing spring.
—Isaiah 58:11, NLT

Do whatever you feel is best for you," my husband lovingly said when I told him I planned to quit my job. Then Ron laughed before continuing, "How many people can actually say they've lived out their fantasies like you have, Deb?"

After thirty-five years of marriage, Ron knew me pretty well. I can't recall (perhaps it was pillow talk) when I shared about a dream I frequently had as a child. I would dream that I'd been accidentally locked in a supermarket overnight. Though scared to be all alone, I still had lots of fun going around eating treats from off the shelves. When morning came, someone would open the door. I'd leave fully satisfied with a mile-wide smile on my face, ready to share with others, as did Miss Goody Two-Shoes, a generous child from an old children's story.

I've indeed lived out part of my dream because I worked as a demo person in a large discount superstore. I enjoyed the pleasure of sampling delicious "free food" while being paid to promote products to passing customers. It's not often that a Christian can publicly witness about their love for Jesus so openly in the workplace. Yet I was able to do this for more than three years. As I shared with coworkers about my faith and family, blessings flowed. I felt the presence of holy angels as they connected our hearts in friendship. I'm sure some of the ladies instinctively sensed that Heaven had brought us together to share sunshine and laughter, gifts of encouragement, and hope. My coworkers brought happiness and joy into my life just by caring. They learned from me how difficult, sometimes unpleasant, it is to be the parent of a special-needs adult child. They understood and shared in my pain.

Yet Jesus knew I lacked willpower to resist snacking on all those demo goodies at work and that being overweight causes me stress. Together we made a wise decision. It was time I left, though wearing my mile-wide smile. December 18, 2005, was my last day as a demo person at the superstore.

I know Jesus gave me that job so I could practice being comfortable and speaking with people I didn't know in preparation for future jobs. So Miss Goody Two-Shoes was good to go—go wherever Jesus would lead.

Today, are you willing to step out in faith and follow Jesus wherever He leads?

Deborah Sanders

Under His Wings

PART 1

He will cover you with his feathers,
and under his wings you will find refuge;
his faithfulness will be your shield and rampart [protective barrier].
—Psalm 91:4, NIV

In April 1963, I had been blessed with a handsome baby boy, weighing nine pounds, one ounce. Monday, September 30, dawned like any other morning. It was raining, and since this was our rainy season, it appeared as a normal day. My husband, Joey, had transported children to school and returned home. He mentioned he suspected it would rain all day. Not having a television or weather radio, we went about our indoor duties. The baby was sleeping, and I was trying to complete my chores before he woke up. Joey was in another room, reading and napping.

I happened to look outside and saw trees swaying wildly; I realized something strange was happening. I woke up Joey and told him. He responded, "Oh, it's just raining hard with some wind." He went back to sleep while I worked quickly to finish my cooking.

Around 11:45 A.M., I heard a loud noise. It was not thunder or lightning! I called out to Joey excitedly, telling him that trees were falling everywhere, and avocados, mangoes, and coconuts were on the ground. He got up, prayed, dressed quickly, and went to check on his car.

Our very modest home was surrounded by trees and located in a hilly village called Mary's Hill, on the island of Tobago. Joey had parked the car a distance from the house due to the rain. He returned thirty minutes later with news that the car was OK, but the roofs of some of our neighbors' houses had blown off! He was very concerned about his parents' home, which was also surrounded by trees. They lived three miles from us, and we had no telephone to call them. The falling trees had blocked the roads, making them impassable, so my husband decided to walk to his parents' home to check on them. Meanwhile, the sun came out and shone in its full radiance, and the sky was blue once again. Now a quiet, comforting, gentle breeze blew.

Then, amazingly, on Joey's way to his parents' house, the storm returned with a vengeance. But God protected us.

We still thank Him for His goodness and for sending His angels to cover us. "The angel of the LORD encampeth round about them that fear him, and delivereth them" (Psalm 34:7, KJV).

Shirley John Blake

"Under His Wings"

PART 2

God is our refuge and strength, a very present help in trouble.
—Psalm 46:1, NJKV

In this life, one beautiful moment can suddenly turn to destruction in the next. A hurricane had wreaked havoc in my neighborhood, but it became calm again. While my husband went to check on his parents, I stayed at home alone with my baby. Glancing outside, I noticed the bright-blue sky had suddenly grown dark and ominous. Hurriedly, I closed all the windows and doors just before lightning flashed, followed by thunder, rain, and ferocious winds. The winds broke windowpanes, swung windows back and forth, and blew open the front door, letting the rain pour in.

I pushed the door shut and positioned a large chair behind it to prevent the winds from forcing it open. I wrapped my sleeping baby in plastic so he would not get soaked and held him close, keeping his face exposed so he could breathe. The rain and winds were coming from all directions. It sounded as if the roof were being ripped from the house. For a moment, I considered running outside should the roof be blown off; however, I decided to depend on my heavenly Father for protection. I sat on the floor with my back against the dresser, holding my baby tightly. I repeated Psalm 91 and sang William Cushing's comforting hymn:

"Under His wings I am safely abiding.
Though the night deepens and tempests are wild,
Still I can trust Him; I know He will keep me,
He has redeemed me, and I am His child."*

As I sang, a feeling of security came over me with the assurance that God would cover us. It was still storming when I heard a knock on the door. My husband's welcome voice called, "Shirley! Shirley! Are you all there?" He said he was walking to his parents' home when the hurricane returned. A large van was parked on the side of the road, so he joined people who took shelter in it. The powerful wind had lifted it up and down. More than twenty people lost their lives on the island that day. We thank God our entire family survived what became known as Hurricane Flora. We praise Him for His faithfulness. Under His wings, we can always find refuge.

Shirley John Blake

---

* William Orcutt Cushing, "Under His Wings," 1896.

My Child—My "Speed Bump"

And all thy children shall be taught of the LORD;
and great shall be the peace of thy children.
—Isaiah 54:13, KJV

I have learned many things from my nine-year-old son, Ted. I always feel proud that he reminds me to do the right thing, which I had taught him in his younger years. One day, as I was cleaning my kitchen, I found some leftovers and wanted to dispose of them. So I told my son to go and give them to the neighbors. He immediately replied, "Mom, this food doesn't smell good. If we wouldn't eat this, why do you want to give it to others? 'Do to others what you would have them do to you' [Matthew 7:12, NIV]." Dumbfounded, I did not know how to reply. I quietly lowered my head in shame and threw the food into the garbage.

Another memorable incident that is etched fondly in my memory occurred on a Saturday evening. I was washing dishes when my son came to me and said, "Mommy, the Sabbath is not over yet, and you have started your work." I was reminded of these inspired words from the devotional book *Our Father Cares*: "We should jealously guard the edges of the Sabbath. Remember that every moment is consecrated, holy time."* I felt deeply convicted by his words, left my work, and sat down for the evening worship. Whenever I get moving at too fast a pace in life, forgetting what the Lord says to me, my little son is like a "speed bump." He slows me down and reminds me of the little things that the Lord has asked me to do.

Is it possible that our children have a thing or two to teach *us*? Is it possible that their innocence and zest for life give them a perspective that we jaded adults may have lost? I believe so. I believe that if we open our eyes and hearts, we will find much we can learn from our children about God and His desires for us. It's easy for us as parents to take on a know-it-all attitude with our kids. But maybe it's time for us to realize that we do not, in fact, know all there is to know about life. Maybe it's time for us to look at these little people and uncover the nuggets of wisdom they have to offer.

Lord, give us the humbleness to learn from little children because You have said that we must become like little children (see Matthew 18:3).

Esther Synthia Murali

---

* Ellen G. White, *Our Father Cares* (Hagerstown, MD: Review and Herald®, 1991), 73.

Finally Free

"I will be with you; I will never leave you nor forsake you. . . .
"Have I not commanded you? Be strong and courageous.
Do not be afraid; do not be discouraged,
for the LORD your God will be with you wherever you go."
—Joshua 1:5, 9, NIV

When you hear God calling, it's nearly impossible to ignore it. During my junior year of high school, I felt God calling me to a summer evangelistic job that required preaching sermons. Public speaking is something I have always been afraid of, and I have never felt that I am good at it. I was confused when I felt the urge to apply for a job that revolved around public speaking, but I decided to do it anyway. I trusted that God would help me with my fear so that I could preach His Word.

I ended up getting the job, which confirmed for me that God was calling me to work for Him. I began preparing my sermons and, most of all, praying that God would help me when the time came to speak.

The big day finally arrived. This would be my first time preaching, and I began to doubt whether God could use me when I was so fearful of speaking in public. Anxiety weighed on my chest, and all I felt I could do was pray constantly. Yet I chose to go forward and at least attempt what I had committed to do. God helped me complete the sermon.

After I finished preaching, I felt a peace come over me. I knew God's message had touched the hearts of many present. Feeling good after preaching my first sermon, I felt confident that God would help me to deliver His message for the rest of the summer.

That experience taught me that we can actually let fear motivate us as we wait to see God at work in our lives. Trusting that He will take care of our fear is the only way we can truly get rid of it. By trusting God and letting Him use me, despite my fear, I was able to preach His Word and reach many people. I thought I was a terrible public speaker, but He proved me wrong and showed me that amazing things will happen as long as I trust Him.

God tells us in His Word that He is with us wherever we go. We don't need to be afraid of what we feel incapable of doing. If God is calling you, choose to trust and let go of your doubts and worries. Let Him free you from what holds you back from spreading the good news.

Megan Michalenko

Jesus, Our Witness

Verily, verily, I say unto thee, We speak that we do know,
and testify that we have seen; and ye receive not our witness.
—John 3:11, KJV

My neighbor and I try to walk in the morning or evening, whenever we have the opportunity and good weather here in Minnesota. On our walks, we bounce ideas off of each other and pray together. I enjoy our walks and spending time with the Lord. After a morning walk with my neighbor one day, I discovered I could not open the garage door at home. I tried using the keypad several times and failed. My husband came out to see what was happening. He reviewed with me the steps I'd followed in trying to open the door and what I should do the next time. The door opened. Then, along with my neighbor, we walked over to the garden and started a conversation about a blooming hibiscus plant and other flowers in the yard. During the conversation, my husband left with our son for the store and closed the garage door. He was confident that the garage door would open with no problems.

When it was time for me to go inside again, the garage door keypad refused the code. I had been certain the door would open. Now here I was, experiencing the same problem I had previously had with the keypad. My neighbor watched me correctly follow all the keypad-entry steps but with no success. We brainstormed our options. I could use her cell phone to call someone, but I could not remember my family's cell phone numbers. The only solution would be to sit and wait. "Let's pray," I blurted out. "Lord, please help this garage door open!" I again punched in the code on the keypad; immediately, the garage door began to open. It seemed as if on the very last word of my prayerful cry for help, God had responded. We were speechless and happy at the same time.

There is no need to doubt Jesus. He hears and is most attentive to all our needs. Though we know that Jesus is near and trust Him, why are we often surprised at His quick responses? Our Witness (Revelation 3:14) saw our need that morning and acted on our prayer. We paused and thanked Him and then prayed about other challenges we were experiencing.

As we were reminded that morning, Jesus can fix anything. He makes Himself known to us in one way or another and is present in every situation.

Margo Peterson

Reaction Versus Response

The LORD of hosts is with us; the God of Jacob is our refuge.
—Psalm 46:11, NKJV

A while back, I read a news story about a woman who was driving to an appointment in a nearby rural town while her car windows were tightly closed. The sudden scuttling of a little mouse along the inside windowsill of the passenger door caught her attention. Horrified, the woman began to scream. Her deafening shrieks further energized the mouse, which leaped onto the car's dashboard, ran blindly toward the steering wheel, and then disappeared. Locked inside a moving vehicle with a now *invisible* mouse, the woman continued reacting to the appearance—and disappearance—of her unwelcome traveling companion. She repeatedly stomped the vehicle's foot pedals. Waving her arms about, thinking she was now seeing more rodent movements, she let go of the steering wheel. Alas! Her car veered off the road and splashed, grill first, into a roadside lake. Witnesses immediately called 911, and the woman was soon rescued from her car.

Of course, many of life's surprises are often more disturbing than a wayward mouse. Perhaps you and I, at some point, have reacted emotionally to someone else's presence, choice, or behavior that caused us to feel uncomfortable, unsafe, or fearful. Rather than taking an extra prayerful moment or two to decide on a measured and appropriate response, we simply reacted. Instead of making things better, though, our emotional reaction "sank" the whole situation or relationship into some dark "lake." Let's broaden the picture now: in recent months, *beyond*-disturbing global events have taken everyone by surprise. Have we been prayerfully responding or simply reacting? Of course, the key word here is *prayerfully.*

When experiencing a sudden shock or loss, our first reaction is usually fear—perhaps even that God has abandoned us. Yet as both Messianic and end-time prophecies affirm, God knows all about our present and our future. He is never surprised by unfolding events. He provides help and guidance as we weather them. In fact, He is *with* us. David wrote, "You make known to me the path of life." He adds, "You will fill me with joy in your presence" (Psalm 16:11, NIV). I pray we will respond prayerfully to setbacks rather than react to them. May our initial response always be, *Lord, I will trust Your perfect love for me. Take control of my steering wheel. Let my faith in Your presence with me calm my every fear and show me how to respond.*

Carolyn Rathbun Sutton

Sleep to Live

There is a way that appears to be right,
but in the end it leads to death.
—Proverbs 14:12, NIV

B ut it's only ten o'clock," cried Melissa. "And this book is so interesting!"

"Six A.M. will come early enough as it is," I said. "You know your brain functions better when you have eight hours of sleep. It is time for you to go to bed."

"But I can get by on seven hours," pleaded Melissa.

"You may get by," I replied, "but when you get only seven hours of sleep, your brain is irritable and tends to whine, complain, argue, and procrastinate."

"No, it doesn't," Melissa contradicted. "It's my brain, and I know when it's irritable and argumentative."

"That's just it," I replied, repressing a laugh. "Studies show that people who lose sleep are unaware that their brains aren't functioning optimally. Plus, sleep deprivation and obesity are linked, and obesity tends to shorten one's life. How long do you want to live, Melissa?"

"At least one hundred and twenty-two years, one hundred and sixty-four days, like Jeanne Louise Calment of Arles, France," she said.

"The California Human Population Laboratory Study's number one recommendation for living longer and with better health is sleep," I said. "It is the single most important determinant for longevity. You need to give that wonderful brain, leased to you for use on this planet, the sleep it needs. I'd like you to make good choices, Melissa."

Melissa sighed. "I'm arguing right now, aren't I? And I just don't want to admit it! Maybe my brain is tired, after all!"

This time I did laugh.

"There is a way that *seems right* to a person, but it can shorten your life and negatively impact all your relationships. I know you want to do better than just 'get by.' "

"I *do* want to take good care of my brain and live a long time, so I'll put my brain to bed right now. I'm sorry I argued." Melissa smiled and closed her book.

Dear Lord, help me to be as willing to course correct and do what I know to be right as this child.

Arlene R. Taylor

You Can Dissolve Prejudices

That thy way may be known upon earth,
thy saving health among all nations.
—Psalm 67:2, KJV

In Brooklyn, New York, lived an eighty-plus-year-old woman who had a live-in home supervisor, whom I'll call Elena (not her real name). Elena's job was to supervise home health aides sent to care for the elderly woman. I worked for an agency that assigned me a four-day live-in schedule in that home. Due to circumstances, I was an unemployed chaplain but a functioning medical missionary. I was content to work as a home health aide for income and as an outlet for medical evangelism.

One Monday part of my duty was to prepare a meal for all three of us: the elderly woman, Elena, and myself. I faithfully prepared the food and drink and then set the table for two. Elena inquired about what I would eat. She was surprised when I informed her that I had brought my own food since I don't include meat and meat products in my diet. Intrigued, she said, "I will eat what you eat." Without reservation, I shared my food with her. She was incredibly pleased, seeming to enjoy it. My meatless diet generated a chain of questions regarding lifestyle issues. When I told her my denomination worships on the seventh day of the week, she said, "No wonder!" Then she shared with me her childhood experiences related to my church while growing up in her country of origin. I listened with rapt attention and some sadness as she unraveled some of her misguided prejudices regarding my denomination as well as Christianity in general. She had decided to become an atheist. Eventually, she shared her entire life story and said, "God purposely sent you here to rescue me because I was dying!"

Before I left that Friday, she asked, "Could you come and pick me up tomorrow? I will go to church with you." I was excited to be able to take her to church! I gave her a Bible and other books. Though Elena was overweight and had other health challenges, she made changes in her lifestyle practices and lost more than ten pounds within two weeks. How happy she was! She now attends church with me and is taking Bible studies. Ellen G. White wrote, "When people become interested in this subject [health], the way is often prepared for the entrance of other truths. If they see that we are intelligent [about] health, they will be more ready to believe that we are sound in Bible doctrines."* With whom can you share a health tip or two?

Ekele P. Ukegbu-Nwankwo

---

* Ellen G. White, *Counsels on Diet and Foods* (Washington, DC: Review and Herald®, 1938), 76.

Depressing or Uplifting

*Praise the L*ORD *forever! Amen and amen!*
—Psalm 89:52, NLT

This morning I read Psalm 88 in the New Living Translation. The introduction read, "For the choir director: A psalm of the descendants of Korah. A song to be sung to the tune 'The Suffering of Affliction.' A psalm of Heman the Ezrahite."

I soon saw why this psalm would be sung to the tune "The Suffering of Affliction." It starts with a positive line—"O LORD, God of my salvation"—but quickly goes downhill. Although the song mentions God, it really is all about Heman and his troubles:

> I cry out to you by day.
> I come to you at night.
> Now hear my prayer;
> listen to my cry.
> For my life is full of troubles (verses 1–3, NLT).

Then Heman blames God and accuses Him: "You have driven my friends away" (verse 8, NLT). "Why do you reject me?" (verse 14, NLT). "Your fierce anger has overwhelmed me" (verse 16, NLT). He ends in depression. Speaking of death, he says, "Darkness is my closest friend" (verse 18, NLT).

Wishing for something more encouraging, I read on. Psalm 89 starts out: "I will sing of the LORD's unfailing love forever!" (verse 1, NLT). The writer speaks of God's unfailing love, His faithfulness, His promises, His might, His glory, His justice, His truth, His wonderful reputation, and His righteousness, among other attributes.

In verses 38–48, the psalmist looks at the things he doesn't understand, and in verses 49–51, he expresses his concerns. He ends in triumph: "Praise the LORD forever! Amen and amen!" (verse 52, NLT).

Wow! What a contrast! What was the difference?

The first was written by Heman the Ezrahite, the second by Ethan the Ezrahite. So the two had the same family background. They each addressed their frustration, but one's words felt depressing, and the other's, uplifting. As I read the chapters again, I realized Heman was focused on emotions. In contrast, Ethan brought his feelings to God but focused on God and truth.

I've often heard it said that we become like what we focus on. "God," I prayed, "help me to recognize the truth about myself and my challenges, but let me focus on You and truth. Help me become like You. Make my words, even the expression on my face, uplifting, encouraging."

Helen Heavirland

A Godly Man

My . . . [daughter], keep my words,
And treasure my commands within you.
Keep my commands and live.
—Proverbs 7:1, 2, NKJV

It was 2018 and Father's Day again. What a joy it was for me to dial that familiar number to hear my daddy's voice. I could almost see the twinkle in his eyes. I heard his laughter as he recognized my voice. I was his seventh child, and I knew he loved me as dearly as he loved the other nine. I felt special as if I were the only one, but all the others knew they were special too. I expressed my Father's Day greeting with gratitude to my Father in heaven, knowing that it was His special mercies that kept Dad for his 103 (soon to be 104) years.

Though it was still fairly early in the morning, I knew his routine upon rising: a glass of water with lemon juice, a chapter from the Bible, followed by his morning devotions, and a walk before breakfast. Dad's time with God is not negotiable—even if the queen were visiting. The foundational principles that were established in our home were based on the Bible first and then supported by the inspirational writings by Ellen G. White.

Along with that firm spiritual foundation came lessons of love, compassion, generosity, and all the virtues Dad claimed from God's Word. His wardrobe is still always assembled with meticulous thought so that when he emerges from his bedroom, dressed for all occasions, heads turn, and eyes light up. His greatest joy is the fact that all his children have followed in his footsteps. As the saying goes, "We are products of our environment."

Conversing with Dad led me to think of the relationship Jesus has with His Father. In John 10:30, He said to the disciples, "I and My Father are one" (NKJV). They shared in the creation and redemption stories and the plans for the universe. Yet, because of His love and compassion, Jesus gave up His status and became a servant so that we could regain our status as sons and daughters. Jesus, our older Brother, knows that we are also products of our environment. His consistent prayer life, which sought His father's strength, and His life of service are our examples.

Each day let us celebrate Father's Day with our Father in heaven, giving thanks for His unconditional love. His admonition to us: "Keep my commands and live."

Sonia Kennedy-Brown

Recalculating
Due to the Coronavirus

For I the LORD *thy God will hold thy right hand,*
saying unto thee, Fear not; I will help thee.
—Isaiah 41:13, KJV

I t has happened before. With an address plugged into our map app on a smartphone, we begin driving to our destination, only to discover somewhere along the way that there is an accident or road construction that will not allow us to take the normal route. The map's program signals that it is recalculating to show us the best alternative route. We are not always happy to learn of the change—and sometimes the delay—but we really have no other option, so we adjust our plans and journey on.

So it has been as the COVID-19 pandemic struck our world, our nation, then our state, and finally even our communities! For our safety, we have had to readjust our thinking and change our normal activities, even our long-range plans, in light of the pandemic. We are inconvenienced by the closing of schools, businesses, and churches and disappointed that special events have been canceled and just about any gathering of more than ten people. But since these are uncertain times, we adjust in order to comply and move forward as suggested. "Sheltering in place" and "social distancing" are new concepts we need to practice because the safety of our families and every citizen of our country is the most important thing to consider.

Some wonder, *What is happening to our world? Is this pandemic something we might expect near the end of time?* Without question, people are fearful. Of what, they aren't quite sure, but their actions confirm it as they stand in line to stock up on food, water, and other necessities.

We who believe God is in control sometimes have moments of fear too. If it isn't fear of COVID-19, it is likely fear of something else. Let us arm ourselves with the comforting promises of scripture: "Cast thy burden upon the LORD, and he shall sustain thee" (Psalm 55:22, KJV). "I sought the LORD, and he heard me, and delivered me from all my fears" (Psalm 34:4, KJV). And finally, "Do not be anxious about anything, but in every situation, by prayer and petition, with thanksgiving, present your requests to God. And the peace of God, which transcends all understanding, will guard your hearts and your minds in Christ Jesus" (Philippians 4:6, 7, NIV). *Thank You, Jesus.*

Bernadine Delafield

When God Chuckled

But God in heaven merely laughs!
He is amused by all their puny plans.
—Psalm 2:4, TLB

Having experienced significant back-to-back losses, I was rather surprised that I was now facing another. It had started in October 2012 with my beloved brother's death from cancer. Nine months later, my husband of forty years had a fatal heart attack while returning home from a weeklong celebration of his retirement and sixty-fourth birthday. Eighteen months after that, I lost my job of nearly two decades as an elected county court judge. I thought that under those circumstances, it was OK for me to be a little surprised that another loss was in the making.

My removal from the bench should not have caused the Florida Bar to seek revocation of my license to practice law. But almost immediately after I opened a law office, I received notice of their intent. The force of that news was just a hairbreadth less than what I had felt when I called my husband's cell phone and intuitively knew he was dead.

I had a conversation with God while waiting at a stoplight as I drove to my office the next morning. I told Him that I thought I had been rather faithful, steadfast, and trusting during each of the above-mentioned ordeals, especially throughout the investigation and trial that resulted in my removal from office by the Florida Supreme Court.

He answered, agreeing with me. My next question was, "Then why this new trial?"

I heard Him chuckle as He said, "You got promoted!"

Quite honestly, my first response was also to chuckle. God compared His leading to educational progress; the goal of each year's hard work is promotion to the next level. Failure to progress is a disappointment and cause for alarm. With that divine insight, I suited up for yet another round of a demonic-inspired attack, which ended with a nine-month suspension, rather than the revocation of my license as sought by the Florida Bar. It would be wonderful if I could tell you that my season of trials ended with the restoration of my law license, but it did not; other "big promotions" were scheduled for the upcoming year.

But I can end the recounting of this part of my journey by testifying that God proved true to His promise: "I will never leave thee, nor forsake thee. So that [I] may boldly say, The Lord is my helper, and I will not fear what man shall do unto me" (Hebrews 13:5, 6, KJV).

Judith Warren Hawkins

My Falls

Do not gloat over me, my enemy!
Though I have fallen, I will rise.
—Micah 7:8, NIV

Over the past three years, I have fallen five times. Fortunately, in only one fall was my body damaged more than my pride, so I can laugh at myself as I describe these falls to friends. You may be wondering, *Why is this woman falling?* Well, I recently discovered that many of my retired friends and I are falling due to imbalance. The wonderful thing is, so far, we all got up!

Let me give you more details of my falls. Once I was heading toward a parking lot to get my car. I had no reason to be hurrying because I was going home with no time limit for getting there. As I neared my car, I started trying to retrieve my car key from my handbag. Doing so distracted me from focusing on the pathway to my goal. I stubbed my toe and fell to the ground, flat on my face. My body and face showed evidence of that fall for days. Thanks be to God, my injuries were reparable, but the experience has kept me more focused as I walk daily.

Prior to another fall, I was too proud to seek help in hanging a line across my back patio. In order to hang the line, I needed to be higher, so I chose to climb onto a folding stool. Fortunately, I had the sense (or divine intervention led me) to place the stool against a firm support. The stool folded beneath me. When it folded, I was able to cling to that support and gracefully slide to the ground. Once again, I got up. I recognized, painfully then, the danger of pride and also that at seventy-two years of age, it's now time for me to let the younger ones climb while I guide and instruct.

On three occasions, I lost my balance and fell. In one instance, two relatives were close enough to grab and support me, soften the fall, and lift me to my feet again. In another, it was a total stranger who helped me up. In yet another, I was all alone when I hit the ground; I just sat there and prayed before moving. Thanks be to God, He got me up.

Sisters, my falls have spiritual applications for all of us. We must take care not to fall because of life's distractions, personal pride, or imbalance. We need to learn to accept help from God and from those He sends to our aid. So, today, let us resolve to empathize with, help, and restore those among us who fall spiritually, because when we least expect it, we, too, may fall!

Cecelia Grant

Vengeance Is God's

"Vengeance is mine, I will repay," says the Lord.
—Romans 12:19, NET

Have you ever been tempted to take revenge on someone after he or she hurt you? Yet God tells us that doing so is not our responsibility.

God appointed John the Baptist to prepare the way for Jesus, calling people to repentance. When John spoke truth, not everyone was pleased, especially Herodias, the unlawful wife of Herod, her brother-in-law. After John said that Herod's marriage was really a matter of adultery, the prophet was arrested. Herodias wanted to take revenge on John for speaking the truth. When the dancing of her daughter at a great feast pleased Herod, he promised she could have whatever she wished. After consulting with her mother, she requested the head of John the Baptist. Aghast, Herod felt he could not refuse her request in front of all the people. In this sad story, history records that often when we are told the truth about ourselves, we want to deny it, justify ourselves, or blame someone else. But true vengeance (judgment) belongs to God.

First, God's judgment is "according to truth" (Romans 2:2, KJV). He is not biased as we are; He sees the whole picture.

Second, His judgment is according to "works" (Revelation 20:12, KJV). He knows if our works are built on foundations of "gold, silver, precious stones" or on "wood, hay, stubble" (1 Corinthians 3:12, KJV).

Third, God is no respecter of persons (see Romans 2:11) in His judgments. Our God is merciful and loving, and He is objective. He judges with insight and knowledge.

Finally, Paul tells us that "God shall judge the secrets of men by Jesus Christ" (verse 16, KJV). Our relationship with Jesus will affect His judgment of us. May God help us see our mistakes and confess them to Him. Then we need not fear His "vengeance" or judgment because His mercy is greater than any mistakes we have ever made.

Mothers, ladies, girls, let's be careful not to cause others to sin. Mums, may our children be a blessing to others and not a curse.

Lord of heaven, help us to know You and do Your will that we may not be banished and end our days in shame and exile. We request this in Jesus' holy name. Amen.

Pauline Gesare Okemwa

On Guiding a Tree

"Yet at the scent of water it will bud
and put forth shoots like a plant."
—Job 14:9, NIV

I stood outside the gate of the elementary school that my granddaughter, Soffía, attends. I stood, trying to keep my balance as strong Santa Ana wind gusts came swooping down on me. Once I found my footing, I noticed a tall, newly planted tree right next to me. I couldn't even tell what kind of tree it was as it bravely stood there, bereft of all its leaves, barely moving, no matter how strong the wind. Fortunately for the tree, it was surrounded on three sides with sturdy wooden poles that were strapped individually to its thin trunk and then tied one to the other to create a circle of poles and tape that would ensure the tree would grow tall and straight.

Looking at that tree, I was reminded of the many Bible references comparing trees to humans. In Psalm 1, we read that a person who delights in the Lord "is like a tree planted by streams of water" (verse 3, NIV).

And here I was, standing in front of a school for children. I asked myself: *What will it take to ensure they grow straight and tall and healthy?* It takes the water of love from caring parents who guide their offspring with the Word of God and the Trinity of heaven: God the Father, God the Son, and God the Holy Spirit. Those three supporting poles will keep the "tree" from losing its way.

Job was like a well-watered tree, growing straight and strong and gathering his children under the shade of his faith. But one day his tree was shaken to the core, and it seemed that this giant tree had been cut to the ground forever. But Job understood that a tree that has been guided by the Word of God and faith in Jesus cannot lie fallen for long.

"If it is cut down, it will sprout again. . . . At the scent of water it will bud and put forth shoots like a plant" (Job 14:7, 9, NIV).

A mere "scent of water" will revive the stump of that tree, and it will soon continue its growth, straighter and taller than ever before, because it's a worthwhile investment of time and care to guide a tree to its full potential.

Lourdes E. Morales-Gudmundsson

A Facet of God's Love

Let no one seek his own, but each one the other's well-being.
—1 Corinthians 10:24, NKJV

I have always thought that in Bible characters we could find lessons for our lives. Rereading the book of Ruth in detail, I marveled at the way in which the central characters of the story—Ruth, Naomi, and Boaz—are related. I think they are an example to follow regarding how family relationships can work and produce happiness for all members. This is especially true if we follow the principle in today's theme text.

I see in Naomi a generous woman who, though in her old age and loneliness amid great misfortune, does not "blackmail" her daughters-in-law to take care of her. Rather, she encourages them to return to their people to have the possibility of obtaining a better future. Notice how she puts their interests above hers: "Return each to her mother's house" (Ruth 1:8, NKJV); "Turn back, my daughters" (verse 11, NKJV); "Go—for I am too old" (verse 12, NKJV); and to Ruth specifically, "Look, your sister-in-law has gone back to her people and to her gods; return after your sister-in-law" (verse 15, NKJV). In response, Ruth replies, "Wherever you go, I will go; wherever you live, I will live. Your people will be my people, and your God will be my God. Wherever you die, I will die, and there I will be buried" (verses 16, 17, NLT).

Ruth could have chosen to look after her own future and not return with an old woman for whom she would have to care and work, making a living for them both. Yet she made the loving choice, even knowing there would be additional hardship in leaving her own country to live in an unknown country. I admire the love that exists between the two women and how they put the well-being of each other first.

In this world of selfishness and abuse, where many values are being lost and the family is in crisis, we look at these two women and their decisions: they modeled the principle of not seeking their own comfort but rather "the other's well-being" (1 Corinthians 10:24, NKJV). What a breath of pure, clean air for us!

May the Lord help us to have these same family relationships where love flows in both directions. Let's give and receive, because mutually caring relationships are the ones that provide happiness. They demonstrate a facet of God's love.

Maite Lavado

Angels Are Watching Over You

*The angel of the LORD encampeth round
about them that fear him, and delivereth them.*
—Psalm 34:7, KJV

On the island where I was born, there are extremely venomous and vicious snakes, ranging from six to seven feet in length and as thick as a man's arm. Few people survive if bitten by these snakes. Suffice it to say, we all were terrified of them.

Back in those days, my father rented parcels of land where he planted vegetables to supplement the household income. Before planting season, he cleared the area of weeds that had overrun the property. On many occasions, he encountered these terrible reptiles; however, God was always watching over him. These snakes have sensitive nerves at the bottom of their bellies that allow them to sense a person's presence. Thus, they can position themselves by pulling their entire body in one spiraling coil, with their head at the top, ready to strike a person before the person is aware of their presence.

On one such occasion, my father was cleaning dead leaves from around banana trees while backing up to a fallen tree. Later, he recounted that he had suddenly heard someone call his name. This startled him because he knew he was the only person in the field.

He quickly turned around to see who was there. It was then he found himself facing the biggest snake he had ever seen. He prayed and slowly backed up to lengthen the distance between himself and the serpent. Fortunately, he was able to reach for a long stick with which he killed the dangerous reptile. But he was so frightened by this encounter that he returned home early after realizing how close he had come to being struck by that snake.

Had it not been for the Lord's protection, my father would have been killed. We were all grateful to God for His watchful eye over him. We had no doubt that an angel of the Lord had called my father by name, thereby saving him.

The Bible tells us that Satan is waiting for any move that we may take away from the protection of our heavenly Father, and he's ready to strike with fury. I thank my heavenly Father who protects, delivers, and keeps us safe from Satan's fangs.

Flore Aubry-Hamilton

Joy Is the Flag

Always be full of joy in the Lord, I say it again—rejoice!
—Philippians 4:4, NLT

It was my privilege to accompany my husband when he spoke for some ministers' meetings in Norway in the spring of 2014. Norway is one of the most beautiful countries in the world, with majestic mountains, beautiful fjords and lakes, and pristine farmlands. We arrived a few days early to adjust to the time change. On Sunday, we were invited by Dr. Terje Dahl (he said to call him Terry) to go on a day tour of Oslo. Terry strategically directed us to many of Oslo's well-known and favorite sites. After a trip to the Vigeland Sculpture Park, we were delighted to enjoy traditional thin, heart-shaped waffles spread with either homemade apple-plum jam or sliced brown cheese in a garden belonging to Terry's mom. She lives in the same house where she was born, located directly across from the school she attended with the current king of Norway.

Afterward, we headed for the old palace, "a fortress on the water," and then to the new king's palace. As we walked toward the palace, Terry commented, "The king is in residence today because the flag is flying." As soon as he said that, my mind went to one of my favorite children's songs: "Joy Is the Flag Flown High."* It states that the flag of joy is flying in the heart for "the King is in residence there."

As I mouthed the words to this song, I thought, *I will pray every day to be able to display joy as the flag, letting the world know that the King is in my heart.*

I daily offer this prayer from one of my favorite books: "Take me, O Lord, as wholly Thine. I lay all my plans at Thy feet. Use me today in Thy service. Abide with me, and let all my work be wrought in Thee."† I continue, "Let the words of my mouth, and the meditation of my heart, be acceptable in thy sight, O LORD, my strength, and my redeemer" (Psalm 19:14, KJV).

During the day, we may have to pause and pray again because we are so easily distracted by the day's events, but thankfully, we have a God who is anxious and willing to help us get back on track. May joy be the flag flown high in the castle of your heart today!

Rita Kay Stevens

---

* Author unknown, "Joy Is the Flag Flown High," 1978.
† Ellen G. White, *Steps to Christ* (Chicago: Fleming H. Revell, 1892), 70.

Living God's Love

"But I say to you who hear: Love your enemies."
—Luke 6:27, NKJV

Being called to ministry is exciting, but it is also demanding. That is why Jesus told us to count the cost, not in the financial sense but in the followership sense. Am I willing to lead as Jesus led? Am I able to love as Jesus loved?

Jesus' counsel in the sermon on the plain in Luke 6:27–31, 35 is much like His sermon on the mount in Matthew 5:38–48. At the heart of both is God's command to love one another, even our enemies. I can envision Him as He taught the people the principles of kingdom living and the divine realignment of the heart. Those called by Jesus must have hearts that characterize the love of God to those He died to save.

Loving one another is challenging, but loving our adversaries is even more challenging. We all know how difficult this command is.

In my earlier walk with God, it took much prayer and fasting to be able to work with people who pretended to be my friends but were, in fact, my enemies. Constantly, I had to press into the presence of God until the Holy Spirit helped me replace my negative feelings toward them with God's love for them. It wasn't easy.

What did the Holy Spirit impress upon me that helped me tremendously? That I was once God's enemy, yet He forgave me. He came to die not only for me but for my enemies too. When He called me to serve, His divine purpose was for me to share His love. No matter how we are treated, we must be faithful to our calling. When we received Jesus as our Lord and Savior, we also received a divine realignment of our hearts. We became partakers of His nature to love—even our enemies. Hallelujah!

Jesus drew us with His everlasting love by dying in our place. He was beaten without mercy. He was mocked, stripped naked, and taunted to the very end. And so that you and I would have victory, He sent the Holy Spirit to empower us to serve others and share His love.

Dear Father, thank You for Your incredible sacrifice on our behalf. As Your chosen vessels, thank You for giving us the Holy Spirit to clothe us with Your kindness, humility, gentleness, patience, and love for one another, even our enemies. In Jesus' name, amen.

Shirley P. Scott

We Can't Heal Ourselves

Heal me, O LORD, and I shall be healed . . . for thou art my praise.
—Jeremiah 17:14, KJV

I recently underwent emergency surgery to remove adhesions that my body had produced in an effort to heal itself. Adhesions are like Band-Aids that attach themselves to the damaged parts of the body in order to promote healing. Sometimes the self-healing adhesions attach themselves to other organs, causing problems that can result in death. When the potential for this is evident, surgery may be necessary to remove the adhesions and facilitate healing externally. Well-intentioned actions with unintended outcomes happen in our lives every day—physically (as described above), intellectually, emotionally, and spiritually.

Intellectually, God created us to be thinkers and problem solvers. It is easy for these intellectual abilities to slip into an I-can-fix-it mentality that inadvertently disregards our need for Christ. Sometimes our well-intended efforts to "heal" our children, marriages, finances, jobs, health, or ourselves can do more harm than good. We can all think of a time when we felt what we were saying to "help" a loved one hurt them beyond measure.

I am reminded of my desire to ensure my daughter reached her fullest potential, only to realize that she felt I was communicating my disappointment in her. Nothing was further from the truth. The well-intended "Band-Aids" I had produced to heal the damaged parts of her life had resulted in unintended outcomes. I came to realize God is the Master Healer. I thank *Him* for his surgical intervention. My daughter, a remarkable young lady with unbelievable resiliency, is on the way to full recovery through God's pruning for His glory.

Though our children can often cause us the greatest emotional pain (hence, my choice of illustration), this lesson has to be applied to every aspect of our lives. Circumstances often propel women into subconsciously believing we can fix all the hurts of our children, spouses, friends, and ourselves. We can't! Our good intentions can often restrict the functions necessary for the fulfillment of life in others—and ourselves, in particular. We need outside intervention from the Master Surgeon Himself.

If you are spending more time in pain than in the joy of life, the Master Physician is ready to operate. We cannot heal ourselves or all that hurts. We cannot be all things for all people. Yet we can learn to depend completely on Jesus, which ensures our spiritual well-being.

Deborah M. Harris

Food for Kids

"It is more blessed to give than to receive."
—Acts 20:35, NKJV

During the COVID-19 outbreak of 2020, the shutdown of our daily lives was beyond anything we could have imagined. Schools based in the Palmer, Alaska, district were abruptly closed. That meant students who rely on the school's daily lunches would have to go without. Our district transportation team quickly put together a few short bus routes, and as a district bus driver with top seniority, I was immediately offered one of the routes. I was teamed with two wonderful ladies from our nutrition services for our two-hour daily route. We began deliveries on Monday, March 23, 2020. "We want to inform you," one of the ladies said, "that we are very competitive and want to give away the most food in lunches." I was instantly in. Our team quickly grabbed the lead in this friendly competition as these ladies worked hard and engaged well with the families at the various drop-off points along our route. Delivering an average of eighty-eight lunches each day, we found the work to be intense and the boxes of lunches heavy!

On Fridays, we had double the normal amount of lunches so that our students could have a little extra food to eat over the weekends. Families met us in their cars, though one family picked up their children's lunches via a snowmobile. Some came on four-wheelers, others on bicycles, and one on a dirt bike. After delivering lunches from the bus every day, I would load twenty-six more lunches into my car to deliver to nine of my own regular bus-route families, who lived too far away from our route's drop-off points or had small children and couldn't, by themselves, get to our drop-off points. I cannot tell you how grateful these families were to have the lunches brought to them because they would not have received any otherwise. By the end of each exhausting day—and especially on Fridays—I took a much-needed nap in the afternoon. You can imagine that having the Sabbath on which to rest each week was *most* welcome! By the time the lunch-delivery program ended on Thursday, May 21, 2020 (which would have been the last day of the school year), my team and I had given out 3,885 lunches! Yes, we won the informal competition, but more than anything, the joy of being used by God to meet the needs of the children in my school district was an amazing experience.

Whether in a pandemic or some other challenge, what has God called *you* to do for Him?

Sonia Brock

A Tuna Sandwich and a Dollar

Blessed are the merciful: for they shall obtain mercy.
—Matthew 5:7, KJV

"Can you give me a dollar?" Daily he begs—this neat, clean, well-shaved, and stocky man. He sits in front of a bank as he solicits one dollar from every passerby.

Another homeless person—disheveled, dirty, with matted hair and cut-off pants—takes up his position under a tree with sparse shade. The earth beneath him is grassless, but it is his bed at night and his seat by day. He doesn't beg but looks off into the distance, cursing the invisible as he moves restlessly from side to side. All who pass him as they enter the supermarket are aware that he is there.

One day two people were in the marketplace. The first passerby saw the first beggar smoking a cigarette and asking for a dollar. *So that is what he wants my money for—to smoke cigarettes?* Yesterday she had heedlessly passed him by; today he would get a dollar. She hands one to him and returns to her work at the office and tells a friend how good it feels to have given even one dollar and what a blessed feeling of sympathy flows over her.

The second passerby is in the eastern part of the small town. She has always felt uneasy about approaching homeless people, for she figures that mental instability goes hand in hand with being dirty and on the streets. Yet God has been speaking to her: *How could you see your "brother in need" and shut up your "heart from him"?* (1 John 3:17, NKJV). She also recalls that one day "the King will . . . say, . . . 'Inasmuch as you did it to one of the least of these My brethren, you did it to Me' " (Matthew 25:40, NKJV).

She exited the supermarket with her groceries in one hand and a few dollars rolled up in the other. She had saved the change for the young man and stretched it toward him, though she had a nervous feeling in the pit of her stomach. He looked her way and said, "Buy me a cake!" She obediently returned to the supermarket, but upon finding no cake, she bought a tuna sandwich and gave it to him. He took it. With a glad heart, she walked to the car with a sense of well-being that she had helped someone that day. You, too, know the feeling, don't you, when you have done something for Jesus by reaching out to someone else?

Hyacinth V. Caleb

Stormy Weather

"The LORD is my strength and my song;
he has given me victory."
—Exodus 15:2, NLT

On a day off from work at summer camp, I decided to spend my free time with family at home. While I stopped at a gas station along the way, I felt my phone buzzing in my pocket. I pulled it out to read an emergency alert: "Flash flood warning until 5:00 P.M." I looked up and saw sunny skies overhead and friendly clouds floating through the air. I laughed and continued driving. Slowly, however, the sunny skies gave way to gray, billowing clouds. With only thirty minutes left in my drive, I noticed light rain falling on my windshield. Light rain turned to a steady downpour. Now the gray, billowing clouds turned to green, swirling clouds. Eventually, sheets of rain blinded my vision as I slowed to a crawl, passing parked vehicles along the shoulder of the road. Hands trembling and heart pounding, I reassured myself, "I've driven through blizzards worse than this; a little rain won't hurt anything."

Suddenly, I no longer had full control of my vehicle. The wind shook my car, the road became a river, and the green sky glared at me. My mind racing, I pulled to a halt behind a stopped vehicle and thought, *Is this a tornado? Could a giant piece of debris come crashing through my windshield? Is the ditch safer than my car?* I sat, listening to the squeak of my windshield wipers as they frantically but uselessly pushed against the rain. *God, I don't know what's happening out there, but please keep me safe!*

I can't tell you that I had instantaneous peace about the storm or that the rain stopped falling that very moment. No, I still didn't know what might become of me. My car continued wobbling in the wind, and my heart continued racing. Eventually, I made it out of the storm alive and well. Driving the rest of the way home, I saw trees uprooted, lawns flooded, and run-down barns collapsed. As I pulled into my grandparents' driveway, I breathed another quick prayer: "Thanks for Your protection, God."

Reflecting on that experience, I've made a spiritual connection: God wants to guide us through *all* our storms. You might be dealing with storms—literal or metaphorical—right now. If so, I'd encourage you to always look to Christ for protection and strength.

Britni Conrad

I Believe in Miracles!

"It shall come to pass that before they call, I will answer;
And while they are still speaking, I will hear."
—Isaiah 65:24, NKJV

I believe in miracles because I've seen God perform countless miracles for my family and me when circumstances seemed utterly impossible. Recently, He did it again for my husband and me in two different situations on the same day. Since our retirement, my husband and I travel together frequently. Over the years, we have learned that as we grow older, our bodies aren't as agile as they once were, so when we make flight reservations, we allow enough time between our arrival and departure to avoid the stress of having to rush.

Recently, a situation arose where my husband had to travel alone. I didn't realize until it was too late that he had allowed only forty minutes between the time his plane landed and the departure of his next flight. Immediately, I began to express my concern. "What if the plane arrives late or the departure gate is far away, and he misses his connecting flight?" The morning of his departure, he called to say that he was on his way to the airport. Again, I expressed my concern. He doesn't like to carry a cell phone, so when I suggested that he borrow someone's cell phone at the airport to inform me if he had made it on time, he calmly said, "Don't worry about it; it will all work out OK." I continued praying that the Lord would help him make his connecting flight. Later, a notice appeared on my cell phone from the airlines that the flight would depart nineteen minutes late. I shouted, "Thank You, Jesus!"

That morning I was scheduled to speak on the Morning Manna Prayerline and was concerned because my voice had succumbed to allergies. I could speak only in a whisper and cried out to God, "Father, I must speak shortly and can hardly talk. Please help me." Isaiah 65:24 tells us that "before they call, I will answer, and while they are still speaking, I will hear" (NKJV). God heard my prayer, and when the time came for me to speak, my voice had improved. He blessed far beyond my expectations.

Yes, I believe in miracles. God answered our prayers, and we're profoundly grateful. He's still in the miracle-working business. Call upon Him; tell Him all about your problems. He will listen and work out everything for your good, even when the circumstances seem impossible.

Shirley C. Iheanacho

Independence Day

"So if the Son makes you free, you will be free indeed."
—John 8:36, NRSV

Today is known as Independence Day in the United States of America.*
The Declaration of Independence, ratified on July 4, 1776, by fifty-six members of the Second Continental Congress, declared—and explained—why the thirteen American colonies considered themselves free of British rule. Yes, I'd say that freedom runs deep in my American veins, but it runs deeper than nationality. Freedom is a human issue. Human beings can't function without freedom any more than a flag can fly without wind.

Have you heard the freedom story of Edith Eva Eger? She survived the Auschwitz concentration camp during the Second World War. At the camp, her parents died in the Nazi gas chambers. But that was just the beginning of the horrors: a prison guard broke the girl's back. Then she endured a death march through Austria. By the end of the war, Edith had wasted down to seventy pounds (thirty-two kilograms). She was left for dead on a pile of bodies. But an American soldier saw her hand move, pulled her out, and called the medics. Edith lived to tell her story.

Her message focuses on the freedom of choice—something she says cannot be stolen from a person. Recalling how she nearly died of starvation in the camps, Edith said, "I chose to eat grass." She sat on the ground, choosing one blade over another. She kept reminding herself that even amid these dire circumstances, she still had a choice—"which blade of grass I would eat." Though others took everything from Edith, they still could not take her freedom.

So today, in memory of the freedom our nation's fathers died for and in memory of little Edith in the midst of hell on Earth, let's celebrate freedom.

The enemy can take our peace, homes, health, livelihoods, and very lives. But God has built an impenetrable wall around the sanctum of the human will. Circumstances may devastate, yet the treasure of freedom will always be ours. It may not always be the freedom to do as we please; in fact, our human rights may be horribly violated. Yet because One was stripped of everything He had—and in love, hung on a cross for us—we, through Him, have the ultimate say over how we respond to the world around us. How have you used your freedom?

Jennifer Jill Schwirzer

---

* This devotional first appeared as a blog post. Jennifer Jill Schwirzer, "Independence Day!" *Jennifer Jill Schwirzer* (blog), July 4, 2019, https://jenniferjill.org/independence-day/.

Me, Myself, and Why

"There is nothing concealed that will not be disclosed,
or hidden that will not be made known."
—Luke 12:2, NIV

I have a secret.

The person you see in front of you isn't me. I designed that person to fit your expectations—the things I hope you like. Do you want someone who is selfless, compassionate, and smart? *Boom.* I'll drop everything to help you, I'll give you an encouraging word, and I'll agree with you on politics.

I didn't deceive just you. I thought I was selfless, compassionate, and smart too.

But the Real Me only recently came out of hiding. I don't know when I began hiding her. I just kept editing my shell—the person I allowed people to see. The Real Me was unchanged.

She simply crawled deeper and deeper away from my consciousness. She hoarded every insecurity, fear, and frustration that I shoved down into her hidey-hole. The pain and heartache inflicted by family and friends festered within her for years. She's ugly and malnourished now because I refused to confront my problems and face my insecurities.

On the outside, I look good. I wash the outside of my cup. But the inside remains dirty.

So what do I do now?

Well, I must take responsibility and undo the damage I've inflicted on myself. I must stop secretly blaming other people for my pain and resentment. My name may mean "bitterness" (Ruth 1:20), but I don't have to embody that. I can create clear boundaries for myself so that I can grow the Real Me. No one asked me to be a people pleaser. It isn't fair to anyone that I am one.

Worst of all, I'm confronting every insecurity and fear I've buried over the years. They number in the thousands. Most of them are unfounded. Others I need to work through. A few I need to communicate to the people who have "inspired" them.

God knows my insecurities. He understands why I have them, why I've hidden them, and why it hurts to look at them. God knows how angry and disappointed I am with myself. He fully knows every part of me. And God fully loves me. That means He wants to help *all* of me grow.

Maria Kercher

Nearly Two Minutes Too Late

Call unto me, and I will answer thee,
and show thee great and mighty things, which thou knowest not.
—Jeremiah 33:3, KJV

The lawn really needs to be cut; it is too long," I said to my son. "I will phone Tony and see when he can do the job if he is not trucking still," I called over my shoulder as I walked to the phone.

Maybe his mother would know, I thought. When the call was connected, I said, "Hello, Muriel! This is Muriel in McBride [our same-name joke]. Can you tell me where I can contact Tony? For three days, I have been phoning his number and no answer."

She replied, "Haven't you heard what happened to him?" I had not heard, I told her. She continued. "He is in the Prince George Hospital."

"What!" I exclaimed in shock. "Whatever happened? Did this occur while he was mowing someone's lawn or hauling a load of logs up north?" I continued.

His mother sadly replied, "No one saw the lawnmower accident actually occur. Shortly after the accident, a nearby workman saw that something was wrong, ran toward him, and shut off the motor. He endeavored to stop the bleeding. With help, they rushed him to the town hospital, where the doctor applied a tourniquet to arrest the bleeding of his left arm. He was then whisked one hundred and twenty miles [193 kilometers] to the large Prince George Hospital. There Tony was given thirty-plus units of blood to keep him alive. He had lost so much blood the doctor said that two minutes later, it would have been too late to save him."

Tony realized that God had saved his life—by two minutes!

"Muriel," I told Tony's mother, "Mark and I will be going to Prince George on Friday. I am to have surgery, and we'll go early so we may visit him. We will also be praying for him."

On Thursday, we kept our appointments, bought our groceries, and ran other errands. Then we went to see Tony in the afternoon.

Recently, I heard that Tony is able to drive his truck again. He is of good courage and planning for the future. God hears and answers our prayers.

Muriel Heppel

Fenders, Fence, and Faith

Many are the afflictions of the righteous,
but the LORD delivers him out of them all.
—Psalm 34:19, ESV

When I worked for a small nonprofit organization in West Virginia, my commute was forty-five minutes.* Most of the road twisted and turned like a deer path, and there was no cell phone service for most of the drive. One hot summer day, the rain had fallen hard but stopped shortly before I left work. I didn't know anything about road chemistry. It had not rained for several days; therefore, oil and other chemicals had built up on the road, causing it to become extra slick. I saw an S turn coming up. As I rounded the second curve, I lost control, and my car turned sideways, then *wham!* All was still, and nasty-smelling steam rolled out from underneath the hood. As I stumbled onto the road, I realized the passenger door was crunched against a telephone pole. I had also taken out a hundred feet of fencing, and my license plate landed eight feet up in a tree. I walked away with only a one-inch burn on my arm from the airbag. What is possibly even more amazing is that I wrecked a short distance from the only person I knew who lived along my route! There were also two other accidents in the area at the same time as mine. Although it was a bright, sunny afternoon, the road conditions were bad.

God did not spare my car or the fence, but He did save me, and He provided me with the comfort of getting help from someone I knew. As bad as the situation was, it could have been much worse. In our modern understanding of the word *righteous*, most people, including myself, would feel it prideful to claim that description for ourselves. But the Bible uses that word to describe God's followers. This righteousness doesn't come from within us; it comes from the Holy Spirit abiding in us. I believe God saved me not because I was righteous but because He wasn't done working His righteousness within me.

Thank You, Lord, for saving me and allowing me to share how You have worked in my life in order to bolster the faith of others. "Therefore encourage one another and build one another up, just as you are doing" (1 Thessalonians 5:11, ESV).

Deidre A. Jones

---

* This entry first appeared as a blog post. "July 27, 2010," *Highland Seventh-day Adventist Church: Sabbath Thoughts* (blog), July 27, 2010, http://highlandcounty22.adventistchurchconnect.org/sabbath-thoughts-blog /july-27-2010.

Oh Yes, He Cares!

Jesus told them [the parents] to give her something to eat.
—Luke 8:55, NIV

Most of us know what it is to be hungry. *Food*—we all need it! Among other definitions for *food*, we find that it is "nutriment in solid form" and that it "nourishes, sustains, or supplies."* Schoolchildren often arrive back at home with this greeting: "Mom, I'm hungry! What is there to eat?" So caring mothers (and some fathers) have been connected with food in children's minds. The caring Jesus, too, was always concerned that people had food to eat. John 6:1–14 shares the story of how Jesus multiplied the lunch of a little boy in the crowd surrounding Him. The child's mother had probably packed his lunch consisting of five barley loaves and two small fish. The boy unselfishly shared his lunch by giving it to Jesus. Jesus was concerned about the crowd of people around Him being hungry but having nothing to eat. Jesus blessed the lunch and fed more than five thousand hungry listeners with it. Jesus really cares for the needs of people.

On another occasion, crowds of people were waiting to see Jesus. Then a man named Jairus pushed his way through the crowd, begging Jesus to come to his house because his only daughter was dying. Jesus went to the house where everyone was mourning the death of the little girl. He entered the room where she lay, took her by the hand, and said, "My child, it's time to get up." Immediately, she opened her eyes and looked around. His first concern was that she have something to eat (Luke 8:55). Does Jesus care? Oh yes, what a wonderful, caring Lord He is!

At dawn one morning after His resurrection, Jesus appeared on a beach. His disciples in a distant boat didn't recognize Him. As they came closer to shore, Jesus called out to them, "Haven't you any fish?" (John 21:5, NIV). When the disciples said they didn't, Jesus replied, "Throw your net on the right side of the boat and you will find some" (verse 6, NIV). When they did, their net filled with many fish. That's when John realized that the Man on the beach was Jesus. He had built a little fire and was cooking some fish for His disciples. Jesus also had bread. "Come and have breakfast" (verse 12, NIV), He invited them. Oh, what a wonderful breakfast that must have been!

Does Jesus care? Oh yes! He cares for you and me. Jesus is aware of our every need.

Priscilla E. Adonis

---

* *Merriam-Webster.com Dictionary*, s.v. "food," accessed September 13, 2020, https://www.merriam-webster.com/dictionary/food.

God Doesn't Text

For we are God's handiwork, created in Christ Jesus to do good works,
which God prepared in advance for us to do.
—Ephesians 2:10, NIV

Recently, I have been knitting fingerless gloves, which I call texting gloves. I made my own pattern a year or two ago and decided to plan ahead for winter and make a few pairs because our hands get so cold during the winter months. With my kind of gloves, one size fits all. As I was sitting in my chair knitting, I thought about God's hands. There is absolutely no problem that is too big to fit into God's hands. He doesn't do sizes either; we all fit into His hands just fine. From the tiny baby to the big, strapping man, we all fit perfectly. How comforting!

Nearly everyone sends text messages these days, and I am trying to fit into this technological era. It is often the most convenient thing to do, but there is much one can miss when communicating only through text messages: the warmth of the human voice, the vocal inflections, and the personal touch. There is so much you can communicate to another through your voice. But guess what? God uses His *voice* to communicate with us if we can be still enough to hear it. One of the ways He does this is through His Word. Our world is a busy place, and our lives reflect the stress of hurriedness. Yet it is comforting to know that God is right there in the thick and thin of our everyday lives. He is not texting (as we do); He is whispering. How sad that we are often so busy that we miss His quiet presence! We need to develop a focused, childlike faith—a faith that takes time to insert itself into every area of our lives. We need to tell God exactly what is on our minds, as children do.

Just the other day, I read about a little boy who was asked how to make his mother happy. He replied, "Tell her she is beautiful even if she looks like a dump truck."

Through Paul, God reminds us that "we are God's handiwork" (Ephesians 2:10, NIV). Genesis 1:27 assures us that "God created man in his own image, in the image of God created he him; male and female created he them" (KJV). Even when someone else might think we look like a dump truck, God reminds us how He views us—as beautiful, one-of-a-kind masterpieces. So, as I sit here knitting gloves that will help people communicate with one another during the winter, my Creator communicates to me that I am unique, special, and beautiful—as are you!

Grace A. Keene

God, Maow, and I

Yea, though I walk through the valley of the shadow of death, I will fear no evil:
for thou art with me; thy rod and thy staff they comfort me.
—Psalm 23:4, KJV

Maow, the cat we adopted three months ago, has a curious morning ritual. Having been a stray before we adopted him, he regards the home litter box with absolute disdain and instead insists on going to the nearby park for his morning business. But because of his frequent scuffles with the community cat (which counts our cul-de-sac as his territory), Maow "meow-calls" me early every morning to shepherd him through the danger zone to the relative safety of the park. Instead of being guarded, he now struts along, trusting me to ward off the rogue cat. As we play out this amusing little scene every day, I realize how like my relationship with God this looks. As David sings, "The LORD is my shepherd; I shall not want" (Psalm 23:1, KJV).

Coming out of our front gate is the most treacherous spot on our walk to the park. Peering under parked cars, I look out for the lurking enemy cat threatening to strike. I think of 1 Peter 5:8: "Your enemy the devil prowls around like a roaring lion looking for someone to devour" (NIV), just like the community cat who often appears suddenly, making a lunge for Maow. In these instances, I try to pick up my cat so that he can remain safe. But he wriggles so fiercely, demanding his freedom, that I often let go of him—only to have to race again to his defense from his lithe enemy. At these times, I am reminded of Jesus' words about His desire to shelter even an unwilling Jerusalem as a mother hen gathers her chicks under her wings (Luke 13:34). Seeing myself in Maow's "shoes," I realize my complete dependence on God is the key to being able to navigate safely from life's "front gate." God has told me to trust Him with all my heart and follow the path as He reveals it to me (Proverbs 3:5, 6). There are times when I may be impatient, but waiting for God to walk me through the gate is safer (Isaiah 40:31). When I do things my way, though, and subsequently get crushed by marauding "alley cats," I run back to Him, and He comforts me (Psalms 23:4; 34:18).

Friends, we have recently stepped through the COVID-19 pandemic gate into the unknown. So, as Maow trusts me for safety, let us wholeheartedly trust in the Lord. Let us "acknowledge Him" in all our ways, and "He shall direct . . . [our] paths" (Proverbs 3:6, NKJV).

Jessy Quilindo

Stop, Listen, and Connect

I call on the LORD in my distress,
and he answers me.
—Psalm 120:1, NIV

I like to begin the day by praying that I will be in the right place at the right time to be a blessing to God's people. It is rather like walking on a road. God can put people right in our path, and we have a choice: stay on our side of the road and help, or cross over to the other side and don't help. The parable of the good Samaritan in Luke 10:25–37 is a good example of a Jewish "neighbor" being loved by a very unlikely person—a Samaritan passerby.

The interesting thing to me as I review this story is that God allowed three people the opportunity to help someone in their path: a Jewish priest, a Levite, and a Samaritan. The priest and the Levite crossed to the other side of the road to avoid coming in contact with the injured man. That was a conscious decision. They thought, *No, I'm not going to help!* The Samaritan, on the other hand, did not cross to the other side of the road. He chose to help, even unselfishly. We assume he knew he was doing what God would want him to do. Even the expert in the Jewish law who had asked Jesus, "Who is my neighbor?" had to reluctantly admit the Samaritan was the one who "had mercy" (verse 37, NIV). He stopped, looked, and connected with the injured traveler.

Recently, my friend Rose and I set out on a bike ride along a dirt trail in eastern Oregon. Eventually, we arrived at the end of the trail and spent some time at a beautiful waterfall. Then, since a rainstorm appeared to be approaching, we decided we'd better hurry back. Rounding a switchback in the trail, we saw a woman walking quickly. She called out, "Have you seen a little girl?" We hadn't. She hurried past. A man right behind her breathlessly explained, "Our daughter is missing! She is nine and [holding out his hand] about this tall."

Rose replied, "We'll help you look, but first, I want to use the restroom up the trail." I pedaled off *down* the trail, praying and trusting in the promise of Psalm 120:1 (today's text). Circling back a bit later, I met up with Rose. She said, "As I approached the restroom, I heard a child inside singing. It turns out she was that couple's missing girl!" Because Rose and I had stopped, listened, and connected with these parents in distress, God used our prayers and outreach to these "neighbors" to reunite a family.

Diane Pestes

Left Behind

Behold, I stand at the door, and knock: if any man hear my voice,
and open the door, I will come in to him,
and will sup with him, and he with me.
—Revelation 3:20, KJV

My husband, a pastor, was recently transferred to a new church, so our family moved to a new town. It was again time to make new acquaintances and get used to our new surroundings.

One day our neighbors across the street came over to welcome us to the neighborhood. I noticed a beautiful orange tiger cat sitting in their driveway and asked them what its name was. "Oh, he's not our cat," they said, "but we call him Cammie. Some years ago, the cat's owners moved from the neighborhood and simply left him behind." I love animals and felt sorry for him, so I decided I would befriend and feed Cammie. I started feeding Cammie every day. Soon he allowed me to pet him as he ate.

One exceptionally cold morning, Cammie met me at the door and tried to get into the house. I longed to let him inside so that he could get warm, but I was afraid that once he got in, he wouldn't really be happy. He's used to having his freedom outside and would probably find living in a house to be too restrictive. Though he thinks he wants to be inside, he has really become a wild cat and won't even let me pick him up. Cammie would not understand my rules about not scratching the furniture or getting on tables. No, I'm afraid he wouldn't fit in, especially since I have a fourteen-year-old cat that is already established with us. Having Cammie inside the house would destroy both our peace and his.

This situation reminded me of how Jesus longs to let all the people He has created into heaven. In fact, He tells us in 1 Timothy 2:4 that our Savior "desires all men to be saved and to come to the knowledge of the truth" (NKJV). The problem is, if they don't let Jesus change them first, they will not be happy there. Not only would they find it impossible to fit in, their presence would destroy the peace of those around them.

Just as we couldn't let Cammie into our house because he wouldn't change to fit in, Jesus can't allow into heaven sinners who refuse to change. Sadly, He must leave them outside the heavenly gates and on this earth. May each one of us confess our sins, accept Jesus' gift of salvation, and allow His Spirit to change us now so that we won't be left behind when He comes.

Christa White Schiffbauer

The Sticky Note

"Ask, and it will be given to you; seek, and you will find;
knock, and it will be opened to you. For everyone who asks receives,
and the one who seeks finds, and to the one who knocks it will be opened."
—Matthew 7:7, 8, ESV

Hang on, guys. Something's wrong with my computer mouse. I have to figure it out," Mr. Mosher said at the beginning of geometry class.

Five minutes passed, and he hadn't found a solution. Ten minutes, and Mr. Mosher still couldn't find the cause of the problem. We all expected him to ask for help, but he kept searching for the answer on his own.

Fifteen minutes had passed when he finally picked up his mouse and looked underneath it. He began to laugh. He had found my prank.

You see, Mr. Mosher and I had a bit of a prank war that went on throughout my high school years. This was my prank on him: I had taped a sticky note to the sensor of his computer mouse that read, "Your move! LS :-)." At the time, I had thought he would figure out what I had done in a couple of minutes. Instead, he had spent a full fifteen minutes trying to solve the simple problem.

Often in our walk of faith, we act like Mr. Mosher. We know there's a problem in our relationship with God, and we do everything we can to figure out what's wrong on our own. We search for the source of the problem and inevitably come up empty. We get discouraged and think about giving up on God altogether.

That's when we realize what the problem is: something's blocking our connection to God. Whether it is an addiction, social media, or the difficulties of life in general, we constantly find that our connection with God is being tampered with, just as the sticky note was blocking the mouse from working.

When we realize there's a block between ourselves and God, the solution becomes clear: Pray to Him. Talk to Him about what's blocking our path to Him. All He ever needs from us is an invitation, and He will swoop in and save the day in one way or another. All we ever have to do is ask Him. With His help, we can find and remove any sticky note that perplexes us.

Lacey Stecker

Slow Down

Draw near to God, and he will draw near to you.
—James 4:8, ESV

One morning during the 2020 COVID-19 pandemic, as I prepared for my daily devotions, I prayed that in whatever I read, God would lead me to understand and be able to apply it to my life. I prayed about the pandemic and asked that—however it might affect my life, even if it were to take my life—my trust in God would remain strong.

Upon opening the book I had been reading, the title on the page leaped out at me: "Life on Pause." Yep, that's the way many of us were feeling. We certainly felt that way if we were trying to put into practice the social-distancing and isolation recommendations being given by government officials and healthcare workers appearing on television newscasts each day in an attempt to limit the spread of the dreaded disease. In Leviticus 13, God gave the first social-distancing guideline to limit the spread of infectious diseases.

But the text that the devotional writer had chosen for that day gave me a boost of hope and assurance. "Be still, and know that I am God" (Psalm 46:10, KJV). In other words, the Lord is saying, "Calm down. I'm in control. No need for worry."

So, in that time of a little less connection with the people around me, God had just offered me an increased opportunity to connect with Him and make my relationship with Him grow stronger. And this is just what I will need to see me through these last days before Jesus returns for His faithful children.

There's nothing I want more than to be ready for that blessed day. Taking advantage of the opportunity to know Him better, learning to walk closer to Him with more sure footsteps, working with Him in sharing the gospel of the kingdom, and increasing my faith in Him—these are my goals for the rest of my time on this earth.

It's sometimes very hard to make oneself settle down and take the needed time each day to gather strength from the only Source of living bread and water for our spiritual sustenance. But I can't face the hardships and uncertainties of this life on my own. I need to know and trust the One who supplies all my needs. Please join me in taking advantage of moments like these to come more fully into the Divine Presence.

Sylvia Sioux Stark

Heavenly Tears

"He will wipe away every tear from their eyes, and death shall be no more,
neither shall there be mourning nor crying nor pain anymore,
for the former things have passed away."
—Revelation 21:4, RSV

Recently, I waited at an airport's international terminal for my friend Ann. She was returning from a visit to Germany. As I watched for her, I got caught up watching the emotional reunions of passengers and their loved ones.

A young woman from southeast Asia held flowers and jumped up as her parents came into view—her mother in a sari and her father wearing a sarong. Smiling, he bowed to her before they hugged.

Next, an airport employee brought an Asian woman through the arrival gate in a wheelchair. Her son took off running toward her, and they touched each other's cheeks, the right one and then the left. Soon they chattered excitedly in Mandarin.

A Caucasian college student, wearing short shorts, tights, and hiking boots, tromped through next. Her thick hair was in dreadlocks. Her father, dressed in a business suit, threw his arms around his free-spirited daughter and her tie-dyed backpack.

When a Hispanic woman appeared, her daughter bent over and touched the top of her shoes two times in a gesture of honor and love. Then their squeals of joy erupted.

By the time Ann came through the arrival gate, tears were rolling down my cheeks. She asked why I looked so sad in greeting her! "Oh," I tried to explain, "these are tears of . . . well, how can I describe it?"

I couldn't. But I decided that when I get to heaven, I'm going to stand in a spot where I can watch as many reunions as I can all at once! I can't imagine that I won't be sobbing. Yet the Bible promises that in heaven, God will wipe all tears from our eyes.

One theory of why we cry here on Earth is that we're experiencing emotional overload, and our tears are a way of releasing some of that emotion. So, when God puts an end to crying, I'm certain it won't be because we're no longer experiencing powerful positive emotions, such as love and connection. It will be because we finally have a boundless capacity to contain and savor them!

Lori Peckham

My Defender

"Do not be afraid, for I have ransomed you.
I have called you by name; you are mine."
—Isaiah 43:1, NLT

Who is Jesus to you? When I was in high school, I would have told you, "Jesus is my Father." You see, I had lost my father, and so God became a father to me. It was a very personal experience—a tender, gentle relationship that got me through some important seasons of life. But over the years, life happens. And if we aren't careful, we can start answering this question with pat answers that are entirely true but have no personal meaning. That's where I have been for a while, which is a hard place because it leaves the core of your soul empty and unprotected. It allows hurt, guilt, and shame to flourish; it did for me.

Shame has a way of controlling and telling us we aren't valuable. It says we are not worthy of love, wholeness, or even a relationship with God. Recently, as I was thinking about shame, I saw myself as a little preteen girl, sitting along a chain-link fence, huddled with my arms wrapped around my knees and my head down. Standing next to me was a strong being whom I presumed to be God. In his hand, he had a long whip made from a material that could cause at least moderate pain. That whip lashed out at me time and again. With each blow, my shame and guilt intensified. I felt scared and trapped. Tension filled me as I waited for each successive blow.

I wondered why this scenario had come into my mind, although it certainly portrayed what I was feeling. At that moment—when I was scared, alone, and beaten down—Jesus stepped onto the scene. Beaming with love and beauty, He held out one hand, put it on the side of my accuser, and effortlessly pushed him away. "Let the children come to me. Don't stop them! For the Kingdom of God belongs to those who are like these children" (Luke 18:16, NLT).

At that moment, I saw the being whom I had presumed to be God become powerless and run away. It had been Satan masquerading as God. But Jesus stepped in and delivered me, though undeserving. At that moment, I felt sudden relief. Peace. Safety. Rest. Deliverance by *His* power, word, love, and decision. And He will step in and rescue you too. Your circumstances might not change. But your confidence in God's love, grace, and acceptance can.

Who is Jesus to me? Once again, the answer has become personal. Jesus is my Defender. Who is Jesus to you?

Jennifer Haagenson

Under Your Wings

He will cover you with His feathers;
you will take refuge under His wings.
His faithfulness will be a protective shield.
—Psalm 91:4, HCSB

One hot summer evening around seven thirty, while I was doing literature evangelism book sales in Houston, Texas, my team leader assigned me to a parking lot plaza. I started talking to people and slowly started selling some magabooks (books in an attractive magazine format). Then I approached a parked car with a man sitting inside. I showed him the books I was selling and told him the money from the sales would help me pay for my schooling. "I think you would be blessed by this reading material," I said with a smile. But he simply looked me up and down and then laughed in a way that made me feel rather uncomfortable.

"That's OK if you can't purchase a book right now," I said. "However, I would appreciate even a donation toward my education." He looked away and didn't seem interested. "May I offer to pray with you before I go on my way then?" I asked.

After I prayed for him, I went my way and saw some other people going to their cars with whom I could share. A little while later, I heard a voice calling across the parking lot: "I'll give you some money." That made me happy. I turned to see that it was the man in the car with whom I had prayed earlier.

"Which book would you like to buy then?" I was not prepared for his diabolical laugh or his offer of twenty dollars to go to a dark area of the parking lot and be intimate with him. Suddenly frightened and feeling worthless, I looked at him and said, "I'm sorry, sir, if you misunderstood me. That's something I will not do." When I walked away, he started to follow me around the parking lot. Trembling and crying now, I started running—right into a woman getting out of her car! As soon as she saw my tears, she asked what had happened.

As I told her, she hugged me and helped calm me down. In gratitude, I gave her one of my books, *Peace Above the Storm*. After that, she prayed for me, and I felt God's protective wings over me. Then I called my team leader to report the incident. Before going to bed that night, I thanked God for sending an angel to remind me to have "peace above the storm."

Diana Celaya

Battered but Not Broken

We are troubled on every side, yet not distressed; we are perplexed, but not in despair; persecuted, but not forsaken; cast down, but not destroyed; always bearing about in the body the dying of the Lord Jesus, that the life also of Jesus might be manifest in our body.
—2 Corinthians 4:8–10, KJV

Many years ago, my mother shared some of her wisdom to prepare me for the world—a world that I was anticipating greatly, not realizing that it has its own rules and only plays to win for itself. Yet I was anxious to step out to discover my own path. Win or lose, I was going to stay and fight. And I did just that.

My mother was very adamant that I must not forget, "You will meet people in life who have different walks, who are more educated, more opulent, and more upscale than you." She continued, "We each have a story, and each is all laced with different trimmings." How true can that be! Her words still resonate with me.

From our first earthly parents until today, we have been creating stories upon stories. One commonality in our stories is that most are tainted with sin, and sin has no respect for anyone. We have been tasting sin that we didn't sign up for.

Perilous times in our lives can open doors that trigger severe storms. No matter how diverse our calamities, we can all testify that we were beaten down at some point with no hope of rebuilding. Yes, "we all have a story," as my mother pointed out, but rest assured that the One who redeemed us from the wreckage of the stories, which give us our testimonies, also has a story. His story is our only hope. Jesus has the best story; it can reignite a wounded spirit. No matter how downtrodden we become, we do not have to cast about because Jesus is alive. He understands our hurt and pain. Jesus may not be physically present with us, but we are not alone. He left us His gospel of peace and His Comforter. He will help us stay on the path to life everlasting.

So allow Jesus' power to be manifested through you. Authorize God's will to become yours; wrap it around you to protect you from the pitfalls of the devil. Trust the One who died for you. Though battered, we need not stay broken. Look to Him, the Victor, for salvation.

Corletta Aretha Barbar

God Answered My Prayer

Ask, and it shall be given you; seek, and ye shall find;
knock, and it shall be opened unto you: For every one
that asketh receiveth; and he that seeketh findeth;
and to him that knocketh it shall be opened.
—Matthew 7:7, 8, KJV

The year 2006 was a challenging year for my husband and me. He was involved in a terrible accident, in which he sustained a mid-spinal cord injury that left him unable to walk. After confinement in the hospital for several weeks, he began rehabilitation. During this difficult season of his life, he was totally dependent on me. We were both active people, but now our movements were restricted. Daily we followed the therapy regimen, and after several months of untiring effort, he was finally able to walk on his own. That was an exciting moment, and we were both thankful to God for this incredible miracle.

One morning I thought, *I need to get back to work.* I had left my job to care for my injured husband. Now I felt that it was time to return to the workforce. *Lord, I need a job, but I am too tired to look for one,* I said.

A week later I was surprised to receive a phone call from a principal for whom I had taught some years before.

"Mrs. Morrow, we have been seeking a teacher for our elementary school. We've put announcements in several papers and made appeals to the churches; however, no one has replied. In our board meeting this morning, it was suggested that we pray. After praying, a number of the board members asked, 'What about Mrs. Morrow?' So I'm calling to offer you a teaching position in the lower division," she said. "Are you available?"

Without hesitating, I responded, "This is an answer to my prayer. Yes!"

"Great! And because we're familiar with your work, we won't need to interview you. When can you come in to sign papers and discuss salary and benefits?" she asked.

In the book of Matthew, chapter 7, we are admonished to "ask, and it shall be given you; seek, and ye shall find; knock, and it shall be opened unto you: For every one that asketh receiveth; and he that seeketh findeth; and to him that knocketh it shall be opened" (verses 7, 8, KJV).

I can testify that God's words are true!

Willietta Ann Morrow

Claim Your New Name

"Daughter, your faith has healed you."
—Mark 5:34, NIV

Jesus was on the way to the home of one of the synagogue leaders to heal his dying daughter. A woman who had an issue of blood for twelve years pressed her way through the crowd to get to Jesus. This woman interrupted Jesus' mission. She was determined that He would heal her.

She could have been beaten or even killed for mingling with others in her condition, yet she was determined to match His heart with her faith. "She thought, 'If I just touch his clothes, I will be healed' " (Mark 5:28, NIV). She finally wedged her body through the crowd and touched Him. "Immediately her bleeding stopped and she felt in her body that she was freed from her suffering" (verse 29, NIV). No matter how hopeless our problems, let's never allow fear to keep us from approaching Jesus with courage.

Jesus identifies this woman when He calls her "daughter": "Daughter, your faith has healed you" (verse 34, NIV). In calling her "daughter," He is speaking to all women. He speaks to our femininity, our hearts, and our potential. Jesus speaks to what we women can be. It is a pronouncement of our futures. It is through our faith that God releases His power and His divine revelation of our purpose.

Let us allow God to orchestrate our destinies. Jesus did not just release the woman from her physical illness—He released her mentally and spiritually! That's why Jesus asked, "Who touched me?" (verse 31, NIV). He wanted her to have a testimony. Jesus wanted her to lay aside her fears and take on a boldness that only He could give. She had interrupted Jesus' passage for a greater purpose.

Sometimes it takes an interruption of our existing affairs to connect with Jesus. What He did for this woman, He wants to do for us! He wants our faith to be enlarged, our dreams to be expanded, and our lives to be full of spiritual interruptions. He desires us to give birth to God-sized dreams, see miracles happen in our lives, and meet people in the kingdom because of our Christian witness and service.

Let's press our way into the presence of the Almighty to experience the joy of having God's heart connect with our faith and claim our heritage as His precious daughters!

Ella Tolliver

The Night Prayer

One of those days Jesus went out to a mountainside to pray,
and spent the night praying to God.
—Luke 6:12, NIV

Does this happen to you sometimes? You find that sleep does not come easily, and you toss and turn in bed—your mind full of irrational fears and worries. Or perhaps the sleeplessness has something to do with your creative soul and all those wonderful ideas and projects you want to accomplish. I have often found myself afflicted by these night spells. Yet luckily for me, my tremendous love for nature brings thoughts of the night garden flooding my mind, instilling in me a new kind of amity toward sleeplessness and acceptance of the night hours. In an instant, my mood changes. A surge of enthusiasm rushes through my veins, taking me to the night garden. I mustn't forget I'm alive. I mustn't forget that God is bigger than my anxieties and fears—now, tomorrow, and the day after that. And I know exactly what I must do.

Outside the quiet garden is shrouded in peaceful moonlight. Over my head, millions of stars dance in the heavens while silvery moonbeams illumine sleepy black-eyed Susans. A puff of perfume lingers in the night air. I hear hushed wings rustling in nearby shrubbery. I walk by sleepy roses and night bloomers—the moon vine, lady-of-the-night, night jasmine—where I pause to say a prayer.

Could this be why Jesus loved to pray in the night garden? The Son of God could have chosen any place to pray with His disciples after the Passover meal. But His clear preference was His favorite garden. He went out to the Mount of Olives, heading eastward to the garden called Gethsemane (Mark 14:26). I can imagine Jesus choosing His prayer corner among the ancient olive trees. I can imagine the same moon that still illumines our nights shining down on Jesus' beautiful head as He poured out His heart to His heavenly Father. That night in the garden, humanity's fate was changed from doom to hope.

So on those nights when sleep is elusive, let us not stay in bed. Instead, let us go to a quiet corner and engage in earnest prayer. Getting out of bed in the middle of the night when you can't sleep may be the key to sleeping more each night. What you do then, in the wee hours, can affect how the rest of your nights—and your life—go. And that could make all the difference.

Olga Valdivia

Rewarded Trust

And we know that all things work together for good to those who love God,
to those who are the called according to His purpose.
—Romans 8:28, NKJV

It was a beautiful spring day. Our pastor and his wife were prepared to go on a holiday to another continent to enjoy time together with their son and his family. When they left, they asked my husband and me to take care of their house and, at least two times per week, to sleep in their house. We decided to go every Tuesday to sleep there. Because I wanted to clean the house a little bit on Tuesday, I arrived there first. Time passed quickly, and evening came. It grew dark! I was still waiting for my husband to arrive. Suddenly, the phone rang. It was my husband. "I cannot come to be with you tonight," he said, followed by an explanation of an issue he had to resolve. Now I was scared! The house felt huge—I just couldn't be alone! It had three entrances, and I felt lost. "Pray to God," counseled my husband, "and then sleep well!" I was scared, but I did what he told me after locking all the doors (which had a combined thirteen special locks). I prayed and slept in a room that was on the first floor.

At an unusual hour of the night, I woke up. I wanted to get out of bed but found I didn't have the strength to do so. I tried again and again—many times—but always in vain. I was conscious, but I couldn't figure out what was happening to me. I didn't feel well and was so weak. As I prayed, trusting in God, He gave me an idea: slide to the floor even though I couldn't get up. Then I dragged myself by my elbows toward the window about twenty-three feet (six to eight meters) away. Once there, I rested a moment until I could get up to open it. Finally, fresh air!

What had happened? The pilot flame of the gas burner had gone out, and gas had leaked into the room, decreasing the necessary oxygen. I'd felt intoxicated! Who woke me up? An angel—at the right time. Otherwise, I soon would have been sleeping for good. And who could have entered the house to help me with so many locks on the doors?

During the three years since then, I've grown to understand that God had a plan for me: serving women as I experience His presence in my life. God calls us all to be ambassadors, using our God-given gifts, empathy, and resources for His glory. He is coming soon!

Dear Lord, help us to trust You and not to lose any time, which is so precious!

Ana Nadasan

Yearning for Yesterday

And Jesus said, ". . . Go and sin no more."
—John 8:11, NLT

Yesterday is my best friend. Sometimes I want so much to go back that I'm paralyzed and unable to go forward. Many times my present is so filled with remorse and guilt that I wish I could return to yesterday and drop the many mistakes or callous choices I made.

One of the shameful decisions I made was to write to a new colleague, explaining to him the importance of politeness. We had an encounter that upset me a bit, and of course, since I was perturbed, I thought he naturally would be too. As the time came for us to work together, I wanted to be proactive and tell him exactly how to behave—even how to greet me. I would not be ignored. You see, sometimes the enemy uses the very gifts that make me special to make me silly. I love people. I am intuitive and observant, and I can uncover sadness and needs and turn them into solutions. And I like to write. In this situation, the devil used those gifts to help me "see" that my new colleague did not greet me and "hear" disdain when he finally spoke to me. I put all my gifts together and blasted him an email. Soon he responded, completely stunned! He vaguely remembered the incident I shared with him, but he really did not connect me to that incident. Then he amazed me: as we worked together, he promised I could count on him to help me succeed in my work and do me no harm. He was gracious and kind but very shocked.

I obsessed over my misstep the rest of the day and woke up the next morning, burdened and bothered by my behavior. I wanted to go back to yesterday at the point where I could have thought better about things. Reason. Pray. Focus on Christ instead of myself. But I could not. Sin is a deadly disease, and it brings so much misery. This was not the first time I wished I could change the past. But God has not called me to do that. He bids me go and sin no more. God gives me a pass for my yesterdays and provides grace for my tomorrows. My Christian walk is fraught with faults, but, like my colleague, God has promised me that He will do me no harm. If I confess my sins, He is faithful and just to forgive my sins and cleanse me from all my unrighteousness (see 1 John 1:9).

Sisters, the longing for yesterday is futile. You can't change the past, but God can usher your bitter dusk into bright dawn. All you need is to admit, apologize, and accept His forgiveness—just for today.

Rose Joseph Thomas

Sabbath

"Remember the Sabbath day, to keep it holy."
—Exodus 20:8, NKJV

In Germany, World War II was raging. So many things had changed since the war began. My father and his twin brother were the oldest boys in a family of nine. Their mother did her best to care for the children while their father was away, serving in the war. Because of the terrible conditions, the family often did not have enough food to eat. Most nights they slept in an underground bunker for fear that the bombs being dropped would hit the house. The family used the bunker mainly at night to sleep in, though it was cramped when all the family members were inside. In fact, it was so cramped that on some nights, my father and a few of his brothers chose to sleep in the much roomier barn that belonged to the farmer next door.

One night my father and his brothers started leaving for the neighbor's barn when their mother stopped them. "My son, remember this is Friday night. Tomorrow is the Sabbath, and we will be going to church just as we do every Sabbath. We need to sleep together tonight so that when we awaken tomorrow morning, we will be prepared to all walk to church together."

My father looked at his mother as she spoke. His gaze shifted from her face to the row of his brothers' and sisters' shoes neatly lined at the entrance of the bunker. Some of the shoes were too small and pinched little feet. Other shoes were too big, so bits of straw were used to fill the gap between their toes and the front of the shoe. Yet all the shoes stood neatly as a quiet reminder that the Sabbath day was different from the rest of the week. Sabbath was holy. Sabbath was the day the family went to church to celebrate a loving Father in heaven who was caring for the family through these most awful times. My father looked away from the row of shoes and back at his mother. He chose to honor her request. He and his brothers would sleep in the bunker with the rest of the family that night.

As the kids settled down to sleep, air-raid sirens began to scream, then bombs fell. They heard a loud crash followed by screams. They remained in the bunker. In the morning, as the family emerged from the bunker, they saw only smoldering ashes where the neighbor's barn had so recently stood. With heavy but thankful hearts, they walked to church that Sabbath morning.

"Therefore the Lord blessed the Sabbath day and hallowed it" (Exodus 20:11, NKJV).

Beatrice Tauber Prior

Bread, Water, and Crows

And the ravens brought him bread and flesh in the morning,
and bread and flesh in the evening; and he drank of the brook.
—1 Kings 17:6, KJV

For the past two months, I have woken to the sound of crows screeching on my balcony. These birds have become a daily fixture in my life. At first, I couldn't stand them. They were loud, dirty, and aggressive, landing on balconies, stealing leftovers off of plates, and getting far too close for comfort. Truthfully, however, I was already familiar with being uncomfortable.

I had never planned to be in this location at all, much less for two months. And with the airport and the world in general shut down, the end of this unplanned trip was nowhere in sight. I was desperately low on funds. And with an island-wide curfew, everything—including pharmacies, shops, and supermarkets—had been closed. I was worried about how long my supply of drinking water would last, when I would eat fruits and vegetables again, and what would happen when my medications ran out. So, really, the crows were the least of my concerns.

I was sitting outside one morning when a particularly intrusive crow landed on the balcony with a large piece of bread in its beak. It brought 1 Kings 17 to mind. Here Elijah is on the run, and God sends him to the brook Cherith, where he lives on river water and food delivered by ravens. I have always wondered how Elijah felt about this situation. Crows and ravens are similar, both being scavengers. I couldn't imagine either of them bringing me anything I was willing to eat. Yet God used these birds to feed Elijah during a desperate time. It made me realize that I was living a version of 1 Kings 17. Like Elijah, I was stranded and completely dependent on God to take care of me. I didn't know what each day would bring but had to wait for God to give me what I needed. And you know what? God always supplied. I never ran out of drinking water. A few weeks into the curfew, local farmers started delivering fruits and vegetables. And not long after, a local supermarket arranged a delivery service.

Though we usually don't want them, we all need these kinds of experiences to help us build a living faith in God. It is the kind of faith that will carry us through all the twists and turns of life.

R. Bowen

It Was No Mistake

*"The Lord himself goes before you and will be with you; he will never
leave you nor forsake you. Do not be afraid; do not be discouraged."*
—Deuteronomy 31:8, NIV

I had ordered something online, but when the package arrived, the company had sent me something else—although the tracking and order numbers were the same as what I had ordered.

I called the company to tell them they had sent me the wrong product. "Sir," I said to the gentleman who answered the phone, "I really have no use for baby wipes. I'm an eighty-six-year-old woman, and there are no babies in our family who live nearby or in this neighborhood."

The man responded, "I'm sorry, but you cannot return them because they did have the same tracking and order numbers as what you wanted. It's our fault, so just keep the baby wipes, and we will give you a full refund." Two weeks later, the case of baby wipes was still in my office when the COVID-19 pandemic hit with a vengeance. Suddenly, people were hoarding toilet paper. *Hey*, I thought, *those wipes might be a good substitute*. And they were, although I had to carefully remember not to flush them. I forgot maybe three times, but God was so good. He kept our plumbing—and all our appliances and the heating—working. We were so blessed.

As I write this, we are still experiencing isolation in our homes, social distancing, and the wearing of protective masks. It is a horrible time in all our lives, but God shows us each day that we need not fear. He loves us, and He cares for each one of us. He is with us. Why, He even sent me baby wipes when I thought I didn't need them. He knew they would be useful.

Yes, eventually, the company that had sent me the baby wipes by mistake shipped the item I had originally ordered. So far, we have not really run out of toilet paper, and our daughter, who gets our groceries each week, has been able to get everything on our shopping list.

We have all our needs met, except the need for hugs from our family, but that will come soon when this virus ends. In the meantime, I keep remembering that God has told us not to fear! Unlike that company mixing up my order, He never makes mistakes.

Anna May Radke Waters

He Knows

You can be sure that God will take care of everything you need,
his generosity exceeding even yours in the glory that pours from Jesus.
—Philippians 4:19, *The Message*

God doesn't always give us everything we ask for, but He has promised to supply what we need. In fact, He knows what we need before we do! Several years ago, my husband, Earl, and I were struggling financially to pay our mortgage so that we could have a roof over our heads. We were also struggling to feed three children and ourselves. Daily, we prayed to God, asking Him to meet our basic needs. One day I was at a large-chain grocery store. I looked at the shelves stocked with food and sundry items that we could certainly use. But the amount of money in my wallet was very limited, so I had to choose carefully and frugally.

Then I noticed a colorful sign posted in the grocery store: "Enter our drawing to win $100 worth of groceries! The winning name will be drawn next Saturday."

I almost chuckled in resignation. *I'd never win anything*, I thought. *But, hey, what do I have to lose?* So I wrote down my name and phone number on one of the entry blanks. Then I dismissed the whole thing from my mind, purchased a very few—but desperately needed—grocery items, and went home to care for my family.

The weekend rolled around. What a relief to worship and fellowship with our church family and not have to think about the cares of this world, although we did ask for prayers regarding our dire financial situation.

We arrived back home a little bit before sundown. As the sun set, we thanked God for another restful day in Him. I was just starting to get the children ready for bed when the telephone rang unexpectedly. I picked up the receiver: "Hello?"

"Is this Mrs. Barbara Fisher?" asked a woman's voice at the other end of the line. When I confirmed that it was, she continued. "I'm just calling with some very good news for you. Today was our store's drawing, and I'm pleased to tell you that you are our winner. You have just won one hundred dollars' worth of free groceries!" I was speechless, though I shouldn't have been. God knew we needed food and other household goods. And now we had enough money to choose whatever we needed the most. Truly He is faithful to supply our needs through Jesus!

Barbara Fisher

Never Alone

PART 1

Behold, a virgin shall be with child, and shall bring forth a son,
and they shall call his name Emmanuel,
which being interpreted is, God with us.
—Matthew 1:23, KJV

August 27, 2015, seemed like just another beautiful day, but it wasn't, not after I heard the gut-ripping news over the phone that my husband—my friend, the spiritual leader of our home, and the father of my two precious teenagers—was dead, killed in a plane crash. The kids and I, in a state of shock, dropped to our knees and called out to our God. On that devastating day, God had to pick up the shattered pieces and carry us supernaturally through the next painful days and months.

While none of us is ever prepared for the shock of suddenly losing one we dearly love or going through any trauma, God is never caught off guard. Unbeknownst to my family, the truth God emphasized to us at the beginning of that year was exactly what we would need to sustain us through our loss. He understood that because of the level of pain this would inflict upon our family and so many others, we needed a deeper, stronger truth—a truth made for the occasion—for that dark moment. Yes, we sing about "God with us" every Christmas season, yet this underrated truth is packed with high-dosage healing power for all of us who have been or will be deeply hurt before this life is over. Ellen White gives us some insights into what "God with us" means to us personally: "Through all our trials we have a never-failing Helper. . . . Though now He is hidden from mortal sight, the ear of faith can hear His voice saying, Fear not; I am with you. . . . I have endured your sorrows, experienced your struggles, encountered your temptations. I know your tears; I also have wept. The griefs that lie too deep to be breathed into any human ear, I know. Think not that you are desolate and forsaken. Though your pain touch no responsive chord in any heart on earth, look unto Me, and live."*

I can never explain what this truth has meant to me over the years. When my husband first heard and understood it, he told the "angel" friend who shared it, "I will be eternally grateful for what you shared with me today."

May the words of that quote comfort you in your time of need, as they comforted me.

Sharon M. Pergerson

---

* Ellen G. White, *The Desire of Ages* (Oakland, CA: Pacific Press®, 1898), 483.

Never Alone

PART 2

Fear thou not; for I am with thee: be not dismayed;
for I am thy God: I will strengthen thee; yea, I will help thee;
yea, I will uphold thee with the right hand of my righteousness.
—Isaiah 41:10, KJV

For many Christians, life has been innocent and safe, and we thank God for those times. Yet we understand that things can happen in this life that are so deeply painful that all we can do is sit at the bottom of a dark closet in complete silence. No one else can go "there" with us and understand the way we feel. As if those moments of anguish were not enough, life often punches us with additional trauma that further agitates the deep pain in the original, unhealed wound.

Alone in our dark corner, we cry out in desperation, "Does God even care or notice our suffering? Does He know what *this* pain feels like?" The answer is yes! He knows and cares—and so much more. He says in His Word that He never leaves us nor forsakes us (Hebrews 13:5). He is always with us (Matthew 28:20). Furthermore, He says what is done to us is done to Him (Matthew 25:40). In all our afflictions, He, too, is afflicted (Isaiah 63:9). "God with us" is His official declaration of permanent union with each of us personally and forever. Wow!

So we silently sit, as it were, at the bottom of a dark closet, astounded at what's happening in our personal lives, shattered communities, divided nation, turbulent world, and bewildered church, yet we know that we are not alone. Our Creator, our Savior, our never-failing Helper is with us—suffering with us. He comes so close that He feels our troubles and gathers our tears unto Himself (Psalm 56:8). He will have mercy on us. What is the ultimate mercy of God? That one day He will avenge all wrongs and make all things new and right. He will take us to the new, safe home He has prepared for all of those who long to live with Him—a home that is gun-free, racism-free, cop-free, criminal-free, violence-free, pain-free, poverty-free, separation-free, virus-free, and death-free. So, until then, let's let Him keep our hearts singing with hope.

Let's allow Him to hold on to us, through every storm thrown against us, and carry us safely to the shores of heaven. There we will gratefully sing the song of "Moses the servant of God, and the song of the Lamb, saying, Great and marvellous are thy works, Lord God Almighty; just and true are thy ways, thou King of saints" (Revelation 15:3, KJV).

Sharon M. Pergerson

Going Home

For he satisfieth the longing soul,
and filleth the hungry soul with goodness.
—Psalm 107:9, KJV

I grabbed my red sweater and went back upstairs to look for Mother and Daddy in the church foyer. I didn't see them or my little brother, Henry, anywhere. I squeezed past the people waiting to speak with the pastor so that I could check outside.

I looked all around. The car wasn't there—Mother and Daddy were gone! I clutched my sweater and hurried back inside. The sanctuary door was closed, but I pushed it open far enough to peek in. I saw Henry with the Andersons! I ran over to him. Mrs. Anderson explained, "Jeanie, your mother needed to go to the hospital. You and Henry will stay with us."

They showed us around their place, then prepared supper. While washing up, I quickly blinked back tears before anyone noticed. It was different here—a refrigerator and running water and the roof didn't leak—but it wasn't my home. Although the Andersons were kind and their two teenage children tried to cheer us, I remained sad. I didn't want to play or go for walks. I didn't want to eat. I just wanted to go home.

One day Mrs. Anderson beckoned to me, "Your dad is on the phone; come talk to him." Since I hadn't talked on a phone before, I hesitated. After Daddy said he'd come for us soon, I heard nothing else.

Finally, one evening Mrs. Anderson called, "Your dad is here!"

Mother was still in the hospital, but Daddy took time off work to stay home with us for a couple of days. Walking out to the car, Daddy reminded us to be careful of the broken springs poking through the car's seat. Along the way, wind whistling through a window lulled me to sleep. When the car stopped, I woke to see the setting sun gleaming like gold on the windows.

Glad to be home, we stood by the potbelly stove to get warm. The bubbly, plopping sounds coming from the kitchen tickled our tummies. Soon Daddy served steamy oatmeal with raisins. He pressed slices of bread onto the side of the stove to make toast. I was home at last!

Soon Jesus will come to take His children home where a warm welcome awaits: "Thou wilt shew me the path of life: in thy presence is fullness of joy; at thy right hand there are pleasures for evermore" (Psalm 16:11, KJV). Home, heavenly home!

Jeanne B. Woolsey

Before I Called, He Answered!

"Before they call I will answer;
while they are still speaking I will hear."
—Isaiah 65:24, NIV

I know it is true that God sends angels to protect us! One Monday my husband was driving me to work on the other side of the island. To get there, you have to go over a mountain via a couple of tunnels, and then there is a hairpin turn near the bottom.

On this day, traffic was particularly light. The road was almost eerily empty. And then it happened. While trying to negotiate the hairpin curve, a car on the other side of the road flipped over the divider! We couldn't believe what we were seeing! Normally, there would have been several cars where this car landed, and there could have been more accidents as cars swerved while trying to avoid the overturned car and each other. If we had arrived at that point just a few seconds earlier that morning, we could have been hit by that car. But praise God, it was a one-car accident, and the driver was able to get out of his car unharmed.

The following Wednesday my husband was driving to his evening class on the freeway near our house. Again, he saw a car flip over the divider just a little ahead of him! Again, only one car was involved, and the driver seemed unharmed. The next week I was taking my usual morning walk around the neighborhood. As I was crossing the street in the designated crosswalk at the traffic light (when I had the walk signal), a speeding van nearly hit me. I had to jump back quickly to avoid being hit. It felt as though angels had lifted me and pulled me back.

A day or two after that, my husband and I went to a grocery store near our house. The traffic light was red, so we had to wait for it to change. When it did, my husband started to turn. At the same time, we heard a very loud engine. Just as my husband managed to put our car in reverse to back up a little, a speeding vehicle blew past us! When we got to the grocery store, we just sat in the car for a few minutes, praying and thanking God that we had not been hit.

In all these experiences, things had happened so quickly that I wasn't able to pray for protection, but God granted it anyway. He is always watching over us! Praise God!

Julie Bocock-Bliss

The Audacity of God

"For My thoughts are not your thoughts,
Nor are your ways My ways," says the Lord.
"For as the heavens are higher than the earth,
So are My ways higher than your ways,
And My thoughts than your thoughts."
—Isaiah 55:8, 9, NKJV

After my brother Ron passed away, I found one of his file folders filled with scraps of paper, each containing hastily scribbled notes. Excitedly, I looked through the file. He'd always been a man with a hundred thoughts boiling around in his brain at once, sparked by something he'd read, a sermon he'd heard, or a conversation with a friend. And here was a treasure trove of them, waiting to be explored further. It was as if we were once again enjoying another thought-provoking conversation! One oblong piece of paper especially caught my eye: "Audacity: a willingness to take bold risks in [an] unexpected way." Below are his thoughts:

- Pharaoh said, "Throw all boy babies into the Nile River." So God put baby Moses into the Nile and arranged for Pharaoh's daughter to train him for God's cause (Exodus 2).
- The Red Sea in front, Pharaoh's army behind, Israel entrapped in the middle, and God says, "Stretch out your rod, Moses!" (Exodus 14).
- Locating Israel on the crossroad of the world, a chosen/favored nation; to bring blessing to all humankind (Deuteronomy 7:6; 26:16–19*).
- Sending a choir out to do battle (2 Chronicles 20).
- Then the most audacious, grace-filled plan of all. God would send Jesus as a babe; to be born of a virgin and placed in a manger; shepherds were the first witnesses of His advent (considered to be unreliable witnesses in their courts; legally barred from testifying) (Luke 2).

I can't wait till we get to heaven; Ron will probably spend the first hundred years getting all these stories firsthand!

Jeannette Busby Johnson

---

* See also Ellen G. White, *Prophets and Kings* (Mountain View, CA: Pacific Press®, 1917), 15–22.

Editor of Our Stories

"And if it seems evil to you to serve the LORD,
choose for yourselves this day whom you will serve."
—Joshua 24:15, NKJV

In Genesis 2:17, it is clear what God's command was to our first parents: "You must not eat from the tree of the knowledge of good and evil" (NIV). We are all familiar with this story. Eve and Adam did eat from the tree—the very tree they were told not to. Although God had commanded them otherwise, He did not thwart their poor choice. Thus, the story of sin unfolds.

It is also clear that diverging from God's will only causes heartache and pain. But He does not rob us of our God-given gift of free choice. Yet, like everything else in our world, the perfect gift of choice was corrupted by sin. We turned our ways from God, indulging in ruthless and abominable acts. If only we had followed His counsel from the very beginning!

Even today, God allows us to choose. He gives us the pen and paper to write our own individual stories. He gives us the title of author. From my own experience in writing, I know how convoluted a story can get. This is the same with our life stories. Our lives get complicated and confusing. As we try to figure things out, it's easy to fall into anxiety and worry as we experience pain and perplexity. I am so thankful that God gives us a promise. He does not ask us to write our stories alone. Instead, He taps softly on our hearts, asking to come in. If we accept this request, God enjoys the title of Editor.

Suddenly, our unruly lives become an organized outline. This doesn't mean our lives become sinless. We are still given the gift to choose. It is then, however, that the Editor's powerful glory is manifested. Through the Cross, our mistakes are righted. Through His blood, our sin is wiped clean, and we can have victory in Him.

Let God be the Editor of the story that He gives you the freedom to author.

Madeleine E. Miyashiro

Secret

O taste and see that the LORD is good:
blessed is the man that trusteth in him.
—Psalm 34:8, KJV

We all have secrets that we hide from the public. A secret might be a sin we are battling with, or it might be a life plan—anything (negative or positive) that matters a lot to us but that we choose not to let anyone else know. Some of us have met with disappointment after close friends revealed our secrets to the public.

I have found Jesus, though unseen by me, to be my best Secret Keeper. I can tell Him everything, and I know He will find solutions quietly. There is no secret that is unreasonable to Him. He handles any secret well and helps me out. Let me share one secret that Christ kept quiet and handled well for me.

I found out that I was pregnant after I had laid plans for the upcoming quinquennial Women's Ministries congress for an area that spanned several African countries.

After my prenatal consultations, I learned my due date would be in July—around the time of the congress, slated for July 24, though I needed to be on site by July 20. *God*, I cried, *Help me deliver my baby at least two weeks before the congress so that I can have the strength to lead out!* Yet, as the time drew closer, it seemed the baby would come later than I had hoped. *Lord*, I prayed secretly, *even if it takes a Cesarean-section delivery for the birth to be two weeks before the congress, that would be fine with me.* That secret prayer was between Jesus, whom I trusted, and me. I could never share it with anyone else, not even my husband (who had lost his only sister during a Cesarean delivery some years before).

On July 5, I went to the hospital with my husband for the final prenatal visit. The doctor shared that the ultrasound had revealed the umbilical cord was wrapped around the baby's neck. This necessitated an immediate Cesarean-section delivery if the baby was to be saved. I was shocked at the way God was handling our secret. Immediately, I agreed to have the procedure and encouraged my husband, who was already crying. To God be the glory, baby Eleazar—a handsome, bouncing baby boy—arrived in good health. Guess what! Two weeks later, I was in Ghana, conducting a women's congress. What a Secret Keeper and Miracle Worker is Jesus!

You can trust your secrets to Jesus, who cares for you. Your secret sins He will help you overcome. And the desires of your heart He will lovingly shape into what is best for you.

Omobonike Adeola Sessou

The Extravagance of God

He counts the number of the stars;
He calls them all by name.
—Psalm 147:4, NKJV

Walking through a beautiful garden one afternoon, I couldn't help but wonder how the Lord must have taken delight in creating such a diverse assortment of plants. I thought about the Garden of Eden and how spectacular it must have been.

When God made the world, He could have given us just one kind of flower, perhaps a lovely rose, and we would have been delighted with it. But He created hundreds of different kinds of flowers. The mixture of shapes and sizes is amazing, not to mention the variety of gorgeous colors. And He infused them with delightful, distinctive fragrances.

If God put only one lovely star in the sky, we'd be out there often, watching it with wonder. We'd marvel at the way it shines and moves across the heavens. Instead, He gave us a sky full of beautiful, twinkling stars on a canvas of midnight blue.

When the Lord put Adam and Eve in the Garden of Eden, He might have been happy having only two earthlings. But the One who made thousands of fantastic flowers and untold numbers of shining stars wanted more than just two people. That's why we're here.

Because God loves us so much, He gave us a priceless gift—the gift of love—so we could appreciate the world that He created and the things He provided for our health and happiness. He wanted us to love and appreciate each other and, of course, appreciate the Lord Himself, knowing that He first loved us. Through the year's changing seasons, the beauties of nature are ever-present reminders of God's love for us. Whether the eye-pleasing beauty and fragrance of a crimson rose, the soothing sounds of a babbling brook, a whip-poor-will's song, or a cooling breeze, brushing gently across one's face on a warm day—all are reminders that the Lord of Creation is also the Savior at Calvary. All these testify of His great love for us.

Marcia Mollenkopf

Hearing God's Voice

"Today, if you hear his voice, do not harden your hearts."
—Hebrews 3:15, NIV

Sometimes I am envious when I hear people testify about receiving clear guidance from God about the things going on in their lives. I longed for that when I was trying to decide whether I should retire from the job I had held for thirty-three years. I even took a day from work to go for a hike and confer with God about what I should do. Even so, I never felt that I had a moment when God's will or answer was obvious. I had to do it the old-fashioned way: weigh the options, consider the consequences, and pray continuously.

I want Samuel's experience when he heard God calling him during the night (1 Samuel 3). I have been known to ask God not to give me the "still, small voice" but to send me a plane with a banner behind it, saying, "Jean, this is what I want you to do."

As with other times when I feel God does not pay me as much attention as He does others, it occurs to me that God has very vividly come to my aid at times. Many of those times have been in scenarios that are inconsequential in the grand scheme of life.

Specifically, I remember being woken up on a Friday night with a throbbing toothache. Of course, these things always happen at a time when you cannot resolve them immediately. Not only was it the middle of the night, but I would also not be able to call the dentist until Monday. I got up and took a painkiller, but the ache was still there an hour later.

I kept praying, asking God to take away the pain so I could sleep. While lying there, I distinctly heard a voice in my head say, "Go gargle some Listerine." What? Gargle mouthwash? Yet I was in pain, and I needed it to stop, so I got up and gargled Listerine. The pain went away; I fell asleep. I did not know that Listerine could stop toothaches. Only God could have told me to use Listerine. I have since learned that antiseptic mouthwash, such as Listerine, temporarily deadens the nerves in the tooth to stop the pain.

Frequently, we are confronted with reasons to doubt God. Life is difficult at times. Clear, distinct guidance from God would be great. But how much stronger do we become when we have to take the time to seek answers through Bible study, prayer, and meditation.

Jean Arthur

This World Is Not My Home

But as it is written:
"Eye has not seen, nor ear heard,
Nor have entered into the heart of man
The things which God has prepared for those who love Him."
—1 Corinthians 2:9, NKJV

During my childhood, my family moved frequently. My mother was a single mom raising three children and always trying to improve our lot in life. I became somewhat accustomed to our frequent moves, but I didn't like them! I cried when leaving my best friend and moving from Colorado to Arkansas when I was eight years old. Thankfully, I had cousins in Arkansas, and we lived close to each other for eight years, although we moved many times within our community.

When I turned sixteen, my brother asked us to come to live with him and his wife for two years. I resisted that arrangement, but off we went—and it turned out to be a great blessing. After finishing my high school years, I returned to the Southwest for college. I was reunited with a number of my old friends there and made many new friends as well.

I must have become more adventurous as I matured because I moved back to Colorado after college, staying for two years before returning to the Southwest. And what did I do once I got there? I kept moving! Eventually, I found my wonderful husband and had our lovely daughter.

I didn't understand this meandering path for many years, but now I can see God's leading. My many homes have made me more adaptable in many ways, and I have wonderful friends all over the country. I picked up new skills as we traveled, and we have found a beautiful long-time home in the Oklahoma City area. I go to a great church, where my talents are needed and where I am loved and included. Yet I know that I have one more move to make—to my eternal heavenly home with God. Maybe He has allowed this discomfort here on Earth so that I will long even more for an eternity with Him!

Robin Widmayer Sagel

Choices

Let us choose to us judgment:
let us know among ourselves what is good.
—Job 34:4, KJV

When I was a child growing up in Jamaica, we lived on a hill. Our driveway was very steep. At times, parked cars needed a stone behind the wheels to keep them from rolling down the hill! We had a neighbor who lived two doors down and across the street, and he often rode his bicycle. One day he came to our house to ask us to ride with him. (I had just learned how to ride a bicycle with training wheels.) My younger siblings, Kryshna, Noel, Apryll, and Joel, were with me at the entrance to our garage when he rode up to visit. We were all having fun.

Soon our neighbor asked me to race him down the driveway. Of course, I said, "No!" because it was dangerous. The driveway was so steep. But he kept asking and daring me to race him. Oh, the pressure! At first, my siblings had mixed feelings but soon were encouraging me to race him so I could win. My resistance eventually broke down.

I finally agreed to the race, and we took off. I was actually standing on my training wheels as I headed down the driveway. Out of the corner of my eye, I saw him take the corner and ride onto the street. But I shot straight across the street, hit the sidewalk, and flipped into a pile of sand. Ouch!

I got up and realized I had cuts on my elbows, knees, and hips—a very painful experience, to be sure. Picking up my bicycle, I headed back up the driveway to our house, crying the whole way. I really regretted my decision to race.

When I got inside our house, I found Daddy in the dining room. He had been looking through the window the whole time and seen the entire thing transpire. He had hoped I would make the right choice—which I did not do. I got a good spanking on top of my cuts and bruises for the wrong decision I had made, especially since I had shot across the street without even looking to see whether any cars were coming. I shed many tears that night but was glad it hadn't been worse: I could have been hit by a car. I am thankful the Lord protected me despite the bad decision I made. I've noticed He often has a way of doing that.

Noella (Jumpp) Baird

God's Care

You will not fear the terror of night . . .
nor the plague that destroys at midday.
—Psalm 91:5, 6, NIV

As I write this, the world is in the midst of the COVID-19 pandemic (I live in the United States of America). I suspect most of us need no explanation since many of us were homebound, at least temporarily, for health reasons and were in the same situation. This disease has closed shopping malls, limited the availability of certain items in grocery stores, closed schools, and canceled sporting events. We are told that the only way to "flatten the curve" (of escalating coronavirus cases) is to stay home. Social distancing means just that—stay away from other people. One Friday evening, soon after the pandemic hit, our pastor decided to host a livestream "hymn fest." My husband and I had gone to our family room to watch the livestream broadcast on TV. While waiting for the hymn fest to begin, my husband ran upstairs to get something and discovered our street was filled with fire trucks and police cars.

We soon learned our next-door neighbor had thrown out some charcoal briquettes that he thought had cooled sufficiently. But they were hot enough to ignite the grass, then the fence connecting our two houses, and finally his house. Someone passing by saw the fire, called 911, and alerted the family. The fire department arrived and extinguished the fire when it was only a few feet from our house. We were so thankful for the firefighters on duty during this pandemic when so many people were not working. And how thankful we were for Jesus' care and protection over our home, for the fire could have traveled either direction along the fence!

Not only is God protective and caring, but we decided He also has a sense of humor. When we finally were able to rejoin the hymn fest, the text on the screen for the song they were singing declared, "It only takes a spark to get a fire burning." We had to agree and say, "How appropriate!" Whether it is a fire burning between two houses or a worldwide pandemic, God sees and cares. As David said in Psalm 57:1, "I will take refuge in the shadow of your wings until the disaster has passed" (NIV).

That is my prayer too.

Sharon Oster

The Loving Heart of Our Wonderful God

And so we know and rely on the love God has for us.
God is love. Whoever lives in love lives in God, and God in them.
—1 John 4:16, NIV

I've been learning over the years to discern God's voice. I know from Scripture that God speaks to His servants in many ways—dreams, visions, audible voice, and the prompting of the Holy Spirit. Joel 2:28 tells us so. And who can forget God's "gentle whisper" to Elijah in 1 Kings 19:12 (NIV)?

Over the years, people have repeatedly said to me, "Thank you for obeying the Holy Spirit." It might have been that I called them or sent some item that they desperately needed.

One particular morning was no different. After my devotions, I had a strong urge to call my younger brother. The call itself was less than a minute long.

"Good morning," I said simply. "I have a message for you. A woman named Jasmine asked me to tell you that she loves you." So why did I deliver my own message in the third person? I did so because that's my way of gift wrapping my love. My brother accepted the gift with a touching catch in his voice. Having delivered the gift, I said goodbye and hung up the phone.

About an hour later, he called back. "I want to thank you for being obedient to the Holy Spirit," he said. My brother has been fighting cancer while still working every day and trying to fight off the fear of either himself or his wife contracting the COVID-19 virus during the pandemic. "I was in very low spirits when I received your call," he informed me.

As I listened to my brother, tears came into my eyes. I, in turn, thanked him for sharing. Feedback is important in God's work because it strengthens the faith of the servant who delivers the message.

My tears were also tears of joy. It's wonderful to know that God loves and demonstrates His love for us, even in such small ways. I contemplated 1 John 4:12: "No one has ever seen God; but if we love one another, God lives in us and his love is made complete in us" (NIV).

These words are so true. Nodding my head, I reminded myself that our Father is the best. I truly thank God for His abundant love and compassion.

Jasmine E. Grant

Where Are My Glasses?

"And when she has found it, she calls her friends and neighbors together saying,
'Rejoice with me, for I have found the piece which I lost!' Likewise, I say to you,
there is joy in the presence of the angels of God over one sinner who repents."
—Luke 15:9, 10, NKJV

I was in Port St. Lucie, Florida, and my scheduled departure for home was February 6, 2020. Since I was flying out of Fort Lauderdale to Edmonton, Canada, with a layover in Montreal, I decided to stay overnight with my cousin in West Palm Beach. The following day I packed my belongings and rechecked the room before heading to the airport.

When I travel, I usually have one pair of glasses in my purse, which I tuck into my backpack. I keep the other pair in the pouch that I wear for easy access.

The flight was late, so I missed my connection. A flight attendant met me at the gate with hotel and food vouchers. Then she helped me collect my bag and took me to the hotel shuttle.

I took the return shuttle to the airport at 6:00 A.M. after checking the hotel room to ensure I had not left anything behind. I had time to spare, so I ate breakfast and read my daily devotions. I finally returned home safely, albeit a day later than originally planned.

At home, I unpacked my suitcase and backpack and emptied my travel purse. *Wait! Where is my new pair of glasses?* I retrieved the suitcase and backpack and checked all the pockets. Nothing! I called my cousins to see whether I had left my eyeglasses in the room, but they were not there. I knew I had not used them in Montreal, so where could they be? I began to pray frantically because I need those particular glasses.

On Sunday, I told my family that I could not find my glasses. I racked my brain, which only gave me a headache.

Then I had a thought: *"Be still and know that I am God."* I focused on other things and went to bed.

Early on Monday morning, I heard a voice saying, *Check your sunglasses case.* I sat up, jumped out of bed, and grabbed the case from the dresser. There were the missing glasses!

Is there anything too hard for God? He will seek and find you too. Hallelujah!

Sharon Long

Swept About but Not Lost

*Are not two sparrows sold for a farthing? and one of them shall not fall on the ground
without your Father. . . . Fear ye not therefore, ye are of more value than many sparrows.*
—Matthew 10:29, 31, KJV

It had been a trying morning with torrential rains and much unexpected stress at work. After leaving early to take care of personal matters, I decided to take advantage of a nice walk, since the morning rain had left a freshness in the air. With each step, I reviewed the events of the day. I needed this walk to process my thoughts.

As I walked up a hill, stepping over large branches that had blown down earlier, crossed the street, and stepped onto the sidewalk, I noticed a small squirrel lying on the ground. I thought it devoid of life until I heard whimpering. He was wet, barely hanging on to the little bit of life left in him. He must have fallen out of the tall tree in the morning storm. When I knelt down, our eyes met, though his were barely open. I knew how he felt; like him, I felt nearly lifeless, blown about by life's winds that morning.

I gently picked him up and cradled him inside my coat. I talked with him as "we" walked home. Once home, I cradled him anew in a warm, soft washcloth and laid him in a box under the heat of a small table lamp. Later that evening, I offered him some water with an eyedropper and some pieces of a nut. He just slept. I stayed up through the night with him, swaddling him in the washcloth and laying him against my chest so he could feel my heartbeat. I also wanted him to have a sense of peace. He slept like a baby, and then I dozed off to sleep myself.

The next morning the little squirrel appeared to be a bit more alert and accepted some food and water that I offered. I took him to my local animal rescue center for care. I knew he would be happy there. Rehabilitated, he would enjoy scurrying up the trees with other furry and feathered creatures.

God is good. That day I was cold, wet, windswept, and drained of life from my morning experience. He brought me face-to-face with myself in the form of a nearly lifeless creature lying on the sidewalk. God showed me how much He is aware of my trials and how He will sit with me all night if need be—and let healing take place.

Victoria M. Shewbrooks

Living in Limbo

"What no eye has seen,
what no ear has heard,
and what no human mind has conceived"—
the things God has prepared for those who love him.
—1 Corinthians 2:9, NIV

Life is at a halt due to COVID-19 lockdown regulations. It has been like taking a train through a long tunnel, hoping that when it comes out on the other side, everything will be just fine. The problem is, waiting for the train to be in the light again is taking much longer than we expected. In the meantime, we live in limbo, waiting for a miracle to dispel the nightmare that so many people are currently experiencing. Waiting is not something we like to do, but we usually know what we are waiting for. Now we are waiting for the end of something that is totally incalculable.

As believers, we have been waiting for a long time for the glorious advent of our Lord as King of kings and Lord of lords and our new home with Him. Yet we don't really know what heaven will be like. In Bavaria, many people imagine heaven as a small cloud on which a sweet little cherub with bare feet, dressed in a white nightgown, plays the harp all day long. But who wants to sit on a cloud all day, playing the harp? After all, life on that little cloud is almost like waiting for something to happen, and nothing ever does.

How long will we have to wait for our train to get through the dark tunnel of this world's problems? It really doesn't matter, as long as we are aboard this train on the way to our heavenly home. The best thing about heaven is that Jesus will be there. He will embrace us—no more social distancing!

During this pandemic, some folks are just waiting for time to run out, living from meal to meal, morning to evening, and through each long night; others are eagerly waiting to see how their Savior works out His plan.

What gives meaning to your day?

Don't be discouraged. As the apostle Paul said, "I will come back if it is God's will" (Acts 18:21, NIV). We will make plans with family and friends again if God wills. So don't give up! As long as we wait patiently for and with the Lord, this time will pass. And in the long run, seeing our Savior's face and feeling His arms around us are well worth waiting for.

Hannele Ottschofski

Back and Forth

Each of you should use whatever gift you have received to serve others,
as faithful stewards of God's grace in its various forms. . . .
So that in all things God may be praised through Jesus Christ.
—1 Peter 4:10, 11, NIV

I swim every weekday morning. Although it's a good way to keep moving—especially when the ground is icy and the wind cold—I find that swimming laps is boring. Back and forth. It's a slog. Back and forth.

I used to count laps to make sure I'd complete my daily goal, but often I'd forget whether I was on lap twenty-five or twenty-nine. Now I just swim for a certain length of time. Back and forth. Back and forth. Although my newer system is less frustrating, it doesn't make the laps more fun.

One bleak January morning when the snow was swirling, I had to struggle to convince myself to leave my flannel sheets and go to the pool. "Sure, it's cold outside. Sure, swimming laps is boring. Just *do* it!"

I grabbed my swim bag, pushed my feet into boots, and trudged to the car. Inside the gym, I shed my coat and thought about going home. "No, I'm going to do this," I vowed. "Back and forth. It's boring. But that won't stop me. Back and forth."

I pulled on my swim goggles and stepped into the water. *Brr!* It was colder than usual. I'd have to swim hard to stay warm.

"Back and forth. Back and forth," I said grimly as I pushed off to fulfill my morning task.

Arriving at the far end of the pool, I saw a yellow plastic duck perched at eye level on the edge of the pool, grinning at me.

Who left it there? I wondered. I returned the grin, made my turn, and swam back. My frustration vanished.

Back. Grin. And forth.

I swam with joy because that silly duck greeted me each time I completed a lap—each time I was victorious over my boredom.

On my last lap, I began to wonder whether I could be like that duck. Could I be there for others, cheering them on and offering my support? Changing their lives?

Denise Dick Herr

Wilderness

"He found him in a desert land
And in the wasteland, a howling wilderness;
He encircled him, He instructed him,
He kept him as the apple of His eye."
—Deuteronomy 32:10, NKJV

Wilderness places are dry and uninviting. In fact, wildernesses are places that we all try to avoid. Yet, in my experience, God was waiting to show His love in my wilderness of despair. I was spiritually dry, and for so long, I had fought feelings of aloneness as I lived in a remote area, ministering to other people's needs. One day I read about a missionary searching for a deep connection with God. Her friends asked her whether she had ever heard God's voice or asked God for something "with her name on it." In my desperation, I prayed, "God, give me something—for me personally—with my name on it." I didn't expect anything would happen right away. But I was desperate.

One morning I was at my church, preparing for a children's class, when something unusual happened. Amid my hurried preparations, a church member stepped in with an envelope with my name on its blank front. I tore it open hurriedly, eager to get back to work, uninterrupted. Just then, a check for one thousand dollars slipped out. I pushed it back into the card in the envelope, certain I had not seen correctly. My heart raced as I read the words on the card—words of encouragement with Bible verses that told me I was special to God and I was cared for. The check was no mistake, and neither were the words that told me Someone saw what I was doing and the ministry I was trying to do for His glory. As I looked at my name written on the envelope, I knew that God had heard my cry for a revelation of Himself.

Each of us knows in a superficial way that God cares. But claiming His compassion and grace in our own lives may seem radical. We know God is there for us, but we often choose other sources of stability. But I learned that anyone who comes to God will find a fresh revelation of His grace. Sometimes God takes us through the wilderness to show us who we are without the luxuries of life, the friends, and the things we hold dear. When we take our eyes off our troubles and look up, we find who we are when the Almighty is on our side. We see that what matters most is who travels through our wildernesses with us—the One who knows our name.

Anne Crosby

August 15

Loved by Grace

For by grace you have been saved
through faith . . . ; it is the gift of God.
—Ephesians 2:8, NKJV

We had just bought some run-down acreage. I was eager to help my husband improve the property but didn't have a lot of physical strength. When I saw the new riding lawn mower, I quickly announced I would take over the mowing. My husband looked dubious and reminded me not to get into the mud next to the pond. I proudly made a few circles and thought, *This is easy. Just one more clump of long grass near the pond.* In an instant, I was sucked into the mud. The mower stopped right before landing in the pond. My husband and his brother had to get the tractor to pull me out of the muck. My brother-in-law made a few unintelligible comments in his native Newari, but my husband said not a word.

My next adventure involved mowing the horse pasture. My husband explained the intricacies of the brush cutter on the back of the tractor and reminded me to stay away from the fence. The tractor still had the loader attached. Long prongs were attached to the front. It only took two rounds before I had hooked the fence with one of the prongs. Damage included one broken corner post and two broken wires. My husband said not a word. Ah! I would make it up to him. In town one day, I washed his beloved 1990 Toyota and filled it with gas. As I put my hand on the ignition, I had a strong inclination not to turn the key. I looked down and realized I had just filled his priceless old relic with unleaded gas instead of diesel! A ride on a tow truck and US$300 later, the gas tank was clean and full of diesel. My husband said not a word.

The next summer I backed our new-to-us car out of our new-to-us garage. It required a ninety-degree turn to head down the drive. Oh, well, the car has a backup signal if you get too close to something, right? True, but that doesn't necessarily warn you if you are hitting something at an angle. The warning buzz came just as I felt the car crash against a column on the porch. For a moment, I knew what Samson felt like while waiting for the roof to collapse. It didn't, and my husband ordered a new taillight.

My husband has my total love and gratitude for putting up with my messes for thirty-seven years. Our heavenly Father is like that. He watches us make mistakes again and again but still loves and redeems us. That is what grace is all about!

Sherry Taujale Shrestha

234

Isolation

"Fear not, for I am with you;
Be not dismayed, for I am your God.
I will strengthen you,
Yes, I will help you,
I will uphold you with My righteous right hand."
—Isaiah 41:10, NKJV

Only now, in my elderly years, do I realize how much I, as a child, relied on my father for faith and protection. He was a pastor in Mauritius, where I was born and raised. I had a peaceful, happy life in a warm, sunny country. But when cyclones beat the island, I was scared even with my dad around. Once we listened to a local radio broadcast until the last words—"Bonne chance! [Good luck!]"—were spoken. Then the transmission went off the air. We were isolated, alone in the dark, to fight against the vicious elements of destruction. Of our four-bedroom house, one bedroom remained intact, and in it, seven kids huddled on the double bed, waiting for the cyclone to leave.

Our house had front and back verandas. On each side of the house was a gate leading to a walled path toward the back of the house. Once, strong winds destroyed our front veranda, shattering all its windows. One side of the house started to bow in as if the wall were about to crush it. My dad lifted his arms in the air and called on God to stop the wall from falling on our wooden house. It stopped. We were safe—isolated but safe in God's care.

As I write this in March 2020, COVID-19 is a plague on this earth. People are dying while world leaders are trying their best to stop this virus from spreading. But people continue to die. People are told to isolate themselves, and in some places, soldiers are ready to enforce the law. Children are well aware of the situation because they can't attend school, socialize with friends, or go to playgrounds. Most businesses are closed. Isolate! Isolate! Yesterday's local news depicted schoolchildren crying because they'd had no time to say goodbye to all their friends before going into isolation. All this is a reminder of our need to connect with Jesus and draw closer to Him as we isolate from evil and repent of our sins. He doesn't mind everybody drawing close to Him. The more, the happier, for all of us—and for Jesus. He promises to care for us. Let's believe in Him and trust Him more than anybody or anything. He is in control and is our only safety!

Monique Lombart De Oliveira

My Help

My help cometh from the LORD.
—Psalm 121:2, KJV

I have always been an emotional person. I cry at movies and commercials—anything that tugs at my heart—as well as situations and circumstances that I cannot control. In fact, when I testify at church, the ushers know to pass me the box of tissues. But over the years, I have been crying less. I am learning to trust God and rejoice more.

God has blessed me with my own company—a training facility for adults with intellectual and developmental disabilities. I enjoy what I do. When the COVID-19 pandemic hit, however, the state of New Jersey mandated the closing of all nonessential businesses. At first, I was not allowed to work, nor were my employees. My first thought was to cry, but I couldn't. The tears just wouldn't come. I said, "OK, God, what's my next assignment? Because if You allowed this to happen, surely You have something else You want me to do." I shocked myself at this verbal declaration. After all, I knew that everything would be lost if I could not work: no work equals no income. Our facility being closed would cause hardship for the employees and the parents of those we trained by limiting the use of our office building and our new van. These concerns flooded my mind, but God gave me such peace I could not cry, even if I wanted to.

In my fifty-plus years of living, I have realized God is in control of all things. The Bible tells us that "all things work together for good to those who love God" (Romans 8:28, NKJV). The Bible is filled with many of God's loving promises that we can trust. We can take Him at His word. God's love for us amazes me! He is concerned about whatever concerns us. And He did indeed bless my business, for the state allowed us to reopen as long as we didn't meet in large groups. The agency could continue to function if we worked with our clients one-on-one. With these allowances, I was able to keep some staff and even hire two more employees!

COVID-19 has tested the faith of us all at some point, but there is peace in knowing that God's got us, and He is going to provide. I thank God for the peace He has given me. Isaiah 26:3 promises, "Thou wilt keep him in perfect peace, whose mind is stayed on thee" (KJV). Mighty Jehovah God has blessed me to still be able to work and not miss a paycheck. To Him be all the glory! God has been a blessing throughout this whole pandemic, His wonders to perform.

Avis Floyd Jackson

"Be Anxious for Nothing"

Be anxious for nothing, but in everything by prayer and supplication, with thanksgiving, let your requests be made known to God; and the peace of God, which surpasses all understanding, will guard your hearts and minds through Christ Jesus.
—Philippians 4:6, 7, NKJV

When I have faced crises on previous occasions, being free of anxiety was definitely not on my list of things to accomplish that day! If someone told me that I should not be anxious, I would quickly say with just a hint of frustration, "That's impossible!" When God says that we should "be anxious for nothing," is He just giving us a helpful suggestion, or is it actually a command? I reflected that in addition to the "be anxious for nothing" command, God has given us other commands that He will enable us to follow. For example, we have the Ten Commandments, and not one of them is impossible to obey (at least some of the time). After all, what kind of parent would tell a little child to do something that was impossible for the child to accomplish?

One day in my Bible study time, I came across a very encouraging text from the words of Jesus: "The things which are impossible with men are possible with God" (Luke 18:27, NKJV). The important word in this text is *with*. The word *with* generally means to have an association or connection with someone or something. If we only have an association or connection with other human beings, when someone suggests that we not worry or be anxious, it would be quite easy to say, "That's impossible!" Yet if we are daily walking and talking *with* God, nothing that He asks us to do will be impossible.

After the apostle Paul exhorted us not to be anxious about anything (Philippians 4:6), he gives us this reassurance: "And the peace of God, which surpasses all understanding, will guard your hearts and minds through Christ Jesus" (verse 7, NKJV). How encouraging that the peace of God will watch over and defend our hearts and minds! This same peace will also preserve and protect our hearts and minds in a relationship of rest and quietude in Christ Jesus. When we are greatly upset about something, there is little possibility of keeping our hearts and minds from anxiety—without God. Only His peace can do that in us. I want to be able to say, "God, by Your grace, I choose not to be anxious about this situation. Your Word says that if I make that choice, then You will keep my heart and mind at peace."

Terry Wilson Robinson

Showers of Blessing

Who giveth rain upon the earth,
and sendeth waters upon the fields.
—Job 5:10, KJV

This past year I observed a tree within one block of my house during my daily walks. Its bare silhouette stood out against the backdrop of verdant trees. No leaves appeared on its branches in any season. I kept thinking, *That tree is dead. Why doesn't the owner cut it down?*

Finally, one autumn day, some loggers appeared with heavy equipment on a truck and started cutting down the tree. The following day they returned and ground the stump before covering the area with fresh soil. When the landscaper arrived later that day, he sprinkled some seeds on the area from which the tree had been removed.

Since we had not had rain for the previous two weeks, I thought, *Some birds are going to feed on those seeds. They're lying right on top of the soil.* I wondered why the landscaper hadn't sprinkled a thin layer of soil over the seeds to protect them.

Two days afterward, it rained all day. When I took my walk the following day, I could already see tiny green shoots pushing up through the soil. Two days later, rain fell again for the entire day.

The following day, as I walked past that same spot, I spotted grass beginning to cover almost the entire area where the dead tree had been. In that short period—just two days with rain—the seeds had sprouted, and blades of grass almost one inch in length had sprung up. Now there was enough grass to cover the whole patch of soil.

As I pondered the process I had witnessed, I recalled Paul's letter to the Corinthian church. In it, he stated, "I have planted, Apollos watered; but God gave the increase" (1 Corinthians 3:6, KJV).

I pray that we may spread seeds of love, joy, truth, peace, and graciousness every day so that the Holy Spirit can bring "the increase"—springing up blades of trust in the hearts of men and women who will, in turn, bear witness to the marvelous light of God. I pray they will be prompted to ask about the difference they see in our lives, compared with those who don't know Jesus. May we each feel privileged to be coworkers with God in growing His kingdom of grace here on Earth in preparation to enter His kingdom of glory when Jesus Christ returns.

Florence E. Callender

ASK

"Ask and it will be given to you; seek and you will find;
knock and the door will be opened to you."
—Matthew 7:7, NIV

For me, the acronym ASK represents the three promises given in Matthew 7:7. Listed in order, they are ask, seek, and knock.

What encouraging words for us who are living in a world where innumerable needs for help abound! Even more amazing is that even while we are in the process of asking, seeking, and knocking at heaven's door, God is in the process of preparing His responses for what we have requested.

Reading my email one morning, I came across a request for devotional articles. I welcomed the opportunity to contribute an article or two and prepared to write. But after long minutes of sitting before the computer, not one word could I coax from my brain. A couple of days passed. I prayed for ideas, experiences to recall, or something worth writing about and sharing. Nothing. On the morning of the third day, as I prayed, besides my thanksgiving and requests for the day, I reiterated my plea for help with the writing project. Just then, ideas popped into my mind, one after another like fireworks in the sky on a night of celebration. I paused in my prayer to note each one. Then I ended my prayer and immediately listed the ideas on paper before they vanished from my mind. Through this experience, I concluded that the word *persist* is deeply embedded in Matthew 7:7.

Similar experiences have also happened in the past. Some of them had to do with speaking appointments that one gets from time to time when working in a school. Whether the topic had been provided or not, my task was to decide what points to include and how to organize the concepts. As I knelt in prayer to ask for help, the ideas paraded into my mind. At one time, I had considered thoughts such as these to be interruptions to my prayer, but then I recognized them as answers to what I was praying for. So I would linger in that position as long as the ideas kept coming before concluding the prayer.

God is faithful when we persist in asking, seeking, and knocking. He waits to bestow the needed resources, solutions, answers, and opportunities.

Bienvisa Ladion Nebres

It's a Jungle Out There

*Be alert and of sober mind. Your enemy the devil prowls
around like a roaring lion looking for someone to devour.*
—1 Peter 5:8, NIV

It was the punch line of an advertisement, but what caught my attention in the ad was the picture of a lion lurking behind the trees of a thick forest—because lions do not live in forests. They prefer grassy plains, dense scrub, and open woodlands, mainly in parts of sub-Saharan Africa. They move stealthily in their surroundings, and their yellow-gold coats provide camouflage so that these predators go almost undetected by their prey. During our stint as missionaries in East Africa, we enjoyed viewing lion prides from the safety of our vehicle.

Lions or no lions, it's a jungle out there. Listen to the news. Nations continue their search for elusive peace. We are inundated with movies, television shows, and video games that portray scenes of violence, hostility, and crime that desensitize our brains and distance our thoughts from what is pure and honest. Many idolize performers who are barely clothed or whose music speaks of disrespect to other humans. Ellen White wrote, "The desire for excitement and pleasing entertainment is a temptation and a snare to God's people, and especially to the young."*

A jungle provides a dwelling place for many species of wild and dangerous animals. Likewise, this world is like a jungle that harbors various kinds of temptations. Big temptations are like giraffes, towering high above the savanna, obvious and easy to avoid. Yet crouching in the shadows are little temptations, such as the tendency to engage in hurtful words, a hateful spirit, judgmentalism, and gossip; all of these can destroy relationships with others. "Satan is a persevering workman, an artful, deadly foe. . . . He is in every sense of the word a deceiver, a skillful charmer. He has many finely woven nets . . . to entangle the young and unwary."†

It's a jungle out there, all right! But the Lord has promised He will protect us from the snares of the devil. First Corinthians 10:13 says that "God is faithful; he will not let you be tempted beyond what you can bear. But when you are tempted, he will also provide a way out so that you can endure it" (NIV).

Evelyn Porteza Tabingo

---

* Ellen G. White, *Counsels to Parents, Teachers, and Students* (Mountain View, CA: Pacific Press®, 1943), 325.
† White, *Counsels to Parents*, 325.

How's Your Hiding Place?

Your word I have hidden in my heart,
That I might not sin against You.
—Psalm 119:11, NKJV

When I was a kid, I liked to play hide-and-seek, as I'm sure many of you did. The one who is the best at hiding is the one that wins. As I was reading my devotional this morning, I found myself thinking about hiding, specifically about what we hide and our motivation for doing so. The devotional I read highlighted the story of Josiah—one of Judah's good kings who came to the throne when he was eight (2 Kings 22). Hilkiah, the high priest, found the book of the law hidden and forgotten in God's temple. He had it read to the king. Josiah was convicted of his and the nation's sins. He tore his clothes in remorse. When the book of the law was read to the people, they repented of their sins and returned to worshiping God.

I was impressed from the Bible's stories that people hide things for three reasons: First, for protection, as when Moses' mother hid him in river reeds to protect his life, or when David hid God's Word in his heart to protect him from committing sin.

The second reason people conceal something—usually for less than honorable purposes—is so that others won't know or find out. For example, Achan stole and hid the forbidden spoil that the Israelites were not to take when conquering Jericho. He ended up dying for that action (Joshua 7:10–26).

The third reason people hide things is to forget or not be held accountable for something. That brings us back to King Josiah. When the hidden book of the law was found, the Israelites realized they were now accountable. When they eventually rejected God's commands, their "reward" was to be taken into captivity by the Babylonians, where they would learn their lesson the hard way.

So how about you and me? What kind of hide-and-seek are we playing? And why? If you are like me, you have probably hidden at some time in your life for one or more of the reasons listed above. But the good news, dear sisters, is that if you find yourself hiding in the wrong place for the wrong reason, there is still time to change your hiding place. God is ever patient with us, not willing that even one should perish (see 2 Peter 3:9). As David did, let's all strive to hide God's Word in our hearts and keep our hearts hidden in Jesus. *Let us never forget You, Lord.*

Debra Snyder

Rudy

The LORD has heard my supplication;
The LORD will receive my prayer.
—Psalm 6:9, NKJV

When I arrived at Rudy's home for my initial visit as a hospice caregiver, he was sitting slumped over in his wheelchair. His wife, Margaret, welcomed me and introduced me to Rudy. I knelt in front of him and assured him I would do all I could to help him be comfortable. Rudy nodded now and then but said little. I told him I would enjoy helping his wife take care of him.

Days passed. Margaret and I had fun caring for Rudy, doing household chores, and visiting. I learned that Rudy was ninety-eight years old and had gotten his high school diploma at the age of ninety-two! He was a man of many talents and the joy of his six children.

When Rudy died, I attended his service at a local church. After the service, his son, Marv, smiled and came over to me.

The first thing out of his mouth was, "What did you say to Dad?"

The blank look on my face surprised him as I asked, "What do you mean?"

He replied, "You know, when you first met him."

I still had no clue.

Marv continued, "Something you said to Dad made him such a good patient after he'd been difficult for the rest of us." I shook my head, saying I didn't know what he was talking about. Then two of his siblings approached me with the same question. Marv said, "Just don't tell Mom! Let her think you are wonderful in that you could handle Dad when the rest of us had trouble!"

Hospice patients often feel that they are imposing on family members with their care; this may have been the case with Rudy. But the real secret, I believe, was my many prayers for Rudy. God definitely softened his heart, big time, because I certainly don't have that talent!

Marybeth Gessele

Troubles

"I have told you all this so that you will have peace of heart and mind.
Here on earth you will have many trials and sorrows;
but cheer up, for I have overcome the world."
—John 16:33, TLB

Amid the COVID-19 pandemic of 2020, with so many losing so much, I, too, had my own frustrations, especially during one week. Waking up at three o'clock on a Friday morning, I rehearsed all that happened during the week and wondered how I was going to face the day with no solutions to any of the problems that had developed.

A month before this, I had fallen, bruising my lungs, and I was still hurting. I had not been able to give our dog a much-needed bath, and she needed a haircut. On top of that, my clippers needed replacing. I also needed to take her to the vet for an exam and necessary medication.

But stores were closed, and nonessential businesses weren't open.

In addition, our computer wasn't running smoothly and kept freezing up, so I needed to find someone to fix it.

In the meantime, our bank called, saying there was a recurring charge to our account that we didn't make. We were told not to use the charge card again, and new ones would be mailed.

Soon after, when trying to make an appointment with my doctor, I found out the office was closed for the weekend. When we received our mail, the thermostat we ordered online was the wrong one, so I had to contact the company and straighten that out.

Lord, where are You in all of this? I questioned. It was so discouraging not to be able to do much of anything. The house wasn't getting cleaned, and I couldn't fix much for meals. Lying around in pain was a new experience for me. It was overwhelming.

By the end of Friday afternoon, the Lord answered, *I've been with you all day—busy solving your problems.* And He did. One by one, He sorted out what was important enough to fix immediately and what could be let go until the following week. I was able to enjoy rest of mind and body over the weekend.

The good, the bad, and the ordinary—nothing in this world lasts forever, but in heaven, we will experience only that which is good.

Donna J. Voth

In Our Will, We Will Fail

Many are the plans in a person's heart,
but it is the LORD's purpose that prevails.
—Proverbs 19:21, NIV

Nearly every woman has dreamed about finding her "prince," the one man who will sweep her off her feet and show her what true love is. But when you have been hurt, used, broken, humiliated, and left feeling like damaged goods, pure love seems like a lie.

After two years of courtship, I found myself planning a wedding, even though something inside me left me feeling as if I were making a mistake. But I was determined to do my own will, and I ended up shutting down God's voice.

One month before the wedding, I decided to go for a walk to clear my head. On my walk, I had a "come to Jesus" moment. I prayed and asked God to bless my marriage. I wanted my "happily ever after." As I walked around the neighborhood, I heard someone calling my name. I stopped to look around, but I could not see anyone. I continued walking, but the Voice kept calling my name. After the third time, I stopped and responded, "What?" I concluded that God was trying to talk to me. I leaned against a wall and said, "What, Lord?"

The Voice responded, *"Do not get married."*

What? I was in shock. Everything was organized, and the invitations had been sent! The Voice responded, *"I will be with you. Be strong, and don't be afraid."* As I headed back home, I was not sure what to do. I was scared and confused. Soon after that, I learned that my fiancé was seeing another woman.

Looking back, I'm glad I trusted God and listened to His voice. Sometimes our pursuit of what we want blinds us. The Holy Spirit did provide courage and strength. And a year later, I received abundant blessings through the marriage I had dreamed of.

This experience taught me that we must learn how to trust God's voice and follow His instructions. Even when some decisions might be hard to make, we must trust our heavenly Father. All our desires must be aligned with God's purposes, or we will fail. Only His love can complete us. His voice will never lead us amiss. We might think we know what is best, but we often do not. I am glad His plans for me prevailed. My advice: Let go and let God.

Esther Siceron-Reyna

Let the Spirit Pray for You

*Likewise the Spirit also helps in our weaknesses. For we do not know
what we should pray for as we ought, but the Spirit Himself makes
intercession for us. . . . Now He who searches
the hearts knows what the mind of the Spirit is.*
—Romans 8:26, 27, NKJV

I was blessed recently by two articles answering a teenager's question: "What should I do? I don't feel like praying." These articles not only reminded me of some important prayer principles but also taught me several new ones.

First, the Bible instructs us to pray continuously (1 Thessalonians 5:17). But the question is, How—especially when we don't feel like praying and when our heart is too heavy, pained, or angry to even think of what to say? Yet this question is answered in today's theme text.

Second, prayer is more than just asking for something, thanking God, or praising Him. Prayer starts when we accept God's presence. Romans 8:26, 27 tells us that God's Spirit is right there with us, making prayers out of our wordless sighing and groaning. Often, we feel that we don't know how to pray or that we are so sinful that God can't hear us. But He can. God says, "Be still, and know that I am God" (Psalm 46:10, NKJV).

Third, some prayers can be understood only by God when desperation and pain are seeping out of our hearts. When we have tried everything we know to try, when we have been obedient, and when we have followed all the steps that have been laid out in sermons, books, and articles, God may still seem silent. Yet even then, He hears and understands our wordless prayers.

These are the times when we just go to Him, acknowledging that He is with us. We sit quietly, cry, and let our minds unwind, not worrying about forming the right words. God's Spirit will do that for us. Jesus said, "Blessed are the poor in spirit" (Matthew 5:3, NKJV). In our humility and sense of defeat, when we can't talk to God or hear His answers, we can still expect His promised blessing. Even when our faith is running dry, the Spirit will reach into our hearts and form our unspoken pain into heavenly language to present before our Father. Hannah, greatly desiring a child, prayed wordless prayers of pain and grief in the tabernacle. At first, the priest, Eli, did not understand her behavior. When he did, he blessed her and told her God would grant her wish, and God did (1 Samuel 1:9–20)! These are promises to hold on to.

Elizabeth Versteegh Odiyar

A Strange Reason to Praise

*In everything give thanks; for this is the
will of God in Christ Jesus for you.*
—1 Thessalonians 5:18, NKJV

I often envied church members who would testify of the joys they experienced as they spend much time in morning devotions. I would sit in church and quietly ask God for that type of experience, telling myself it was good to covet *good* things.

My situation was that I had a one-hour commute to work and had to be there by 7:00 A.M. every day. I usually got up at 4:30 A.M. To have a devotional time and get prepared to leave home at 5:45 A.M. was a hustle. Something would have to suffer. But I have learned that we must be careful what we pray for because when we ask, God keeps His promises, and no good gift does He withhold.

I worked at my island's offshore petroleum company and had assumed this would be my place of employment until retirement. But in August 2018, the country was shocked by some devastating news: this company, which had been around for more than sixty years, was going to retrench all its workers because it had become a financial strain on the government.

This was not the news anyone expected to hear. This would be terrible financially, emotionally, and economically. Thousands of families would be affected. What good could come out of this? I found myself jobless with two young-adult sons who were still studying and pursuing expensive career paths.

But would you believe that God gave me a reason to give thanks in the situation? Yes, I was now able to spend quality time in morning devotions, and this time was so refreshing. The prayer ministry department of our church had weekly Wednesday morning services that I was able to attend. I developed a closer relationship with God, of whom I could never get enough.

We women know that life can become difficult at times. When tough times come, we may not feel like giving thanks. But if we take a good look, we will find a reason to give thanks.

Sisters, let's purpose that even in the midst of tears, we will have an attitude of gratitude. We can give thanks in everything because this is what God desires of us. When things go right, praise because you feel like it; when things go wrong, praise *until* you feel like it.

Jill Springer-Cato

The Rahab in Me

*Wait on the LORD: be of good courage, and he shall
strengthen thine heart: wait, I say, on the LORD.*
—Psalm 27:14, KJV

I must say, I thought long and hard when naming this devotional. As you know, Rahab had a career that is still looked down upon by the "churched" and the "unchurched." We don't hear of any parents naming their child Rahab. You may be thinking, *Yes, I may not have always done everything right either, but to call me Rahab—that's just going too far!* But please, before you attempt to tear this page out of the book, lend me your ear.

The Bible does not share with us how Rahab became a prostitute. You may be like me and wonder what led her down that path, but the point of this story is not why but *in spite of.* When Rahab saw the two men of God within the walls of the pagan city Jericho, she recognized her salvation had come. Rahab was told that Jericho would be destroyed, but if she hung a red cord from her window and didn't leave the house until the day of salvation, whoever was in her house would be saved. She didn't ask how long she had to wait, she didn't go out to look down the street to see whether anyone was coming, and she didn't even send one of her relatives to look. The Bible doesn't share how long they waited—whether it was a few days, weeks, or months. She may have wondered whether the Israelites would ever come. But she never left the house. Rahab had only heard about what God had done for others, but she still believed. She recognized those Israelite spies as men of God and wouldn't let them go until they swore she would be saved under the stipulated conditions. She was determined, by God's grace, to change her life.

Just like Rahab, through circumstances that may or may not be of our own making, God can and will save you. Rahab waited, and her miracle came. God made her an honorable woman by allowing her to get married during a time when it was unheard of for a righteous man to marry someone of her profession. God also gave her a son—the awesome man of God, Boaz. The greatest honor of all is that Jesus came through her bloodline. Yes, I do want that "Rahab faith" in me; faith that may not know when or how my change will come but, by faith, I know it will!

D. Reneé Mobley

Who Is That Woman?

PART 1

A Samaritan woman came to draw water.
—John 4:7, TLB

Jesus chose a shortcut from Jerusalem to Galilee so that He could pass through Samaria and meet a woman at Jacob's well. As He sat by the well, a woman came to draw water. Who was that woman? The Bible writer does not tell us her name. He does inform us, however, that Christ's disciples had gone to buy food. So Jesus was sitting alone when she arrived. He said, "Give Me a drink" (John 4:7, NKJV).

Curious and startled by His demand, she replied, "How is it that You, being a Jew, ask a drink from me, a Samaritan woman?" (verse 9, NKJV). More than seven hundred years of religious and racial prejudice had separated the Jews from the Samaritans.

Jesus continued, "If you knew the gift of God, and who it is who says to you, 'Give Me a drink,' you would have asked Him, and He would have given you living water" (verse 10, NKJV). Yet He had nothing with which to draw water.

Jesus said, "Whoever drinks of the water that I shall give him will never thirst" (verse 14, NKJV). The woman immediately asked Jesus to give her His living water so that she would no longer thirst or have to come to the well to draw water. His response was to request that she go and bring her husband to join them. The woman admitted that she had no husband. When Jesus agreed that the woman had spoken the truth, He revealed He already knew her story. Then He added, "You have had five husbands, and the one whom you now have is not your husband" (verse 18, NKJV).

Whew! Pure astonishment must have been the woman's response to what the Master had just said. She said she perceived He was a prophet. The woman felt naked before Him and correctly realized that her loose morals were exposed. She changed the subject by stating that the Samaritans worshiped on a designated mountain, though the Jews said Jerusalem was the place for worship. Jesus then told her that the location of a worship place was not as important as the heart and faith of the one worshiping. When the woman said she knew the promised Messiah would reveal all spiritual things when He came, Jesus said, "I who speak to you am He" (verse 26, NKJV).

Though this woman had multiple moral failings, Jesus still went out of His way to seek her out and reveal Himself—and His salvation—to her. Will He not do the same for you and me?

Patricia Hook Rhyndress Bodi

Who Is That Woman?

Part 2

But none of them asked him why,
or what they had been discussing.
—John 4:27, TLB

While Jesus and the woman at the well were still conversing, His disciples returned from town and marveled that He was talking with this Samaritan woman. Yet no one questioned Him.

As soon as Jesus revealed Himself to be the Messiah, the Samaritan woman left the well, leaving her water pot behind. Into the city she went to share what she had just experienced and bring others to meet the Savior. John 4:39 reveals that "many of the Samaritans of that city believed in Him because of the word of the woman who testified, 'He told me all that I ever did' " (NKJV).

This story is not found in the synoptic Gospels—Matthew, Mark, and Luke—John alone shares this story. Now let me tell you why I chose to highlight the woman at the well for this devotional reading.

In 1988, after a twenty-seven-year absence, I returned to my denominational roots. At a church camp meeting in Mount Vernon, Ohio, I met the woman at the well. One night at the evening meeting, after recounting a powerful testimony of someone like me, speaker Dan Matthews made an altar call. To my surprise, I responded—but ever so slowly, taking a circuitous route and seating myself about twelve rows away from the platform. But Dan had observed me, and when he was finished talking to all the people down in front, he walked back to where I was seated. We had a wonderful Spirit-filled conversation. He told me the story of the Samaritan woman who had strayed, how she met the Savior at the well, and of her life being changed. Though I had attended a Christian elementary school for two years, church high school for two years, and a Christian college for more than two years—*and* attended church and Sabbath School for many years—I had no recollection of ever having heard this story! That evening I was parched and ready for renewal.

After Dan offered a special prayer for me, he initiated a prayer covenant with me—a commitment to pray for each other for one month. We corresponded several times. I was finally rebaptized in 1990, largely due to his intercession for me, and I have never looked back.

Who was that woman at the well that Jesus came to find? I am that woman!

Patricia Hook Rhyndress Bodi

No More Tears: God Is Faithful

"And God will wipe away every tear from their eyes;
there shall be no more death, nor sorrow, nor crying.
There shall be no more pain, for the former things have passed away."
—Revelation 21:4, NKJV

March 29, 2020, marked the twenty-second month since my husband of thirty-five years had passed away, and I still didn't understand his death. I know death is very much a part of life on this earth, but I also understand that death was not God's original plan for us; with sin came death. I was not even questioning why Chris died. I was trying to grapple with the concept of death and dying. I thought I needed to understand. Chris's death was not my first encounter with death, by any means. My parents and some other relatives had died. I grieved my losses, but I rationalized that they had lived fulfilling lives, dying at ages that indicated they had met the allotted "threescore years and ten" (Psalm 90:10, KJV). On the other hand, Chris was so young, so very athletic, and so very vivacious. But death came, and I accepted it, not quite understanding how or why. During those months, I attempted, in vain, to understand the concept of death or dying, but I understood that God is faithful. He has kept His promises to fulfill my every need.

Instead of enlightening me on the intricacies of death and dying, my heavenly Father has given me a peace "which surpasses all understanding" (Philippians 4:7, NKJV). Instead of clarifying death's mystery, God increased my faith so that I can trust Him; even "though I walk through the valley of the shadow of death," He will be with me (Psalm 23:4, NKJV). Instead of justifying Chris's death, my Father has given me the blessed hope—the hope of a new heaven and a new earth and the glorious resurrection of the faithful when "the dead in Christ will rise first" (1 Thessalonians 4:16, KJV). I still don't understand how a living, active person lies down to rest and doesn't awaken. But my faithful Father has taken me beyond the desire to understand. He's given me a peace that the world doesn't understand, increased my faith in Him (even when I can't see Him), and given me the blessed hope of a world made new with life everlasting.

My dear sisters, in your life-changing situations, unexpected experiences, and unplanned circumstances, trust our heavenly Father. Nothing surprises Him because He knows the end from the beginning. He has promised that He will be with us. He is faithful. I am a witness today.

Valerie Knowles Combie

God Is Relevant

The LORD is my rock and my fortress and my deliverer;
My God, my strength, in whom I will trust;
My shield and the horn of my salvation, my stronghold.
—Psalm 18:2, NKJV

Have you ever asked yourself, *Is God still relevant to my life today?* Sometimes people say the Bible is for another time and that the stories and words are not for us today. Some call the stories in the Bible nice tales but, nonetheless, fiction. How sad! I have been reading my Bible all my life, and each word, each phrase, and each story teaches me something relevant for my life today. Let me share one with you.

God is my Rock. Our verse for today says that God is our Rock, Fortress, Deliverer, Strength, Shield, Salvation, and Stronghold. Wow! God is all of this and more. But let's focus on the description that God is my Rock. The original Hebrew uses the words *Jehovah Sela*, which means "The Lord is my Rock." A rock is an inanimate object, but when you look at huge rocks, such as those we see in mountain ranges or beside crashing waves, these immovable giants give me a wonderful image of the God I serve. God is immovable, stable, and dependable. This is the God we serve, and I praise and thank Him for being my "Rock." Throughout my life, I have often run to my immovable, faithful, unchanging Rock, Christ Jesus.

I know that some of my sisters have called on God in times of trial and have not felt His presence or received an obvious answer from Him. I've had those times also. But I remember the story in Mark 4:35–41 when Jesus was asleep in the boat during the storm while His disciples were struggling to save themselves. The lesson I learned from that story is that God's silence does not mean He is absent. Once I invite God into my life each day, He travels with me through all the ups and downs of that day. When I call on Him, I do so because I know He's there. God has promised never to leave us (Hebrews 13:5). So I affirm my faith in the knowledge that God is present, even if He has chosen to be silent. Why is God silent? I can only surmise that it is for my good, for He always works for my good.

Don't be discouraged, my sisters. God is real. God is your Rock. God is relevant. Invite Him into your life each day and believe His Word.

Heather-Dawn Small

Faithful— No Matter the Consequences

*If it be so, our God whom we serve is able to deliver us from the
burning fiery furnace. . . . But if not, . . . we will not serve thy gods.*
—Daniel 3:17, 18, KJV

In 1941, Mother was only seventeen when Nazi forces invaded Ukraine,
rounding up young people to ship like cattle to labor camps in Germany as
slaves.* Now a captive worker in a U-boat battery factory, she determined to
continue keeping the Sabbath day holy, whatever the consequences. The presiding
Nazi officers became infuriated. "We will chop off your head," they threatened,
"if you don't work on Saturdays!" When the German interpreter explained to the
officials there was only one "Sabbath keeper," a Nazi officer said, "You can rest on
your holy day—but you won't get your food ration that day for the week." That
left Mother with just one loaf of hard bread (made with added sawdust) for the
whole week. As it was, she normally didn't eat much, as the food was prepared
with horse meat and pork, which are unclean foods according to the Bible.

One evening after work, Mother walked, alone and tearful, toward her
barracks. Her stomach was so empty she felt sick. Suddenly, at the end of the
corridor, a door flew open. A strong hand grasped Mother and roughly pulled
her through the doorway and into an unfamiliar room. Stunned, Mother looked
into the face of a Nazi officer. Too shocked to do or say anything, she watched the
officer reach under his shirt and produce a small sandwich. He handed it to her;
his silent gestures sternly cautioning her to be quiet. They could both be hanged.
He reopened the door and quickly motioned for Mother to leave. She hastily hid
the sandwich under her shirt and walked on; tears now freely streaming down her
cheeks. *My Father in heaven, You are so good to me. Your ways are unsearchable. It's
incredible how You impressed this officer to give me food when I was so hungry. Lord,
You are faithful to me. I will always be faithful to You. I love You, Lord. You are my
All in all.* Mother kept her promise to be faithful to the end.

Though her reward awaits her on resurrection day, Mother's example and
legacy, especially in these uncertain times, continue to encourage us to remain
faithful and obedient to God and His Word—no matter the consequences.

Galina Gritsuk

---

* Adapted by the author from her published article, "My Mother," *News 'n Views* (Grants Pass Seventh-day
Adventist Church newsletter), July 2018.

Broken Shells

He healeth the broken in heart, and bindeth up their wounds.
—Psalm 147:3, KJV

M omma, why don't people collect broken shells?" asked five-year-old Arya. "Probably because they don't look beautiful enough," Momma answered. "Momma, I think broken shells are beautiful. From now on, those are the kind of shells I would like to collect," Arya stated.

Broken shells can be symbolic of our life's journey. At some point in our lives, we all feel broken. In brokenness, Sarah, Rebekah, Rachel, Hannah, and Elizabeth cried out to the Lord for a child. These women teach us to wait patiently and prayerfully on the Lord during times of brokenness. Abigail, Naomi, and Ruth, though sorrowing, found strength through sharing with others despite their brokenness. Naomi and Ruth, especially, teach us to face the future through giving and not grieving. Then there were women broken by sexual misuse—Tamar, Dinah, and Bathsheba. They experienced undeserved shame and a subsequent time of silence, yet their stories encourage us to help abuse victims and survivors find their voices by offering them God's everlasting peace. Both Mary Magdalene and the Samaritan woman acted out their brokenness through promiscuity. Yet they found healing through the righteous love that Jesus, our faithful Companion, offered them. Mary, facing the possibility of being a single, unwed mother, found healing through her Son, who later died to save the world. These broken-shell stories remind us that God's grace and healing are for all.

Although we are tested in every way, God will not forsake us (2 Corinthians 4:8, 9). He is our Comforter (Psalm 23:4) and Physician who heals the brokenhearted (Psalm 147:3). God is calling us to His rest (Matthew 11:28, 29). He will never allow us to be broken beyond repair. So especially in our brokenness, let's keep pressing on in faith (Philippians 3:14), knowing He will make us new (Revelation 21:5). God picks us up and lovingly nurtures us (Psalm 34:18) and restores us as we come to Him in complete surrender through prayer (James 4:10). He died for us all, He loves us with an everlasting love (John 3:16, 17), and He will never stop seeking after more broken shells (Luke 19:10; Ezekiel 34:11).

Suhana Chikatla

Crash in the Night

But godliness with contentment is great gain.
For we brought nothing into the world, and we can take nothing out of it.
—1 Timothy 6:6, 7, NIV

It was a normal night for us, and we followed our nightly rituals, ending with our study of the Sabbath School lesson and prayer. As usual, we went to sleep quickly. Our days had been busy, so we were glad to fall into bed and looked forward to blissful sleep.

Around three thirty, we were awakened by a loud crashing noise. We had felt safe because of our security alarm, but what was that noise? Was an intruder trying to get into our home? My husband got up and went toward the locked door. He opened it and listened but heard nothing. I remained in bed, frightened and sinking deeper into the bedding while I pulled the covers higher up over me. We heard no further noise, no footsteps, and no sound of an intruder. What would make that clattering noise? My husband turned on the lights and headed toward the bathroom. He glanced to his left, and there was the culprit. Two closet shelves had fallen! Our clothes plus the other things on the shelves had been too much weight on them! What a mess! We laughed with relief. The "intruder" had turned out to be inanimate.

We were safe, but this incident proved we needed to go through our closet and reduce some of our wardrobe. We discovered clothes we seldom wore. Instead of cleaning out the closet when we purchased new items, we had just kept adding to what was already there. That's why the shelves were overflowing. Now in the wee hours of the morning, our shelves had crashed, spilling clothing, hats, and purses all over the floor. We were forced into action: we would have to declutter our closet.

This incident also made me think about all our other stuff. Do we need so much? Should we start buying less and giving more away? Do you, like me, have too much clutter in your closet? Jesus, our Example, had only the necessities of life. Our frightening experience that night seemed to provide another opportunity—to assess my life's activities. Did I have too much clutter in my life as I went at a frantic pace, doing many things but missing what was important?

Our crash in the night had two lessons for me. I needed to declutter not only my closet but also my life. God turned a fearful event into a golden opportunity. Praise the Lord!

Edith C. Fraser

The Night God Answered the Phone

In the day of my trouble I will call upon You,
For You will answer me.
—Psalm 86:7, NKJV

I've been thinking about our heavenly home lately. How nice it will be to be surrounded by everyone I love in an atmosphere of peace and holy joy with no worries about natural or man-made tribulation. Think about prayer meetings led by God Himself! In Revelation 21:9–27, John describes that home. How amazing that though the walls of the Holy City are made up of twelve different precious stones, all the gates are pearl. Since certain mollusks create a pearl sac to seal off a threat—or tribulation, if you will—it would seem that we also must pass through tribulation to get home.

One year was especially a year of tribulation for us. Mom's increasing cognitive decline was more than just aging. My ninety-year-old father had his hands full with caring for her and their disabled grandson, so my husband and I moved our nephew in with us. Shortly after, my husband was diagnosed with lung cancer. Then Dad fell while sweeping the porch, cracking ribs and scapula, and sustained a life-threatening brain injury. A round of tests followed, along with transfers from one hospital to another. I spent my days with Mom at the hospital and took care of home needs in the evenings. Dad had always been my problem-solving resource, and I was definitely feeling in need of his wisdom. Now he couldn't be relied upon to know where he was or how to use the bedside phone. One night I got home from the hospital and couldn't stop crying. Exhausted and overwhelmed with all the responsibilities and decisions that now fell upon me, I had a word with my heavenly Father. Then, with little hope of success, I called Dad. He answered on the second ring. "Hi, baby, what's the trouble?" With complete clarity, we spent the next twenty minutes discussing the location of important papers, how to access funds to care for Mom, and outlining principles for his care. He assured me of his love for the family and me, lifted me up in prayer, and encouraged me that God would strengthen me for whatever lay ahead. The next morning found him as mentally muddled as ever.

That miraculous phone call often reminds me that my heavenly Father loves me enough to handle my tribulations now and will ultimately see me safely through those gates of pearl.

Vicki Mellish

September 6

From Fishermen to Introverts

I can pray this because his divine power has bestowed on us everything
necessary for life and godliness through the rich knowledge
of the one who called us by his own glory and excellence.
—2 Peter 1:3, NET

Due to a series of unexpected events, I have spent the last two months living in a fishing village. It has been an interesting experience for me—the quintessential city girl who can't tell a tuna from a tilapia. As with every situation in my life, God has used it to teach me something.

The fishermen here live interesting lives. They often go out to sea very early in the morning, never knowing what the night will bring. Sometimes they don't sail out very far and catch a lot. Sometimes they go out for miles but find nothing. Sometimes they catch lots of small fish, which aren't worth much. Occasionally, they catch something big that almost sinks their boats. They need to be strong to pull in those large catches, persistent through difficulty, and not easily discouraged by trips that bring in nothing. They also need to be resourceful, learning to subsist on little during those stretches when they don't catch much.

A friend once asked me why Jesus chose several fishermen when selecting the twelve disciples. Now I think I see how the skills and experiences they had as fishermen would help spread the gospel. Their strength and ability to subsist on little would have helped them on the long journeys as they brought the gospel to different areas. Their persistence and resistance to discouragement would be necessary as they faced persecution and rejection. They had everything they needed to be workers for God.

With my naturally introverted personality, it is not easy for me to chat with strangers or make friends with everyone in the room. Sometimes I feel that this puts me at a disadvantage for sharing the gospel. But actually, God has used my introverted personality to help me be a good listener and build good relationships with people, which later allows me to share Christ with them. The way God has made me helps me to be a light for Him.

I think we all have everything we need right now to be workers for Christ. He will use everything we are willing to give Him to build His kingdom for His glory. We are ready to be workers for Him if we are willing to let Him use us.

R. Bowen

Why I Stayed and Why I Left

For God hath not given us the spirit of fear;
but of power, and of love, and of a sound mind.
—2 Timothy 1:7, KJV

I think most girls dream of their wedding day and being married. We play house, and we have crushes on the neighbor boy. I was married for eighteen years to a man I met at the gym. It was a rebound relationship. During our courtship, I knew there was something not quite right about the relationship, but we both stayed out of fear. He proposed to me after I broke up with him. He was afraid of losing me, and I felt I needed to reward him for buying me a ring. Months later, we got pregnant. I did not want to embarrass my mother or church family any further because my unmarried sister was also pregnant.

When my boyfriend refused to zero in on a wedding date, I realized the ring was just a token to hush me. I gave him an ultimatum: get married at the courthouse before the baby was born or else. He reluctantly agreed, and we did get married. Then he rebelled! He cheated; I cheated to get revenge. But we both stayed out of fear. I was afraid of being alone. I was afraid of being a divorcée and a single mother with our now four children.

But there was something inside of me that wanted something better. I held on to the dream of being loved in a healthy way. I was tired of the cheating, disrespect, criticism, arguing, fighting, facade, and pretending in front of the children. I was tired of the silent treatments, the cold side of the bed (as he slept on the couch), and going to church alone. I wanted something real and deep. The emotional pain of being married only on paper took its toll.

After the last time he cheated on me, I filed for divorce. Miraculously, I was able to file for free when years before I had been denied. It was all about God's timing. God was with me every step of the way. He sent people in my path to soothe me, exhort me, encourage me, and comfort me. I am grateful for the people He placed in my life.

I never expected to be a divorced and single mom in my forties. It has not been an easy road, especially for my ten-year-old, who misses his dad very much. Yet it seems like God brought me back to my teenage years, teaching me how to wait with expectancy on my new chapter with the eyes of faith. I no longer live in fear. Fear kept me in my own cage for years. I am now at peace and content, living in the freedom of God's salvation and hope.

Raschelle Mclean-Jones

September 8

A Spiritual Lesson From COVID-19

*Abraham . . . was confidently waiting for God to bring him
to that strong heavenly city whose designer and builder is God.*
—Hebrews 11:10, TLB

As I write, most of us are experiencing a global pandemic's realities for the first (and hopefully only) time in our lives. For me, the reality of COVID-19 slowly started with snippets of news items in places far away before overtaking the local news media. Many changes—some happening quickly—were made to help keep us healthy. In less than a month, most of us had little choice but to adjust to a world much different from what we were used to.

Simple pleasures, such as taking children or pets for playtime at a park or shopping for anything, especially groceries, were no longer pleasurable. Venturing outside of the home took way more planning and preparation than we could have anticipated. There were times when I procrastinated or rationalized away an outdoor venture until the event became unavoidable. Extremes of human behavior came to the surface. Random acts of kindness, such as young people volunteering to shop for those in more vulnerable situations, warmed our hearts. On the other hand, people's unfortunate acts of selfishness ranged from hoarding items to refusing to maintain a safe physical distance, thus putting more vulnerable people at greater risk.

As jobs and businesses were categorized as "essential" or "nonessential," some people were able to continue their work—though within very different parameters. Others saw their livelihoods dry up like withered leaves in the fall. The insecurity all these rapid changes brought was palpable. For some, their church family and their usual go-to place of worship and comfort were no longer available to them in the usual manner. Many people were ushered, feet dragging, into a brave new world of technologically assisted support. Telemedicine, live-streaming, and Zoom conferences became the new norm—an uncomfortable, intimidating norm for some, especially those who had managed to live without these "novelties" of modern life.

After about a month of experiencing the new realities of the pandemic, I was grateful to be able to mentally step back and reflect that, indeed, this world is not our home. It was a time to compare the new life I was living with the old ways. Further, it has also been a time to consider that the promise of eternal life in heaven is even more desirable now than ever before!

Doreen Evans-Yorke

Frustration and God

For I know the thoughts that I think toward you, says the LORD,
thoughts of peace and not of evil, to give you a future and a hope.
—Jeremiah 29:11, NKJV

I woke up frustrated. I rarely oversleep, but I had that day. I'd had a tough night spent dreaming about all the things I hadn't gotten done at work, after an evening of frustration and feeling like I let a friend down. Circumstances beyond my control or ability to change prevented me from helping her out as I had planned. Now I would not have time for both God *and* the gym if I wanted to get to the office on time. I chose God and unpacked my gym bag.

Then came the text and the phone call.

My brother's mother-in-law had died of the cancer she had so valiantly fought. He was on his way to the office to tie up a few things before heading to the airport to pick up his sister-in-law. His wife was helping her father walk through things that needed to be done. My beautiful sixteen-year-old niece was home alone. I was sure her heart was breaking. She so loved her "mom-mom." Hanging up from my brother, I texted my niece to see whether she wanted to go out for a cup of hot chocolate. She instantly responded, and I headed to her home instead of the office. We sat and talked for a while. I dropped her off at home just in time for a friend to pick her up and take her to her sister's.

As I headed to work much later than anticipated, I realized that if I had gone to the gym, I wouldn't have been in a place to take my brother's call or go and hang out with my niece. God had orchestrated details that had left me frustrated and beating myself up at first because I didn't see the big picture. But He had.

"I know the plans I have for you," says the Lord.

It's a much-quoted promise. A favorite used to encourage people. We forget to whom and when it was given. The leaders of Jerusalem have just been taken into captivity. Their prophets tell them it will be OK; God will soon rescue them. But God's message is different. He is not going to rescue them for seventy years—seventy years of captivity. He tells them to build houses, plant gardens, raise children, enjoy grandchildren, and pray for the place where they are captive. They are going to be there for a while. Then He promises, "I know the plans I have for you."

Tamyra Horst

Contentment

Now godliness with contentment is great gain.
—1 Timothy 6:6, NKJV

Camping was very enjoyable to me as a child. When I was nine years old, my parents bought a tent, sleeping bags, cots and air mattresses, a portable stove, a lantern, camping stools, and other equipment to make camping more enjoyable. Usually, we made local trips, but one summer our family of five traveled from the northern plains to the West Coast of the United States of America!

Yellowstone National Park in Wyoming was one of the locations my parents chose to spend a night. After entering the park and registering, we were warned about bears being seen at this very campground! How exciting!

When the tent was up and everything in place for our night's stay, my mother began preparing supper.

My father, my two older brothers, and I set out to find our bear. We searched in vain. Disappointed by our failed mission, we returned to the very place we had left earlier, only to be surprised by a group of people standing near our campsite, pointing and laughing.

Next, we recognized my mother in the group.

Then our eyes traveled to our picnic table where a *bear* was removing the plastic lid from a metal container. He helped himself to the contents and then ambled off when he was finished. Soon the crowd left us alone to eat our delayed supper.

So we saw our bear but not where we thought we would locate him. While we looked elsewhere, the bear came to our own campsite, proving that sometimes what we search for in other places is best found at our own spots.

Happiness comes from being content where we are.

Have you heard people complaining about not having enough of this or grumbling that someone else's life is easy when their road is so rough and difficult? We may have a spring of living water right under our feet. And the added treasure of being in God's will brings contentment. While chasing the proverbial rainbow, the rainbow might be in our own backyard. Even though life may be hard—sometimes downright difficult—just knowing that God is with us and that He cares brings thoughts of satisfaction and contentment. God truly is enough.

Valerie Hamel Morikone

Faithfulness

"Have I not commanded you? Be strong and of good courage; do not be afraid,
nor be dismayed, for the LORD your God is with you wherever you go."
—Joshua 1:9, NKJV

What a year 2020 was! Having nearly the whole world shut down by COVID-19 has given authorities much power to decide how we live. And it all happened so quickly! Many travel plans were canceled; all hospitality venues were affected. Church camp meetings went digital. Yet we were thankful for the communication technologies already in place, plus the creative ways that our church work moved forward.

This got me to thinking about some Bible times when there were lockdowns. Joseph was used to his freedom, roaming the hills of home as a young boy. Being thrown into a pit wasn't his idea of freedom nor was being sold as a slave in Egypt. But he didn't become a victim. Instead, he did his best to please his new master— no wallowing in anger or bitterness. Potiphar gave Joseph a taste of freedom. That fell apart, though, when Joseph was falsely accused and imprisoned. But Joseph trusted God to see him through. And we know the story ends with Joseph becoming the second most powerful ruler in Egypt, after the pharaoh.

Esther's story is a bit different, but she, too, was in a lockdown situation. Chosen as a candidate to be the new queen of Persia, Esther first lived for a year in the palace to prepare for her important night with the king. Life had changed drastically for her. She was surrounded by women vying to be the one chosen as queen. Talk about competition! Would Esther make new friends here? She was lonely. The secret of her Jewish nationality added pressure. But because of her upbringing, she trusted God. When selected as the new queen, Esther soon found her life, along with that of all the Jews, being threatened by palace intrigue. Yet she remained faithful to God, spending time in prayer and fasting. He responded by giving her the necessary wisdom to devise a clever plan that allowed the Jews to defend themselves. The Lord must have given Esther nerves of steel to follow through with the plan suggested by her wise cousin, Mordecai. She gave it her all, and God blessed her.

May we, too, live above our fear, especially in circumstances beyond our control, and remain faithful, trusting in God.

Louise Driver

Animals Are Teachers Too!

"Now ask the beasts, and they will teach you."
—Job 12:7, NKJV

We got a new addition to our family, and the most excited one was Lily, our dog. She trembled with excitement when she first saw (the delicately named) Roundbutt, a male guinea pig. The back bedroom was considered the safest spot for a guinea pig on account of our cats. We bought a rabbit cage, bedding material, timothy hay, and treats for our newest pet, which was our son's until he joined the army.

During the daytime hours, when the cats are outside, we bring Roundbutt's cage to the kitchen. This is where Lily and Roundbutt first got better acquainted. At first, Lily would whine excessively to the point of being annoying. She wanted to be close to Roundbutt, but the cage door was closed because we wanted to supervise and be sure the guinea pig wouldn't get hurt by Lily's exuberance. Lily began to lick at Roundbutt through the wire cage, and the guinea pig liked it.

Now we open the cage door, and Lily sticks her head inside to socialize with Roundbutt. It's so cute. Roundbutt makes these purring sounds and nibbles on Lily's ear and collar. He enjoys the attention Lily gives him. The guinea pig moves around the cage but always comes back for more attention, and all the while, Lily wags her tail like a whip.

Lily is accepting of other animals that are not like her at all. She is a forty-three-pound (nineteen-plus kilogram) dog, and the guinea pig weighs about a pound (less than half a kilogram). Lily immediately bonded to him. Not only that, but she is also protective. If our cats come into the house, they know to make a wide circle around Roundbutt's cage. If they don't, Lily will growl and lunge at them. She knows instinctively that Roundbutt needs protection. Roundbutt, on the other hand, is oblivious to the danger. You would think he would run into his hut to hide, but he stays outside in full view. Fortunately, Lily lets us humans pet and get near Roundbutt, but she has to be right there in the middle so that she gets petted too. If Lily were a human, I think she would make a great Christian. God created animals for a purpose; we can learn from them if we take the time to observe. With our animals, we learned about friendship, loyalty, and even boundaries. We weren't looking for a guinea pig as a pet and didn't know everything that one involves, but we're glad Roundbutt is now part of the family. *Thank You, Lord, for our pets. They indeed teach us!*

Rosemarie Clardy

Angels Appointed to Watch Over Us

For he shall give his angels charge over thee, to keep thee in all thy ways.
—Psalm 91:11, KJV

In 1972, I was in my first year of junior high school in Florida. Our family had recently emigrated from Cuba. I didn't fit in culturally, linguistically, or in the way I dressed. I felt very lonely. School anti-bullying programs did not exist in those days. In public school, you either sank or swam. That's when I stumbled into mean-girl territory, and the bullying started. I was pushed, laughed at, and mocked for the way I talked and dressed. One day I received a "death sentence." The bullying girls said, "Tomorrow morning, when you get to school, we'll be here waiting for you."

What would I do? Run? Hide? Ask an adult to handle my problem? No, doing that would certainly paint a big bull's-eye on my back. What other choice did I have? That evening at home, however, I learned about the power of angels watching over us. God gave me a new "sentence." You see, Mom was a woman of faith. She loved her Savior and truly believed He watches over us with the deepest affection. Mom took me to her room, pulled open the top drawer of the small dark-green nightstand by the side of her bed, and took out her large, old Bible. She introduced me to the world of angels and God's protective care over His earthly children.

As Mom's fingers traveled swiftly through the pages of her Bible, God's promises became more and more real—and precious—to me. I knew that my best weapons the next day were going to be the faith and the trust I'd place in the care of my heavenly Father.

When I arrived at school the following morning, those girls were already waiting for me. Half of them had placed themselves on one side of the door I had to walk through, while the rest stood on the other side, flanking the entrance. No adults were supervising, and there was no turning back. Then something inexplicable happened. As I walked through the doorway, the girls stood in front of me as if in a trance. Unable to make a move or even speak, they just stood and watched in silence—as if seeing something or someone I could not see. I've always believed they saw my guardian angel walking by my side that morning.

I was never again victimized or bullied by these girls. All bullying stopped, and I graduated from junior high school as a conqueror in the Lord.

Olga Valdivia

Obeying God's Spirit

*Trust in the L*ORD*, and do good;*
so shalt thou dwell in the land, and verily thou shalt be fed.
—Psalm 37:3, KJV

Every time I think of God asking what seems to be an unthinkable request, I'm reminded of the biblical patriarch Abraham. God told Abraham to sacrifice his promised son, Isaac. From our viewpoint, this seems like an unlikely request because Isaac was the son through whom God said He would build a great nation. Did our Lord know what He was doing? Obviously so, as this story is one of our best examples of how someone listened to and faithfully obeyed God's Spirit. At the point of sacrifice, the angel of the Lord called out to Abraham, "Lay not thine hand upon the lad . . . : for now I know that thou fearest God, seeing thou hast not withheld thy son, thine only son from me" (Genesis 22:12, KJV).

Over the last few weeks, I, too, have sensed God's presence in a way I didn't expect. Since my husband and I are retired, our incomes are fixed. But we are blessed that there is enough to live on with some extra. Tithe and offerings come off the top, plus we support a few charities. So, when God's Spirit whispered to me to do more, I was, in a word, surprised. In retrospect, my argument seemed trivial: "Father, I'm doing what is requested and a little extra. I don't think there are any additional funds to work with." That's when God called my attention to the checkbook tucked away in my purse. Sure enough, there was a little more than usual in our account after the monthly bills had been paid and savings securely tucked away. Resigned to God's leading, I asked, "What would You have me do?" The answer came immediately. The COVID-19 pandemic was raging across the globe, and I personally knew someone who was financially impacted through the closure of her small business. My first step was to send her a check. Then there were others whom I know who had lost loved ones. They, too, received a donation to help with likely expenses. But God wasn't finished. Since our little conversation, I have been convicted that every time the funds left over from our obligations reach a certain amount, a needy person will benefit from them.

God is so good. I personally can't thank Him enough for His love, mercy, and blessings to me. I'm just ecstatic to be called His child!

Yvonne Curry Smallwood

Promised Prosperity

Beloved, I pray that you may prosper in all things
and be in health, just as your soul prospers.
—3 John 2, NKJV

It wasn't God's plan for pain, suffering, sadness, aging, or death to be part of our lives. Despite the entrance of sin, God is tenderly watching and is still supremely in control.

Approximately three years ago, my usually healthy body began to decline. Even after much medical investigation, no accurate diagnosis could be given, and my symptoms worsened. One night I cried to God out of the depths of my sorrowful heart. My prayer was brief: "God! Help me!" Shortly after the three-word prayer, I fell into a deep sleep and had a beautiful dream. In my dream, God appeared to me in the form of a very tall man. He had the most pleasant face and personality I had ever witnessed. God held my hands and invited me to tell Him what was worrying me so much. I told Him all and noted how attentive, patient, kind, compassionate, understanding, and loving He was as I related my long, depressing story. Still holding my hands, He said, "Jackie, everything is going to be all right." I felt at peace, and my dream ended. When I awoke, I had mixed feelings. I was happy for the assurance that I would be OK again, but I missed my time with God in my dream—I wanted to return and remain with Him forever.

About a week later, I underwent an echocardiogram. The results of this test led to a sleep study, and I was diagnosed with a severe form of sleep apnea, which proved to be the root cause of all my medical symptoms. God again intervened and provided me with over half a million Jamaican dollars, so I was able to purchase a sleep machine for my therapy. My health is being restored gradually, thanks to the Triune God's watchful care. My health may never be fully restored to its original state in this life, but the best is yet to come because Jesus has promised to make all things new. He will wipe out—and undo—every negative loss or pain that sin has caused us. I can hardly wait for this change to come. The promises in the Bible are sure and true. Let's embrace them.

"And God will wipe away every tear from their eyes; there shall be no more death, nor sorrow, nor crying. There shall be no more pain, for the former things have passed away" (Revelation 21:4, NKJV).

Jacqueline Hope HoShing-Clarke

Staying Connected

But since we were torn away from you, brothers,
for a short time, in person not in heart,
we endeavored the more eagerly and with great desire to see you face to face.
—1 Thessalonians 2:17, ESV

When I was a young girl, I had a pen pal. I don't remember her name now, but I remember we wrote back and forth a few times. She once sent me a little knitted doll that I still have, but I don't remember that I kept any of her letters. When I got a little older, my family moved away from my grandparents, but my grandmother often wrote to me. When I left for college, her letters kept coming, as did those from other family members. Though busy, I still tried to stay connected. I did better with phone calls. I phoned my mom fairly frequently after leaving home. I also remember my dad calling every Sunday morning at eight o'clock without fail, beginning when I was a teenager and then well into my adult married years. When Facebook came along, I was excited to reconnect with distant family and old school friends. It's much easier to scroll through Facebook than sit down and write a long letter to someone. It's also less intrusive in another person's life than a phone call. But I can still stay connected.

Today we have so many more ways of staying connected. I often text my kids, attend Zoom meetings, and often FaceTime with my dad, daughters, or granddaughter. And during the recent pandemic, I was very glad that my husband, who is a pastor, was able to hold a church service that was livestreamed for our members and others so they could stay connected.

But you know, the older I get, the more I realize the best way to stay connected is just to *be* with someone. Talking to people face-to-face, seeing their expressions, and being able to hug them—that's what we were meant to do. That's the way God created us. He created Adam and Eve, and then He came and spent the day with them in the Garden of Eden. FaceTime, texts, phone calls, and letters are OK, but they are only the next best thing to *being* there. Two arms wrapped around me in a huge bear hug—that's the best!

I can view my spiritual life in this same way. Journaling my prayers and reading the Bible are great ways to stay connected to God. Yet I am really looking forward to the day when I can feel His strong arms around me—in person—and hear Him say, "Welcome home!"

Kathy Pepper

Praise Him!

Make a joyful noise unto the LORD all ye lands.
Serve the LORD with gladness: come before his presence with singing.
Know ye that the LORD he is God.
—Psalm 100:1–3, KJV

The COVID-19 pandemic has forced many people to change their daily living activities. It has given us more time to view the things around us, particularly the wonders of nature. Spring has brought the blooming of flowers and leaves. Birds are singing and flying from tree to tree, mating, and building nests in the bushes. Squirrels and chipmunks are running to and fro. Insects, such as bumblebees, are doing their usual dances. Deer and other animals are wandering in the nearby underbrush.

I am in awe of the marvelous way God created these things. He said in Matthew 6:25–34 to consider the world He has created and not worry about tomorrow. In the wake of COVID-19, many worry about their health, families, stock market fluctuations, and other significant matters.

While my mind was contemplating the activities of God's creatures, I asked myself, *Why do we worry, despite knowing that God is faithful to provide?* Although the earth is marred by sin, both animate and inanimate creation follow the laws instituted by God. The sun rises and sets every day; the moon and the stars show up in the evening; the wind blows at its appointed time—all under the guidance of the Creator.

One of the creatures that captured my attention the most was a bird. There is a tree at the back window of my bedroom, and every year a bird wakes me up around three thirty in the morning. I hear it tweeting and singing. I imagine it is talking to its chicks while praising God for life and the food He provides it each day.

How about us? Do we focus just on the pestilences flying around us, forgetting that we need to praise the Lord and let Him take care of our needs? Or is gratitude also an important part of our lives? I've come to realize that the most important thing we need to do is trust our powerful God to shelter us under His mighty wings. Psalm 100:1–3 says to "make a joyful noise unto the LORD, all ye lands. Serve the LORD with gladness: come before his presence with singing. Know ye that the LORD he is God" (KJV). So let us praise Him in songs and psalms.

Flore Aubry-Hamilton

The Missing Purse

"What woman . . . if she loses one coin,
does not . . . search . . . until she finds it?"
—Luke 15:8, NKJV

I honestly don't remember what I did with my purse one stressful afternoon as we left a restaurant in Cleveland, Tennessee, on our out-of-state trip to take care of the estate of our late son-in-law. All I remember is that as my husband drove us toward that day's destination, I suddenly realized my purse was missing—with all my credit cards, debit cards, and iPhone. When I alerted my husband, he glanced at his phone. The Find My Friends app was blinking, communicating with my phone, wherever *it* was. In the car, we "followed" the moving dot via the map on his cell phone. Needless to say, we were both praying. When the dot stopped moving, we found ourselves in front of a building with a Keep Out sign on its locked gate: a city refuse collection center. We called the police for help and to file a report. A kindhearted police officer responded, going inside with my husband's phone to locate mine. In a pile of rain-drenched refuse, Officer Lawson dug down as far as he could, ruining his shoes. When his search was unsuccessful, my husband and I decided to give up. After all, phones can be replaced.

But we soon learned that my purse *had* been found! A city street sweeper, Roy Stinnett, found it in his sweeper when he was unloading and washing it out. Not only was the purse hanging from a latch inside the sweeper apparatus, but the purse was still closed! When a public works employee gave me my now-battered purse, looking as if it had been tossed about in a cyclone, all the contents were there! Cash, credit and debit cards—everything except for the iPhone. The next morning Roy, the same public works employee who had found my purse, returned to the refuse collection center with a shovel and the resolve to find my phone, which he eventually did with the assistance of a fellow employee. Our daughter was able to retrieve my phone for me. Though battered and with a cracked screen, it still worked! A second answer to prayer!

When I gratefully recall how God answered our prayers through the honesty, compassion, and selflessness of these city employees in their everyday tasks, I wonder something: I wonder whether we are as conscientious as they in fulfilling the responsibilities God gives *us* each day.

After all, we aren't just seeking a lost phone or purse—we are searching for lost souls.

Jeannine Fuller

No Coincidence

For the LORD taketh pleasure in his people:
he will beautify the meek with salvation.
—Psalm 149:4, KJV

In 2012, my husband and I were invited to a surprise birthday party for one of our friends. We did not know the hostess, and she did not know us. Eight years later, I was summoned to speak at the final Sabbath day celebration program of our denomination's Ten Days of Prayer initiative. One feature of the program that I used was promises, interspersed with music, testimonies, and prayer. The congregation was instructed to write subheadings for the promises with corresponding scriptures. They were to exchange their list with that from an unfamiliar congregant. I descended the platform and gave my original handwritten copy to a guest. I asked her to meet me at the end of the service. After the postservice ritual of greeting each attendee at the door, I realized my recipient had not participated. In fact, she was nowhere to be found.

In bewilderment, I explained my disappointment to the Women's Ministries director, who had asked me to be the day's speaker. She replied, "She said to tell you she could not wait because her husband had an appointment." I was dejected. The Women's Ministries director then added, "She is my friend. Do you remember when you attended my surprise birthday party? She was the hostess. She says she will give you a call." I felt so much better.

The next morning my cell phone rang. A woman introduced herself and explained how God had worked on her behalf. "In the service yesterday," she said, "I was inadvertently overlooked by the ushers who distributed the pens and writing pads. And I had none of my own. What a terrible feeling! So I really needed those promises that you gave me."

Over the next weeks, I received another call from her, stating she had made several copies of my promises and mailed them to her friends. Her contacts informed her that they were so blessed and were, in turn, making copies and sending them to their friends and families. I directed her to a website where she and her friends could have unlimited access to God's promises. What a life-changing experience! Today we continue to be on the battlefield. She is now my prayer partner and a godly support. Our God is all knowing.

Pauline A. Dwyer-Kerr

September 20

Losses Not Lost

Even though the fig trees are all destroyed, and there is neither blossom left nor fruit;
though the olive crops all fail, and the fields lie barren;
even if the flocks die in the fields and the cattle barns are empty,
yet I will rejoice in the Lord; I will be happy in the God of my salvation.
—Habakkuk 3:17, 18, TLB

The loss of relationships by betrayal, drawing apart, or death is universal. The loss of material things seems to be increasing exponentially because of natural disasters. Other losses are due to hazards caused by human action or inaction, including the consequences of society's advancements, such as faulty airplane designs and industrial pollution. Observant Bible students see the fulfillment of Jesus' words in Matthew 24:6–8 and are encouraged to "lift up . . . [their] heads; for . . . [their] redemption draweth nigh" (Luke 21:28, KJV). When the losses are personal, creating new normals for our lives, we struggle to make sense of these experiences. Sometimes the losses come in quick succession, such as Job's period of suffering. And if the truth be told, they probably are like that.

I experienced such a season from 2012 to 2017, when the deaths of five close family members and a friend, coupled with the losses of my job and professional credentials, spawned economic instability, health issues, and heartaches. This season of great outward instability gave me only a few moments to catch my breath and regroup after one loss before the next one arrived. In retrospect, I know that Jesus sustained me because every one of these events was enough to challenge my faith in, trust in, and obedience to God's Word. An underlying matrix anchored me: God permitted each trial and test for my good and His glory, to paraphrase Romans 8:28. His vision of my eternal future required shifting my priorities, reliance upon family members and friends, and sense of independence. Yet my losses must not be *lost* as I consider my spiritual development and growth. Meditating on the following words comforts me: " 'In everything give thanks: for this is the will of God in Christ Jesus concerning you.' [1 Thessalonians 5:18]. This command is an assurance that even the things which appear to be against us will work for our good. God would not bid us be thankful for that which would do us harm."*

Judith Warren Hawkins

* Ellen G. White, *The Ministry of Healing* (Mountain View, CA: Pacific Press®, 1942), 255.

God Sees Me

When Jesus saw him stretched out by the pool and knew how long
he had been there, he said, "Do you want to get well?"
—John 5:6, *The Message*

Recently, my husband gave me something that I had wanted for quite some time—Logos Bible Software. I am still learning how to navigate the home page, library, and tons of resources, but it's so exciting! Whenever I hear someone expound on a text critically, it gives me a strong desire to know the Bible in that way too. I have always loved to take a scripture text and ponder it. I remember when I first started public speaking, I was very excited about my discoveries. On occasion, I would see Dr. Benjamin Reaves (our college president at the time) get out of his car to go to his office. I would hurry to chat with him about my speaking engagement and what I was learning. He would smile and become excited with me. I recall his words to me: "Chew the bone." That is, get every ounce of meaning from the passage that you possibly can.

The Word of God has many lessons that we can "chew" on and apply to everyday life. That is true with the above verse and the question Jesus asked a sick man before He gave the command. This miracle is the third of Jesus' recorded in the book of John. The invalid had no idea who Jesus was when he was asked the question, "Do you want to be made whole?" Nor did he know about the miracles Jesus had performed.

Why did Jesus choose this man? There were many invalids and blind and broken people that day at Bethesda, which means the "house of mercy." Why did Jesus take note of this man when there were so many others? The man did not ask for healing. Since I wanted to get a better understanding, I kept chewing, and the Spirit brought to my mind the story of the widow of Nain. There it was: In that vast crowd in the town of Nain, the Bible says, "Jesus saw her" (Luke 7:13, *The Message*) and had compassion on her. I'm encouraged because that lets me know that Jesus sees me, and He wants to do the impossible in my life too. Working in ministry, you sometimes wonder whether Jesus sees you, especially when life gets challenging.

Father, I thank You for the assurance that You see and take note of where I am and what I face from day to day. Each time I open Your Word and seek to understand it, I find myself drawn closer to the God who sees me.

Shirley P. Scott

Operation Bear Hug

"For the Holy Spirit will teach you in
that very hour what you ought to say."
—Luke 12:12, NKJV

My youngest daughter, Kristin, and I traveled to Magadan, Russia, in the summer of 1992 to be part of Operation Bear Hug. In Russia, we were to hand out copies of *The Desire of Ages*, along with invitations to a health fair and evangelistic meetings at a recently built church. Interpreters would go door to door with us in apartment buildings and seaside homes, although I had studied beforehand a sheet of conversational Russian words. So I felt confident.

Many of the people I met were so appreciative of the books. They'd gaze, tears streaming down their faces, at the picture of Christ on the cover. They'd hug the book and invite us in.

Down by the seaside with my young interpreter, I felt quite confident (overly so) about going to the doors alone, so my interpreter and I split up to cover more territory. As I came out of one home, a man with a heavy scent of alcohol came toward me. He angrily shouted words I'd not heard and which certainly were not on my vocabulary sheet. I sent up silent prayers because of his threatening gestures. About that time, my interpreter appeared. When she saw and heard the man, she explained his anger. Many people had been told by local religious authorities that we were doing evil work and our books should be burned. At that moment, I believe the Holy Spirit calmly spoke through me. To the man, I said, "God has given each of us beautiful minds to think and discover truth. We should never take what someone else says as truth without studying it for ourselves." The man completely calmed down, apologized, and asked for a book. As we visited another home, the man of the house excused himself because someone was banging on his gate. He returned and said someone wanted to see me. It was the previously angry man! He was so excited—but now in a wonderful way. He had stopped an ambulance driver and had told him all about his new book. The driver now wanted one also!

God is always present, unseen, watching over us, ready to help when we recognize our need. His Holy Spirit wants to use us. When we are willing, the Spirit will take over our thoughts and words. I will never forget the sense of calm that came over me when I should have been terrified and how the words given me calmed an evil spirit that had taken over that man. "For the Holy Spirit will teach you in that very hour what you ought to say" (Luke 12:12, NKJV).

Susan Anderson

You Never Know

Finally, all of you, be like-minded, be sympathetic,
love one another, be compassionate and humble.
—1 Peter 3:8, NIV

D id you have a good Christmas?" we asked the waiter at our favorite Mexican restaurant in early January. He hesitated, then said, "It was OK." We asked if he was all right. He then told us it had been a year since he had lost his younger brother. Tears were in his eyes; we shared a special moment with him. Later that same week, we encountered several other people who were going through challenges.

It is so important to greet people wherever you are and ask how they are doing. Why? Because doing so can change someone's life. I pray daily that I can always be a blessing to others. Sometimes just a smile, a quick greeting, or a hug can make a difference in a person's day. And I have found that when I am feeling down and other people ask me how I am doing, it always makes me feel better.

My sister had an experience years ago with a man she was dating. They decided one evening to walk to a lake in their hometown. It was getting dark. They had a flashlight, but they didn't switch it on. They soon discovered they were in total darkness yet sensed someone was nearby. They called out and asked if someone was there. When a man answered, they started a dialogue. They stood for over two hours talking to him. Eventually, all moved on. But it wasn't until they got back to a lighted parking lot that the man revealed he had a gun. "I had planned on committing suicide tonight," he told them. "But your interest in talking to me saved my life."

We never know what people are going through. Sometimes we mistake someone's gruff attitude as an indication that the person is mean or uncaring; then, we find out this person is going through a big challenge in life. In church, sometimes we put on our Sabbath happy faces, even though we may be going through a difficult time in our lives. During those times, it is so important to talk to someone and ask for help.

God is always with us. He wants us to treat people with kindness. So, as we continue God's work, let's demonstrate the golden rule. "In everything, do to others what you would have them do to you, for this sums up the Law and the Prophets" (Matthew 7:12, NIV).

Jean Dozier Davey

Lesson From a Squirrel

Henceforth there is laid up for me a crown of righteousness,
which the Lord, the righteous judge, shall give me at that day:
and not to me only, but unto all them also that love his appearing.
—2 Timothy 4:8, KJV

Too often, we ignore the contemporary relevance of ancient wisdom. One day, as I watched a black squirrel try to climb a bird feeder pole, a wise old saying came back to me: "He who repeats the same activity the same way is doomed to failure."

The squirrel evidently remembered that he had once been able to climb the bird feeder pole and walk around above the feeders. But he had not yet figured out how to drop onto a feeder after we installed a metal cone around the pole to discourage him from climbing. Yet the squirrel continued racing up the pole as high as he could go, then the cone would stop him. He would drop to the ground, sit upright on his haunches, and stare up at the feeders. Again, he would try to race up the pole, only to be stopped. One rainy day he found himself sliding down the wet pole, but he continued his daily assaults. He has not yet given up. He knows that there is food just out of his reach. For now, anyway, it is still unreachable.

I think that I am all too often like that squirrel. I get an idea in my head that something must be done in a particular way. No one else can give me acceptable advice as to a better approach. I continue doing the same thing the same way. It seems to take a major event to get me to change my mind or consider other options.

Then one day, a light comes on in my brain. I wonder why it has taken so long to figure out the resolution to my problem: all I need to do is let go of my ideas and let God lead me to the right solution. Suddenly, my problem seems insignificant. The solution has been there all the time. I just had to let go and let God show me the way.

Paul wrote he was not going to give up until he reached the eternal prize. He would not depend on his own wisdom to push through obstacles on the metal "pole" of life. Instead, he would continue depending on the Lord to guide him. "Henceforth," Paul says, "there is laid up for me a crown of righteousness, which the Lord, the righteous judge, shall give me at that day" (2 Timothy 4:8, KJV).

If we want that crown, we, too, must seek God's ways, not depending on our own wisdom.

Patricia Cove

God's Interruptions

Speak unto Rehoboam, the son of Solomon, king of Judah,
and unto all the house of Judah and Benjamin, and to the remnant
of the people saying, Thus saith the LORD . . . this thing is from me.
—1 Kings 12:23, 24, KJV

After two years of renting in an apartment complex, I felt it was time for me to consider purchasing a home. I went to the Lord in prayer for guidance and devoted half of a night to fasting and prayer.

A few days later, I noticed a real estate flyer on the notice board in the lobby of my office building. I contacted the real estate broker at the telephone number listed, asked questions about the process, and decided to get started. I was assigned an agent. We viewed listings weekly. One evening, while viewing a home, I had the distinct feeling that this was the one for me! I shared my assessment with the agent. But she encouraged me to consider other homes that she had selected.

We visited another property weeks later, and I was impressed with some of its features. But it was my second choice. Evidently, there were reasons why my first choice seemed to be unavailable, according to the agent. A closing date was set for the second-choice house, though the seller was to do some renovations on the property before the closing.

Two days before the closing, the broker called to inform me that the seller had reneged on the sale. I turned to the Lord about the situation. After prayer, I experienced a sense of peace and believed that this was God's doing (1 Kings 12:23, 24). During this time, my agent had taken leave to care for her ailing mother in another state. While awaiting her return, the broker contacted me. He informed me that the house in which I had initially shown interest was still available. I was delighted and agreed that we should move forward on an offer. A closing date was scheduled, and the house that God had chosen for me was now under my ownership.

As I reflected on this interruption, I praised God for temporarily removing the agent during the process, allowing the disappointment of my first offer, and ultimately placing me in the very home He had chosen for me.

This thing was from the Lord!

Claudine Houston

September 26

Saving Our Children
PART 1

"I will save your children."
—Isaiah 49:25, NKJV

In late spring, my husband returned from one of his early morning walks with news of five goslings in one of the goose families that live on the pond just behind our house. So naturally, it was my great delight to go out to visit them when we walked together later that day. As we approached, we saw the fuzzy little gray goose toddlers exploring the banks of the pond, looking for tasty morsels in the short grass. Then to our horror, we noticed that one of the little siblings was flipped over on his back, struggling without success to regain his footing. Time after time, the little one tried to right himself. He flailed his one free leg and wing and thrashed to flip over but could not flip right side up. It was evident that his goose parents were quite concerned but obviously incapable of helping him.

We thought it odd they didn't do more to help. We have seen geese pull their babies from danger many times before. But this couple had failed. Why wouldn't they help him, we wondered, when they obviously were devoted to him and anxious about the situation? They paced back and forth, surveying the situation. As they kept watchful eyes on the other four in their little brood, they still responded every time the one in distress tried to flip over or gave out his little half-chirping, half-squealing cries for help. It soon became clear that they had done all within their power to help him get back on his feet but just could not help.

After we returned home, I still could not help but regularly revisit the pondside to check on the unfortunate little gosling. Every time I went out, the situation was the same. This went on for several hours, and I became more concerned as intense sunlight shifted to bear down directly on the helpless creature. The little gosling was trying to right himself, and the parents were trying to help him but to no avail. Time was running out for him, so I determined that if the parents left him, I would go down and do for him what they could not: flip him over.

Undoubtedly, you, too, have encountered situations that brought consternation, sadness, and uncertainty as to whether or not to act. How blessed we are that in any situation, we can trust the One who said He would instruct and teach us how, when, and even whether to proceed! Only He is "able to do exceedingly abundantly above all that we ask or think" (Ephesians 3:20, NKJV).

Ella Louise Smith Simmons

Saving Our Children

PART 2

*"I'm the one who's on your side,
defending your cause, rescuing your children."*
—Isaiah 49:25, *The Message*

Late in the afternoon, on a trip out to investigate the struggling gosling's predicament, I found several of my neighbors trying to intervene. The one man in the group was down near the goose family, trying to approach the little one. But each time he drew near, the parents launched a full, wing-flapping attack. They were doing all in their power to protect their baby. Then the man's wife drew the family away by luring the other four siblings with bread crumbs. The parents followed to protect the four of them from this new "danger." With the goose family diverted in the opposite direction, the man knelt over the one that had our concern. What the rest of us could not see—or the geese understand— was that there was a nearly invisible trap holding the little one down from which he could not escape, nor his parents free him.

The man called out that the gosling was trapped in a transparent plastic mesh and declared he would need scissors to free the gosling. My house was the nearest, so I quickly obliged. In short, with the parent geese out of the way and the right tool, the man was able to cut the shackles that bound the little one. Within a few minutes, he had freed the little gosling and placed him upright on his feet to everyone's relief and sheer delight.

There are many times in life when our children—whether toddlers, teens, or adults—through carelessness, recklessness, or just ignorance get themselves ensnarled in the entrapments of sin. Most parents give their all to rescue their children and free them from danger. But, as with the geese, we often just don't have what it takes to achieve the rescue. On numerous occasions, many of us have experienced the anguish of helplessness that results from our human frailties. It is then we have had to be reminded that we needed a man to intervene; no, not their earthly fathers but the man Christ Jesus, the only One who can help in such times. Take a lesson from the geese. Let us not hamper His rescue efforts by our insistence on hovering in the way. Remember, we cannot save our children under any circumstances. Only He who shed His innocent blood and died on the cross for them can save them, and He has promised to do so. I claim that promise today.

Ella Louise Smith Simmons

The Unexpected

Ye are of God, little children, and have overcome them:
because greater is he that is in you, than he that is in the world.
—1 John 4:4, KJV

The COVID-19 virus came and changed the way we view and operate in this world. As we all know, it was a pandemic that affected people around the globe physically, emotionally, financially, and socially. How could this be? Our new normal was to stay at home indefinitely. This pandemic caused us to use our homes as our offices, schools, and shopping centers. We celebrated birthdays and had family reunions virtually. Outside contact was prohibited, except for getting groceries or medical necessities. Many wondered when this devastation would end. I was really concerned about the course of our lives. I had just started a new job. With any new job, you try to shield your misgivings and insecurities while, with guidance, you learn the lay of the land. For me, learning the lay of the land was grabbing my computer and propping myself on the bed to do the best I could do with the work I was given.

I knew I had made the right decision to start a new normal, but I was doubting my expertise. My husband gave me the encouragement I needed for each day. But the next morning I would get up feeling anxious about my workday. I prayed that God would be my inspiration, but I still felt defeated. I was also frustrated with myself as the news described the desperation of communities losing loved ones and their jobs.

One morning, as I lay in bed battling my discouragement, my heavenly Father, through a calming breeze, reminded me that I was not alone in this unexpected adventure. He was and would be with me all along the way. I lay in bed a little longer, reciting Psalm 121. Later that evening, my husband and I were reminiscing about the last few weeks at home. We had gotten to enjoy the company of our children. Instead of rushing past one another, we now had the opportunity to share a meal, tell stories, and quietly reflect on God's awesome mercies.

Of course, we are still coping with the unexpected. Some days are better than others, but we do know that we are not alone. God is faithful and merciful. He is right by our side as we tackle this new, unforeseen normal. As you attempt to cope with your challenges, may you find comfort in today's verse, knowing that the One within us is greater "than he that is in the world."

Diantha Hall-Smith

The Impression

Whether you turn to the right or to the left,
your ears will hear a voice behind you, saying,
"This is the way; walk in it."
—Isaiah 30:21, NIV

One Sabbath morning in spring, I awoke early to find sunshine streaming through my window. This was a pleasant change after several days of rain. On this particular Sabbath, I was scheduled to sing at church. While I was having my morning devotions, however, I had a sudden and distinct impression that I needed to get into my car and drive to a nearby town in the opposite direction of the church.

This doesn't make any sense at all, I thought. *Why should I go for a drive in the country now, when I need to be getting ready to go to church?* But even after I ate breakfast, the impression would not go away. Finally, I decided to just go ahead and make the drive because it really was a beautiful day.

As I drove toward a smaller town nearby, I saw a car parked by the side of the road. When I passed the car, I noticed two ladies getting out of it, so I pulled over and asked, "Do you ladies need any help?"

"Yes!" they replied. "Our car broke down last night. It was so late we decided to sleep in the car and then try to find help in the morning. We've been praying that God would keep us safe and show us how to get help."

"Listen," I said, "I know of a gas station with a mechanic in the town where I live. May I take you there?" The ladies gladly got into my car. I drove them to the gas station. Soon the mechanic was able to tow their car to his shop and start working on it.

I explained to the ladies that I needed to go to my church to present special music for the worship service. They understood. By the time I told them good-bye, I had already missed part of the Sabbath School program. After I sang for the church service, I returned to the gas station to check on my new acquaintances. The mechanic had just finished repairing their car. They were extremely grateful that I had stopped to help them and profusely thanked me. I responded, "It was God who answered your prayers for help. I am just pleased that He used me to be a blessing in your time of need." *Dear Lord, help us always to follow through on Your divine impressions.*

Christa White Schiffbauer

God's Amazing Mathematics

*When I brake the five loaves among five thousand,
how many baskets full of fragments took ye up? They say unto him, Twelve.*
—Mark 8:19, KJV

Do you recall those mathematic problems that teachers assigned to your class when you were in school? Some students quickly grasped the math principles, while others struggled. For students who were not avid readers and whose learning style was not audiovisual, word problems may have posed difficulty. The problem was intensified when students were required to solve such problems without the aid of a calculator or paper and pen.

Interestingly, Jesus once gave His disciples a mathematical word problem: "How many baskets full of leftover fragments did you pick up?" His question was based on two miracles that Jesus previously performed. The first was the day Jesus taught a multitude until evening. Jesus perceived they were hungry and instructed the disciples to feed them. They responded that the cost of bread for this vast multitude was beyond them. Jesus asked whether anyone in the crowd had food; a lad had five barley loaves and two fish. Jesus blessed the food and instructed His disciples to distribute it among the crowd. Miraculously, more than five thousand men plus women and children were fed, and twelve basketfuls remained. The second time throngs had been with Jesus for three days. This time Jesus blessed seven loaves and a few fish, which fed more than four thousand people, and seven baskets of food were left over.

"The miracle of the loaves teaches a lesson of dependence upon God," notes author Ellen White. She continues, "But when . . . we are brought into strait places, He will deliver us. We are not to give up in discouragement, but in every emergency we are to seek help from Him who has infinite resources at His command."*

During the 2020 COVID-19 pandemic, many people suffered a shortage of food and other essentials. Many lost jobs and even loved ones. Yet how comforting to know that God can take care of any crisis or emergency we may face in life. He has promised to supply all our needs, and we will undoubtedly still have basketsful remaining. That's *His* mathematics!

Whatever crises you may be facing, simply trust Him because He cares for you.

Gerene I. Joseph

---

* Ellen G. White, *The Desire of Ages* (Nampa, ID: Pacific Press®, 2005), 368, 369.

Adoption

For you did not receive the spirit of bondage again to fear,
but you received the Spirit of adoption by whom we cry out, "Abba, Father."
—Romans 8:15, NKJV

It was a bright and beautiful Sunday morning when Brinkie, the last and only female cat of Grandma's second set of kittens, came for her meal. She was now two years old and had given birth to her first set of kittens in the hills. After she returned to her babies, I heard loud noises, yowling, meowing, and actual screaming and clashing between two cats. Sometime later, I noticed that Brinkie was going back and forth, meowing, and seemed very frightened, sad, desperate, and helpless. So my husband and I went into the hills in search of her kittens. We cried, "Meow! Meow! Meow!" but without any success. After losing all her kittens, Brinkie came home and adopted her mother's and sister's kittens that were already weaned. They accepted her, and she lovingly and tenderly bathed and fed those big kittens as if they were her very own.

Have we been adopted into the family of God? There are some steps to follow, but first, let us note Isaiah's prophecy (Isaiah 9:6) and also listen to what the apostle John said about the Servant King and Messiah who would come to live on this earth as a babe, suffer, and then die on a cruel cross to pay the ransom for our adoption from sin. John the Baptist preached in the wilderness about repentance and baptism. By baptizing Jesus, he gave us an example regarding our own adoption. Nicodemus heard John the Baptist's message and read the Scriptures and then went to Jesus by night to ask how he could get adopted. Jesus told him that he had to be "born of water and the Spirit" (John 3:5, NKJV).

Today we also may be asking, "How can I be adopted?" To obtain the benefits of adoption, we need to acknowledge God as the Creator and Sustainer of the world, believe and have faith in Jesus, our Redeemer, and be washed in His blood. The first step is repentance (Acts 3:19), then confession (Proverbs 28:13), followed by consecration (Jeremiah 29:13). Then, we ask God to help us grow in faith through the power of the Holy Spirit (Ephesians 3:16).

As it was with Brinkie and her three sets of adopted kittens, so it is with God's people. Some of us may have been adopted into church fellowship more than once. Let us not give up. Our heavenly Father is still waiting to welcome us home into His everlasting kingdom.

Bula Rose Haughton Thompson

God's Guidelines or "Luck of the Genes"?

There is a way which seemeth right unto a man,
but the end thereof are the ways of death.
—Proverbs 14:12, KJV

A few years ago I was flying to the East Coast to teach a healthful cooking seminar. My airplane seatmate was a gentleman in his early forties. We exchanged the usual polite greetings. Further conversation revealed he believed in God. He also believed that our bodies were created in a way that could handle any food or substance because it was the "luck of the genes" that determined our longevity and health, not necessarily our choices. Guess what background this man came from? He shared with me that he was the son of the owner of one of the largest tobacco production companies in the United States.

Does it matter how we take care of our bodies or what type of fuel we put into them? I believe that it does! God designed our bodies to be healthy. In His Word, He provides guidelines for their care and maintenance that will result in optimum health.

We are careful to put the prescribed kinds of gasoline and oil into our vehicles, according to the manufacturer's instructions. How much more diligent we should be, then, to follow our Creator's "instruction manual" since we are "fearfully and wonderfully made" (Psalm 139:14, KJV). God desires that we enjoy good health (3 John 2). Someone once said that the Holy Bible is the world's best medical textbook. In fact, in it, God gives us eight laws of health: (1) Eat healthy, nutritious food (Genesis 1:29; 3:18). (2) Briskly exercise daily (Genesis 2:15). (3) Rest properly each night (Mark 6:31). (4) Enjoy sunlight daily in small doses (Genesis 1:4). (5) Drink plenty of water every day (Nehemiah 9:15). (6) Get plenty of fresh air every day (Genesis 2:15). (7) Live a temperate, drug-free life (Genesis 2:16, 17; Revelation 22:17). And finally, (8) trust in divine power (Proverbs 3:5, 6).

In the Bible, we can find hundreds of references to health principles, starting with the diet and lifestyle God gave to humankind in the Garden of Eden as recorded in the book of Genesis.

I hope you agree that good health is much more than mere "luck of the genes." Today, why not resolve anew to follow God's guidelines—all of them—for life and health?

Marcella Lynch

A Child's Perspective

"So do not fear, for I am with you;
do not be dismayed, for I am your God.
I will strengthen you and help you;
I will uphold you with my righteous right hand."
—Isaiah 41:10, NIV

For many years, I have remembered things and events in my mind the way I thought about them as a child—seemingly too big and impossible to be true. I was born and lived my early childhood in a small village in North India. It is the hottest place on Earth; at least, that is what I thought. Our family lived in a secluded area with only one neighboring compound. Our compound was surrounded by a very, very tall wall. Again, that's what I thought. As an adult, I revisited my first home in North India. To my amazement, the wall was only about three and a half feet tall! I was so shocked and surprised that I asked the man accompanying me—a friend with whom I had grown up in the small village—whether this was the same wall. He assured me that it was. I sat down to straddle the "very, very tall" wall. With one foot on the ground, the other foot could almost touch the ground on the opposite side, and I'm only five feet, two inches (157 centimeters) tall! And the village isn't the hottest place on Earth.

Sometimes we humans never outgrow that same childish perspective I had about the very, very tall wall. We tend to think that many things are way too big or impossible to achieve. We have self-doubt and uncertainty about many other things. Our walls are too high. Just like my perspective changed after visiting my old home, my thinking has changed as I've grown closer to God and matured in my Christian walk. I have learned I need to stop looking at my life and my problems like a child (or an anxious adult) who sees no way out and no way to scale the very, very tall wall. Now I turn my eyes upon Jesus, and all things have become possible through Christ.

No matter how difficult, tall, or big the problem is, Jesus makes it possible for us to get past the obstacle blocking our path. He helps us climb over the situation, go under it, or go around it, and sometimes He even lifts us up to carry us through it in His mighty arms. Being held in His arms is my new perspective.

Nancy A. Mack

God's Language

"Behold, I will pour out my spirit to you;
I will make my words known to you."
—Proverbs 1:23, ESV

G ood day, Oline! It's morning and time to awaken!"
"Only a minute more, Ollie; the pastor's sermon is almost finished!"
Thus began my grandparents' conversion to biblical truth. Oline Olsen had emigrated from Askim, Norway, as a young woman. A young man, Oliver Benson, had emigrated from Oslo. They had not known each other in the motherland, though. Providential timing provided their meeting, marrying, and welcoming children to their home in Portland, Oregon, in the United State of America.

A series of religious meetings had been advertised to be held soon in a tent, and out of curiosity, Oline decided to attend. When she discovered the presentations would be in Swedish—not her native tongue but close enough—she was blessed by the nightly studies from God's Word. Some of the nuances, fine points, and verb tenses were lost; however, she followed the topics and was convinced that the minister spoke the truth. And that is where a loving God revealed His abundant grace: Each night in a dream, Oline heard the entire sermon again in Norwegian! All questions cleared up! All possible misunderstandings explained! An honest seeker honored with divine blessing. (Does the word *miracle* come to mind?)

Soon it was summer, and the family attended a church camp meeting in Gladstone, Oregon (under yet another tent!), where Oliver came to a decision: his pipe would no longer be a part of a healthier lifestyle. There followed a joyous baptism.

Their daughter was welcomed as a student at an Oregon Christian boarding high school, followed by study at a Christian college in Washington State. There she met a ministerial student. Following graduation and marriage, the young couple was invited to join a team of traveling evangelists, bringing full circle their conversion-to-outreach experience via tent meetings. Their many visionary endeavors eventually led to the Bible in Living Sound ministry, which continues to spread the good news of God's love. If ever anyone experienced the "gift of hearing," it was my grandma Oline. *Thank You, Father God, Savior God, and Comforter God, for speaking all dialects, brogues, accents, and especially the language of heaven!*

Darlene Joy Grunke

Ready or Not?

"Do not store up for yourselves treasures on earth. . . .
For where your treasure is, there your heart will be also."
—Matthew 6:19, 21, NIV

After experiencing four hours of weather delays at Orlando International Airport in Florida, United States of America, our plane took off for Newark, New Jersey. We knew we could possibly miss our international connection to Venice, Italy, so as soon as the plane doors opened, we pushed our way out of the plane and ran as fast as we could to our next gate. Lightning storms along the East Coast had also delayed the Venice flight, so we had just enough time to board. Once settled in our seats, I began to wonder whether our luggage would have had time to transfer. We hoped for the best. In Venice, we stood patiently watching the bags come down the conveyor belt. Just when we thought the last had been unloaded, my husband's bag appeared! As I had feared, though, my bag didn't make it.

Our ride to the cruise ship waited while we filed a claim. There were no more flights to Venice that day, and the ship was scheduled to leave port at 5:00 P.M. I had planned for this trip for months and had carefully packed everything that would make this nineteen-day cruise perfect. My only hope was that the bag would catch up with us at the next port.

Nine days later, after nearly giving up on ever seeing that bag again, we opened the door to our stateroom and almost stumbled over my suitcase. I was overjoyed! But the strangest thing had happened over the first leg of the journey. I discovered that I was able to get along with a lot less than I ever imagined! I, the lady who likes lots of variety and appropriate choices, was able to survive by buying only a few basic necessities.

In a weird sense, it gave me hope that maybe this experience was preparing me for what is yet to come. This world is temporary, and our earthly home is for but a brief moment in time. Just before Jesus comes, we will be faced with a decision: either we choose Jesus and leave everything behind, or we take the easier path of compromise.

Remember Lot's wife? She hesitated between choosing to leave and give everything up or stay where she was, compromising her faith, blending in with the crowd, and not standing for God. She looked back for one last glimpse of home, trying to decide what was more important. She hadn't lived in a way that made the choice easy. Let's choose Jesus and live simply now.

Bernadine Delafield

A Little Bang Trim

*And if . . . any of you does not know how to meet any particular problem he has only
to ask God—who gives generously to all men without making them feel foolish or
guilty—and he may be quite sure that the necessary wisdom will be given him.*
—James 1:5, Phillips

"Mom, don't Kathy's bangs need trimming?" I asked. At nine years of age, I had started to notice things like that.

"Yes, I'll get to them soon," she agreed. We lived at our church youth camp, where my parents worked for the summer. A day or two later, after swimming in the lake, I again noticed six-year-old Kathy's bangs.

"Why don't I just trim your bangs?" I wondered aloud to Kathy. When she questioned my ability, I said, "Sure, how hard can it be?" My optimism overcame my trepidation.

She sat down on a stool in the cabin. Reaching for the scissors, I began to snip. But why couldn't I get them straight? They kept going uphill. First one direction, then the other. And they were getting shorter and shorter. This was harder than I thought. My former confidence gone, I tottered on the brink of panic and despair when a familiar sound caught my ear. Mom opened the door, taking in the situation at a glance. "Mom, I thought I'd help you trim Kathy's bangs, but it's not going well," I confessed. "Can you do anything with it?"

No words of censure and reproof. "Well, I should have gotten at that earlier. Let's see what we can do," and Mom took the scissors. "There's not a lot left to work with. *Hmm.*" She straightened what was left of Kathy's bangs, but there was only so much she could do.

"The good thing about hair is that it grows," Mom offered optimistically. "I'm sorry, Kathy, but this is the best I can do with what's left."

Not long after this incident, I trimmed my own bangs, more successfully this time. Later, Mom asked, "Rhonda, do you think you could trim my hair?"

How easily this could have turned out differently! Mom's matter-of-fact, solution-oriented, redemptive attitude gave me the confidence to try again. And God promises that when we come to Him, He will not make us feel foolish or guilty either. He is willing and able to help us. He redeems our mistakes and uses them for good.

Rhonda Bolton

Meeting Their Needs

I, Paul, am under God's plan as an apostle,
a special agent of Christ Jesus, writing to you faithful believers in Ephesus.
—Ephesians 1:1, *The Message*

I was surprised when my son phoned me: "Mom, I have joined the Naval Reserves." *Almost thirty-one, married, working at a good job, and he now joins the reserves? He will be gone six months for boot camp and training, then home with a one-weekend commitment a month to the reserves. But he is an adult, right? He can make his own decisions.*

I was frustrated. Then I received a letter from my cousin Allen. "Charlotte," he wrote, "I understand your being a bit disappointed by Benton's decision. I noticed many years ago that I don't really enjoy watching other people make their choices. And sometimes it's worse if it's your kid. But at this point, it's probably best not to try too hard to fix it. Try to be supportive, and maybe someday you might be able to say, 'Thank you for your service.' Yet pray that this might be one of the 'all things' God can use for good in his life [Romans 8:28] and maybe in the lives of others as well." That letter really made a difference in my life.

My son had told me his wife was behind him in this decision, so I knew, as his mother, I had to support him too. Not long after, he sent his sister and me a letter. "A friend here in boot camp doesn't get any letters. His family doesn't support him, so I'm wondering if you could send him some letters and encourage him. He has noticed all the letters I get. Could you help?"

I love writing letters, so why not? But what do I say to a young man who isn't my son? I guess one starts with prayer, asking for God's help. So my daughter and I wrote some letters to this young man. My son wrote us again, asking, "Hey, could you write another letter to a couple of other guys who found out you wrote to Kyle? They said no one is writing them either; they would like some letters. They said your letters are interesting, and, yes, they are serious." *Really?*

So my daughter and I wrote them letters, too, to encourage them and, hopefully, keep up their morale. Coming from a generation that wrote many letters, I know how important letter writing is. My daughter also loves to write letters; many from her generation don't. Maybe my son's joining the Naval Reserves would also help us by calling on us to use a gift God has given us that would encourage some young men far away from their homes.

Charlotte (Swanson) Robinson

October 8

Resilience in Isolation

"LORD Almighty, the God of Israel, enthroned between the cherubim,
you alone are God over all the kingdoms of the earth.
You have made heaven and earth."
—Isaiah 37:16, NIV

We often experience joy in the morning upon waking from our sleep. Each day brings new life, health, and strength from the Lord. But being in isolation due to fear of an invisible enemy, such as during the 2020 COVID-19 pandemic, produces uncertainty and paranoia. Yes, there are benefits to resting for a while, as when Jesus asked His disciples to come to a deserted place and rest from their busy days when they hadn't even had time to eat. Everyone needs rest and time away from stress and work in order to maintain good health and sanity. But being locked down for a long time with no productive work or activity causes rest to lose its benefits, especially when partnered with fear and uncertainty. People feared not being able to provide for their families. Students needed to continue their education. Struggling with uncertainty can lead to a loss of strength as one wonders, *When will it end?*

Thankfully, Paul reminds us, "We know that suffering produces perseverance; perseverance, character; and character, hope. And hope does not put us to shame, because God's love has been poured out into our hearts" (Romans 5:3–5, NIV). So we learned to be resilient as we dealt with isolation. Cell phones, tablets, and computers became avenues for connecting with each other, though we still missed the personal touches, hugs, and kisses. We practiced social distancing and visited outside, giving air hugs and elbow greetings instead of real hugs and handshakes.

I encourage you to cling to what God has promised us:

But those who hope in the LORD
　will renew their strength.
They will soar on wings like eagles;
　they will run and not grow weary,
　they will walk and not be faint (Isaiah 40:31, NIV).

Edna Bacate Domingo

Is Your Faith Strong Enough?

A furious squall came up, and the waves broke over the boat,
so that it was nearly swamped. Jesus was in the stern, sleeping on a cushion.
The disciples woke him and said to him, "Teacher, don't you care if we drown?"
He got up, rebuked the wind and said to the waves, "Quiet! Be still!"
Then the wind died down and it was completely calm.
He said to his disciples, "Why are you so afraid? Do you still have no faith?"
—Mark 4:37–40, NIV

When the disciples frantically woke Jesus, who was sleeping through the massive storm that threatened to sink their ship, they were dealing with a real problem. The wind and the waves were very real and very scary. The water that was filling the boat faster than they could bail it out was also very real. Many of them had spent most of their lives on the Sea of Galilee as fishermen, and they knew the difference between a small storm and a serious tempest. And this was a tempest, and it frightened them.

Despite the real danger of the storm, Jesus was sound asleep. How could Jesus sleep with such turmoil all around Him? What is even more shocking is that after the disciples woke Jesus up and after He calmed the sea, He rebuked them for their lack of faith. Excuse me? This dangerous storm had strong winds and tossing waves that filled their boat with water, creating the likely possibility that they would sink and drown.

Jesus did not question the nautical judgment of His disciples or disagree that the situation was serious. Instead, He questioned their lack of faith. They needed to learn, as do we, that faith is never dependent on our circumstances. Faith believes what God has said, no matter how things look around us. Faith recognizes that God is still in control, even in the worst of storms. Faith believes that God is able.

When we are walking in faith, we will not walk in fear. "The LORD is on my side; I will not fear: what can man do unto me?" (Psalm 118:6, KJV). Faith is not the belief that nothing will ever go wrong. Rather, faith is the belief that God is for and with us, and He will never allow us to endure something that He cannot ultimately use for our good and His glory. So today, have faith. The winds and the waves still obey His voice, and He is saying to you, "Peace, be still."

Beverley Martin

Hugs From God

He which hath begun a good work in you will perform it.
—Philippians 1:6, KJV

As I spent time with Jesus this morning, I looked over at my little table and saw six books. I realized that each one had a bookmark in it. Some of the books had bookmarks halfway through the book, others were a third of the way through, and some almost at the end of the book. Oh, my! Had I really started reading all these books and not finished even one of them? After a big sigh of disgust and guilt, I methodically looked at each one and thought, *Which one should I finish first?* I decided it should be the one someone in my small group had given me to read a while back. I remember really getting into this book and how the person who let me borrow it had underlined practically the whole book because he loved it so much. So I picked it up to read again, and guess what? The very next chapter was exactly an answer to a prayer I had prayed to God that morning. It spoke to me loud and clear, and I knew this was a hug from God.

Sometimes we look at our lives and see chaos, uncompleted projects, failures, and bumps in the road that divert us on our path. But sometimes, it is good to step back, look at your life, and recalibrate. It might be something as small as deciding to finish what you started. God has not abandoned you! Even in the midst of chaos, He is there with a little word of encouragement, a hug, or a gentle push ahead. Wherever you find yourself, He can move you forward in love and encouragement.

"Being confident of this very thing, that He who has begun a good work in you will complete it until the day of Jesus Christ" (Philippians 1:6, NKJV). That is really a faith statement! Put your name in this promise today. If you have accepted the gospel of Jesus Christ, He has begun a good work in you. As you spend time with Him every day—in His Word, in prayer, and in "doing life" together with other believers—He is in the process of completing that good work in you until He comes. Be assured of that!

I am not going to worry so much about the books I have started and not finished. I will eventually read them. Instead, I am going to wake up each day and praise God for what *He* has started and will get done!

My Jesus is faithful.

Lee Lee Dart

Master Puzzle

Who among you fears the LORD
and obeys the word of his servant?
Let the one who walks in the dark,
who has no light,
trust in the name of the LORD
and rely on their God.
—Isaiah 50:10, NIV

When we were little, we were fascinated by puzzles and building blocks. We felt very proud when we finally completed our masterpieces after hours or days of hard work. Today, as an adult going through a struggle, I often wonder how this fits into God's puzzle for me. This is not to say that God sees us as a game or as a means to have fun. Yet He puts events, places, and people in our lives to help us grow, move forward, and heal from wounds. In these times, we also see His mercy and blessings in our lives. We do not deserve His love, but He showers us with it anyway. I can certainly say that when I look back, even though I have had negative experiences, God has allowed both good and bad into my life so that I could learn to cling to Him, bring my heart to the cross, and surrender my life to His perfect will.

I like to think that God feels proud of any progress we make and will be joyous when the pain and evil in this world are over. We will spend eternity with Him as perfect masterpieces, made and redeemed by Jesus Christ, His Son. No matter where we are today or three years from now, we can trust that every piece of life's puzzle has been put into place by Jesus if we are living in Him. Though we do not have a picture on a box cover to preview what the fully assembled masterpiece will look like, the Holy Spirit is with us to guide and comfort us. He will bring encouragement even in those times when all we can see are pain and anxiety, when things are not going the way we may want them, or when our lives seem to be in a mess.

May we open our hearts to God today. His way is perfect—always. So the next time doubts come to mind and you feel discouraged, just remember, "I know I will not be put to shame" if I "trust in the name of the LORD" and rely on Him (Isaiah 50:7, 10, NIV). We are works in progress in the hands of the Master!

Yvita Antonette Villalona Bacchus

I Never Shall Forget

He will ever be mindful of His covenant.
—Psalm 111:5, NKJV

I recall a song from my childhood that repeats, "Oh, what He's done for me!" It ends with "I never shall forget what He's done for me!"* This song came to mind while reviewing my life, especially the past sixteen years, pausing in September 2005.

In September 2005, I had undergone a PET scan and had received the results. Finally, my husband, the rest of my family, and I could breathe a tremendous sigh of relief—the colon cancer had been beaten into submission by the mercy of my loving Savior and the care and prayers of my husband, our sons and their families, my doctors, and our wonderful friends.

A few months after receiving the good news, I approached my surgeon yet again and asked that my colostomy be reversed. For eight months, it had been a constant reminder that my body was not operating normally. Yet I had held on to the hope that this would all be over one day, and I would be able to return to business as usual.

My surgeon did not recommend a reversal. "I believe that keeping the colostomy would be far less problematic than a reversal," she told me. I could not envision my life postreversal and did not ask for details. But, eventually, the surgeon honored my request. She would perform the procedure if I agreed to take responsibility for whatever lay ahead.

My surgeon was partially correct. I refer to those things that could be labeled problematic as challenges—not problems. I live with those daily challenges, and sometimes they occupy my entire day; home is where I spend most of my time. Yet I think back to the words of the song: "what He's done for me" and *continues* to do for me. For every challenge that has come my way, God has provided a solution—a solution that allows me to leave the availability of home conveniences and even venture out occasionally.

Over the years, I have been blessed to welcome six grandchildren into the family, which is so remarkable because of my very close brush with death. My colon surgeon told me a year after my recovery that she never expected me to live. The details of what God has done for me on this journey in the midst of challenges are so amazing. I never shall forget what He's done for me!

Marea I. Ford

---

* Congregational praise song, "Oh, What He's Done for Me."

God Breathes From the Guango Tree

And when he had said this, he breathed on them,
and saith unto them, Receive ye the Holy Ghost.
—John 20:22, KJV

I suffered from a vein-related ailment for many months. The doctors advised that healing was probable but perhaps not for a long time because vascular issues take a while to heal. They can also cause great pain and suffering. I spent many days at home, away from my usual, active lifestyle. Having to slow down and wait for healing provided me with an opportunity not only for physical healing but also for healing of the mind and spirit. I reflected on God's goodness and grace but also prayed daily for complete healing.

One day during this time, a friend took me on an outing so that I could experience a change of scenery and be refreshed. We went to an old town close to the sea, where we leisurely moved about, viewing and enjoying the artifacts and remnants of this beloved historic town. After a while, I felt tired and was grateful for the seats that were provided in a large area beneath a giant guango tree. Its branches spread far and wide, ever ready to provide shelter to those who would find rest in the shade of its expansive canopy.

As I sat resting, a refreshing breeze such as I had never felt before wafted through the branches of the tree, swirling about as if coming to rest upon me. It was special. I felt renewed and reassured. Of all the experiences I had that day, this was the most memorable. As we departed, I was at peace in my heart that God had breathed from that towering guango tree and touched me.

It does not matter what we go through, be it fire, storm, or flood. God always finds a way to touch His children, bringing comfort and peace. Jesus and His disciples had just gone through a season of suffering and uncertainty. After the Crucifixion, Christ's followers were assembled behind shut doors "for fear of the Jews" (John 20:19, KJV). He knew they needed reassurance and comfort, so He appeared to them and strengthened them. God may not stop our fire, storm, or flood, yet He has promised to be with us through it all, bringing comfort, healing, and peace.

Join with me today in longing for, waiting for, and being renewed by His touch.

Elizabeth Ida Cain

Safety Is of the Lord

And it shall come to pass, that before they call, I will answer;
and while they are yet speaking, I will hear.
—Isaiah 65:24, KJV

A soft blanket of snow had fallen as we slept. My husband, Norman, woke me, saying, "I don't think you will be able to volunteer at the hospital today." Yet I was thankful when the road conditions improved, and I was able to go after all. The pastor phoned and asked Norman whether he could plow the snow in the church parking lot. Norman readily agreed to go but a bit later. Before I left, he asked me to come straight home when I finished at the hospital. The roads might be slick.

My trip to and from the hospital was uneventful. As I came closer to home, however, I began to be concerned for Norman. I picked up supper for him, turned into the church driveway, and began heading up the hill. Soon my car began to slide sideways, forcing me to a halt. Getting out of the car, I started walking but quickly realized I was on solid ice! I returned to the safety of the car and looked for Norman's tractor.

Oh, dear! I'm in a mess. I'll try to call him. But my cell phone signal was weak. "Oh Lord, I need help. Please show me what to do," I prayed aloud. Again, I began walking in the direction of the church building since I had the pass code that would enable me to get in. But I found myself in calf-deep wet snow. "Please help me, Jesus," I breathed. Then I saw the headlights of the tractor and began waving wildly! Norman stopped and asked, "What are you doing here?" I held up a soggy Taco Bell bag and weakly said, "I brought you some supper." Norman gently helped me inside the warm church.

He saw that my car was sitting on solid ice. As we rode home in his pickup, he said, "You could have been in real trouble."

"But I wanted you to have some supper," I said sweetly. My answer seemed foolish then.

As I look back on my decisions that day, I realize they were not bad decisions but rather foolish ones to make during inclement weather. I had let my love and concern for Norman jeopardize my own safety. Despite my flawed judgment, the Lord had answered my cry for help and delivered me that cold night on the dangerously slick hill of the church driveway! I'm surely glad that our prayers are heard and answered in *all* types of weather, aren't you?

Rose Neff Sikora

Pennies From Heaven

"For the LORD your God is living among you.
He is a mighty savior.
He will take delight in you with gladness.
With his love, he will calm all your fears.
He will rejoice over you with joyful songs."
—Zephaniah 3:17, NLT

I have this thing I do. I've done it since I was a kid. In fact, my mom used to say I must have inherited the tendency from my grandpa because he did it all the time. Most of my friends can tell you what I do: I pick up spare change. Whether I'm out for a walk or out shopping, when I see loose coins on the ground, I pick them up. I've even done it on hikes and during visits to other countries. Wherever I am, I have a knack for finding coins.

Last year I collected more than sixty-eight US dollars in this manner. As a kid, I supplemented my allowance by picking up coins. I've collected for an international development and relief agency and for church projects. When our church was renovating its social hall, I was teaching in one of the children's classes. We had a box in the classroom where children and teachers could put loose change or dollar bills as our way of contributing to the building fund (inspired a bit by the story of King Joash in 2 Chronicles 24:4–16). We leaders wanted the kids to feel like they, too, were contributing to this church endeavor. We also wanted them to know that every gift, large or small, is precious to God. I told those kids who didn't receive any allowance or couldn't think of any way to raise money to look for spare change. I also brought in the spare change I found.

Beyond the nice fact that money found on the ground is free money, I like to see these pennies (and nickels and dimes and quarters and sometimes dollar bills, not to mention foreign currency when I'm in other countries) as little gifts from God. Sometimes when I'm feeling down, they are messages of hope from my heavenly Father to remind me that He is always with me. When I'm worried about something, He uses the money to remind me that He is in control. When I am happy, they are reminders that God is good, and He rejoices with me.

God uses so many ways to show us His love and care. Let's look for them today! Collect them, and share the stories with others to encourage them too.

Julie Bocock-Bliss

Lean on Him

It is of the LORD's mercies that we are not consumed,
because his compassions fail not.
—Lamentations 3:22, KJV

Our journey through life may not always be smooth; it may be thorny or rough. So it's no wonder the Bible tells us that "to every thing there is a season, and a time to every purpose under the heaven" (Ecclesiastes 3:1, KJV).

Pain and sorrows can make one doubt that there is even a God. But God is our Sustainer. He is gracious and faithful to us. The great deceiver still works tirelessly to make us feel alone through the travails we sometimes face. Yet we can hold on to God's promises that will keep us going. "Weeping may endure for a night, but joy cometh in the morning" (Psalm 30:5, KJV).

In all the pain, struggles, and heartaches we may have been through—or the ones we are passing through—God knows all our weaknesses and needs. He will not abandon us, and when we wait upon Him, He will hear us. Even when it seems God is taking too long with an answer, we can always lean on Him. Personally, I know God is good. I have had a near-death experience, but God saw me through it. I prayed, and He answered. If He has not yet answered about an issue we have, He is still aware of our setbacks and is with us. His ways are different from ours.

I remembered when I once took an aptitude test for an international company. My name was neither on the list of those who had failed nor on the list of those who had passed. My name was completely omitted. I know now that had I been given the position, it would have kept me too busy to serve God. Our loving God knows how to supply our needs; He will not let us down. I am grateful I learned to trust Him because He has been sustaining me. It is important to lean on Him, for He is the only One who can keep us from falling. Friends may let us down, our spouse may not be there for us, and our kids may seem to abandon us. But know that God is there for us to lean on. He will carry us through all our struggles and suffering.

If God could give Sarah a child at the age of ninety, your problem won't be difficult for Him to resolve. If God could save Rahab the harlot, He can save you. If God could restore Job's losses, He can restore all that you have lost—many times over. Let us lean on and trust God. He will make us happy.

Elizabeth Oluwaseun Adebayo

Wherever We Are

Whither shall I go from thy spirit? or whither shall I flee from thy presence?
If I ascend up into heaven, thou art there: if I make my bed in hell, behold,
thou art there. If I take the wings of the morning, and dwell in the uttermost parts
of the sea; even there shall thy hand lead me, and thy right hand shall hold me.
—Psalm 139:7–10, KJV

In this world, temptations will assail us, and trying circumstances will test our faith, weaken our endurance, and deaden our ears to God's whispers of saving grace and strength. The duties and trials of the hour cause us to falter and sway toward the enemy who always stands ready to lead us astray and entangle us in making decisions to our own detriment and woe. Over time—days, months, perhaps years—as we yield to what we want, God's pleading voice becomes less audible. Eventually, desperation and a sense of unworthiness grip our entire being. The strong hold of sin is relentless. We are blinded to the way back home. We cry out to God, wondering whether He is still there, ready to forgive and restore.

One morning, as I opened my refrigerator's freezer compartment, I noticed that the ice-maker container had far surpassed its capacity. The ice cubes were frozen in place, making that feature totally inoperable for its designated work. After some maneuvering, I removed the ice container and emptied its frozen-together contents into the sink. What followed unfolded to me a revelation of God's grace, patience, and constant seeking of us, regardless of our pretense not to hear and our willingness to stray. At first, as I turned on the faucet's hot water, its stationary flow in place, the ice remained frozen and resistant to change. But then the water's steady stream began to initiate crackling sounds in the ice clumps nearest the downpour. A quiet pause. I mused, *Is the ice too frozen in its self-sufficiency to yield to the flow of the hot water?* Wait! The ice clumps began separating, moving one at a time. You see, undiscerned by my watchful eye, the flowing hot water had been extending its reach in all directions, regardless of the distance and resistance. Then the stronghold of resistant ice totally surrendered to the warmth of the water, bringing release and, in the spiritual sense, forgiveness—living waters flowing freely to bring newness of life wherever we are. God hears our cry for forgiveness wherever we are. He clothes us with His robe of righteousness and welcomes us home.

Cynthia Best-Goring

Words Can Hurt or Heal

A word fitly spoken is like apples of gold in pictures of silver.
—Proverbs 25:11, KJV

You're looking especially lovely today," the greeter at the church door remarked as he handed me a bulletin one Sabbath morning. *Me? Lovely?* I felt especially unlovely that day, though wearing a pretty, green summer dress with a matching jacket and nice white sandals. But his kind words did make me feel at least 75 percent better.

One day my sister, her daughter, and her granddaughter (a college student) were visiting me. During one of our discussions, the granddaughter very softly commented that she was not pretty. I overheard her but said nothing at the time. A few days later, I wrote her a little note, assuring her that she is a pretty young lady and should not underrate herself. I found out that she was so touched by the message that she cried. She later replied, thanking me for lifting her spirits and making her feel better about herself.

The old saying "Sticks and stones may break my bones, but words can never hurt me" is definitely not true. Some time ago, my phone rang. When I answered, I was taken totally off guard when the adult daughter of close friends accused me of saying hurtful things about her father's mental state. I told her truthfully that I had no idea what she was talking about. From her cold reaction, though, I don't think she believed me. The man's wife told me later that he had been having problems and was seeing a neurologist, but I had not been aware of it and had neither thought nor said such a thing. I'm glad to say that we are still friends.

Even though it hurt to be falsely accused, it did no physical damage to me nor even leave lasting hurt feelings. How different it was with Jesus at the hands of those He had come to save! Not only were there those who falsely accused and condemned Him, but wicked men pushed a crown of thorns down upon His head, struck Him, mocked Him, and spat in His face. Then Roman soldiers nailed Him to a cross. Even then, the mocking did not stop, for the chief priests, scribes, and elders joined in taunting Him to prove God's favor by coming down from the cross. What a temptation that would have been for my human nature! Yet because He so loved the world, He endured the agony of the cross so that whosoever believed in Him might have eternal life (see John 3:16). *Thank You, Jesus, that "whosoever" includes even me!*

Mary Jane Graves

The Professional

But our homeland is in heaven, where our Savior, the Lord Jesus Christ, is; and we are
looking forward to his return from there.
—Philippians 3:20, TLB

I can now laugh about this event; however, it was significant and potentially devastating at the time. After being away on holiday, my husband and I returned home to out-of-control and dense weeds in the garden. Wearing gloves and work clothes, I began the job of pulling the waist-high weeds, leaning into them to grab them from the roots. It was pure drudgery. As I worked, I noticed burrs attaching to my clothing and hair. I thought there were only a few burrs and kept going to get the job done. After about three hours, I finished the job, only to realize I was covered with burrs! My husband, Bret, seeing a tight helmet of tiny, troublesome green burrs covering my head, exclaimed, "What on earth have you done?" Naturally, I tried to take care of these burrs myself. I took a shower, using conditioner and then vegetable oil. But neither worked. Bret tried to pick out the burrs by hand, removing only about fifty of the estimated four thousand burrs. I began to think I would never get these burrs out of my hair! My thoughts went back to when I had lost my hair after chemotherapy treatment for breast cancer. The thought of having my head shaved again brought back bad memories, and the tears came.

That Sunday night we realized that we had to call a professional. My long-time hairdresser had come to our house previously to shave my head during chemotherapy. We made an emergency call to her. She couldn't see me until the following day after work.

She almost fell to the floor in amazement when she saw my hair, but she knew exactly what to do. She (later together with her mother) worked methodically to remove each burr, taking over six hours to get my hair soft and smooth once again. What a relief to have all the burrs finally gone!

We all have "burrs" in our lives—things that get stuck to us, sins we cannot shake, toxic people, bad decisions with damaging consequences, and occurrences that leave us in a mess. We all need to go to a professional—a Savior who alone can remove these burrs, these sins, and heal the damage and the mess. We may try to fix ourselves, but it does not work. Our Savior, Jesus, is the only One who can forgive and provide a clean and undamaged life. We need to go to our Professional, our Savior, daily.

Karen Dobbin

The Shadow of Death

Yea, though I walk through the valley of the shadow of death,
I will fear no evil: for thou art with me;
thy rod and thy staff they comfort me.
—Psalm 23:4, KJV

As I write this, we are in the throes of a pandemic. COVID-19 has turned our world upside down and forever changed the way we relate to one another. I was home in Jamaica until March 30, but a sense of duty and responsibility made me leave my safe haven with family to travel alone to the New York tristate area, which was the epicenter of the virus. I am a labor and delivery nurse and had scheduled myself for work throughout April. I could not bring myself to cancel my shifts and leave my frontline colleagues short-staffed at the height of the pandemic. I guess this is how people feel when they sign up to go to war, despite knowing that it could change their lives forever. I left home not knowing when I would return to my family or see them again. I left knowing that my sister, with whom I live when I am in the United States of America, had been significantly exposed and might be positive for the disease. Fear gave me headaches for days before my arrival, but I felt that I needed to return.

One day, shortly after I returned to work, I became so anxious trying not to contaminate my personal belongings that I locked my ID in my locker. The ID had the key for the lock on the locker. On the same day, I learned that my sister had tested positive for COVID-19. Thankfully, she was not ill, but here I was, wondering whether I would be positive, too, and how I would fare if I came down with the disease. That day I kind of lost it. Unable to function, I left work early.

The experience took me to a place where I realized that all human effort to protect myself from this scourge would be in vain. To survive and function to the best of my ability, I would have to trust in the God who helped David pen the words of the text above. It is a text I often quote during the flu season when infected colleagues and patients cough with impunity around coworkers. Now, more than ever, we must quote this text, repeat it, believe it, and live it.

I pray that those of you reading this have come through the pandemic unscathed. We may have lost friends or loved ones, but even when we walk through the valley of the shadow of death, God still comforts and leads us with His rod and His staff.

I pray that He will bless you with His mercy, comfort, and protection.

Raylene McKenzie Ross

Look and Live!

And Moses made a serpent of brass, and put it upon a pole,
and it came to pass, that if a serpent had bitten any man,
when he beheld the serpent of brass, he lived.
—Numbers 21:9, KJV

COVID-19 has overtaken our lives! What we wear, what we do, where we go, and when we go are determined by instructions or requirements from our local governments and the Centers for Disease Control and Prevention in the United States of America. Some supermarket shelves are empty. Many people have lost their jobs. Others have lost their lives to this deadly disease. Many hospitals have no available beds. States are recommending (or requiring) that people wear masks when they leave their homes and practice social distancing when they encounter others.

In the Bible, the children of Israel were in the Sinai Desert when they experienced an infestation of serpents. Many were being bitten by the snakes and immediately becoming sick—some to the point of death. But God told them through Moses that if they would only look at a brazen serpent that Moses was lifting high on a pole, they would live. Simple!

The temperature in my state is rising, and the Memorial Day holiday is fast approaching. Many people are thinking, *Spring is here, and we want to party as usual! The best beach locations are awaiting our arrival! We have been quarantined for almost two months. Who knows whether face masks and social distancing are making a difference? One state official did say that swimming in a pool is acceptable. No masks or social distancing allowed at our beach party!*

Yet those in the Sinai Desert who debated the merits of looking at the brazen serpent died. All they had to do was look at the uplifted serpent and live. In our pandemic, many who ignored the requirements to practice social distancing and wear face masks so that they could party at the beach soon contracted the virus. All they would have had to do to stay well was remain at home or simply don a face mask and practice social distancing.

When will we open our eyes and hearts to accept the subtle pleadings to live—live eternally with our Lord and Savior? "Look at me. I stand at the door. I knock. If you hear me call and open the door, I'll come right in and sit down to supper with you" (Revelation 3:20, *The Message*). It's simple: look to Jesus now and live!

Sylvia A. Franklin

Do We Always See When Our Prayers Are Answered?

Now therefore give me this mountain, whereof the Lord spake in that day;
for thou heardest in that how the Anakims were there,
and that the cities were great and fenced: if so be the Lord will be with me,
then I shall be able to drive them out, as the Lord said.
—Joshua 14:12, KJV

One hot summer day, as I drove out of the multilevel parking garage of my place of employment to go visit clients, I prayed, "Please, God, provide a parking space for me on the ground floor when I return." I also hoped that the parking space would be one into which I could easily maneuver. If I had to park on the top level of the structure, I wouldn't have a roof over me, and I needed to get some groceries on my lunch break to leave in the car for the remainder of the day. This would save time at the end of the day. The temperature on the ground floor was much cooler and more ideal for keeping groceries than was the warmer temperature on the top level.

But I am not good at reverse parking. Wherever I go, I try to pick spaces where I can just drive in and drive out easily. If I have to back up, I try to find a space with no other cars parked on either side of me. I also become very flustered when trying to back up for a parking maneuver if I see another vehicle driving by. How I wish I could reverse park!

On my return from the trip, I drove into the parking structure, circling through to see whether any of my favorite spaces were open. Alas, they were all taken. My heart sank. *Now I will have to do my shopping after work,* I thought, *which will put me home later. Evidently, my prayer was not answered.* To my amazement, I suddenly spotted a parking space, though not my favorite, between a parked car and a concrete column. I said to myself, *This space is for me. Wow! My prayer has been answered, after all! And if this is the only space available, that means I must reverse park. God did His part; I must do mine.* Another car pulled up and stopped. The driver waited patiently for me as I started trying to park my car. After a few attempts, I was successful.

This experience taught me a valuable lesson. I prayed but didn't see an immediate answer. Yet when we pray, are we expecting our needs to be met with no effort from ourselves? In the Bible, Caleb, though old, had faith that God would help him obtain his promised inheritance despite great obstacles. Let us be like Caleb and remember that the Lord is with us. He will help us conquer our mountains. I now ask God to open my eyes to see His answers.

Jenetta Barker

A Better Sleeping Place

"Let not your heart be troubled. You are trusting God, now trust in me.
There are many homes up there where my Father lives, and I am going to prepare them
for your coming. When everything is ready, then I will come and get you, so that you
can always be with me where I am. If this weren't so, I would tell you plainly."
—John 14:1–3, TLB

Why do we live in houses?" My third-graders looked a bit puzzled when I posed this question.

One student raised his hand and said, "That's a good question because Adam and Eve didn't live in a house, right?" That was exactly where I wanted to go. Today we live in houses for the sake of safety. We need protection from the weather and danger. This is so different from the Garden of Eden, where everything was safe. There was absolutely nothing to worry about.

Jesus knew that we need a place of safety, and it is exactly what He promised. In today's verse, we read that He is preparing houses in heaven for us to live with Him. I could tell that morning my students liked the thought. But being born in Switzerland, they did not long for it the way another student of mine had some years earlier. I had been teaching in a remote village in the Philippines. Jomel was about ten years old. His family was one of the poorest in the village. Their house stood literally in a swamp of dirt and trash. Under the leaking roof, there was not much except a smoky cooking area and a platform for sleeping.

One morning we talked about God's plan for us and how He wants to save us and live with us in heaven. The children memorized John 14:1–3, and we discussed it. When asked, "What is Jesus doing in heaven now?" Jomel suggested Jesus is preparing a "sleeping place." How precious for him to know that God is preparing a sleeping place for him! I think Jomel understood something very important that I sometimes miss because I have everything I need.

Are you longing for the better place that God is preparing? Whether you live in an ugly place you detest or have a beautiful home you love, God is preparing something far better for you. We can't even imagine how wonderful. I'm looking forward to the sleeping place my God is preparing especially for me, like He once did for Adam and Eve! God would love to prepare one for you, too, if you decide to let Him take you. Make that decision today!

Simea Kübler

Let Me Be His Hands

And He took them up in His arms,
laid His hands on them, and blessed them.
—Mark 10:16, NKJV

Life is hard for women in Nepal. Girls are married very young and often are so unhappy that they try to end their lives. They long to move on to the next life, hoping it is better than their current one. I see this often at the hospital where I work.

One young girl was married to a man who was not faithful to her. To make matters worse, she bore him a daughter instead of a son. The baby girl died at birth. Then this woman was not treated as a wife in her husband's home but as a slave. After a woman marries, she is no longer welcomed back into her parents' home, even if something goes wrong or her husband is mean to her. Instead, she is blamed for any problems in the marriage and is thought to bring dishonor to her family. So this young woman stayed. Eventually, she died. Her death caused a big riot in front of the hospital's emergency room. The girl's family fought with the husband's family; each blamed the other for her death. The police were called to help stop the fighting. My heart ached for God's daughter, and I pray for others in situations like hers.

One day a woman came to the hospital to have her baby, which was not yet full term. Yet she was happy after giving birth to a son, though premature and tiny. We put him, so small and precious to God, in an incubator and prayed for him. After several weeks, his lungs just couldn't keep going, and he died. The baby's mother was devastated and then suddenly left the hospital. Her deceased baby was also gone. We waited for her to come back. When she didn't, we called the police to look for her. We never did learn what became of her or what she had done with the remains of her baby.

It is hard, sometimes unbearable, to see such sadness and evil in the world. I pray for these women and children and hope that someday they will know the God of life and His joy. My prayer is that they will know Him personally. I also pray they will know that He will come back someday soon and make everything new. Until then, I ask Him to help me be His hands and words and care for those who are hurting and struggling.

Dear Jesus, Lover of children, I know that You look after all children in this world.
Today, please help us show even one person how much she is loved by You. Amen.

Susen Mattison Molé

A Nasty Turn and a Bible Verse

*"So My Word which goes from My mouth will not return to Me empty.
It will do what I want it to do, and will carry out My plan well."*
—Isaiah 55:11, NLV

Life can seem quite normal, and then one day, looking back sometime later, you come to a realization and say, "I see now that God was preparing me for this."

For me, that hint came on a Sabbath morning. Our senior pastor joined us in our French-speaking Sabbath School class. Now that was unusual because he felt more comfortable speaking German or Spanish. We enjoyed his insights during the discussion, but I soon forgot what he said. What he shared at the very end, however, I did not forget. It was either completely out of context or a very original way to close the discussion. He read and commented on Romans 12:21: "Do not be overcome by evil, but overcome evil with good" (NASB).

During lunch, my husband and I talked about the text and our surprise that the pastor had brought it up. "Why did he bring up that verse?" Little did we know.

On Sunday, life went as usual. Monday: *Hmm, this lump hurts. I'll call the doctor.* "Yes, we need a biopsy." Tuesday: *I won't say anything. My husband is flying to the United States today, and I don't want him to cancel this trip.* Wednesday: *This must be some cyst; I won't worry.* Thursday: "You've got breast cancer."

What? Can't we rewind and start over again? Even though the doctor's words were clear, it took a while for them to sink in. But some days later, I remembered that Bible verse shared in Sabbath School. Now I understood why our pastor had come to our class that Sabbath (of all Sabbaths) and shared that verse (of all verses). It was as if God were telling me: *"Now do all you can, think all you can, and be all you can to overcome this evil with good."*

I did not know then what the outcome of my cancer would be. But I did know that Romans 12:21 would be my cancer story verse. I shared it in my videos. I talked about it. And I praised God for having prepared me for the shock I received on that cold and rainy January morning. Now I praise God because I am healed and because I know that, with Him, I don't need to fear unexpected turns. My Father—and your Father—knows. And He will give us His grace and His Word to face whatever comes.

Lorena Finis Mayer

October 26

God Placed a Comma

Many are the afflictions of the righteous,
but the LORD delivers him out of them all.
—Psalm 34:19, ESV

At the age of thirteen, I lost my mom. The best writers in the world could not have found words to describe how I felt that day. I can recall thinking that I would never be able to bounce back from my devastating situation. At the time, my mother was the only parent I knew. My father was not in the picture, so her death meant that I was an orphan. After that, my mother's family did an exceptional job raising me, but I still felt lonely. I remember being told that "this too shall pass." How many times have you heard that line during a tragic situation? "This too shall pass" became another cliché that people shared to encourage me somewhat. But it meant nothing to me because the more years that passed, the more alone I felt. Eventually, I disconnected from God.

I can recall sitting at home in my room one night, having a pity party for myself when a message popped up on my phone from an old high school friend. She encouraged me to read the book of Esther because this queen reminded her of me. Esther, an orphan, lost both parents and lived with an old cousin—nothing short of a tragic weight for a child to have to bear. But Esther's story didn't end there. In fact, God appointed Esther to become the queen of Persia, and He used her, along with her cousin, to save the lives of His exiled people, the Jews, living in Persia at that time.

My sisters, I know the phrase "this too shall pass" seems to be overused at times, but believe me when I say that weeping does not last all night. It will pass. There really *is* joy in the morning (see Psalm 30:5). Like Esther's story, mine did not end in heartache and sorrow. God has given me the gift of evangelism and leadership. He uses me to preach to those who are lost so that they can find comfort in my testimony and draw closer to Him. It is because of this that I have the assurance that your storm, too, will pass! God has a major plan for you, just like He had for Queen Esther and for me! So my sisters, don't you dare put a "full stop" [a period] where God has placed a "comma." Remember that He is the Author and Finisher of our faith, and He lives!

Allow God to write your story, and watch Him turn your test into a testimony!

McKella O. Wiggins

The Boy God Wanted

Trust in the LORD with all your heart,
And lean not on your own understanding;
In all your ways acknowledge Him,
And He shall direct your paths.
—Proverbs 3:5, 6, NKJV

He was eighteen months old when my husband and I first saw him. This toddler had bowed legs, swollen hands, jaundiced skin, and drainage tubes inserted in his infected ears. Nor was he acting normal. Yet we adopted him. Having been turned down for adoption by many families already, this child would have been placed in foster care had we not intervened. He became our second son; we had previously adopted our first son.

Not all our family and friends accepted our sons. One church member told me that when we adopt, we should get "the best."

As my second son grew older, his legs straightened out. Medication cured his jaundice, swollen hands, and ear infection. I found out he was acting strangely only because he was imitating another child. When our son was about five or six years old, he would have a Bible in his hands and give "Bible studies." This continued until he was an adult.

After graduating from high school, he informed me he was going to college. I tried to discourage him because I didn't feel he was ready. He pointed to the sign on his bedroom door that said, "I can do all things through Christ which strengtheneth me" (Philippians 4:13, KJV).

He was right. Both my sons graduated from college, married two great ladies, and produced my three fantastic grandchildren.

Did God answer my request to have children? Of course, He did—just not in the way I expected. I have read devotionals about childless women who prayed about having a baby, and God answered yes to their requests. What about women, like myself, who pray for children, but God answers no? We feel like failures. We go through the stressful, psychological, and emotional trauma of trying to have children. Is this God's plan or ours? Years ago, I read that God made some couples childless so that children who are parentless could have a family. I appeal to women who are childless: please consider adoption. This is a great missionary work.

Ruth Cantrell

He Answered

Before they call, I will answer;
and while they are yet speaking, I will hear.
—Isaiah 65:24, KJV

A few weeks ago, while at my appointment with the cardiologist, I was told I had only four more years before I would need another open-heart surgery. *I do not want another open-heart surgery!* I thought. When I got into the car, I said to my husband, "I am going to buy something big and nice for myself."

Immediately, I was ashamed that my first thought after coming out of the doctor's office was to get something for myself. I knew that there was nothing I needed or wanted. But then again, our car had 125,000 miles (201,168 kilometers) on it. Even though it ran smoothly with no problems, I really wanted a back-up camera in a car, especially since I had almost hit a lady when backing out of my sister-in-law's driveway.

Silently, I prayed, *God, I really don't think I am worthy of a new car, but if I could have one with lower mileage than on this one, that would certainly be nice.* I reflected on how our previous car had had 88,000 miles (141,622 kilometers) when we purchased it. I "heard" God say to me, *"Other people buy new cars and think nothing of it."* But I still felt unworthy and simply left my heart's desires in God's hands for His decision.

As my husband and I talked about our vehicle, he became excited about having a newer car. In addition to a car with a back-up camera, it would certainly be nice to have one with lower mileage. My husband thought about it and came up with additional features he would appreciate in a car: the same color as our current vehicle, heated seats, and a nice radio—at a reasonable price we could afford. After some research, my husband found a car for sale only forty-five miles (72 kilometers) away and with all the features we desired. So we went shopping.

As we drove home in our newer car with only 8,000 miles (12,874 kilometers) on the odometer (along with its new car warranty because of its low mileage), I thought, *Lord, You were there when this car was manufactured seven months ago, even before I almost had an accident. Even though my original thoughts were selfish, You made sure everything my husband and I wanted in a car was provided for us. You even added special features neither of us had thought about! How much You love us! Thank You for answering our prayers even before we call upon You.*

Avonda White-Krause

Have You Washed Your Hands?

The law of the LORD is perfect, converting the soul.
—Psalm 19:7, KJV

Lunch preparation completed, I called my three small grandsons inside. Since they were coming from the sandbox, I reminded them to wash their hands. Moments later, they burst through the door, charging toward the bathroom. Not wanting the washup to be a drip-and-dry event, I stopped them before they reached the table. Bending down, I individually clasped their little hands in mine, asking, "Have you washed your hands?" Quickly, they shouted in unison, "Yes!" The first two passed Grandma's feel-and-sniff test as their hands were still semi-moist, clean, and fragrant. The third reluctantly held out his hands for inspection. They were dry, dirty, and smelled terrible. But from that day forward, all were able to honestly say "Yes!" when asked whether they'd washed their hands. Though immature, they were learning to respect Grandma's rules and develop character traits of honesty, responsibility, and cleanliness.

Our Father in heaven has given us ten foundational rules of conduct for character development. These principles are found in Exodus 20:1–17. God gave these precepts, knowing that because of our love and respect for Him—and by obeying them through the indwelling of His Spirit—we might develop characters that reflect His and be blessings to others. These precepts show us, like a mirror, when and where our characters are distorted or unclean, just as the feel-and-sniff test revealed whether or not the dirty hands of our grandsons needed attention.

Through His life of surrender and obedience to the will of His Father, Jesus Christ showed the excellence of character that He wants us to develop through a loving relationship with Him. Psalm 19:7 tells us, "The law of the LORD is perfect, converting the soul" (KJV). Therefore, if the law that reflects God's character is perfect, it is changeless and eternal. Scripture shares with us that not one letter is permitted to be changed within the law of God (see Matthew 5:18). Logic tells me that the original "document" engraved in stone and written by God's finger cannot truly be altered by even one stroke of a pen or any human decree. Any such attempt to do so by human beings is a forgery—the falsification of a legal document given by the God of heaven and Earth and sealed by the blood of Jesus Christ upon the cross of Calvary.

Dottie Barnett

October 30

The Sin of Ingratitude

And Jesus answering said,
Were there not ten cleansed? but where are the nine?
—Luke 17:17, KJV

Have you ever done all there is that you could do for someone—maybe a child, sibling, coworker, or even a parent—and he or she acted as though you had done nothing for him or her? This person showed no appreciation for your effort! Well, consider yourself fortunate if you have *not* encountered someone like this in your family, at work, among friends, or—God forbid—in the Christian church. Even Jesus experienced ingratitude when only one out of ten healed lepers returned to say thank you. Many of God's servants dealt with the hurt of ingratitude. Ezra, Nehemiah, and Joshua, to name a few, did all they could to help the ancient Israelites remain faithful to God and avoid the consequences of their actions. Yet as complaining mounted among the unthankful people, the faithful servants of God must, at times, have been discouraged.

Moses experienced his share of ingratitude as well. The very people he loved turned on him, rebelled against him, and threatened to elect another leader to take them back to Egypt. Joshua witnessed their rebellion. It must have been a challenge for him when God chose him to be the successor of Moses and lead the offspring of rebels into the Promised Land.

The prophet Isaiah witnessed the people of God fall deeply into sin. They forsook God and His instructions. Isaiah warned the children of Israel and their kings to repent of their wicked, idolatrous ways so they would not have to suffer God's judgment by being taken into captivity by the Assyrians. But the people of Israel and their kings were so depraved that when warned, they simply turned a deaf ear. They turned on God's messengers and imprisoned a number of them. Christian tradition has it that Judah's most wicked king, Manasseh, even ordered that the prophet Isaiah be sawed in two (many believe this is referred to in Hebrews 11:37). How ungrateful they were to God's merciful call!

Today many still behave in ways similar to those of ancient Israel. We carry the sin of ingratitude in our DNA. Only the transforming power of God can change our stony hearts and replace them with hearts of flesh—soft hearts that will love Him and manifest an attitude of gratitude. *Lord, help us to truly appreciate all You do for us every day.*

Kollis Salmon-Fairweather

No More Black Fabric

"The bin of flour shall not be used up, nor shall the jar of oil run dry,
until the day the LORD sends rain on the earth."
—1 Kings 17:14, NKJV

I was sewing with my sewing machine one day when my good friend Angie said, "Why don't you start making some masks?"

"That sounds like a good idea," I said.

This was during the COVID-19 pandemic. I knew many people who would need a mask, especially since my daughter and stepdaughter are nurses.

We found a mask pattern on the internet. The masks needed black cotton fabric for one of the four layers. To my surprise, we found on my fabric shelf a whole bolt of black cotton fabric that I had never used. I began making masks with the help of my daughter. She would cut out the patterns, and I would sew them together. After sewing nearly two hundred masks, I needed more black cotton fabric. I looked on my fabric shelf—and found more!

When this black cotton fabric was gone, my friend and I got on the internet to order more, but we had no luck. It was midnight when I prayed, "Lord, what am I going to do?" I looked on my fabric shelf and found more black fabric! "Look, it's a miracle!" I excitedly showed my husband. When he asked whether I really thought God did a miracle just for me, I answered, "Why not? God did it for Elijah and the widow of Zarephath when He blessed them with continuous flour and oil until He knew it was time to send rain." So I kept sewing masks until I ran out of black cotton fabric once again. As I walked slowly to my fabric shelf, I prayed, *Lord, I know my husband doesn't believe You did that just for me, but I need more black fabric again.* I looked on my fabric shelf and saw something black. Yes! It was even more black cotton fabric! In excitement, I ran upstairs to share with my husband. "Look!" I told him. "God did it for me. Just for me!" Finding black cotton fabric on my shelf had happened yet again!

I continued to sew until the day that the very last of my black cotton fabric started getting low again. *What am I to do now?* Just then, I heard a knock at my front door. It was the mail carrier with a package. To my surprise, it was more black cotton fabric that my daughter had ordered for me. What a miracle! God is still in the miracle-working business—especially in times of need.

Charlotte Williams

"Showers of Blessing"

Then you will call upon Me and go and pray to Me,
and I will listen to you. And you will seek Me and find Me,
when you search for Me with all your heart.
—Jeremiah 29:12, 13, NKJV

May 15, 2014, is a day that I will never forget. At home on sick leave, taking advantage of sleeping in, I was awakened by my mobile phone vibrating. I quickly answered the phone call and discovered my sister on the other end of the call. Her message was heartbreaking: "He has aggressive cancer, and there is nothing the doctors can do."

My brother-in-law Paul had been admitted to the hospital the night before for an exploratory laparotomy (surgical incision through the abdominal wall). He had been complaining of abdominal pain and suffered weight loss for several weeks. On that day, thoughts raced in my head: *Paul is forty-six years old. He and my oldest sister are to celebrate their twentieth wedding anniversary in September. They have three children. How are they going to cope?* I prayed, "God, Paul doesn't even believe! How is my sister going to cope on her own?"

I quickly pulled on my gym gear and decided to go for a walk to spend some time with God. One side of the sky was a beautiful blue with white fluffy clouds, while gray clouds darkened the other side of the sky. Thoughts continued to race: *My sister is going to be a widow—she is only forty-five!*

As I was trying to absorb this terrible news, it started to drizzle a gentle shower. The words of a hymn flashed across my mind: "showers of blessing." At that moment, I remembered that I have a God who loves my family and will be with us every step of the way. A God who, regardless of what the future holds, is there with us, holding our hand, comforting us, and being our Rock of strength.

I am glad to say that Paul gave his heart back to God and enjoyed that sweet fellowship for ten months before losing his battle with cancer. During those ten months, our family experienced showers of blessing through food parcels, kind words, additional days off from work, flowers, prayers, and hugs from friends and church family. We were enveloped in God's love, and His love sustained us through this painful journey. With sadness in my heart, I have this wonderful hope: my family will see Paul again when Jesus comes. Showers of blessing will flow then!

Jenny Rivera

Obsessed With Masks

You know we never used flattery,
nor did we put on a mask to cover up greed.
—1 Thessalonians 2:5, NIV

During this time of social distancing due to the COVID-19 pandemic, people are looking for things to do. Some say their homes have never been so clean. Others go through their wardrobes and drawers to help fill the Red Cross's clothes containers. I sew face masks. I don't know how many times I got fed up and said, "It's enough! I won't sew another mask!" Yet here I am, at it again. After stitching more than 140 pleated masks, I am trying the fitted masks. I will probably be at it for a while.

I started sewing face masks early in the pandemic, expecting the time would come when we would need them. In serial production, I used leftover material I had at home. I sent masks to family and friends, but there were still a lot left over. What should I do with them? The church was closed. Then the idea came to send masks to church members since the need would come at some point. That meant more masks were needed, and another skilled seamstress took up the task of making another 110 masks to put in surprise parcels. In addition to the masks, the packages included encouraging reading material and craft ideas and surprises for the children. Many members contacted church leaders to thank them for their surprise parcels.

We are hoping church services will resume after the shutdown. What it will be like, we don't know yet, but at least we have sufficient masks for the church's members and guests.

I have often thought about how we are used to putting on our "Sabbath masks" when we come to church—masks hiding our hurts and pains as we put on a smile to keep others at a distance. Or we wear masks of religious compatibility so that nobody can see what we are really like. Now the community masks we use hide our smiles. But they will not be able to hide our joy at successfully overcoming a difficult phase in our lives. And when we are finally allowed to dispose of our masks, we will appreciate our freedom more than ever. I hope we learn to be authentic and live without our "Sabbath masks" as well. During difficult times, let's fix our eyes on "the Father of compassion and the God of all comfort, who comforts us in all our troubles, so that we can comfort those in any trouble with the comfort we ourselves receive from God" (2 Corinthians 1:3, 4, NIV).

Hannele Ottschofski

Quarantine

Now I saw a new heaven and a new earth, for the first heaven and the first earth
had passed away. Also there was no more sea. . . . "There shall be no more death,
nor sorrow, nor crying. There shall be no more pain,
for the former things have passed away."
—Revelation 21:1, 4, NKJV

When COVID-19 broke out in 2020, people slowly adjusted to a different life. Social distancing, quarantine, handwashing, face masks, and disinfectants became life-saving necessities. Anxiety, fear, and uncertainty prevailed in the minds of many. Meanwhile, the world hoped for a cure.

The regulation confining children younger than five years of age and adults older than seventy hit me hard. I complied with the new rules as well as I could while secretly resenting the restriction on my movements. While fellow teachers taught their online classes from their offices, I taught from my apartment. I missed trips to the market and the shops. But I also knew that the isolation protected me from unnecessary exposure to the pandemic virus. It protected others from me if I was a carrier. Containing the virus depended on everyone's cooperation. Meanwhile, everyone had to exercise patience and prudence.

The prevailing situation gave me some new thoughts regarding God's plan of salvation. Sin, like a dangerous virus, erupted in heaven. Unexplainable, corruptive, and highly contagious, it began with Lucifer. Unchecked, it could have spread through the whole universe. In His wisdom, God cast out Lucifer from heaven. Then He quarantined Earth, where the virus had already spread because of man's wrong choice to listen to the deceiver. Satan and his work of sin have been allowed to continue here so this vicious sin virus—with its symptoms, cause, and effects—will be so fully exposed and so clearly understood that the danger of reinfection will be eliminated. But God did not abandon the world to perish forever from the plague of sin. He had a remedy ready. The cure cost the life of His Son, whose blood, instead of ours, was spilled for this world that has been in isolation since it fell to sin.

One day the sin problem will come to its final resolution. The quarantine will be lifted. Those who have accepted the cure through faith will experience life eternal with true freedom, complete freedom from sin and its ravages—the life God intended for humankind and for each of us.

Bienvisa Ladion Nebres

Shielded by a Cloud of Dust

No evil shall befall you,
Nor shall any plague come near your dwelling;
For He shall give His angels charge over you,
To keep you in all your ways.
—Psalm 91:10, 11, NKJV

The station wagon sped along the gravel road, sending a thick cloud of dust trailing behind. Godson, the registrar of our college; my husband, Henry; our three-year-old daughter; and I were on our way home to the Christian college near Kampala, the capital of Uganda.

It was 1977. The current president of the country's dictatorship had banned several denominations from operating churches in the country, including ours. During this time, the dictator's henchmen in shiny black Mercedes-Benzes were seizing vehicles and leaving their occupants by the side of the road, though not always alive. This day, however, my thoughts were far from the turmoil of the country. Back seat driver that I am, I kept telling Henry to slow down. But my complaints fell on deaf ears, it seemed, as he raced on down the road.

Reaching our college campus, Henry immediately drove the station wagon straight into the garage. Then he told me the reason for his actions: a black Mercedes-Benz had been tailgating our vehicle ever since we left the capital. It followed closely behind us, even as Henry turned off the paved road onto the narrow, winding gravel road about nine miles (fifteen kilometers) from the college. On the winding curves near campus, Henry had managed to put considerable distance between us and our pursuer. It seems the other driver was blinded by the thick cloud of dust behind us and took a wrong turn at a fork in the road. Arriving at our campus, the Mercedes-Benz had gone the opposite direction from our house. Not knowing where our car had gone, the Mercedes-Benz headed back toward Kampala. A few days later, under cover of darkness along back roads, we safely made our way out of Uganda and into neighboring Kenya.

The God of Moses, who provided the Israelites with the pillar of cloud by day, sent His angels and a cloud of dust to shield us from danger. "Because thou hast made the LORD . . . even the most High, thy habitation; there shall no evil befall thee, neither shall any plague come nigh thy dwelling" (Psalm 91:9, 10, KJV).

Evelyn Porteza Tabingo

"Train Up a Child"

Train up a child in the way he should go:
and when he is old, he will not depart from it.
—Proverbs 22:6, KJV

My parents joined the church when I was nine years old. They have many personal testimonies of God at work through the years as they ministered to others. My father, Noel Jumpp Sr., has been a lay evangelist since I was in high school.

We have a lot of memories of attending evangelistic series throughout the years. My mother, Marilyn, was (and still is) his projectionist in charge of the slides my father uses for his sermons. He was (and still is) a very engaging preacher. And I, along with my four siblings, either sang or provided moral support.

Our family really enjoyed meeting new people and going to new places. I know that the memories we made as a family are still with us today and have helped both make our faith stronger and keep us all in the church.

We did many other things together as a family, and as we did so, we strengthened the family ties over the years. One of my favorite memories is when Daddy would take us to the beach or seaside on Friday evenings for vespers or family worship to usher in the Sabbath. The sunsets in Jamaica were all breathtaking and spectacular. The sound of the waves breaking on the shore is so soothing.

One of the things that I learned during those distant times is the importance of being willing to be available to help or contribute to whatever need may arise. Whenever I was asked to sing or tell the children's story for church programs, I was always willing to say yes. It is a character trait that has stayed with me through the years. Even today, when I am asked to sing or tell a story, my first response is still yes. It's hard to say no because I am always so willing.

I also came to realize that I have the gift of hospitality, which I enjoy very much. I love meeting new people. I love making people feel welcome and at home. And of course, I love to cook food that tastes good. Those early years under my parents' guidance were so important.

I am thankful to the Lord for parents who have been faithful to train my siblings and me in the way that we should go. I never want to depart from it!

Noella (Jumpp) Baird

Hope in Jesus Christ Alone

*Then I saw "a new heaven and a new earth," for the first heaven and
the first earth had passed away, and there was no longer any sea.
I saw the Holy City, the new Jerusalem, coming down out of heaven
from God, prepared as a bride beautifully dressed for her husband.*
—Revelation 21:1, 2, NIV

Dear God,
We are living in the last days—I know this is so from what I read in the Bible and what church pastors often tell us. Events over the last decade seem to confirm this reality. There is an increase in catastrophic earthquakes, hurricanes, and other weather-related disasters. Devastating fires burn for weeks, leaving behind nothing but death and destruction.

Father, the hearts of human beings seem to grow more desperately wicked; consequently, murders and other vicious crimes increase at an alarming rate. The year 2020 brought COVID-19. This formless enemy descended on us like a supercharged war machine, killing people indiscriminately and leaving survivors, households, and communities stunned and stupefied. People quarantined in their homes questioned, "What does it all mean? Where do we turn for answers?"

Lord, for those who read the Scriptures, there are answers—answers that will provide seekers of truth with solace, encouragement, and comfort through Your promises.

Yes, the storms are raging. There is no sign or assurance that these current tempestuous events will subside anytime soon. In fact, our Savior warned, "You will hear of wars and rumors of wars, but see to it that you are not alarmed. Such things must happen, but the end is still to come" (Matthew 24:6, NIV).

Thank You for comforting Your church with these words: "Do not be afraid of what you are about to suffer. . . . Be faithful, even to the point of death, and I will give you life as your victor's crown" (Revelation 2:10, NIV).

Father, whatever state the world is in, Your children can rest in You and be at peace because Your Word promises You will never leave us nor forsake us (see Deuteronomy 31:8). We look to You with expectation and hope and to Your soon coming and glorious kingdom.

Jasmine E. Grant

God Matters Most

But Martha was distracted by all the preparations that had to be made. She came to him and asked, "Lord, don't you care that my sister has left me to do the work by myself? Tell her to help me!" "Martha, Martha," the Lord answered, "you are worried and upset about many things, but few things are needed—or indeed only one. Mary has chosen what is better, and it will not be taken away from her."
—Luke 10:40–42, NIV

Susan* was an adrenaline junkie—not the kind that led to a compulsion to skydive, rock climb, or swim with sharks. It was the kind of adrenaline rush that resulted in Susan constant rushing around to ensure perfection and the timely completion of mammoth tasks.

Today Susan lies in a hospital bed, where the pain shooting through her lower abdomen causes her to writhe in agony. Medical professionals can do nothing for her at this point, except wait for the pain medication to kick in. Susan's hectic schedule has taken a toll on her. She is burned out, to say the least, and now suffers the consequences of her choices. The abdominal pains are symptoms of gastroenteritis due to a weakened immune system. She has also been diagnosed with osteoporosis.

Through her pain, Susan's mind wanders to the many days, stretching into months, when she would work off nothing but adrenaline. Her day typically started at five o'clock in the morning with family worship, after which she would make breakfast, pack the kids' lunch, get them ready for school, get dressed, and be out the door without anything to eat. Susan's hectic work schedule would further compound the problem as lunch breaks were typically taken at the end of her workday. By the time she got home, it was time to switch gears. Barely running on empty, Susan would take on the task of helping her kids with their homework and fixing dinner.

Susan's story isn't unusual. Many of us experience this hectic, harmful lifestyle. We must stop before it stops us. Let us be more like Mary, who sat at the feet of Jesus, feasting on His every word. Let us not busy ourselves into ill health. And certainly, life should never get so busy that we do not have time to develop a personal relationship with God. After all, He matters most.

Jodian Scott-Banton

---

* Not her real name.

Inasmuch

Behold, I make all things new.
—Revelation 21:5, KJV

When my daughter and her two young children visited me and we attended church together, the children always looked forward to seeing Bill.* Bill seemed to have a never-ending supply of chewing gum to hand out—a whole package for each child! More important to me than the chewing gum was the kindness Bill and his wife had shown during my husband's last illness. Such things are not easily forgotten.

Fast-forward thirty-three years after my husband's death. Bill's wife had also died. Bill's birthday was approaching, and I wanted to do something special for him. Knowing his weakness for candy, I decided on a box of chocolates. When the day came, I took the festively wrapped package to where he lived, anticipating his excitement. I found him sitting in the large living and dining room at a table, chewing on a small piece of candy that still had the wrapper on. He seemed baffled by my gift and needed help opening it. An expression of wonder came over his face when he saw the contents. He began, carefully and methodically, placing each piece of candy onto the table, eating as he went. You see, Bill, a World War II veteran and former police captain in a large city, was now in an assisted living home. His memory fading and hearing severely impaired, he depended on others for his most basic personal needs. None of his family lived close; his visitors were few. Life held little pleasure for him. Even though the mountain view from the front porch was beautiful and peaceful, he never cared to go outside.

When Bill started to put the remaining candy back into the box, I knew he was finished. One of the caregivers came to his assistance, assuring him that he could eat the rest later.

I talked to him about the coming of Jesus when he will be reunited with his precious wife. We clasped hands as I offered prayer when it was time for me to leave.

Why do I tell you about Bill? Because there may be someone like him whose day you could brighten, if only for a few minutes. Visiting can be awkward, but the present and eternal rewards are worth it. I rejoice in knowing that the time will come when all things, including Bill and many others like him, will be made new.

Lila Farrell Morgan

---

* Not his real name.

Let It Go, and Move On!

Jesus saith unto him, I say not unto thee,
Until seven times: but, Until seventy times seven.
—Matthew 18:22, KJV

The greatest act of forgiveness ever was when Jesus died on the cross to save us from our sins and give us eternal life. Forgiveness is really about Jesus. For Him to forgive us, we must confess our faults to one another, forgive, and seek forgiveness from God. The Bible tells us, "Be ye angry, and sin not: let not the sun go down upon your wrath" (Ephesians 4:26, KJV). A lot of people go to their graves still holding on to grudges. Yet if you were to ask them what they were mad about, they could not tell you. Some people stay angry out of habit and for no reason.

Forgiveness is a hard pill to swallow. Some people say that they haven't spoken to their family members or friends in years. I say, "Let it go, and move on!" We can't have a meaningful relationship with God or each other if we harbor malice, bitterness, and hatred in our hearts. God can't heal us or forgive us that way. Besides, we are not here to judge others.

There have been many incidents in my life that I had to really pray about and ask God for forgiveness and healing. Every time I saw a certain individual that had accused me falsely, I would go the other way just to avoid them. One instance involved the division of my mother's estate between my siblings and me after she passed. My sister knew how my mother wanted her property and possessions divided among us children. Yet because she had access to my mother's affairs, she and her attorney swindled us out of everything. At first, I was mad, hurt, and upset, but after talking to God in prayer, I began to seek His forgiveness for myself and her. I know that one day she will have to answer to God for her actions. I didn't want to carry this with me for the rest of my life. If I hadn't asked to extend forgiveness, God couldn't have forgiven me.

One of the biggest acts of forgiveness that I have witnessed was in 2019 during a trial for a former police officer who shot and killed her neighbor. At the end of the trial, the victim's brother asked if he could say something. He told the officer that he forgave her for killing his brother. He offered Christ, hugs, and grace. He did what Jesus wants us to do. There were those who criticized what he did, but I'm sure this gave him peace and contentment, which is what God gives to us. "Forgive, and ye shall be forgiven" (Luke 6:37, KJV).

Camilla E. Cassell

Heart's Desire

May the Lord answer you in the day of trouble!
May the name of the God of Jacob keep you safe. . . .
May He give you the desire of your heart,
and make all your plans go well.
—Psalm 20:1, 4, NLV

When I got married five years ago, I lived and worked outside my home country while my husband was living and working at home. The first year of our marriage was tough as we lived apart and could meet only once every several months. We had agreed to look for work where the other person was. Whoever secured employment first would determine where the other spouse would move. But deep down in my heart, I was praying my husband would be the one to move. We both kept this situation on our list of prayer petitions.

One Monday afternoon in February, two months before our first wedding anniversary, I attended our usual Monday lunch-hour prayer time at work. While sharing our prayer petitions, one of the elders said we needed to pray for God's divine intervention as all of us in the room that day were living away from our families. Something stirred inside of me, and I decided to do more. I had applied for a job in one of the international organizations in my home country the previous December. So I decided to begin fasting every Monday, Wednesday, and Friday that month and praying that my job application would be accepted. My first fast was on a Wednesday. On Thursday, the very next day, I received an email from the international organization to which I had applied. The email invited me to complete a written assessment. I was over the moon with joy and praised God for the answered prayer.

Yet I continued with my fast. On the last day of February, which was a Monday, I received another email from the organization, inviting me for an oral interview. I got the job and moved back home in June of that year. I was amazed at God's faithfulness to me, of which I was not deserving. Many previous times, I felt God had not answered my prayers according to my heart's desires. Yet when I remember what He has done for me, I know His answer is for my own good and according to His will.

May you always remember to praise the King of kings for the times He has granted your heart's desires and even for the times you have felt He has not, for His plans are not to harm us.

Chipiliro Chonze Santhe

Drinking From the Living Water

On the last day, that great day of the feast, Jesus stood
and cried out, saying, "If anyone thirsts, let him come
to Me and drink. He who believes in Me, as the Scripture
has said, out of his heart will flow rivers of living water."
—John 7:37, 38, NKJV

She wasn't expecting her day to change as drastically as it was about to. At Jacob's well, a Jewish Man asked her, a Samaritan woman, for a drink of water. Sure, she'd had plenty of experience when it came to men. In fact, she had gone from husband to husband and then to a live-in. As she engaged in conversation with Jesus and He revealed to her who He was, she realized He was quite different from the other men she had interacted with in her past.

This woman's encounter with Christ is one of my favorite stories in the Bible. Her story reveals how quickly our lives can change during an encounter with Christ. From then on, we can drink of the same living water—a relationship with Him—that He promised this woman. In Psalm 34:8, the Lord encourages us to "taste and see that the LORD is good" (KJV). When the Samaritan woman realized Jesus was the Messiah, she didn't ask Him any more questions. Instead, she immediately accepted Him as her Lord. Her life would never be the same again.

Although Christ does not condemn us, an encounter with Him does force us to face who we really are. This self-realization is not intended to make us feel bad or horrible; instead, it lets us see how much we need Christ as our Savior. As with this woman, filling her life with one relationship after another, are you filling your life with things or people you hope will satisfy your soul? They can't. Only Jesus can satisfy. Only the Living Water can provide relief for your thirsty soul. And when we trust Him for power, we can let go of unhealthy relationships, unhealthy habits, and addictions we have been depending on for fulfillment. We will no longer have to go from "husband to husband" in search of fulfillment. The Living Water will fulfill the needs of our souls and make us free to walk in the purpose God has for us.

The Samaritan woman at the well immediately became a spokesperson for Christ after she met Him. She went back to her city and told everyone about the Man she had met. So it will be with you as well. Once you've tasted and seen that the Lord is good, a new joy will flow from your heart, and you won't be able to keep the goodness of the Lord to yourself.

Shushanna Mignott

God's Crazy Idea of Love

"I know that you can do all things;
no purpose of yours can be thwarted."
—Job 42:2, NIV

It was Thanksgiving, and I was not doing well emotionally. I was depressed, and my relationship with God was severed. My bad decisions and inconsistent emotions were to blame. I had lost all hope that I could be loved or be in love. But on that Sabbath, I forced myself to get ready and go to church. I arrived in time for the sermon, but I don't remember the sermon; I was just dreading going back to my miserable life. As I was leaving, someone invited me to stay for lunch. I was relieved because I didn't have anything to eat at home. I was planning to fast.

While eating, I was introduced to a jovial middle-aged pastor. We had a candid conversation, and he asked me to sing for him at his next speaking engagement. I was thrilled because I knew who he was. I had seen him on various media outlets and at other big events. I thought I had made it to the big leagues! I called my mother and told her about this great news. We thanked God for this blessing in disguise.

After singing at several of his events, I noticed that the pastor seemed interested in me beyond just having a casual acquaintance. How could this be possible? I was in my thirties, and he was in his fifties. He soon made his intentions known. I've learned how to listen to God's voice even when He and I aren't seeing eye to eye. So I asked God about the pastor's request to further our relationship. When God seemed to be making Himself clear, I fought Him for several months, wondering if that was truly His plan for me. I kept thinking, *Marry an old guy? Is that what I deserve?*

The Lord responded to my doubts with a question: *"Do you trust Me?"*

I did. After a beautiful courtship, the pastor and I wed. Those years married to him were the best twelve years of my life. Unfortunately, my husband passed away on March 31, 2020, but I'm forever grateful to God for the wonderful plan He had for me. You see, God is a Master of love, and He has creative ways of revealing it to us. Don't be afraid of His ideas. Just sit still and let Him bring you His blessings. He can do things that might seem impossible, even creating love where there is none. Are you ready to let God lead you?

Esther Siceron-Reyna

Learning to Make His Way Mine

PART 1

"Therefore I tell you, whatever you ask for in prayer,
believe that you have received it, and it will be yours."
—Mark 11:24, NIV

I grew up believing that God loves it when I pray. He is always there to listen to me, and He will always answer my prayers. What was a bit difficult for me to understand as I grew older was that sometimes I was not entirely happy with the way God answered my prayers. Yet the answers He gives are exactly what I need. God knows what is best for us, and He gives us exactly that! Often when we pray to God, we already have in mind the way we hope He will answer. So much so that when He does not package our answers the way we want Him to, we become devastated. I was reminded of this fact once when I was involved in an accident.

As we left the house that day, I prayed, asking for God's guidance and protection on the road. Upon getting into the vehicle, I whispered another prayer. Along the way, I silently whispered prayers for protection (something I do not usually do). On our way back home, a vehicle unexpectedly drove into ours! My father managed to pull off the main road, out of the way of oncoming traffic. My exact thoughts were, *God! How could You? I was praying for Your protection!* But that day I was reminded our heavenly Father knows what is best for us and gives us that best at all times, whether we recognize it or not.

In that accident, I had allowed *me* to get in the way of seeing that God had answered my prayer—He *had* protected me! Stepping outside our vehicle, I saw we had only a scratch on the side where I had been sitting, whereas the front bumper of the other vehicle was completely ripped off. Thankfully, there were no casualties! Look at God!

In our Christian walk, as we learn to make His way ours, let's remember that our Father always hears our prayers. He listens. He answers. Sometimes He says no and sometimes yes or wait. There is not a sincere prayer that He leaves unanswered! He knows us better than we know ourselves, He knows exactly what we need, and He knows when and how to give it to us. Therefore, when He answers our prayers in ways we may not want, we can still be grateful that He gave us what was best for us instead. His best will always be the answer!

Renauta Hinds

Learning to Make His Way Mine

PART 2

I cried out to him with my mouth;
his praise was on my tongue.
—Psalm 66:17, NIV

One evening I had just finished having dinner but was still feeling a bit hungry. While washing the dishes, I told my mother, "I feel like eating chow mein. In fact, I'm really craving it!" My family usually prefers rice over pasta. So I, being the only pasta lover, usually cook it when I'm in the mood to do so. That evening, though, I had to remind myself that I had just finished eating and a glass of water should suffice.

But evidently, God thought otherwise. You see, as I was telling my mom about my cravings, God knew the intensity of how my stomach was feeling after this meal. As simple as this sounds (believe me), I made a big deal about it when my father came home later that night and said, "I brought chow mein for you."

I always make a big deal over God responding to me, especially if other people are involved. It is my way of reminding them that we have a heavenly Father who "will meet all your needs according to the riches of his glory in Christ Jesus" (Philippians 4:19, NIV). I turned that "chow mein moment" into a sermonette for my family. I praised God for hearing me though I did not go out of my way to talk to Him about what was on my mind, yet I realized that He always listens to us. It might have been a simple, even unspoken, request, but God treated my desire as if it were important. In the process, He reminded me that He is always listening to me.

When we pray, He teaches us how to make His way ours. Having an intimate relationship with God is truly a blessing. Spending time with God allows for a better understanding of who He is. It allows us to grow with Him and in Him. In any human relationship, we must keep together by communicating. Our relationship with God requires the same: communion with Him. Being careless about our relationship with God has the same result as neglecting those we love and care about. On the other hand, the more time we spend with God, the closer we become.

Why not work on our relationship with God just as hard as we set out to work on our relationships with our spouses, families, and friends? As we learn to walk in His ways, we will find Him to be "a friend that sticks closer than a brother" (Proverbs 18:24, NIV).

Renauta Hinds

I Can't Change!

"And whatever things you ask in prayer, believing, you will receive."
—Matthew 21:22, NKJV

I had been on dozens of diets over the years, but I quickly regained any pounds I lost. I finally decided to be content with my weight. After all, my family loved me the way I was. As my seventieth birthday approached, however, my annual checkup revealed increased triglyceride and cholesterol levels. In addition, I became short of breath walking upstairs, and my feet hurt after only half an hour's shopping.

I knew I should do something, but I couldn't face another diet. *Lord*, I prayed, *I know I should take care of this body You gave me, but on my own, I can't give up the foods I enjoy.*

I'd never asked God for help with my addiction to sweets. It hadn't seemed important enough to pray about. Yet Scripture said, "Pray in the Spirit on all occasions with all kinds of prayers and requests" (Ephesians 6:18, NIV).

That must mean God wanted to hear from me about whatever was on my mind. I didn't have to save my prayers for matters of life and death.

I knew I couldn't change my eating habits on my own—my desire for sweets was bigger than my desire for good health. But maybe God could change my mindset. I began to pray every day, "Lord, help me want to change." Weeks passed. I continued to eat all the things I craved. I stuffed myself with chocolate cake on my birthday but continued to pray, "Help me want to change." I devoured the leftover cake the next day, but still, I prayed.

A couple weeks later, I awoke with the thought, *I want to get healthy. Lord, help me make it happen.* God had prepared my heart for change, so I knew He'd help me succeed.

Although I had my ups and downs, daily prayer kept me motivated to stay on track. I concentrated on eating healthy foods and exercising—not dieting. By my next birthday, my lab work had improved, and I was in better shape than I'd been in years.

I lost weight, but more importantly, I gained the assurance that the Lord listens and responds to whatever we have on our minds. We don't have to wait for a crisis to call on Him. He will help us do what we cannot do in our own power.

Lord, thank You for helping us accomplish what seems impossible. Amen.

Diana L. Walters

I Yelled at God Today

How long, LORD? Will you forget me forever?
How long will you hide your face from me?
How long must I wrestle with my thoughts
and day after day have sorrow in my heart?
How long will my enemy triumph over me?
—Psalm 13:1, 2, NIV

"Close your eyes, bow your head, and fold your hands," my first Sabbath School teacher instructed. "This is how we pray to our King." Being the tomboy I was, I didn't have much poise like the girls kneeling beside me. My attention span usually lasted two-tenths of a second before I would either be back to laughing hysterically or planning something mischievous to eliminate my boredom. I definitely didn't filter my thoughts before speaking. Yet, somehow, I was trained to pray reverently with the rest of my class.

But this manner of prayer did not suit me. I would kneel down in my church dress with my ankles crossed on Sabbath, then resume praying to God my way the rest of the week. Our conversations have always been different from what is normally portrayed in a church setting. I prefer talking to Him while panting on an afternoon run, whispering while sitting by a stream, or shouting from the top of a mountain. This is a less talked-about version of prayer.

Job prayed while sitting among ashes in his despair (Job 2:8). Jacob wrestled with God and wouldn't let go until He blessed him (Genesis 32:24–26). David fasted and lay on the ground, pleading with God for his child (2 Samuel 12:16). So why are we afraid we're going to offend God by praying passionately? He is our King and deserves the utmost respect, but He also desires a raw relationship with each of us. I yelled at God today out of hurt. My relationship with Him is not formal; it's real. I'm allowed to be upset or have some needed space to calm down, just as in any other relationship. What makes the difference is how God responds. He doesn't walk away because He's tired of waiting for me. God doesn't move on to the next relationship and leave me in the dust. He waits patiently and is ready to strengthen our connection. This is why I know I can talk to my God without polishing my prayers. He hears me and chooses to stay. He listens to your prayers as well—no matter the delivery.

Delanie Kamarad

Believing His Promises

Take delight in the LORD,
and he will give you the desires of your heart.
—Psalm 37:4, NIV

My husband and I were married at the age of twenty-three, which was perfect timing for us. We prayerfully decided beforehand that it would not be wise to have children in the first year of marriage. But we did not actively prevent pregnancy, and it never happened. At first, I was happy about that fact, but church members and friends questioned me, "When are you folks going to have children?" One member frankly stated, "Something must be wrong with you since you're not getting pregnant." I usually brushed off their inquiring eyes with a smile or an "I'm not ready." Yet deep down inside, I began to wonder whether their pronouncements were true. *What if I'm never able to experience motherhood? What if my husband is never a father?* Such questions bombarded my mind.

Eventually, I shared this situation with my mother. She advised me, "Take it to God in prayer but only when you are ready." This talk with my mom calmed my fears, and I let it go. Sure enough, following the first year of marriage, I prayed and asked God to bless us with our first child.

For encouragement, I read the story of Hannah. "And she vowed a vow, and said, O LORD of hosts, if thou wilt indeed look on the affliction of thine handmaid, and remember me, and not forget thine handmaid, but wilt give unto thine handmaid a man child, then I will give him unto the LORD all the days of his life, and there shall no razor come upon his head" (1 Samuel 1:11, KJV).

God, I told Him one day, *if You could do that for Hannah, You can do it for me.* Months later, I noticed I wasn't feeling like myself. After much prayer, I took a pregnancy test, which confirmed my suspicions. I was pregnant! Nine months later, I gave birth to a healthy baby boy.

Is there anything too hard for God? No! Today, if there is a mountain in your life that is insurmountable and you feel hopeless, trust God. He is a kind and ever-loving Father who is willing to listen and answer our prayers if we will only believe.

Why not trust Him today? He is able.

Deidre Lanferman

Assurance for the Fearful

Whenever I am afraid,
I will trust in You.
—Psalm 56:3, NKJV

We all have innate fears. From the time Adam said to God that he was afraid, fearfulness has often dominated our lives. If responding to a poll, many would admit to having fears, real or imagined. We are fearful when a perceived threat seems beyond our control. We fear people, the dark, failure, being alone, public speaking, or even the smallest animals.

Once, after torrential rains, I stepped outside to place the garbage into our bin. As I lifted the lid, I sensed a movement and quickly stepped back. There, to my horror, I saw a snake. It was about four feet (1.2 meters) long and coiled around the rim of the bin. The fear that gripped me is indescribable. In my panic, I screamed, "A snake!" Fortunately, my neighbor, who was outside at the time, came running with a machete and killed it. Later that evening, when I related the experience to my husband, he assured me that perhaps the poor, harmless snake was more afraid of me than I was of it. But the threat of being bitten by a snake, especially knowing its dangerous potential, fueled my fear and overwhelmed me. I had felt helpless. That is what fear does. It can make us feel powerless, afraid, anxious, and worried about the unknown.

But God has wonderful promises that are a source of comfort, confidence, and hope when we are faced with fear. Here are several from Psalm 91:1–5:

> He who dwells in the secret place of the Most High
> Shall abide under the shadow of the Almighty. . . .
> "My God, in Him I will trust."
>
> Surely He shall deliver you from the snare of the fowler
> And from the perilous pestilence.
> He shall cover you with His feathers. . . .
> You shall not be afraid (NKJV).

Are you fearful about something? Do not hesitate to claim God's many promises. *Heavenly Father, we thank You for the assurance that if we are afraid, we can put our trust in You.*

Annette L. Vaughan

Blessings in Motion

*"For I know the plans I have for you,"... "plans to prosper you
and not to harm you, plans to give you hope and a future."*
—Jeremiah 29:11, NIV

There are defining moments in our Christian journeys that remind us of God's love and ever-present involvement in our lives. Some of these moments occur so unexpectedly that they often take a bystander to point out the motion in the moment and the blessing in the minute.

This morning has found me alone in a new city and new apartment—2,184 miles away from family—and a week away from a new post as a hospital chaplain. As I unpack boxes, I am reminded of how different life is when compared to just a few months ago. Nobody could have predicted how COVID-19 would affect hospitals, communities, and people. Late in the morning, desiring to become acquainted with my surroundings, I walk the unfamiliar two blocks toward my new hospital. The walk is a welcome break from unpacking. Some items do not travel well in a move—fragile items. Why do I feel so fragile?

At the first intersection, I wait for the flashing pedestrian light to indicate it is safe to cross the street. The light is not working. I shake my head and decide to return at a later hour. As I turn, I see a lady behind me wearing hospital scrubs. I cannot remember her name, but she assisted me with the onboarding process. "A cop will show up soon and direct traffic," she says with a smile. "New chaplain, right? I remember. I am curious: How did you choose Los Angeles?" With that one question, I realize the narrative is not complicated, but it feels fragile. I tell her my story. She listens and says, "God's timing is amazing! You move away for a chaplain job, the pandemic begins, the job changes, but in one day, you receive chaplaincy endorsement and leave that job. Then before you get home, God directs you to a place that needs you: here. Only God can plan that!"

There it is: the motion in the moment and the blessing in the minute. A defining moment in my Christian journey, where God's love for me is evident: God has witnessed everything that brought me here, and God directed it all. *Heavenly Father, when we feel alone and fragile, do not let us forget You are leading in our lives. These moments of motion and blessing are precious and planned for each of us individually with mindful detail and love.*

Dixil Lisbeth Rodríguez

Triumph by Remembering the Past

Give praise to the Lord, O my soul; let not all his blessings go from your memory.
—Psalm 103:2, BBE

Though all are daily blessed by God, not all remember to praise Him for His mercies. Ingratitude and forgetfulness of God's goodness and mercy come all too easily. King David warns us not to forget because God forgives sins and heals diseases. He is our Redeemer; He is our Provider and Source of mercy. And only He can deliver us and judge those who would oppress and persecute us (see Psalm 103:3–6).

The devil was the first being to exhibit ingratitude and a lack of remembrance for God's goodness and mercy (Isaiah 14:12–15; Ezekiel 28:11–18; Revelation 12:7–9). These same two sins often dictated the Israelites' choices as God faithfully continued to lead them to the Promised Land (Exodus 17:1–6; 32; Joshua 7; Judges 3; 4). Yet, whenever the people of Israel remembered God as their Sustainer, Deliverer, and Provider, He blessed them.

As people in spiritual Israel today, we must not allow the devil to have his way with us as he did with the children of Israel. Under God's inspiration, author Ellen White counsels us not to forget God's leading in our lives. She wrote,

> In reviewing our past history, having traveled over every step of advance to our present standing, I can say, Praise God! As I see what God has wrought, I am filled with astonishment, and with confidence in Christ as leader. We have nothing to fear for the future except as we shall forget the way the Lord has led us, and His teaching in our past history.
>
> We are now a strong people, if we will put our trust in the Lord; for we are handling the mighty truths of the word of God. We have everything to be thankful for.*

Truly, the way to be triumphant throughout both present and future challenges is by remembering how God has led us in the past and then never forgetting His numerous blessings when we arise every morning and fall asleep every night.

Lord, please bless us and make us overcomers as we daily remember You and Your leading while going about our everyday lives. In Your name, amen.

Joy Bakaba Igwe

---

* Ellen G. White, *Testimonies to Ministers and Gospel Workers* (Mountain View, CA: Pacific Press®, 1962), 31.

The Dead Tree

*My dear friends, I want you to know that what has
happened to me has helped to spread the good news.
The Roman guards and all the others know that I am here
in jail because I serve Christ. Now most of the Lord's followers
have become brave and are fearlessly telling the message.*
—Philippians 1:12–14, CEV

The Bible study group I attend is focused on the book of Philippians, written by Paul while in a Roman prison. Quite an appropriate book to read while we are in quarantine. Paul points out that God is always with us. He loves to bring the dead to life and surprise us, showing His hand at work in all things.

There is a dead tree in our backyard. The men we asked to remove it have counseled, "Just leave it. It will eventually fall down in pieces." A couple of years ago, the top quarter of the tree fell off. But the coolest thing is that the dead tree helped me better understand God as I have struggled to define *success*. Though many use careers to define their success, I, by human definition, really don't have a career. Yes, I've held jobs in similar areas, and I do see patterns as I assess my current and past positions, but they are not what I would want to define me. I have chosen to focus on my children and my music ministry. Though neither pays well, the rewards are *priceless*! Paul wasn't planning to be in that prison, and twenty years ago, I wasn't planning most of what has happened in my own life, but *God* knew. His plan is always good.

I have stayed home, at least part time, with my children for twelve years. I have been part of a music ministry for more than thirteen years, and I have always been outspoken regarding my faith in Jesus Christ. God is using me. I see it in my children, and I see it in those blessed by the songs that I sing. So, as I look up at the old, dead tree today, I see a woodpecker flying into a hole where she is feeding babies in her nest. Flying frantically back and forth, she is doing what she can to care for her family, harbored by the dead tree.

Sometimes we feel small, as if we are not large and successful according to the world's standards. Yet God measures us differently and uses the unlikeliest of things—an old dead tree—to remind us that we are successful when we place ourselves in His hands. "If I live, it will be for Christ, and if I die, I will gain even more" (Philippians 1:21, CEV).

Joey Norwood Tolbert

"The Just Shall Live by Faith"

I will . . . watch to see what he will say unto me, and what I shall answer
when I am reproved. And the LORD answered me, and said, Write the vision,
and make it plain upon tables, that he may run that readeth it. For the vision
is yet for an appointed time, but at the end it shall speak, and not lie:
though it tarry, wait for it; because it will surely come. . . . Behold, his soul
which is lifted up is not upright in him: but the just shall live by his faith.
—Habakkuk 2:1–4, KJV

My best friend, Yvonne, had taken a short travel assignment to California and was enjoying the beautiful weather and hospital where she was working. On her birthday, the Sabbath morning dawned sunny and beautiful. She went to church but felt overwhelmed by loneliness, though the service was a blessing. As she exited the church, she wondered where God was in all her loneliness. As she stood alone with her heart hurting, a car pulled up carrying two ladies from the church. One of the ladies introduced herself and asked Yvonne where she was visiting from. Yvonne said that Orlando was her home. "Well, then, would you join us for a nice Sabbath lunch?" Not knowing the women, Yvonne was hesitant but, after exchanging pleasantries, accepted the invitation. During the drive, Yvonne shared a little about herself and that it was her birthday.

At the lady's house, Yvonne met other people from the church. Dinner was wonderful, and everyone was very friendly. Yvonne was surprised to learn they were celebrating her birthday! She received a birthday cake and a gift! They even sang "Happy Birthday" to her! She was truly blessed because total strangers were thoughtful enough to celebrate her birthday with her! God had had it all planned, even when it seemed He hadn't cared about her loneliness.

My sisters, God cares about us, and He knows what our needs are. At times, we may feel so alone with burning questions: *God, where are You? Why am I alone? When am I going to get that job that I need? When are my children going to give their hearts completely to You?* In those times, we must trust His wonderful promises and hold on to our faith that He will answer our prayers according to His divine will. We needn't go on with all the questions because God has the answers for all the *why*s on our hearts. He will answer in His own time, not ours. He loves us.

The Lord wants us to keep praising and thanking Him, especially when it seems He is not answering. He wants us to be grateful for who He is, not just for what He can do for us!

Jannett Maurine Myrie

No Way! I Am Waiting

Not giving up meeting together, as some are in the habit of doing,
but encouraging one another—and all the more as you see the Day approaching.
—Hebrews 10:25, NIV

My husband, Milton, and I are always thrilled when we can spend treasured time with our granddaughters, Azoya and Kyrah. This past Thanksgiving holiday was no exception. Our home was filled with happy voices and eager feet wanting to explore our new place.

One evening we were left alone with the grandchildren when their parents left for some well-deserved alone time. As it got closer to bedtime, Kyrah became more and more fretful and wanted the comfort of her mom. "Where are my parents?" she inquired. "Where is my mom?"

We completed the bedtime routine: putting on pajamas, brushing teeth, reading a story, and praying. When we prepared to tuck Kyrah into bed, she declared, "I want to sleep in Mommy's room, where I will wait until Mommy gets home." When I lay down beside her in an attempt to comfort and coax her into my room to wait, she defiantly exclaimed. "No way! I am not going into your room! I'm staying in Mommy's room!" Soon my little darling was fast asleep, and I transferred her to my room, where I could keep a watchful eye on her.

As I later shared the incident with her parents, I could not help but relate her defiance—and determination—to our wait for the return of our precious Lord.

No way will I be distracted by the length of time He is taking to return!

No way will I forget His promise of a sure return!

No way will I forget to tell others of His return!

No way will I neglect to be ready!

No way!

As promised, Azoya and Kyrah were picked up by their parents after their trip. Our precious Lord has also promised to return, and He will. In Hebrews 10:37, we read, "For yet a little while, and he that shall come will come, and will not tarry" (KJV). These words are comforting to me.

Dear Lord, help us to wait patiently for You and in no way be distracted. Thank You for the promise of Your sure return.

Gloria Barnes-Gregory

A Time to Dance

To everything there is a season,
A time for every purpose under heaven: . . .
A time to weep,
And a time to laugh;
A time to mourn,
And a time to dance.
—Ecclesiastes 3:1, 4, NKJV

"Everything Has Its Time" is the heading for the third chapter of Ecclesiastes in my NKJV Bible. The words of verses 1–8 cover virtually everything we humans do or accomplish in our lifetimes. These observations of King Solomon are often read at funerals. Pete Seeger put this scripture passage to music. The song was titled "Turn! Turn! Turn!" It became a hit on the music charts for quite a while during the 1960s. Even now, it is still a much-loved piece of music.

As a hired musician, I play piano and organ for two churches on Sundays and volunteer at my own church on Sabbaths. When I can fit it in, I'm a volunteer pianist on the grand piano in the lobby of a nearby hospital. The desk and security personnel enjoy the music. So do the passersby and others who must sit and wait on loved ones undergoing surgery or other medical procedures or are waiting to visit sick friends or relatives in their rooms. Recently, eight family members were waiting to learn the outcome of their family patriarch's heart surgery. Three children, a boy and two girls, were too young to go upstairs. Everyone listened as I played music especially for children, such as Sunday School songs, nursery rhymes, and folk tunes.

When the desk clerk announced that Grandpa's surgery had gone well, I stopped playing for a moment. The children had been tapping their toes and clapping their hands before. When they heard the good news, they broke into a spontaneous dance! Their joy was evident as they hopped, skipped, jumped, and twirled. They were full of the sheer joy of living and thanksgiving.

As they smiled and laughed, everybody there smiled back.

Sometimes, we adults should be more like children. Life has its share of troubles. But even those times can be interspersed with some beautiful moments. And there is nothing wrong with embracing the joy when we can and showing we have overflowing, thankful hearts!

I am glad that I was there to share in their happiness. I will always remember the afternoon when the children in the lobby cheered the hearts of everyone with their dancing. I'm sure God smiled, too, as He watched them from heaven!

Bonnie Moyers

Never Grow Old

"They will build houses and live in them. They will plant grapes and eat their fruit.
They will not build a house and another live in it. They will not plant and another eat."
—Isaiah 65:21, 22, NLV

After my mother-in-law's funeral, our family wanted to take one last look at the farm in Missouri that had impacted so much of our lives. The weathered chicken house held not only memories of tiny yellow peeping fowl but also outdated farm essentials. Among the treasures were two Ford Model T wheels.

Seeing the old farmhouse brought back a trove of memories, but memories alone could not hold up the aging, sagging building. In recent years, family members had painted and patched the house. They had repaired and replaced siding, shingles, and windows. The floor itself had to be replaced, for there was no proper foundation. The goal was to keep the old house livable for as long as Mom would need it. And family members achieved that goal, for she was able to shelter there until the day came when declining health dictated her needs would be better met if she lived in a nursing home.

But the family farm was more than buildings; it included everything that grew there. The acres of soybeans had been essential for the family's livelihood, as well as the fields of hay. The decades-old oak trees in the front yard had shed wheelbarrows full of acorns. The trees had also provided shade for Sabbath afternoon relaxing. Every summer there were pots of moss rose in the closest part of the backyard. Tulips grew in an old tire for a few years. At one time, lilacs had grown beside the driveway in the front of the house. Eventually, however, the lilacs had to go because there was not enough room for the combine to pass by.

The postfuneral visit to the farm was a time for reflection. Our daughter wanted to have a living piece of her grandma. Nothing had been blooming around the house since it had been vacated, except for the purple iris by the garden. She found a spade and began digging. These flowers were taken across the country and are blooming again in Oregon.

Today, buildings decay and collapse. Trees often outlive the buildings they surround, but eventually, they, too, will fall. Jesus is preparing mansions for us that will not decay. He has promised that we will eat from the tree of life and never grow old.

Even so, come, Lord Jesus.

Barbara Huff

Put Things Right

I have seen you in your sanctuary
and gazed upon your power and glory.
—Psalm 63:2, NLT

At times in my life, I thought I was a very responsible mother, not knowing that the father's responsibility was also mine when I needed to fill in the gaps to raise wholly balanced children. I say this because I spend more time with my children than their father can. The Bible story of Ichabod challenges me. I realize that life is fragile and ought to be handled with prayer. The glory of God can depart if I am not careful in my parenting and other choices.

An unnamed pregnant woman in the Bible was married to Phinehas; he was a corrupt son of Eli, the priest in the tabernacle at Shiloh where the ark of the covenant was housed. Eli's only reprimand to his evil sons seems to be a rather mild one (1 Samuel 2:22–25). Sadly, the sons neither heeded their father's warning nor followed his counsel. When Israel was defeated by the Philistines in a battle, the elders of Israel asked that the ark be brought from the tabernacle to the army camp, hoping the ark's presence would give them victory. The wife of Phinehas was aware when her husband and brother-in-law, Hophni, left with the ark. She appears to have known this was not in accordance with the way God had instructed His people to reverence His ark and especially His presence, for He dwelt "between the cherubim" on the ark (1 Samuel 4:4, NKJV). Soon after, this woman learned Israel had been defeated by the enemy. Even worse, the ark of the covenant had been captured, and Phinehas, her husband, killed. Furthermore, when the aged Eli, waiting back in Shiloh, learned of his sons' deaths and especially the capture of the ark of the Lord, he fell backward, broke his neck, and died as well.

Hearing the news of these multiple losses, starting with the capture of the ark, Phinehas's wife, "due to be delivered, . . . bowed herself and gave birth, for her labor pains came upon her" (verse 19, NKJV). She birthed a baby boy. But she did not name him after his father. Instead, she named him Ichabod, saying, "The glory [the presence of God in Israel's midst] has departed from Israel, for the ark of God has been captured" (verse 22, NKJV).

May we, especially if parents, daily live our lives with the same reverence for God that the mother of Ichabod had and, by faith, ever live in the constant glory of His presence.

Pauline Gesare Okemwa

The Kookaburra's Song

Sing to the LORD *a new song;*
sing to the LORD, *all the earth.*
Sing to the LORD, *praise his name;*
proclaim his salvation day after day.
Declare his glory among the nations.
—Psalm 96:1–3, NIV

One of the things I've learned to appreciate here in Australia is the abundant birdlife and how the birds have adapted to living amid the many developments that have intruded into their space. When I moved to Australia and heard the kookaburra for the first time, I wondered whether there were monkeys in the area. The kookaburra's strong bass vibrato sounded more like a monkey than a bird. Though small and with a rather plain coat, the kookaburra nevertheless sings a song that you cannot miss hearing.

This morning, before any of the other birds could come to life, the kookaburra decided to start its song just outside my window. I woke up and listened as it sang out loud and clear, oblivious that its song was crude and rough in comparison to the sweet, melodic songs of the many other birds it lives with. It sang from its heart at the break of dawn. There was no assurance that this kookaburra would live to see the next day, as many a bird has been hit by passing vehicles. But today, it sang with all its might. As I lay in bed, I couldn't help but think about the kookaburra's song. Although it was not yet the heart of winter, it was still cold. I snuggled under my quilt and talked with the Lord. The day was breaking for me, too, but on a very different tone. Unlike the kookaburra, who didn't care about its natural beauty, I was conscious of myself and how I may be perceived in this new country. This morning, however, the kookaburra taught me that I must use my voice for God wherever I may be and regardless of how I define myself, be that as a foreigner, woman, mother, student, or something else.

What about your voice? Is there anything that is holding you back from singing? Are you able to lift your voice in praise to God so that it rings out loud and clear for His glory?

Lord, touch my lips that I may sing Your praises, for You dwell in the midst of praise. May my voice be used for You and for Your glory. Amen.

Grace Paulson

Bonus Baby

For I know the thoughts that I think toward you, says the LORD,
thoughts of peace and not of evil, to give you a future and a hope.
—Jeremiah 29:11, NKJV

When I delivered our third child, I was delighted. I had this pleasant feeling of having completed our family. Two vibrant sons and an adorable daughter—I wouldn't ask for more.

When our daughter was sixteen months old, I conceived again! The nine months of pregnancy were not easy. I was exhausted from years of pregnancies and breastfeeding. The previous pregnancy was still so vivid in my head. I was anxious and worried that something might go wrong during delivery or the baby might have some abnormalities. I often calmed myself with the fact that God had seen me through pregnancies three times before, and I strongly believed He had a purpose for this pregnancy.

One week past my expected date of delivery, the contractions started. I soon realized that labor was progressing very fast, so we rushed to the hospital.

At the hospital, when the midwife was examining me, she froze. Then she asked her assistant to make sure oxygen was ready for use and told my husband to wear gloves and be ready to help. I asked her what was going on.

Calmly, the midwife explained, "I am touching the cord, which can fully prolapse and impair oxygen delivery to the baby." That was not good news! Being a pediatrician and fully understanding the implications of what she had just shared, I could only imagine the worst. I was frightened for a moment until I remembered Matthew 6:27: "Can any one of you by worrying add a single hour to your life?" (NIV). I prayed and then relaxed as I let God take charge. *May Your will be done, Father.* In less than an hour, a strong cry filled the room. I praised God as I looked at our baby, pink and active. God gave us a bonus—a second daughter! As I write this, our bonus baby is now four years old. Every time I look at her, I realize that our family would not have been complete without her.

Beloved sisters in Christ, God is always there to answer our prayers. He has the best plan for our lives. We can always count on Him to give us the eternal peace that surpasses human understanding (see Philippians 4:7). May we always rejoice in His presence!

Lulu Chirande

Abiding

So we have come to know and to believe the love
that God has for us. God is love, and whoever abides
in love abides in God, and God abides in him.
—1 John 4:16, ESV

If God is love, and if abiding in Him means abiding in love, today's text is sort of a big deal! Think about it. John says that those who experience the kind of love that he is about to explain abide in God Himself! Abiding in His love means we grow within it. Here is an illustration.

I was worried! The tents at a women's congress in Africa were packed with women from many countries. Many languages needed translation, yet few women were available or even trained to speak as translators. I prayed, "God, you have someone here to help me. Send her!" From a distance, I heard a voice. I turned toward the kind voice that said, "Sister Raquel, use me. I am not perfect in English, but I felt impressed to accept the challenge." What a joy! We ministered together that day. Many women heard the message in their own language. This is the power that one woman, working with God, can have—the power to do mighty things.

Returning to my room later, I reflected on this young woman, so full of the Holy Spirit and so full of God's love. The words of John came to mind: "Whoever abides in love abides in God, and God abides in him." This is love that moves you beyond your capacity. Love that leads you to anticipate a need. Love that empowers you to serve despite your limitations. Love that compels you to respond to God's calling to serve others.

In this chapter, John helps us understand this love. First, we discover that the Son of God died for our sins because God loved us before we loved Him (1 John 4:10, 19). Second, God's love empowers us to love (verses 11, 12). Third, the love of God is perfected in us to give us confidence (verse 17). Fourth, when we know God's love, we do not experience fear because "perfect love casts out fear" (verse 18, NKJV). Fifth, whoever loves God must also love her sister (verse 21). Hugging this young woman on the last day of our congress, I said to her, "You showed what it is to love others."

Smiling, she replied, "No, Sister Raquel, *God* showed His love through me." She went back home to Togo, but her empowered service and love for her sisters remain.

My prayer this morning is, "Lord, send me someone to love today." And He will.

Raquel Queiros da Costa Arrais

The Dreaded Elevator

And it shall come to pass, that before they call, I will answer.
—Isaiah 65:24, KJV

The elevator door opened, and I moved to enter. "I can't get in there today. Let's walk up the stairs," Mother announced.

"As religious as you are, you're scared of the elevator? Don't you think the Lord can take care of you in there?" was my sarcastic comeback. Well, here I am, forty years later, anxious about getting into an elevator, and I certainly won't get in one alone. I have stood by an elevator and waited for someone to appear so that we could ride together. I have asked a person to ride up to my floor and then back down to his or her floor. I have no shame! Friends who have been stuck in an elevator love telling me their stories—all of which are absolutely frightening to me. Once Walter, my husband, got locked in a bathroom stall at church when the door jammed. After that experience, I became anxious about locking bathroom doors in any unfamiliar location. I've never thought much about the anxiety disorder of claustrophobia, but I clearly have a fear of having no escape, which could result in a severe panic attack.

One day as I was getting dressed for my eye appointment, Walter asked, "What time are you leaving? I'm going with you."

My first thought was, *Why?* But I was too overjoyed to ask. On the way to the doctor's office, he shared that a voice kept telling him to go with me. He figured that if he didn't go and something happened to me, he would never forgive himself. Oh, dear! All kinds of thoughts raced through my mind. Were we going to have an accident? Was the car going to stop? Was I going to get sick? Were we going to get robbed in the parking lot?

It was early, and the large parking lot was almost empty when we arrived. The security guard who usually rode up the elevator with me was not at his usual post. No other patients or employees were in sight. We were all alone. The Lord knew I would be too anxious to ride the elevator alone, so He had already provided a ram in the thicket. What a mighty God we serve!

The following year I witnessed Mother getting into the elevator with no hesitation. "Oh, I decided that the Lord would take care of me," was her response to my questioning look.

With God's help, I'm looking forward to that day too.

Shirley Sain Fordham

Dressed to Impress

I put on righteousness, and it clothed me:
my judgment was as a robe and a diadem.
—Job 29:14, KJV

Each day that life is extended to us is a huge blessing. It is not because of our own power or righteousness. It is because of God's righteousness, mercy, grace, and compassion. As we go about our daily lives, how do we dress to reflect His character and goodness? Are we careless in our walk and speech? How about the way we treat others, our bodies, and the environment? Do we exude the same love as Christ?

Allow me to take you back in time to one of the great apostles: Peter, the fisherman with a fiery tongue and spirit (Matthew 26:74). One day he met Jesus and noted Christ's humble garb and the way He walked, preached, taught, and performed miracles. Jesus' compassion and relationship with His heavenly Father spoke volumes as to the real "garment" He was wearing. The more time Peter spent with Jesus, the more his "garment" was transformed to better reflect that of the Master. Of course, this transformation didn't take place in just one day. Peter often failed, even vowing to protect Christ just before the Crucifixion. Hours later, this same disciple denied Jesus (Luke 22:54–62). But Peter realized his mistake and, with great remorse and bitter weeping, repented of his sins and was forgiven. That was a turning point for him as he fully committed to "dressing" like Jesus through his daily walk, speech, and deportment. He chose to abide in Jesus for the rest of his life (John 15:7). Jesus heard the cry of his heart and responded.

You, too, can cry out to Jesus like Peter. If you're not clothed in Christ's righteousness, you can go to Him with a contrite heart as did Peter. Do not dress to impress through outward adorning. Immerse yourself in the spotless purity of Christ. Trust Christ to change you, and do not give up when you fail Him. He is patient. Stay committed and focused. Spend time with Him each day in His Word. Others will notice you are no longer wearing the garb of the past, for you are changing into a new creature, clothed in the righteousness of Jesus (2 Corinthians 5:17). Surround yourself with like-minded sisters whose mission is to be stewards for Jesus in a world that is not your final home (John 17:16). Jesus will help you live as He did in a sinful world but not be tainted by its influences, wisdom, or ways. For you are wearing the garments of grace.

Corletta Aretha Barbar

Compassion: The Heart of Love

Praise be to the God and Father of our Lord Jesus Christ, the Father of compassion and the God of all comfort, who comforts us in all our troubles, so that we can comfort those in any trouble with the comfort we ourselves receive from God.
—2 Corinthians 1:3, 4, NIV

Thirteen years passed after I left graduate school before I could embark on doctoral studies because I wanted to wait until my daughter was at least ten years old before I began further rigorous study. The reward of such a deep commitment would be new discoveries added to evidence-based knowledge in my nursing profession. The commute from a state university in San Bernardino, California, United States of America, to a parochial university in San Diego took one and a half hours if I moved right along. Every time I arrived in San Diego, I would express my joy and gratitude in this prayer: "Lord, I will do my best; please do the rest." Toward the last year of research work, I drove to San Diego right after teaching my morning classes in San Bernardino so that I could use the computer lab for my research. One day, in the midst of some research due that day, the computer I was using crashed. I had not yet saved my work, so I lost everything I had written!

Tears flowed down my cheeks. I didn't realize that anyone entering the back door of the lab would be able to see me where I was seated. Unexpectedly, my professor came through the door. She saw me crying. Immediately at my side, she touched my shoulder and asked, "What happened?" I told her. She took a chair and sat beside me with an expression of compassion on her face. She looked at the black screen of my computer and kindly said, "It's OK, Edna. You can submit your work tomorrow." What a relief! I told her she was a lifesaver.

Though my teacher was not of the same denomination as I, she (as with many other teaching personnel at this university) gave me a better insight as to what love is and its relationship to compassion. I gained a deeper appreciation for the importance of living out one's simple faith in Jesus and often witnessed down-to-earth compassion modeled in the classroom. Love was extended to everyone, empowering the students to pursue and receive a quality education. The respect, compassion, and humility that Jesus demonstrated on the cross He desires His followers to manifest toward all others. Peter wrote, "Be like-minded, be sympathetic, love one another, be compassionate and humble" (1 Peter 3:8, NIV).

Edna Bacate Domingo

Having Clear Vision

*My prayers: that the God of our Lord Jesus Christ, the Father of glory, may give to you
the spirit of wisdom and revelation in the knowledge of Him,
the eyes of your understanding being enlightened; that you may know what is the hope
of His calling, what are the riches of the glory of His inheritance in the saints.*
—Ephesians 1:17, 18, NKJV

For years, I walked around with poor vision but did nothing about it. I believed I could navigate the world perfectly with concentration. I know what you are thinking: *Is she kidding?* Yes, I am. I was content to walk around with blurred vision until I began to experience migraines and watery, itchy eyes. I remember that when I first got glasses, I saw things so clearly: I could read street signs while driving and fine print on a page. Colors were brighter; shapes were sharper. I could see! How amazing was that! No more squinting or invading others' personal space to read something. *If only I had done this sooner!* Though I enjoyed seeing the world clearly, I developed bad habits, such as not wearing my glasses. Without them, I had to rely on my blurred perceptions or on others to see what was in front of me.

In our Christian walk, we sometimes develop blurred vision. We try to look at God through our earthly and failing sight, expecting to see Him clearly. We go around, squinting and rubbing our eyes in hopes of catching a glimpse of His love. He is patient as He waits till we are ready to get our sight adjusted. Jacob knew of God because of what his father and grandfather had taught him. After all, Jacob was Abraham's grandson. I can only imagine how many stories had been passed down to him. Yet that was not an indication that Jacob clearly saw who God was. Even after having a dream in which he saw angels ascending and descending a ladder stretching from heaven to Earth (Genesis 28:12), Jacob commented, "Surely the LORD is in this place; and I knew it not" (verse 16, KJV). But sometime later, when Jacob wrestled with God, he finally saw with spiritually clear vision: "I have seen God face to face, and my life is preserved" (Genesis 32:30, KJV).

We cannot see God's goodness clearly or fully understand His love with poor spiritual eyesight. Only God's touch can heal blurred vision. Allow God to open your eyes today so that you can see and appreciate Him for yourself.

Diantha Hall-Smith

The Shoelace Story

Do not conform to the pattern of this world, but be transformed
by the renewing of your mind. Then you will be able to test and approve
what God's will is—his good, pleasing and perfect will.
—Romans 12:2, NIV

Every day as I wore my gorgeous new shoes, I wondered about a slight manufacturing fault. *How come they made them in a great color, trendy, and comfortable, yet this one thing they didn't take care of?* There was something about these shoes that was not only bothering me but also hurting me.

The shoes had fancy shoelaces with metal tips at the end—the icing on the cake, except for this fault: after a few steps, these metal tips would flip around and get stuck between the shoe and my foot. No walking technique could unstick them. Once there, they remained, hurting my foot. The only way to release them was to stop walking, stoop down, and move the tips away from my foot. That brought relief for only a few steps. A real nuisance. *Should I return the shoes to the manufacturer and ask for a refund?* I pondered. Returning shoes is a hassle; since my work did not require a lot of walking, I bore the discomfort. For three months! Then something changed. No, the manufacturer did not send me a new and improved pair. I simply asked myself, "Can I do something different?" I tried tying the shoelaces a different way. I made the bow bigger and the ends shorter. Although this went against my ideal—having both the same length—it worked! This change in my tying technique completely transformed my shoe-wearing experience! The metal tips never got stuck again.

That glorious success prompted more questions. *What other ways of doing things—thought patterns or relationships—am I stuck in that make my life painful and do not allow me to enjoy life to the fullest? Do I believe that somebody else is causing my pain, while all this time, I have the power to change?*

How about you? Do you feel stuck? Are you, like I was, blaming somebody else?

Your transformation, like mine, may start by asking questions: Why am I doing this? What other way can I think about this? Can I do something different to make my relationship with this person better? Why not? Then listen for the answer. God wants to renew your mind.

Danijela Schubert

Mother's Witness

But my God shall supply all your need
according to his riches in glory by Christ Jesus.
—Philippians 4:19, KJV

My parents lived in British Columbia (BC), Canada, and my father, a pastor, had predeceased my mother. Before Mother passed away, I made prearrangements with a funeral director, Andre, whom we knew and trusted. When Mother died and the time came for the memorial service, I informed Andre that, due to illness, I would not be able to travel from my home in Ontario for the service.

My mother had been living with my sister Carolynn for several years in BC and would be interred there, alongside my father. Andre and I came up with a plan to use Skype* so that I could "attend" Mother's service through that means.

Andre set up a laptop computer in front of the pulpit in the chapel so that I could hear and see everything from where I was.

I had invited a close friend to keep me company. She arrived, and we were all ready at my end. Half an hour before the service was to begin, I logged in to my Skype account so that I would be ready. To my dismay, I saw a notice posted on that site informing customers that Skype services were down and had been that way for several hours. I was further dismayed to see no indication of when the service would be up and working again. At that time, according to Skype, 74 million people who used Skype were currently without their services.

Only eight minutes remained before my mother's memorial service was to start. I was praying fervently, as were many others of our family and friends. After prayers were offered, I asked Andre to try Skype again. To my great relief, it was up and available for us to use!

Of course, everyone was happy for me. As word spread about the preservice happenings, I believe Mother was able once more to "witness" for Jesus about the power of prayer as she had done all her life. The service director and his staff were all talking about it being a miracle. This experience reminded us that Jesus really does care for us whether our problems are big or small. All we have to do is ask in faith that He will keep His promises.

Kathleen (Cooper) McEwan

---

* A worldwide communication service available on the internet whereby one can make video calls.

Five Senses

But the LORD is the true God;
he is the living God, the eternal King.
—Jeremiah 10:10, NIV

Scripture points out the crucial difference between the true God and the myriad false gods and idols that many people have chosen to worship over the course of history. The true God is a living God, while the others are merely man-made contrivances. "They have mouths but they cannot speak. They have eyes but they cannot see. They have ears but they cannot hear. They have noses but they cannot smell. They have hands but they cannot feel. They have feet but they cannot walk. They cannot make a sound come out of their mouths" (Psalm 115:5–7, NLV). The true God, however, exercises all the senses with which He created His human children.

God can see the circumstances of both individuals and nations and can hear and respond to them. When He saw the mistreatment Hagar experienced, He sent her encouragement and help. In fact, Hagar named Him "the God who sees me" (Genesis 16:13, NIV). Likewise, the psalmist affirms that "the eyes of the LORD are on the righteous, and his ears are attentive to their cry" (Psalm 34:15, NIV).

Scripture also records that God could smell the "pleasing aroma" of sacrifices offered by genuine worshipers (Genesis 8:21, NIV) but complained that the rituals of the insincere were "a stench" to Him (Amos 5:21, NIV). Similarly, He uses the flavor of salt to illustrate how believers are to influence those around them (Matthew 5:13). The Lord touched Jeremiah's mouth to confirm his calling as a prophet (Jeremiah 1:9). In fact, Jesus' healing touch was one of the most significant features of His earthly ministry.

We, in turn, need to make use of our senses on our spiritual journey. Like past heroes of faith, we should trustfully see ahead to the fulfillment of God's promises (Hebrews 11:13), keeping our eyes fixed on Jesus (Hebrews 12:2) and our ears ready to listen for His voice (John 10:3). If we let Him touch and change our hearts, we can become the fragrance of life to those He wants to save (see 2 Corinthians 2:15, 16, NIV). Friends, let us not fail to accept and share the wonderful invitation to "taste and see that the LORD is good" (Psalm 34:8, NIV)!

Jennifer M. Baldwin

Unstoppable Giver

*Great is the L*ord *and most worthy of praise;*
his greatness no one can fathom.
—Psalm 145:3, NIV

In 2017, I traveled from Canada to Brazil to visit my parents, Giacomo and Guiomar. After spending the end-of-the-year holidays in the big city, we went to their apartment on the coast. Dad bought the plane tickets with the agreement that I would pay him back. But once we got there, he refused to accept payment. Then I had an idea. To avoid fighting with my dad over repayment, I would *spend* that money on them for groceries, gas, treats, restaurants, and whatever else I could. The plan was working well, but what I didn't expect was Dad's reaction. He noticed. After a few days, he would give me more money even over my protests. Instead of arguing with him, I decided I would spend that new money also on them: aqua fitness classes, gifts, flowers . . . Yet I couldn't spend it all because Dad wouldn't stop giving me more.

When I was on the plane returning home and reminiscing about this, I remembered how God blesses us more than we know. "Now to him who is able to do immeasurably more than all we ask or imagine" (Ephesians 3:20, NIV). He keeps pouring out His blessings again and again.

"My kindness shall not depart from you, nor shall My covenant of peace be removed" (Isaiah 54:10, NKJV). "Yet the Lord longs to be gracious to you; therefore he will rise up to show you compassion" (Isaiah 30:18, NIV).

And the more we give back to Him, the more He generously blesses us. "And God is able to bless you abundantly, so that in all things at all times, having all that you need, you will abound in every good work" (2 Corinthians 9:8, NIV). "How much more will your Father who is in heaven give what is good to those who ask Him!" (Matthew 7:11, NASB). He gave everything He could, even His Son. "For God so loved the world, that He gave His only begotten Son, that whoever believes in Him shall not perish, but have eternal life" (John 3:16, NASB).

So as we start this day, be confident of God's blessings. You can never outgive Him. Even in difficult situations, He is showering us with His blessings. He delights in giving because He is love. Praise God, for He is wonderful! He is an unstoppable Giver.

Eunice Passos Molina Berger

A Beacon of
Hope Amid Darkness

And the LORD, *he it is that doth go before thee;*
he will be with thee, he will not fail thee,
neither forsake thee: fear not, neither be dismayed.
—Deuteronomy 31:8, KJV

When darkness surrounds us on every side, and we cannot see what the future holds . . .

When our worries become impassable mountains that weaken our ability to hold on . . .

When we just don't know what to do or how to survive . . .

When our prayers to God seem weak and ineffectual, it is during these moments that God is closer to us than ever before. Yet we must not give up praying. Ellen G. White wrote, "Keep your wants, your joys, your sorrows, your cares, and your fears before God. You cannot burden Him; you cannot weary Him. . . . He . . . is not indifferent to the wants of His children. . . . His heart of love is touched by our sorrows and even by our utterances of them."*

Since our mother's death on March 14, 2019, my brother and I have been preparing our parents' house to sell. Fast-forward to April 9, 2020, and our world is now immersed in a global pandemic causing sickness and death, overwhelmed hospitals, and millions to file for unemployment. During this time, my brother and I were finally authorized as corepresentatives of our parents' estate. As I searched for a cleaning service to clean the house one last time before selling it, I asked God for guidance. He sent me the perfect cleaning team in answer to my prayer, and later, I realized He sent me to that team to answer their cries to Him for help. The team manager shared her worries: no jobs since the COVID-19 shutdown of business; no money to pay her boss the monthly US$350 (my US$450 for the manager's services would mostly benefit her boss). "How will I survive?" she exclaimed. My heart sorrowed as I searched for faith-comforting words to ease her anxiety. I responded, "Perhaps a tip," and said that I would be waiting outside.

The manager and her team prepared to leave. My plan was to give her a fifty-dollar tip, but God said, "Two hundred dollars." When the woman glanced at the check, tears of disbelief, joy, and gratitude spilled on her cheeks. In that unforgettable moment, showers of blessing enveloped both her and me. God had used me as a beacon of hope amid the darkness in her life.

Cynthia Best-Goring

---

* Ellen G. White, *Steps to Christ* (Washington, DC: Review and Herald®, 1977), 100.

Snowflake From Heaven

And whatsoever ye shall ask in my name,
that will I do, that the Father may be glorified
in the Son. If ye shall ask any thing in my name, I will do it.
—John 14:13, 14, KJV

The tears had scarcely dried on my cheeks before I began to negotiate with my husband, Norman, about purchasing a new German shepherd. Our twelve-year-old shepherd, Angel, had become gravely ill. We reluctantly agreed with the veterinarian that putting her down would be the merciful thing to do and sadly said our goodbyes.

It was early December, but I couldn't get excited about decorating for the holidays. My heart was lonely for my furry companion. I then began to discuss a new pet with my husband. He expressed reluctance, but I was not to be discouraged. One day I made my rounds to animal shelters in our area, contacted two breeders, and even investigated a dog being trained by prisoners—all without success. I stopped and prayed, "Dear Lord, help me find the right dog for us. Let it be a young dog that is obedient, already trained in basic commands, good natured, leash trained, a lover of cats [since we had one], and house trained."

Now I realize this was a long list, but God says nothing is impossible for Him!

In early February, my stepdaughter, Sherry, called, saying, "I've found a dog for you and Dad." It was an eighteen-month-old white German shepherd named Zena. Sherry and her husband went to meet Zena and sent videos. Our hearts were captivated! We agreed to take her. Sherry volunteered to drive to Washington State and bring Zena to us.

Zena was everything I had asked God for. We nicknamed her Snowflake From Heaven. Norman and I both bonded with her so well and loved her! We were overjoyed to have our home complete again.

Now, you might think this is just a story with a happy ending, but this answer to prayer has become a profound witnessing tool for me. Our pastor allowed me to bring Zena to church for the children's story. I frequently have been given the opportunity to tell many people of God's wonderful answer to my prayer. So when you pray, please know you will receive an answer. He sees the big picture and knows what is best for everyone concerned. In His time and as He sees fit, He will surely answer!

Rose Neff Sikora

The Two Live Crew

For there is no respect of persons with God.
—Romans 2:11, KJV

Every day the radio at work is tuned to one of the most popular stations. A weekday afternoon program features a male and female team who call themselves the Two Live Crew as they cohost the program. Their broadcasts are interactive, entertaining, and filled with relevant information. The program caters to people of all ages and backgrounds, as evidenced by the variety of listeners who call in to the program every day.

One day devastation struck. Listeners expressed shock and sadness upon hearing the announcement that the male cohost's brother had been fatally shot. Two weeks later, a close friend of the female cohost was fatally shot while defending himself against attackers. The grief was much to bear for these two people who bring such joy to their listeners each weekday. We ached for them as we heard about their ordeal.

Though most of us enjoy listening to stories of the famous, we sometimes forget that famous and popular people are also human beings. They, too, experience emotions of pain, hurt, sadness, joy, and loss. The horrific losses of the Two Live Crew cohosts reinforce the fact that we all need Jesus. We all live in a broken world where God is our only hope and the answer to all our problems. And it does not matter who we are because God does not show favoritism (see the Bible text for today). He hears our cries of pain when bad things happen. He welcomes our expressions of joy, praise, and honor when we experience obvious blessings from His hand of goodness. On this earth, we will never understand the workings of God in all the circumstances of life, but we can come to Him for reassurance, deliverance, healing, and help.

While we battle with the circumstances that affect our lives each day, we can find a greater joy if we remember to put into practice a thought expressed each weekday by Two Live Crew on their broadcasts: "It's nice to be important, but it's much more important to be nice." Jesus encourages us to treat others as He does—without favoritism. He considers the way we treat others as the way we treat Him (see Matthew 25:31–40).

Sisters, let us touch someone today with the love of Jesus. Share a word of kindness, smile in the face of sadness, and give a needed gift to make this world a better place.

Elizabeth Ida Cain

A Personal Trainer

For physical training is of some value, but godliness has value for all things,
holding promise for both the present life and the life to come.
—1 Timothy 4:8, NIV

In recent years, I have watched several older relatives get to the point where their health issues caused them a lot of pain. While watching them, I suggested to my husband that although I understood I wasn't going to live forever, it was time to start taking better care of myself in hopes of aging with less pain than my older relatives.

We have had a treadmill and a stationary recumbent bike in our basement for years and have used them with some frequency (my husband more than I). We have a floor mat and some weights that I used regularly for a while. But I needed some accountability. So we decided to purchase a membership for each of us at a local fitness center. I didn't know much about the gym equipment, but I began using the treadmill and several other fitness machines. I soon realized I wasn't accomplishing much because I didn't know what I was doing. Recognizing I needed help, my husband signed me up with a personal trainer as a Christmas gift that year. And for the next six months, I worked! I often told Cara I thought she was trying to kill me, but at the end of six months, I was much stronger than I had been at Christmas (or in my whole life). Cara was the accountability I needed.

I worked out faithfully until the gym was closed due to the COVID-19 pandemic. During the shutdown, my motivation went away. Yes, the treadmill, bike, floor mat, and weights were still in our basement. It was nice enough outside to go for a walk, but I didn't exercise as much or intensely as before. When the gym reopened two months later, I immediately realized I couldn't just pick up where I'd left off. I needed to start slowly again. This time I am motivated not by a person but by something inside that feels better when I exercise.

This morning while I was physically exercising, I reflected on my *spiritual* exercise program. Long ago, I realized my day just goes so much better when I spend time with the Lord before doing anything else. He is my personal Trainer. He is the accountability I need. He tells me what I need to do, and then He helps me do it. And the more time I spend with Him, the stronger I become, and *that* gives me a great feeling inside!

Kathy Pepper

A Mouse in the House!

Cast thy burden upon the LORD, and he shall sustain thee.
—Psalm 55:22, KJV

Many years ago, when my husband was the youth director for our church's Colorado region, we stayed in a nice little cabin in the mountains during the summer camping season. We ate our meals in the camp dining room but had a kitchenette that we could use if we needed or wanted to. One summer a little brown field mouse decided that our home should also be his home. We didn't agree, so we used a broom to herd him out the door. We were amused and a bit sympathetic when we found him running back and forth in front of the door, trying to find a way back in!

In the basement of my current home, we once found evidence that we were sharing space with some mouse-type critters, so my husband set some traps. Whenever one was caught, the man of the house took care of dispensing with it. Our great-niece, who was visiting, saw the traps and was upset because she thought of mice as cute little creatures!

Now there is no longer a man of the house, so when I found that the corner of a big bag of birdseed in the garage had been gnawed open, I knew I had an unwelcome guest. When our pest control agent came for his once-a-year treatment for termites, I told him about the mouse problem. He set a poison trap rather than one that would have to be emptied.

Over time, his trap seemed to have taken care of the situation until I went down to the basement one day. There I found a tiny, lifeless body lying on the floor. Now what was I going to do? Even though I didn't want to deal with the dead mouse, there was no one else to take over. It was up to me. So I eventually got up my courage, picked up a broom and dustpan, and, with these, was able to gingerly place the mouse in a bag to be discarded. So far, there seem to be no more invasions of mice.

I wonder, though, how much I allow Satan's "mice" to take up residence in my life. I could come up with a long list! Perhaps you have a list of your own. I know I need help dealing with those pesky sins but not by setting traps or putting out poison. There is One who has promised that "if we confess our sins, he is faithful and just to forgive us our sins, and to cleanse us from all unrighteousness" (1 John 1:9, KJV). Nothing could be better than that!

Mary Jane Graves

Acknowledge Him

In all thy ways acknowledge him, and he shall direct thy paths.
—Proverbs 3:6, KJV

While shopping in a chain superstore a few years ago, I ran into an acquaintance. He excitedly shared some good news. "I quit smoking!" he said.

"That is wonderful! Praise God," I responded.

With a genuine, incredulous, and puzzled look on his face, he asked what God had to do with it. "He gave you the victory," I replied, equally puzzled he didn't realize that.

"God didn't have anything to do with it; I quit on my own," he retorted.

Not one to let a comment like that go unacknowledged, I stated, "Oh, just as you awakened yourself this morning."

"No, I didn't wake myself up this morning; my alarm clock woke me up," he shot back.

At this point, we both started laughing. But he was serious about feeling that overcoming his addiction was something he'd done strictly on his own. And, granted, perhaps he'd never asked God for help, yet God is the Giver of all good things (James 1:17).

This conversation reminded me of another person who had the same outlook on life: Nebuchadnezzar. He felt that he had accomplished everything by himself. Nebuchadnezzar's words were, "Is not this great Babylon, that I have built for a royal dwelling by my mighty power and for the honor of my majesty?" (Daniel 4:30, NKJV). "By my mighty power" is an ultimate statement of ignorance concerning God's power and supremacy and daily mercy to us. The king was humbled before God and men before he sincerely acknowledged God's might and dominion.

Wow! We shake our heads in disbelief that a person could be so arrogant and ignorant, but are we not all capable of feeling the same about our accomplishments if we're not careful to give God the glory? When we let go of God and His Word, we're treading on dangerous ground.

I don't know why finite man hesitates to give God the glory and honor He alone deserves. And I don't know if that conversation with my acquaintance caused him to think about his relationship with God and his need for God in his life, but I sure hope it did.

We serve a wonderful God! *Father in heaven, help us to remember and acknowledge how wonderful You are every moment of every day!*

Sharon M. Thomas

We Are Called by God

For if I preach the gospel, I have nothing to boast of,
for necessity is laid upon me; yes, woe is me if I do not preach the gospel!
—1 Corinthians 9:16, NKJV

Have you ever felt God urging you to do something that was not comfortable for you, but the urging was so strong you had to move forward? That has been the story of my life in Women's Ministries. The call to work in this department was so strong that I could not say no to God's leading at the time. Through the years, that call has only grown stronger. Even after I am no longer officially working in Women's Ministries, I will continue working to support my sisters in the church and community. The call God placed on my life reminds me of today's verse. Paul says that he preached the gospel because God laid a "necessity" on him, and he knew he could not refuse the call. That is how I feel about working with my sisters.

God places a call on each of His children, and that includes His daughters—you and me. We are called to represent His character to all with whom we come in contact. We are called to love others as Jesus did on this earth. We are called to speak kind, encouraging words to build up those around us. We are called to listen to the pains and sufferings of those God brings into our lives. And we are called to share the hope of the gospel that Jesus has given to each person.

The call of God is general to all believers, but it is also specific. He calls us to do the above in different ways and environments. Through my travels around the world, I have heard so many stories and learned so many ways my sisters are carrying out their call from God. Some women sew scarves for other women who have lost their hair from cancer; some make beautiful, tiny coverings for mothers whose babies were born prematurely or miscarried; some cook for those in need; and some serve meals to the homeless or visit those who are sick. Others visit orphanages to hold babies and toddlers so they can feel the love of God. I can go on and on.

You are called by God, my sister. Never doubt your calling. If you do not know what God has called you to do, then ask Him. If He does not answer immediately, then do what you love to help others. Sew, knit, or crochet, and then give what you make to underprivileged mothers who need clothes for their children. If you love to read, then read God's Word to the elderly or visually disabled. Whatever it is, *do* it. And God will do the rest.

Heather-Dawn Small

Footie-Pajama Friends

Two people are better off than one, for they can help each other succeed.
If one person falls, the other can reach out and help.
But someone who falls alone is in real trouble.
—Ecclesiastes 4:9, 10, NLT

I've known my friend Rachelle since before I was born—at least, that's what I always tell people. Our parents were good friends, and we spent a lot of time together while growing up. One of my favorite memories of our families occurred when I was only two years old. Rachelle's family came over and stayed late. Our parents took us upstairs and got us ready for bed. Rachelle and I, however, were not tired in the least. We found a winter hat on the floor and took turns putting it on. We shrieked with laughter at how funny we looked wearing it. Next, we jumped up and down on the bed and sang, "If you're happy and you know it, clap your hands" at the top of our lungs. Our parents came up and took the cutest pictures of us in our matching yellow footie pajamas—those are still my favorite pictures ever.

When I was five, we moved away, but I've never lost touch with Rachelle. Every Tuesday we call each other and pray together. We have helped each other through hard times. We can go from laughing about embarrassing moments to talking about deep spiritual topics. I know God gave her to me, and I am so thankful for her.

The more I grow up, the more I realize the importance of friendship and community. God doesn't want us to "do" faith alone. That's why He created friendship. I love knowing that I can rely on the people around me. It's important to build a good group of friends because we become like those we spend the most time with. God uses us to reach the people around us. It's easy to feel alone and as if we are the only ones struggling with challenges, but that couldn't be further from the truth.

God will send us the people we need in our lives to help us grow closer to Him. Think about the people in your life and ask yourself whether they help you grow closer to God. Also, think about yourself. Are you being the kind of friend you need to be to those around you? Pray for your friends and the people around you, then thank God for His friendship—not just with you but with all the friends He has put into your life and for whom you are praying.

Ashley Halvorson

The Satin Nightgown

*"If you then, being evil, know how to give good gifts to
your children, how much more will your Father who
is in heaven give good things to those who ask Him!"*
—Matthew 7:11, NKJV

Some years ago, I had been given some money and decided to treat myself to something special from a large department store in town. While browsing in the lingerie department, I spotted a beautiful, long, emerald-green, satin-finish nightgown with delicate cream-colored lacy shoulder straps. Although it's been quite a while since that department store encounter, I can still picture the loveliness of that garment. I saw no price tag, which suggested it was expensive. Nonetheless, I was there to treat myself, so I gently picked up the nightgown, carefully draped it over my arm, and headed to the nearest cashier.

As I stood before the clerk, ready to pay, I commented on the garment's beautiful satin finish. Then I asked the price and reached for my purse. The clerk seemed puzzled over the amount and answered, "You wouldn't be able to afford it anyway."

"Don't worry," I nonchalantly replied, "I'll have it." After all, hadn't God already abundantly provided? As I remember, the clerk wrapped it without making further eye contact with me and scanned it through the register. It was mine!

I love the way God blesses us out of His bounty. He is a generous, kind, loving God who loves to elevate us as His children. Our Father in heaven has a very large purse.

Just recently, my daughter inquired of someone about the cost of marketing one of my publications. The honest response from this very nice man was, "Your mum wouldn't be able to afford me." I immediately thought, *I have been here before. Let us see what God can afford!* I have seen churches buy plots of land and companies, eventually congregations, grow despite little or no money.

Our God is a great big God, and He is not limited by lack of earthly financial resources. He is the God of provision. One of the Bible names for Him is Jehovah-Jireh, which means "the Lord will provide," and it is exciting to see Him manifest His goodness by doing so.

"Look at the birds of the air, for they neither sow nor reap . . . ; yet your heavenly Father feeds them. Are you not of much more value than they?" (Matthew 6:26, NKJV).

Laura A. Canning

Nothing Can Separate Us

For I am convinced that nothing can ever separate us from his love. Death can't, and life can't. The angels won't, and all the powers of hell itself cannot keep God's love away. Our fears for today, our worries about tomorrow, or where we are—high above the sky, or in the deepest ocean—nothing will ever be able to separate us from the love of God demonstrated by our Lord Jesus Christ when he died for us.
—Romans 8:38, 39, TLB

It was my duty and privilege to preach to more than two hundred women in a Kenyan prison one Sabbath. The women wore striped uniforms. Embroidered red and blue labels on their backs designated their crimes. Small children scurried around their feet as they sat in the dust outside their long dormitory cell block. I felt totally inadequate. They were there for various reasons; some seem most unfair. One woman was imprisoned because she had poured boiling water over her husband after seven years of his beating her. Another was there because the raiding police found drugs under her seat in the bus she was on. Another had been accused of murdering her baby, even though the baby lived with its father and his girlfriend. Many of these tales were horrific. It didn't seem right that those women should be incarcerated. Most did not have money for advocates to plead their cause, so they stayed in prison. Those with babies could keep them only until they were three years old. Then the babies were sent back to husbands, grandparents, or other relatives. If no one could be found, they were delivered to an orphanage.

Before going to the prison, I had prayed earnestly for God to show me what to say. He had led me to the scripture in Romans 8 that assures us nothing can separate us from God's love. I read those scriptures and urged the women to hear them in their hearts. I watched their faces as the women listened to my words. I kept praying that God would open their hearts to receive this message of love. When they sang, it was with great enthusiasm and determination. They knew the Christian songs and burst forth with clapping and dancing and raised hands toward God, worshiping Him as their only hope and salvation. I believe they knew the real meaning of worshiping Someone they could trust.

My prayer was—and still is—that God will hear their cries, give them peace, and envelop them in His love, saving them and their children for His kingdom. I hope this will be yours too.

Joy Marie Butler

Faith Versus Fear

The LORD God is my strength . . .
And He will make me walk on my high hills.
—Habakkuk 3:19, NKJV

Impala is not only a car that Chevrolet made; it is also the name of an African animal that can jump ten feet (three and a half meters) high and cover a distance of more than thirty feet (nine meters). But there's something unusual about these animals. In spite of their incredible jumping ability, impalas can be kept in an enclosure in any zoo with just a three-foot-high wall. The reason: *These animals will not jump if they can't see where their feet will land!*

We're not much different from impalas, are we?

Many of us reach great heights and cover vast amounts of distance in our lives. But that one small wall can stop us dead in our tracks.

I'm familiar with that wall. That wall is fear. That wall has kept me from many good things in life.

That three-foot-high wall held me back from pursuing God's purpose of *ministry* for my life because I was afraid I wasn't good enough, didn't know enough, and wasn't smart enough.

That three-foot-high wall has held me back from pursuing God's purpose of *joy* for my life because I was afraid of what others would think of me.

That three-foot-high wall has held me back from pursuing God's purpose of *freedom* for my life because I was afraid I wasn't strong enough to go where I couldn't see where my feet would land.

What is your three-foot-high wall? I would imagine that many of you, like me, have allowed that three-foot-high wall to keep you from fulfilling God's purpose and vision for your lives.

Faith and fear have more in common than we think: *they both demand to be fulfilled.*

What will we allow to be fulfilled in our lives?

Like the Israelites who crossed the Red Sea by placing their feet in the water—*then* watching the sea split apart—we will find the following step will reveal itself after we take our first step. Only in stepping *over* the wall will we see where our foot will land. We may not see every step, but we can be assured that our faith will be fulfilled as we move forward!

Bonita Joyner Shields

It Was Time

"I am with you all the days—till the full end of the age."
—Matthew 28:20, YLT

Moments last longer in a woman's heart as she awaits the outcome of an intense surgery performed upon the body of the man she loves. When a surgery lasts from noon until eight o'clock in the evening, the Lord can hear and understand the repetitive, sweet scent of true, honest prayers whose impact no one on Earth can fully feel.

Such was the case when John thought he was looking at one type of surgery—a laryngectomy. But during the presurgery exam came words no one wants to hear from a doctor's mouth: "This is much worse than when I last saw you and planned this surgery. I need to call in three more specialists."

Although I am a praying woman, I uttered unexpected words from my own mouth: "I have not said enough prayers nor broken enough dishes for this." John smiled. I shook my head. The doctor explained the reasons additional specialists would be needed.

We prayed, cried, laughed, and then turned this serious situation over to the only Power who could love and strengthen us through it. The previous Sabbath our church family had surrounded us with prayer and anointing. On the day of John's surgery, Pastor Sandro stayed with me far into the evening, as did our friends, Bev and Bill. At 9:00 P.M., the surgical nurse took us to a quiet room for an update. She said that John was on life support during the surgery as his throat was vivisected to separate the nose and sinus. His mouth was now connected directly to his stomach. Where the larynx used to be, there would now be a new opening, a stoma, for breathing. Life would never be the same for him: breathing, speaking, or eating. Pastor Sandro went with us into the ICU room where John was awake though connected to wires, draining tubes, and a full rack of bottles and bags hanging from a rolling metal stand. On a whiteboard, he wrote, "Praise the Lord." Most reacted with joy and relief, but I only felt fear. During the night, I contacted the pastor. Calmly, he asked, "Why are you, a woman of faith, in such a panic?" I now allowed myself to love John fully, no matter what the future held. It was then I relaxed. The answer to my prayers was that it was time—time to trust God to take over more completely than ever before. Yes, it was time.

Sally J. Linke

A Divine Leading

Search me, O God, and know my heart: try me,
and know my thoughts: And see if there be any wicked
way in me, and lead me in the way everlasting.
—Psalm 139:23, 24, KJV

One day as I was praying and asking God to search my heart, He reminded me of a girl who sat next to me in homeroom class when I was in junior high school. I liked her, but because she was not American, other students made fun of her, calling her one name in particular. I never called her that name, of course, but sometimes I laughed when others did. We, whether young people or adults, can be cruel and not even realize it. I started to ponder how that must have felt to my homeroom classmate. But it had been at least thirty years since I had seen my friend, and I didn't know how I could tell her I was sorry, though I had asked God to forgive me. I was now a different person, no longer living a wild life. Back then, I didn't know how to have a relationship with God; I just called on Him when I was in trouble. But God was always there, wooing me toward Himself.

I moved away from my hometown a couple of years after I became a Christian. After marriage, my husband and I moved around the country, working in ministry. Then he had a call to pastor in West Virginia; this put us closer to our hometown and allowed us to return and visit with our family occasionally. When visiting our hometown shortly after I'd prayed and asked God to search my heart, I decided to visit a Whole Foods store because we don't have any near where we live. Since the store was not near where I'd grown up, I didn't expect to run into anyone I knew. As I was walking in, though, I noticed someone who resembled my former homeroom classmate. When I called out her name, she turned around. It was she! I knew that God had put this meeting together. After talking a few minutes, I told her I'd become a Christian. Then I said, "I want to apologize to you for the names that students called you. Though I never said those awful words, I laughed along with the kids, which was just as bad. I am truly sorry." She told me not to worry about it. But then I noticed a tear in her eye. After all these years, I believe it still hurt her. I hugged her and told her God loves her and brought us together so that I could apologize to her. Friends, we should always ask God to help us say we are sorry to those we have hurt. Then let's let them know how much God loves them.

Elaine Buchanan

The "Being Present" Christmas

On coming to the house, they saw the child with his
mother Mary, and they bowed down and worshiped
him. Then they opened their treasures and presented
him with gifts of gold, frankincense and myrrh.
—Matthew 2:11, NIV

Several years ago, a young friend of ours, Mark, had been on a recent travel adventure. When I asked what time would be good to phone and hear about his experiences, his immediate response was, "I don't want a call. I want to be *present* with you!" My husband and I made a dinner date with Mark at a local restaurant and had the opportunity to "be present." We not only heard his adventure stories but also saw the sparkle in his eyes. This was a great lesson for us, though we are old enough to be Mark's grandparents. Since the holiday season was just beginning, we decided to "be present" intentionally with friends; we visited some of them in their homes, and we met others for dinner dates in restaurants. No prep or cleanup—just being present. We let them know how important they are to us and how much we value their friendship.

This holiday season, I felt impressed to host a baby shower for a young woman who is new to our church family and couldn't go home for Christmas because of the baby's due date. I texted names on our list of invitees. The response was rather discouraging as person after person couldn't participate: test week, conflicting holiday events, and sickness. What to do? Should I cancel the shower? No, I would invite some "mothers in Israel" to be present at this shower, even though they didn't know this young woman. I prayed for ten. Eleven came with gifts and cookies but mainly to be present and get acquainted with the wonderful young mother-to-be! Seeing the joy and the excitement of the women bonding and encompassing this young woman brought me so much joy and happiness. It was the best "being present" I have been part of in a long time!

I thought of the Christ Child and His parents, Joseph and Mary, being in poor, humble circumstances. Perhaps they were a bit lonely and felt far away from family and friends. Then the Magi came, bringing gifts and being joyfully present! They could have sent their gifts with servants, but they came in person. Their visit affirmed and encouraged this young family that God cared, was providing for their needs, and would always be present with them.

This holiday season, why not take the time to search for someone who needs *your* presence?

Bonnie R. Parker

The Women and the Shepherds

"All authority has been given to Me in heaven and on earth.
Go therefore and make disciples."
—Matthew 28:18, 19, NASB

They had seen the empty tomb and had run to tell the disciples that Jesus was alive. It was too good to be true, and they understood the disciples' doubts. Or perhaps not. In any case, it was all so hazy and surreal; their emotions were all over the place.

The women who had followed Jesus had been given the unique privilege of being eyewitnesses to the glory of God at the entrance of the empty tomb. Thirty-three years before, humble shepherds had also been given the unique privilege of seeing and hearing the wonderful news and music announcing Jesus' birth. Women and shepherds—not really considered first-class human beings at that time. But they went and shared anyway with anyone who would listen.

Now these women, following the Lord's command, made their way to Galilee (Matthew 28:10) to meet many other believers and then the resurrected Jesus Himself. The hills were peaceful, and the walk, unforgettable. Then, as all the followers were together, Jesus appeared.

"I have received all the power and all the authority in heaven and on Earth. Go therefore." As I walked among those hills once, I wondered how the disciples—men and women—felt when they heard the authoritative words and command of Christ. I tried to imagine being there, listening to His words myself. Every time I read this story, these memories come back to me.

Jesus' power and authority always work out things in my life in such a way that I can, without fear, go and tell the story of what He has done and is doing for me. Big things. Small things. But all of them are important things because Jesus is part of that story.

I admire those women who followed and obeyed Jesus. And I admire the shepherds in the hills of Bethlehem. Society may have looked down on them, but they went out and told their story anyway. Some of us may sometimes think that we're not good enough, we're not educated enough, or we're not strong enough emotionally to go and make a difference. What if, when in doubt and fear, we remembered the women and the shepherds?

It works for me, along with the words of Jesus on that serene hill in Galilee: "All power and authority are Mine, dear daughter. Go therefore, share your story, and be a blessing today."

Lorena Finis Mayer

The Christmas Concert

For unto you is born this day in the city of
David a Saviour, which is Christ the Lord.
—Luke 2:11, KJV

Don't forget to come back Friday for the Christmas concert," Mama had said urgently. "It's going to be very good!" Her eyes sparkled as if I were a long-awaited Friend she'd been expecting for years. At ninety-two, she was still beautiful, could sing and whistle, and was an active member in her church, attending since 1942. She loved life! It was Friday, Christmas Eve. I was rushing! *I must hurry!*

The Christmas concert at the assisted living facility would soon start. I saw Mama and six other women and men I knew wearing their beautiful red-and-green outfits. The ladies wore colorful Christmas earrings, headbands in their white hair, and bright-red lipstick. They all wore big smiles! I expected to see lots of these stalwart singers' family members. After all, it was the Christmas concert! But no one came.

The concert began. One lone lady sang carols to a CD player. Where possible, others sang along with her. Mama leaned over and exclaimed, "Isn't this good?" I replied, "Yes," and thought, *Is this it?* I'm the minister of music at my church. Our Christmas concert consisted of a hundred thousand dollar audiovisual system, an opera singer singing Handel's *Messiah*, a trumpeter, a mass choir, and lots of attendees!

"Esta, you said your daughter would be here," the lady said. "Why don't you two lead us in the next song?" Mama beamed! So, with me singing soprano and Mama singing alto, we began to sing "Silent Night." I couldn't stop the tears as Mama held my hands tightly in hers. Those hands that could no longer grip a switch, a crochet or knitting needle, or a hymnal. I looked around at the six, struggling to remember words they once knew so well. Then I realized this *was* "*the* Christmas concert"! I sang slowly. I sang thankfully for Mama and these beautiful people. It reminded me of the birth of my Lord and Savior, Jesus Christ: two people and some animals. When we returned to her room, Mama whispered, "I told you that you'd like it."

I whispered back, "Yes, Mama, it's the best Christmas concert ever!" I hugged her hard and long for all the days gone by and all the days ahead when she would be sleeping "in heavenly peace."*

Edna Thomas Taylor

---

* Mrs. Esta Pearl Saunders Thomas died on August 20, 2015.

She Gave Birth

And she gave birth to her firstborn, a son.
She wrapped him in cloths and placed him in a manger.
—Luke 2:7, NIV

For me, the last six weeks of pregnancy felt like being the proverbial beached whale. My sister delivered both of her children six weeks early, so whenever I declared it was hugely uncomfortable to be pregnant at the end, she never understood it.

In the birth story of Jesus, the innkeeper is often vilified for closing his door on Mary and Joseph. Surely, I would have given up my own room, wouldn't I? It must be obvious to the innkeeper that the woman is uncomfortably pregnant and exhausted by her journey. Isn't her condition worthy of finding a room or space in the house for her?

No, it is not the concern of the innkeeper. The innkeeper is acutely aware that the space will become contaminated with the uncleanness of birthing. A homeowner needed a separate space for a baby to be born. Uncleanness lasts for one week with the birthing of a boy and two weeks for a girl, but the mother must continue in separation for further purification—a total of forty days after birthing a boy and eighty days after birthing a girl (Leviticus 12).

What homeowner has enough spare room to take in a traveling woman who is ready to give birth? Even if a spare room is isolated, one never knows how long it will take before the mother is ready to travel home with her newborn baby. The innkeeper knows that Mary's pregnant condition doesn't excuse breaking the law when his family and other guests are gathered under his roof. The innkeeper won't risk his livelihood with the birthing at his inn.

Through the forced global lockdown in 2020 due to the coronavirus, we can understand what the loss of livelihood for forty to eighty days means for a small business owner and his employees.

Do I consider the dilemma of the innkeeper when he chooses to follow the Torah, shutting his door on Mary and Joseph? What if following God's Word seems foolish or contradicts civil law? Do I know God's voice well enough to let it guide me without regret? Or do I act on what I think is right without consulting the Law and the Prophets? Am I prepared to keep God's commandments, no matter the cost?

Rebecca Turner

God With Us

Devise your strategy, but it will be thwarted;
propose your plan, but it will not stand,
for God is with us.
—Isaiah 8:10, NIV

Do you ever feel that sometimes you pray and pray for something, but nothing seems to happen? Maybe Paul felt that way about getting to visit Rome. In his letter to the Romans, whom he had not met yet, Paul told them he was constantly remembering them in his prayers, and he was praying "that now at last by God's will the way may be opened for me to come to you" (Romans 1:10, NIV). Apparently, Paul had prayed this for a long time, but it just hadn't happened.

We know that Paul did get to Rome several years later, but he went as a prisoner. No doubt he prayed for a safe journey, and he did arrive safely in Rome but not before being arrested, shipwrecked, and bitten by a poisonous snake. Paul's experience illustrates that when we pray sincerely, God does answer but sometimes in ways and timing we don't expect! God knows what is best for us. His ways aren't our ways. God is wiser than we are because He sees the end from the beginning.

Later in his letter to the Romans, Paul assures us that "in all things God works for the good of those who love him, who have been called according to his purpose" (Romans 8:28, NIV). Notice, God works "in" things that happen to us; He doesn't always keep us from going through and experiencing some things we never thought we would face. Yet He's there with us—always in the middle of it with us!

That's the story and real beauty of Christmas. Jesus is our Immanuel, "God with us" (Matthew 1:23)! He walks with us—sometimes carrying us—through the ups and downs of life. We rest assured that Jesus knows the desires of our hearts, the worries, the cares, and the joys. He promises never to leave us nor forsake us (Joshua 1:5) and to be with us always until the end of the world (Matthew 28:20). His second advent reverses the transformation and location of the First Advent. Now Jesus transforms us and takes us to live with Him for eternity. Forever God with us!

Myrna L. Hanna

The Scholarship

Jesus looked at them and said, "With man this is
impossible, but with God all things are possible."
—Matthew 19:26, NIV

It was late March 2013 when a friend phoned, saying, "Let's apply for a scholarship." The following day, after we secured our scholarship application forms, I noticed that the criteria for obtaining a scholarship necessitated a prerequisite in mathematics that I didn't have. My heart sank. We had only two full days to get everything in order before the deadline. When the final day arrived, I had only one out of two forms completed and none of the supporting documents copied and certified. Upon my arrival at the scholarship board, I tried to fill out the rest of the forms, but thoughts of not having the math prerequisite dampened my spirits to the point of changing my mind. I told my friend that I would apply again next year after I studied math.

While walking back to my vehicle, I felt a sense of calm enfolding me. I prayed, *Lord, if You have a scholarship for me, let one of my friends call me to go back to apply.* Five minutes later, the same friend called. "Debora, come back. You already have most of what they need. Just try and see what happens. I will hold a place for you." I was dumbfounded and elated at the same time. I had only one hour to get everything together. Yet, when it was my turn, I didn't even have the names of those who could be my sureties—those who would be legally and financially liable for me. After I submitted everything, the scholarship board personnel asked me to provide them with the names of my sureties. I never did, thinking I would not receive the scholarship. Three months later, my same friend called me, asking, "Why didn't you tell me you got the scholarship?"

"But I didn't receive one," I responded. When my friend said she'd seen my name in the newspaper, I immediately purchased a copy. With my own eyes, I saw I was one of the 2013 scholarship board's scholarship recipients. Though three of us had gone together to apply, I was the only one who hadn't met all the requirements—and the only one who received the scholarship! I give God thanks and praise for qualifying me for what I wasn't qualified for.

Heavenly Father, thank You that Your eyes see us and Your ears are attentive to our prayers. Help us be mindful that we can trust You with every detail of our lives and cast all our cares upon You because You care for us. In Jesus' name, amen.

Debora Ramona Hughes

A Present Help

Now unto him that is able to do exceeding abundantly above all that we ask or think.
—Ephesians 3:20, KJV

The year I turned twenty-one, my mom passed away. That was also the year I started working on my college degree and got baptized. Each child in the family received a lump sum of money from our mother's life insurance. I used my sum to pay tuition for my first year of schooling. At the beginning of the second year of college, I managed to get funds for registration but failed to secure money to pay the rest of the fees. As the year ended, I started to despair, but the hype of social gatherings during the university break and festive season made me temporarily forget my worries. In January, everyone around me was excited about the new year, but dark clouds of foreboding overshadowed my heart. My excellent academic records testified of the hard work I had put into my first and second years, yet I was on the verge of losing it all.

All human help seemed inaccessible. God was my only solace. He inspired me to go to the university and find out the exact amount that I owed. I started off on my one-hour journey to campus and was soon queuing at one of the financial office counters. When my turn came, I handed over my student card and requested the amount due. After a few moments, the lady informed me that I had a credit! "Do you need a printout?" she asked. At first, I stared back at her in confusion, mentally struggling and trying to recall the basic difference between the meanings of the words *credit* and *debit*. My thoughts racing, I concluded that she had made an error in her fact-finding and had provided me with another student's financial information. I voiced my concern to her.

With a trace of impatience in her voice, she confirmed the details of my account and provided the same response as before. In a bewildered tone, I explained that I had not paid my fees that whole year and sought an explanation. At this point, she stormed away in irritation. A nearby teller came to my aid. She reviewed my account and calmly explained that a philanthropic organization called Rhodes had sought out and identified financially struggling students with exceptional academic records—and settled their accounts due! It was evident that before I had even started praying, God had already answered my prayer!

Regina Nakanjako Mngumi

Exploding Tires

The LORD will keep you from all harm—
he will watch over your life;
the LORD will watch over your coming and going
both now and forevermore.
—Psalm 121:7, 8, NIV

My first missionary experience was from 2006 to 2012, when I served as a physician in a Christian hospital located in a remote village in Western Zambia, Africa. The hospital is five hundred miles (eight hundred kilometers) from Lusaka, the capital city. During the dry season, one travels over sandy tracks with huge potholes; during rainy season floods, travel is by pontoon boat. Since electricity is available only in the hospital and campus homes, I had to walk in the dark on night calls. I was ever fearful of encountering a hippopotamus from the nearby river, grazing on the hospital grounds. Spitting cobras are also common there. On several occasions, my husband, Harville, experienced the fury of a spitting cobra with the venom landing on his pants. Others have not been so fortunate. I also feared the black mamba—a snake that chases its prey.

One day we had to make the twelve-hour trip by car to Lusaka. Four hours into our trip, the rear right tire exploded. Replacing it with the spare tire, we continued our journey. Two hours later, the left rear tire exploded. In the process of removing the tire, the wrench broke. With no auto shops nearby and cars rarely traveling along this highway, all we could do was wait for help. After what seemed like hours, a car drove by, and the driver loaned us his tire wrench so we could remove the left rear tire. With two damaged tires, we slowly drove the 121 miles (195 kilometers) to Kaoma, the next town, where we purchased the only available—and old—tire before the shop closed for the night.

Having no place to sleep in town, we continued our journey through Kafue National Park, Zambia's largest game park and home to much dangerous wildlife. Luckily, another commuter was traveling the same route, so we drove together in case either of us had car trouble again. We prayed that this stranger was not a wolf in sheep's clothing who intended to harm us. After sixteen hours on the road, we finally reached Lusaka.

The Lord promises to watch over us and keep us from harm and danger (Psalm 121:8).

Ellen Porteza Valenciano

Life Without Mother

"Honor your father and your mother, that your days may be long upon the land which the LORD your God is giving you."
—Exodus 20:12, NKJV

Sallie Mozelle, in the seventh month of her 103rd year, fell asleep. Mother had been a constant companion in my life. I admired her wit, joy, and generous spirit, so it was my delight to brighten each day of her life with love. Mom's smile was contagious. She traveled everywhere with our family, and we loved the joy she brought on each journey. We shared everything, especially Christian reading material. She was indeed my best friend. I couldn't imagine life without her. I often asked God to let us be together when "separation" drew near. During our times together, I often looked at her in the passenger seat, observing her joy, listening to her, or watching her doze off, as I attempted to capture that moment in my mental archives. (I even wrote a devotional, "Honoring Parents," included in the 2009 devotional book *Sanctuary.*)

At that time, Mom was ninety-three years old, living alone, independent, and maintaining a vibrant life. After work several times a week, I visited her to assist with household chores, personal needs, and appointments. When she was ninety-nine, I realized it was time for her to live with my husband and me. The transition had its challenges because, at that time, my ninety-five-year-old Aunt Annie Bell was also living with us. Huge adjustments had to be made. It was only by the grace of God that all worked out according to His will.

As my mother's health declined, I considered seeing whether my aunt, who had been living with us for seven years, could move closer to her own family. It was a difficult decision. I prayed continuously, asking God for direction as both my aunt and mother needed my undivided attention. I believed that if it were God's will for my aunt to transfer, He would work it out. At that time, I was still working outside the home, and stress was a major factor, although I wanted to bring joy to them both. God led in my aunt's successful transfer.

Then, on a crisp, bright, and glorious Sabbath morning in December, my dear mom departed this life, slipping into a peaceful rest. As I held her hand, I thanked God for Mother. I couldn't imagine life without her, but, you see, my God granted me the peace that "passeth all understanding" (Philippians 4:7, KJV), peace that I had never known. Our heavenly Father will do the same for you.

Sylvia Giles Bennett

When Your Raft Flips Over

And this hope will not lead to disappointment.
For we know how dearly God loves us.
—Romans 5:5, NLT

After a long drive through endless traffic and a sleepless night full of anticipation, it was finally here. I was going to go white water rafting for the very first time! The weather was picture perfect. The blue Carolina sky hugged fluffy white clouds and held a brilliant ball of sunshine. My friends and I climbed into the raft and *swoosh*! Off we went, flying—at times, weightless—carried along by the relentless river flow. Laughter, water spray, and a little apprehension filled the air as we tried to navigate the rapids. At the end, only one question remained: When can I do this again? Life couldn't get any better than this.

And then my husband of fourteen years, traumatically and unexpectedly, exited my life. By choice. The rapids I once excitedly anticipated now seemed threatening and menacing. As I tried to navigate the river with only one oar, the formerly fun, adrenaline-filled challenges suddenly rose like dark specters, clouding my vision. My raft had flipped over, unceremoniously tossing me into the churning, icy waters.

I gasped when the first wave violently crashed over me. My only conscious instinct was to attempt to avoid being smashed by the hidden boulders—custody hearings, attorney's fees, the necessity of moving, isolation, loneliness, loss of friends, and an apparent loss of purpose—which relentlessly came at me with no seeming end. At irregular intervals, the river would grudgingly release its sucking grip, and I would gulp a life-sustaining breath before being pulled back under.

I don't know why I ended up here, tumbling, struggling to perceive the light that provides direction through the churning waters to the surface and survival. I don't know whether I will make it to the river's shore and be able to walk back up to the starting point or continue to be swept along and eventually plunge over the looming waterfalls. The multitude of unknowns is overwhelming. But what I do know is that God knew this was going to happen. He still has a plan for me—a plan to give me hope and a future (see Jeremiah 29:11, NIV). So in between each hard-fought breath and the fight to grasp this seemingly elusive hope, this promise nurtures my teeny-tiny mustard seed of faith. And for now, that has to be enough.

Charmaine Houston

Don't Worry, Be Happy!

*Be anxious for nothing, but in everything by prayer and supplication,
with thanksgiving, let your requests be made known to God;
and the peace of God, which surpasses all understanding,
will guard your hearts and minds through Christ Jesus.*
—Philippians 4:6, 7, NKJV

Have you ever had one thing after another go wrong, and it seems that you just can't get a break? That was my experience when my husband and I relocated after our retirement. We had just moved to a new state and bought a house. The following week after closing on our new home, my husband had to travel out of the country. Now I was alone. After he left, I spent all the next day cleaning the house. Everything seemed to be in good order. All appliances and the air conditioning and heating units were working as they should.

The following day I returned to the house and noticed that the inside of the house felt more humid than expected. As the day progressed, it grew hotter inside the house. I realized the air conditioning unit was not running. While I struggled with that problem, I was also trying to find out where our belongings were because the shipping company transporting them kept giving me the runaround regarding a delivery date. On top of all that, I had lost the keys to our van. It just seemed as if nothing was going right and that my world was falling apart.

But with all that was going on, strangely enough, I didn't feel overly anxious. This surprised me because I am a worrier. Yes, things didn't seem to be going right, but as each problem presented itself, I'd pray about it and leave it in the Lord's hands. I had learned over the years that when I prayed and presented my problems or concerns to God, I should leave them at His feet. Why? Because He just wants me to trust Him when I can't even trace Him.

As I look into the future with all its unknowns, Philippians 4:6, 7 is a source of great encouragement to me. Why? Because I know I don't have to worry or be anxious about anything. God is more than able to take care of me if only I put my trust in Him. He loves me enough to walk with me, especially in the midst of uncertainty.

Won't you trust Him to do the same for you in return for His love and watch care? Don't worry about anything. Be happy that God cares for you. He will guide your feet into safe pathways. And He has promised that when we keep our thoughts on Him, He will give us peace.

Maureen H. Moncrieffe

2022 Author Biographies

Betty J. Adams is a retired teacher in California, United States of America. She has been married for more than sixty-five years and has six children, seven grandchildren, four great-grandchildren, and two great-great-grandchildren. She has written for her church newsletter and *Guide* and works for her church's Community Services ministry. **Mar. 7**

Elizabeth Oluwaseun Adebayo is a woman in her thirties. A teacher by profession, she is married to a pastor, and their union is blessed with three lovely children. She is passionate about doing God's work. She loves ministering to children and mentoring young ones. Her hobbies are reading, teaching, traveling, and cooking. She loves catering and craftwork. She writes from Kwara State, Nigeria, Africa. **Oct. 16**

Priscilla E. Adonis lives in Cape Town, South Africa, and reports she is getting older and slower, but she thanks God for His wonderful love and protection over her day by day. She is grateful for friends who help her where necessary and for her budgies that keep singing no matter what! **Apr. 8, July 8**

Susan Anderson is retired from the United States Department of Agriculture, Forest Service, and lives in the Pacific Northwest of the United States of America. She has been married to Chuck for more than fifty years, and they have two married daughters, a granddaughter, two grandsons, and two great-grandsons. She enjoys writing and spending time with family and friends. **Mar. 25, Sept. 22**

Lydia D. Andrews, CNM, is a retired university professor of nursing. She and her husband, Newton, worked as missionaries in Kenya and Ghana, Africa. She is the mother of three adult children and four delightful grandsons. They live in Huntsville, Alabama, United States of America, and she enjoys cooking, travel, reading, music, prayer ministry, encouraging young people, and spending time with family. **Apr. 29, Apr. 30**

Jean Arthur lives in Silver Spring, Maryland, United States of America. She is an attorney by training but recently retired from thirty-three years of service with local government. She now works as a substitute teacher in the public school system. She is active in her local church and volunteers with the church and in the community. She spends her free time gardening, traveling, bicycling, running, baking, and reading. **May 6, Aug. 5**

Flore Aubry-Hamilton loves the Lord, and she wants her light to shine for Him. She and her husband, George, live in Huntsville, Alabama, United States of America. They enjoy working with disabilities ministries. **June 26, Sept. 17**

Yvita Antonette Villalona Bacchus, a graphic designer, works in the music department of her local church in the Dominican Republic. She is grateful for the opportunity to bless and be blessed through devotionals. **Oct. 11**

Noella (Jumpp) Baird, born in Jamaica, is a registered nurse living in Edmonton, Alberta, Canada, with her husband, Alan, and two young daughters. She loves reading, singing for the Lord, adult coloring, cooking, meeting new people, and entertaining with her gift of hospitality. **Aug. 7, Nov. 5**

Jennifer M. Baldwin writes from Australia, where she works in risk management at Sydney Adventist Hospital. She enjoys family time, church involvement, Scrabble, crossword puzzles, and researching her family history. She has been contributing to the devotional book series for twenty-three years. **Dec. 6**

Corletta Aretha Barbar, a native of the island of Jamaica, West Indies, is a member of the Fayetteville Seventh-day Adventist Church of North Carolina, United States of America, where she resides with her husband, Michael Barbar. She has a passion for writing. Her involvement within the church varies from head of music ministry to being a hospitality team member. In addition to her acquired personal accomplishments, she takes satisfaction in writing, traveling with her hubby, crocheting, walking, sightseeing, and singing. **July 18, Dec. 1**

Jenetta Barker lives in Bedfordshire, England, United Kingdom, with her husband and daughter. She attends Luton Central Seventh-day Adventist Church. She enjoys spending time with her family, reading, walking, writing, and traveling. **Oct. 22**

Gloria Barnes-Gregory is inspired by nature and her precious granddaughters. She seeks to motivate others to make positive life choices. Currently, she and her husband, Milton, serve at the Victory Church in New York, United States of America. **Nov. 23**

Dottie Barnett is retired and lives in a beautiful country setting in southeast Tennessee, United States of America. For more than fifty years, she has been involved in children's and adult Sabbath School leadership. She has written a devotional blog, called *Whispers of His Wisdom,* for the past several years. She loves working with plants and flowers, mowing her large lawn, photography, and camping with her family. **May 14, Oct. 29**

Gyl Moon Bateman lives in Niles, Michigan, United States of America, and has three grown sons. She is recently retired from working as a behavioral medicine nurse at a local hospital. She enjoys pursuing her hobbies, being active in the local community and her church, and helping her sons at their nearby store. **Apr. 22**

Dana M. Bean is an educator from a small, beautiful island in the middle of the Atlantic Ocean—Bermuda. She loves the art of writing, reading, and capturing moments through photography. **Feb. 8, May 2**

Sylvia Giles Bennett recently retired and enjoys the privilege of taking care of others and spending time with grandchildren. She is celebrating almost forty years of marriage with Richard. She enjoys reading and writing. A member of Windsor Seventh-day Adventist Church, Windsor, Virginia, United States of America, she frequently visits Calvary Seventh-day Adventist Church in Newport News, Virginia. **Dec. 29**

Eunice Passos Molina Berger, Brazilian by birth, enjoys living in Ontario, Canada, with her husband, Marcus, and her sister Eliana. She loves her family, friends, and nature. **Dec. 7**

Cynthia Best-Goring lives in Glenn Dale, Maryland, United States of America. She is a wife, the mother of two adult children, a first-time mother-in-law, and a Sabbath School teacher. She enjoys being recently retired from her position as a school principal. **Oct. 17, Dec. 8**

Paula Sanders Blackwell is an educator and writer in Houston, Texas, United States of America. She is the author of a devotional book titled *Lessons From My Hard Head*. She has also authored a ninety-day prayer journal. **Jan. 24**

Shirley John Blake is a retired registered nurse residing in Huntsville, Alabama, United States of America. She loves to travel, go on mission trips, encourage people who have lost loved ones, and visit the sick and shut-in to pray with, sing to, and minister to them. She has four married adult children and eight grandchildren. In 2012, her husband passed away after fifty happy years of marriage. She looks forward to seeing him when Jesus returns. She is thankful to God for allowing her family to immigrate to the United States of America. **June 10, June 11**

Julie Bocock-Bliss lives in Honolulu, Hawaii, United States of America. She works in a library, which makes sense because she loves reading so much! She also enjoys traveling and crafts and thanks God for giving her the time and ability to enjoy these interests. **July 31, Oct. 15**

Patricia Hook Rhyndress Bodi is a happy senior residing in Bonsall, California, United States of America, where she enjoys walking with Jesus every day in the land of eternal summer. **Aug. 29, Aug. 30**

Fulori Sususewa Bola, a retired schoolteacher, is serving as a volunteer with Hope Channel Fiji. She enjoys working with women, being involved in prayer ministry, and working with young people to share God's love through media and television. **Apr. 20, Apr. 21**

Rhonda Bolton is not a hairdresser, but she cuts hair for her family. She lives in Vancouver, Washington, United States of America, with her husband, Bob, and his 105-year-old father. **Oct. 6**

R. Bowen is a Canadian woman, teaching English and living for Christ in Northeast Asia. She enjoys traveling, meeting new people, and watching God work to draw others closer to Him. She is supported by her family living in Toronto, Canada, and her international family of prayer across the world. **July 25, Sept. 6**

Sonia Brock lives in Palmer, Alaska, United States of America, on a little more than nine acres in a small cabin she built. Her dog is her faithful companion. For almost thirty years, she has been privileged to drive a school bus in the rugged but beautiful forty-ninth state. She finds service to her church a joy and privilege, whether it's mowing the churchyard in the summertime or caring for the little ones in Sabbath School class and church service. **Feb. 7, June 30**

Mary Head Brooks, a retired psychiatric nurse, lives in Georgia, United States of America, with her husband, Marshall. She is a member of the Oakwood University Nursing Advisory Council (OUNAC) and enjoys gardening, traveling, and spending time with her grandson, Mason. **May 27**

Elaine Buchanan lives in Rawlings, Maryland, United States of America, with her pastor husband. She has worked side by side with him since they started ministry together in 2002. She is the prayer coordinator for the Mountain View Conference. They love to travel and share their testimonies of how God has changed their lives. They look forward to the soon return of Jesus. **Dec. 20**

Mary Lou Buoymaster lives twenty miles north of Chattanooga, Tennessee, United States of America, where she and her late husband made their home forty-five years ago. Her two sons are grown and married. Her grandson does a little of this and that, and her granddaughter is in the United States Navy, married to a sailor! She rescues, fosters, transports, and cross-posts for dogs in shelters needing homes. She enjoys crocheting and hopes to teach herself piano, which her late husband, whom she greatly misses, played so beautifully. **May 21, May 22**

Elinor Harvin Burks lives with her husband, Winfield, a lay pastor, in Birmingham, Alabama, United States of America. She is a journalism graduate of Wayne State University in Detroit, Michigan. Even before retiring from the City of Birmingham, she and Winfield conducted year-round "Science for Kids" programs at libraries, churches, street fairs, and schools. They love doing crafts. **Jan. 16**

Joy Marie Butler was a missionary to the Pacific Islands and Africa. The former director of Women's Ministries for the South Pacific Division, she is passionate about helping the hurting and abused women of the world. She is a speaker and writer. **Dec. 17**

Elizabeth Ida Cain is an educator by profession, working in human resources and administration, where she finds fulfillment in caring for employees in the workplace as Jesus would do. She is a professional florist who enjoys teaching the art and cheering others with beautiful floral arrangement. One of her spiritual blessings is writing devotionals for the women's devotional books. She lives in Jamaica, West Indies. **Oct. 13, Dec. 10**

Hyacinth V. Caleb was born and raised in Antigua. She attended Seventh-day Adventist universities in Trinidad and Jamaica. She presently resides in Saint Croix, United States Virgin Islands. She is a retired educator who loves reading, writing, and working outside in her garden. **Apr. 28, July 1**

Florence E. Callender is an educational and wellness consultant who lives in New York, United States of America. Her passion is helping mothers of children who learn differently work with their children at home so that they can be propelled from struggle to success in school and in life. In addition, she enjoys going on mission trips with her daughter. **Aug. 19**

Laura A. Canning has written for the women's devotional book for many years, and it is exciting to share her God-given inspirations. She enjoys the unique bond with women across the world who also share their stories. She lives near Windsor, England, United Kingdom, with her pets and has a constant flow of family visitors—both those who pop in for a little while and those who stay longer. Life is never dull. She thanks God for His goodness. **Dec. 16**

Ruth Cantrell, a retired teacher and counselor for Detroit's public schools, lives with her husband in Belleville, Michigan, United States of America. They have two married sons and grandchildren. She enjoys women's ministry, prayer ministry, reading stories, music, organizing programs, and encouraging other church members. **Oct. 27**

Janice M. Turner Carter, born in Atlanta, Georgia, United States of America, became a widow in 2009. She is a mother and grandmother. She enjoys ministry and served as director of the state of Georgia women's ministries for the South Atlantic Conference (SAC) and as the director of the Morning Glory Prayer Ministry for women (SAC). Presently, she travels as a Bible instructor with evangelist Carlton Byrd's team. **Mar. 10**

Camilla E. Cassell, a retired postal employee, attends Berea Temple Seventh-day Adventist Church in Baltimore, Maryland, United States of America. She has two children and treasures her grandson, Amari. She has compassion for families and feels they should spend quality time with each other in love and unity. Unity in the family is union with Christ, which is so important. She enjoys reading God's Word, doing crafts, designing greeting cards, encouraging others in the Lord (especially young people), and music. **Nov. 9**

Diana Celaya is a student at Union College in Lincoln, Nebraska, United States of America, majoring in computer science with an emphasis in web development. She also has minors in communication and information systems. Her home is in Houston, Texas. **July 17**

Suhana Chikatla, PhD, born in India, has two master's degrees in addition to her doctorate. She volunteers in children's, youth, and social leadership positions at her Hanceville, Alabama, church in the United States of America. She is an executive council member for the Gulf States Conference Women's Ministries Department. She and her husband, Royce Sutton, have a beautiful four-year-old daughter, Rehana. **Mar. 26, Sept. 3**

Lulu Chirande, a pediatrician and lecturer at a medical university, lives in Dar es Salaam, Tanzania. She and her husband are blessed to have two sons and two daughters. She worships at Makongo Juu Seventh-day Adventist Church, and she loves gardening. **Nov. 28**

Rosemarie Clardy enjoys nature and is truly blessed to live in the country with her husband and household of pets. In her church, she is currently involved in leading a small group and coordinating a Bible school for her local church. **Mar. 11, Sept. 12**

Jacqueline Hope HoShing-Clarke has been a Seventh-day Adventist educator for more than forty years. She has a PhD in education administration, is the chairperson for the Department of Teacher Education at Northern Caribbean University (NCU) in Jamaica, and serves as an ordained elder at the NCU Church. She is the satisfied mother of two adult children: Deidre Clarke-Jumpp, who is an operating theater nurse, and Pastor Deneil Clarke, who ministers in Lincoln, Nebraska. Her grandchildren are Demetrio, Alayna, and Jude. **Sept. 15**

Valerie Knowles Combie is a professor at the University of the Virgin Islands. She works in Sabbath School classes, plays the piano, and enjoys reading, writing, and gardening. **May 31, Aug. 31**

Britni Conrad is from Wisconsin, United States of America. She currently lives in

Nebraska while attending Union College as a graphic design major with an emphasis in communication. **July 2**

Raquel Queiroz da Costa Arrais is a minister's wife who developed her ministry as an educator for twenty years. Currently, she works as the associate director of the General Conference Women's Ministries Department. She has two adult sons, two daughters-in-law, and four adored grandchildren. Her greatest pleasures are being with people, singing, playing the piano, and traveling. **Feb. 16, May 17, Nov. 29**

Patricia Cove, married for more than sixty years to George, has five children and many grandchildren. She is active in her church, does weekly Bible studies with shut-ins, and is a volunteer chaplain at the Brockville, Ontario, Canada, hospital. She continues writing and publishing. It is all to the glory of God. **Apr. 24, Sept. 24**

Anne Crosby lives in Page, Arizona, United States of America, where her family ministers to the Navajo people. She is a college student and works as a childcare provider and piano teacher in her community. In her spare time, she enjoys writing and participating in children's ministries at her local church. **Aug. 14**

Lee Lee Dart is a pastor at the Adventure Seventh-day Adventist Church in Windsor, Colorado, United States of America. This wife and mother of two is passionate about being a conduit of God's love to others. **May 3, Oct. 10**

Jean Dozier Davey and her husband, Steven, live in the beautiful mountains of North Carolina, United States of America. A retired computer programmer, she enjoys family, cooking, walking in the Pisgah Forest, reading, sewing, photography, and encouraging others. **Feb. 12, Sept. 23**

Bernadine Delafield writes from Florida, United States of America, where she is involved with women's ministries at her church, is an active member of the Sweetwater Oaks Garden Club, and values time spent with family. She loves to travel the world, so she takes every opportunity to do so. **June 20, Oct. 5**

Karen Dobbin writes from Winnipeg, Canada. She is a physiotherapist with more than thirty years of experience, and as a breast cancer survivor, she passionately provides rehabilitation for those diagnosed with cancer. She is married to Bret, and they have an adult daughter, Brittany. Karen has been involved in various capacities at her local church her entire adult life. **Oct. 19**

Edna Bacate Domingo, PhD, MSN, RN, lives with her husband in Grand Terrace, California, United States of America. A retired nursing professor, she is still active running her nursing school. She serves as one of the Sabbath School superintendents at the Loma Linda University Church in Loma Linda. She has three grown-up children and two grandchildren. She loves nature and being with her grandchildren. **Oct. 8, Dec. 2**

Louise Driver is the wife of a retired pastor who still preaches nearly every Sabbath in the state of Idaho, United States of America. Her sister and her three sons and their families live nearby. She enjoys gardening, reading, and traveling. **May 8, Sept. 11**

Pauline A. Dwyer-Kerr holds two doctorate degrees. She is an advanced practice nurse and a professor of nursing. She has received numerous awards. She is an ordained elder in her church. She resides in Florida, United States of America, loves her children and grandchildren, and loves the outdoors. **Sept. 19**

Doreen Evans-Yorke is a Jamaican-Canadian mother of three young adults. She is a certified child life specialist in Montreal, Canada, where she is a member of the LaSalle New Life Seventh-day Adventist Church. **June 1, Sept. 8**

Mona Fellers recently moved to Wyoming, United States of America, where she, her husband, and a couple of close friends are renovating an old schoolhouse into a duplex where they live. They have two daughters, two grandsons, two dogs, and two cats. She serves the Lord in women's ministries and teaching at her local church. **Mar. 31, June 8**

Barbara Fisher lives in the community of Grandview, near Spring City, Tennessee, United States of America. She has two daughters, one son, three granddaughters, and one great-granddaughter. She loves reading books and spending time with friends and family. **July 27**

Sharon Follett writes from the beautiful Sequatchie Valley in Dunlap, Tennessee, United States of America, where she and her husband, Ron, pastored three churches before retirement. She enjoys taking walks in the woods with Ron and their pets as well as singing, leading church choirs, being involved in community events, giving children's piano lessons, and spending time with her granddaughter, Savannah. **Feb. 18, May 4**

Marea I. Ford and her husband, Lee, live in the rolling hills of Tennessee, United States of America. They enjoy spending time with their sons and families, which includes a blessing of six grandchildren. Bible study, quilting, and crocheting are her therapy. **Oct. 12**

Shirley Sain Fordham is a retired educator, wife, mother of three married children, and grandmother of eight. She enjoys family and friends, technology, crocheting, and scrapbooking. She also loves befriending transfer members at her home church in Atlanta, Georgia, United States of America. She has learned to occupy well—living, loving, laughing, and learning until Jesus comes again. **Nov. 30**

Sylvia A. Franklin lives with her husband, Joe, in Rocklin, California, United States of America, and currently works as a human resources analyst for the Sacramento Public Library. She is the administrative assistant to the Women's Ministries director of the Pacific Union Conference of Seventh-day Adventists. She enjoys planning community events and playing games. She was once a contestant on the *Wheel of Fortune* television game show. **Mar. 27, Oct. 21**

Edith C. Fraser is a semiretired college professor. She is a counselor and a family life presenter. She and her husband, Trevor, have been married for more than fifty years. They love to travel and are committed to working with couples and families. **Sept. 4**

Jeannine Fuller and her husband, Glenn, live in Orange Beach, Alabama, United States of America, when not traveling. She is mother to four (including an unofficially adopted daughter from Budapest, Hungary) and grandmother to twelve. She was born to missionary parents in China, graduated from Emmanuel Missionary College (now

Andrews University), and is retired from the teaching profession and Better Than Milk. She has a heart for missions. **Sept. 18**

Claudette Garbutt-Harding has just retired after forty-three years as a Seventh-day Adventist college educator. She has shared forty of those years in pastoral ministry with her husband, Keith. They reside in Orlando, Florida, United States of America. **Feb. 19, May 10**

Lindsey Gendke is a writer, wife, teacher, and mom whose passion is sharing God's redemptive work in messy lives. The author (or coauthor) of three books, she is currently pursuing a PhD in English with an emphasis in composition pedagogy. You can connect with her at LindseyGendke.com. **Jan. 6**

Marybeth Gessele lives in Gaston, Oregon, United States of America, with her husband, Glen. She is a retired hospice caregiver. Donating various sewing projects to charitable organizations is her favorite hobby. **Apr. 25, Aug. 23**

Carol Wiggins Gigante is a former day care provider and teacher at heart. She is an avid reader, photographer, and flower and bird lover and works as a freelance proofreader. She resides in Tennessee, United States of America, with her husband, Joe; their dog, Buddy; and cat, Suzannah. They have two grown sons, Jeff and James. Even so come, Lord Jesus! **Jan. 27**

Kaysian C. Gordon is a mother, author, speaker, and Bible teacher in New York, United States of America. She has published a devotional, *Walking by Faith, and Not by Sight: Learning to Be Still in the Midst of Life's Chaos*. She is also a guest blogger for Devotable, a devotional app and website, and has been included in their published devotionals. She also guest blogs for Recraft Devotional Group, which is dedicated to recrafting lives. She is involved in her church and speaks to various women's groups. **Jan. 7, Apr. 1**

Alexis A. Goring is an author of inspirational books, the founder of the *God Is Love* blog, a devotional writer, a trained journalist, an editor, and a photographer. She loves God, family, friends, church, music, movies, and good food. She enjoys sharing the gospel of Jesus Christ with everyone she meets. **Mar. 28, June 7**

Cecelia Grant is a Seventh-day Adventist medical doctor retired from government service and lives in Kingston, Jamaica. Her hobbies are traveling, gardening, and listening to good music. She has a passion for young people, to whom she is always giving advice. **June 22**

Jasmine E. Grant is a retired social worker who served as a senior counselor for eighteen years among pregnant addicts and addicted mothers in Jamaica, New York, United States of America. She attends the Springfield Gardens Seventh-day Adventist Church and is actively involved with hospitality and women's and family life ministries. An avid reader, she enjoys reading autobiographical, self-help, and natural-cure books. **Aug. 9, Nov. 6**

Mary Jane Graves, a widow, mother, grandmother, and great-grandmother, has retired near Asheville, North Carolina, United States of America, after working as a secretary, librarian, academy registrar, and camp cook! She enjoys reading, writing, table games, gardening, and time with family and friends. She is a longtime contributor to the devotional books. **Oct. 18, Dec. 12**

Glenda-mae Greene writes from her wheelchair at the Sunnyside Adventist Care Centre in Saskatchewan, Canada. Crafting devotionals is her way of sharing the faith she lives by. **Mar. 3, June 6**

Pauline A. Griffith is a retired speech pathologist living in Huntsville, Alabama, United States of America, with her husband of forty-seven years, Dr. Wilfred Griffith. They are the parents of three adult sons. **June 4**

Galina Gritsuk writes from Grants Pass, Oregon, United States of America. From the 1980s through the 1990s, Galina was a translator for speakers and evangelists visiting the Soviet Union from the General Conference of Seventh-day Adventists. She has recently retired from substitute teaching and lives in Oregon with Vitaly, her husband of forty-plus years. They have two adult sons and one daughter. Galina longs for Jesus' return. **Sept. 2**

Darlene Joy Grunke, a retired teacher, quietly passed away in July 2020, not long after submitting her last devotional during the editing process of this book. She served on four scholarship committees plus the boards of NAMI (National Alliance on Mental Illness) and Daughters of Norway. She avidly supported the global church outreach initiative and enditnow®: Adventists Say No to Violence. **Oct. 4**

Jennifer Haagenson is a mom of two precious kids, a pastor's wife, a part-time associate pastor, and a full-time graduate student in a mental health counselor program in Idaho, United States of America. She is also human and has been on a journey of recovery from a season of deep depression. **July 16**

Diantha Hall-Smith is a daughter of God. She is wife to a devoted Christian husband who serves in the United States Air Force and is the mother of two beautiful children. She was born in New York City but now lives in California. She has had the honor and privilege to have lived and visited interesting places, domestically and globally. She enjoys writing, traveling, and spending time with her family. **Sept. 28, Dec. 3**

Diana Halverson lives with her husband in East Tennessee, United States of America, where she is also a mother of four and grandmother of nine. She is a licensed building contractor who retired from the McKee Baking Company as a mechanic. She is currently a state prison chaplain and has been a missionary for more than twenty years in the jungles of Nicaragua. At her home church in Dayton, Tennessee, she directs women's ministries and Vacation Bible School. **Jan. 14, Jan. 15**

Ashley Halvorson, at the time of this writing, was a senior at Campion Academy in Loveland, Colorado, United States of America. She is known for always smiling and loves to spend time with Jesus through music involvement and leading small groups with her friends. She also loves hand lettering and spending time outdoors. **Dec. 15**

Marsha Hammond-Brummel is a teacher living in Claremont, New Hampshire, United States of America. She wrote about her experience during a snow day from school. From May through October, she can often be found at the historic Washington, New Hampshire, Seventh-day Adventist Church and Sabbath Trail where she helps her husband, Ken, welcome guests to the site. **Mar. 1, June 3**

Myrna L. Hanna is the assistant vice president for administrative affairs and alumni and donor relations at Loma Linda University Health. Her favorite things include travel, spending time with family, and encouraging others to make the most of the talents God has given them. **Jan. 23, Dec. 25**

Deborah M. Harris, PhD, is a retired educational consultant. A few years ago, she founded Praying for Our Children, a ministry she is in the process of resurrecting now that she is retired. This prayer ministry is needed now more than ever. Deborah is also known for her inspirational messages when she speaks at conferences and other events. She is also the mother of two and grandmother of four. She lives in the United States of America. **June 29**

Peggy Curtice Harris, born and raised in the states of California and Washington, has lived in Maryland, United States of America, since 1996. She is widowed, retired, a great-grandma, and an author of fourteen books, and she is still active in Destination Sabbath School, prayer ministry, abuse prevention, and creative hospitality in the Beltsville Seventh-day Adventist Church. **Jan. 31, May 19**

Marian M. Hart-Gay lives in Florida, United States of America, with her husband, David. She is a mother, grandmother, and great-grandmother. Knitting and volunteer mission trips are two activities she enjoys. **Jan. 8**

Judith Warren Hawkins has experienced many roles in a courtroom, including being a litigant, a lawyer, and a judge. An author of two books and numerous articles, she is also the founder of Gaza Road Ministries, an umbrella for her motivational speaking, Bible-based preaching, legal or spiritual presentations, and workshop facilitating. She lives in Florida, United States of America. **June 21, Sept. 20**

Helen Heavirland, an author, speaker, and encourager, lives in Oregon, United States of America. Her encouraging story of finding joy in trial, of growing from fear to faith, is told in the book *My God Is Bigger*. **Mar. 18, June 18**

Muriel Heppel has been a teacher and principal for more than thirty years in Canada and the Philippines. She enjoys nature and has a telephone ministry of encouraging others. **Apr. 2, July 6**

Denise Dick Herr, an emeritus professor of English at Burman University in Alberta, Canada, loved teaching but relishes retirement: she has more time to see family, to travel, and to count animals and identify birds. **Mar. 23, Aug. 13**

Renauta Hinds of Guyana is a student at the University of the Southern Caribbean in Trinidad and Tobago. She enjoys teaching, writing, drama, art, music, and being an inspiration to anyone with whom she interacts. **Nov. 13, Nov. 14**

Vashti Hinds-Vanier, born in Guyana, recently celebrated her fiftieth anniversary of entering the nursing profession. She is widely traveled throughout Europe, Africa, and the Caribbean. Her hobbies include cake decorating and gardening. She enjoys spending time with her grandson, Jaden, and resides in Brooklyn, New York, United States of America. **Feb. 13**

Patricia Hines is originally from the Caribbean island of Jamaica. She is now retired and lives in Sebring, Florida, United States of America. She likes to write, enjoys music, and spends much of her day gardening. **Feb. 9, May 9**

Roxy Hoehn is retired in Topeka, Kansas, United States of America, after many happy years involved in women's ministries. She's also a happy mom to three and nana to eleven. **Feb. 20, May 25**

Tamyra Horst writes from Paradise, Pennsylvania, United States of America, where she lives with Tim, her husband of more than thirty years. An author, speaker, and communication director for the Pennsylvania Conference of Seventh-day Adventists, she loves being a mom to her two young-adult sons, being a friend to an amazing group of women, enjoying the quiet with a great book and a cup of chai, and sharing adventures with those she loves. **Feb. 1, Sept. 9**

Charmaine Houston is a health care professional who lives in Pennsylvania, United States of America, with her two children. She enjoys reading and running—recently completing a half-marathon. **Dec. 30**

Claudine Houston currently resides in Georgia, United States of America, and enjoys teaching an adult Sabbath School class at her church. She also enjoys Bible study, reading, and encouraging others. **May 12, Sept. 25**

Barbara Huff is the wife of a retired pastor and church administrator. They have one remaining child and three grandchildren. She is a freelance writer who enjoys finding spiritual lessons from nature. She and her husband live in southwest Florida, United States of America, where wildlife and plant life is abundant. **Nov. 25**

Debora Ramona Hughes writes from the beautiful Caribbean island of Antigua. She is a home economics teacher by profession, working at an all-boys secondary school. In her spare time, she enjoys listening to gospel music, writing, and baking. She is also the mother of an adult daughter. **Dec. 26**

Joy Bakaba Igwe is the associate director of Women's Ministries of the Port Harcourt Conference in the Eastern Nigeria Union. She is an accountant and educator by profession. She is married to Dr. Martin Igwe, and their marriage has been blessed with four children. Her hobbies are singing, making disciples for Christ, and nurturing young women. **Nov. 20**

Shirley C. Iheanacho lives in Huntsville, Alabama, with Morris, her husband of more than fifty-one years. She serves as a church elder, chaplain for senior-adult ministries, and ministry leader on the Morning Manna Prayer Line. She enjoys speaking, writing, editing articles, and encouraging women to write. She is the author of the book *God's Incredible Plans for Me: A Memoir of an Amazing Journey*, available from Amazon.com and in bookstores. She is the mother of Ngozi Bolton, Chioma, and Akunna and grandmother of Nikolas and Timothy. **Jan. 9, July 3**

Avis Floyd Jackson lives in Pleasantville, New Jersey, United States of America, and is a mother of five. She does business out of her home and is a party planner. She is active in her local church and is an Adventist by calling. **Aug. 17**

Rachel Privette Jennings attended Pine Forge Academy and graduated from Kettering College of Medical Arts as a registered diagnostic medical and cardiac sonographer. She is a member of Central Seventh-day Adventist Church in Columbus, Ohio, United States of America. She is passionate about theatrical arts. She has acted, directed, and written plays and devotional messages. **Feb. 2**

Greta Michelle Joachim-Fox-Dyett is a potter, writer, blogger, and educator from Trinidad and Tobago. She is married to her love, Arnold, and the proud mama of an adult daughter. **Jan. 30, Apr. 6**

Elaine J. Johnson enjoys giving testimonies about the goodness of God. She has been blessed to be married for fifty-three years to her best friend. She enjoys reading and writing and has been published in several of these devotionals. She is retired in Alabama, United States of America, after working for thirty-five years with children. **Feb. 6, June 2**

Jeannette Busby Johnson, retired after thirty-some years at the Review and Herald Publishing Association, now lives happily in Miles City, Montana [the "land of her birth"], United States of America, with her daughter's family (which includes a pair of lively twin boys). **May 23, Aug. 1**

Deidre A. Jones and her husband are very active in their small country church in Virginia, United States of America. She has taken on various roles, including communications coordinator, treasurer, and children's ministries coordinator, and since 2017, she has written a blog on her church website. Her hobbies include cooking, sewing, and making others smile. She is a 2009 graduate of Mary Baldwin College. **Apr. 27, July 7**

Gerene I. Joseph is married to Pastor Sylvester Joseph. They have two adult children. She served as the director of Women and Children's Ministries of the North Caribbean Conference for six years. Presently, she is the director of Education in the same conference. She enjoys writing poems and playing the piano in her spare time. She is also a certified lay preacher and has conducted three evangelistic campaigns. **Mar. 12, Sept. 30**

Nadine A. Joseph-Collins, PhD, is a women's leadership expert and spiritual wellness coach and has dedicated herself to full-time ministry. She currently resides in Atlanta, Georgia, United States of America, and travels globally, empowering the prayer lives of others. She appeared on 3ABN Dare-to-Dream Network's *Urban Report* episode titled "How to Pray." This led to a new program: *The Missing Peace.* She recently launched the very first online prayer training program: Creating a WOW Life Through the Power of Prayer. **Feb. 10, Apr. 26**

Delanie Kamarad has enjoyed writing thought-provoking messages for as long as she can remember. She believes personal testimony leads to the most beautiful conversion of a heart. Her dream is to make a difference in the world by giving strength to the weak and encouraging others to fight the good fight in faith. Her home is currently in Colorado, United States of America, while she attends college in Lincoln, Nebraska. **Nov. 16**

Carolyn K. Karlstrom lives and plays in the state of Washington, United States of America. She loves reading, writing, friends, family, husband Rick, and sweet kitty

Dusty. She is a Bible worker, and her blog can be found at carolynkarlstrom.com. **Feb. 15, May 7**

Grace A. Keene was born on December 31, 1935. For twenty years, she lived in New Rochelle, New York, before moving to Florida, United States of America. There she raised her family (and some other people too), whom she still points to the lovely Lord Jesus and His joy and comfort. She resides in a Tennessee retirement center and remains intensely interested in doing what Jesus asks all of us to do: "Go and tell." **Mar. 6, July 9**

Sonia Kennedy-Brown lives in Ontario, Canada, and is a retired nurse. She loves to read, write, and witness to others. Since the publication of her autobiography, *Silent Tears: Growing Up Albino*, she has become a motivational speaker on behalf of albinos and others with other disabilities. To support the book project, contact her at Soniab47@msn.com. **Apr. 16, June 19**

Maria Kercher is a public relations major at Union College in Lincoln, Nebraska. She enjoys reading both fiction and nonfiction, writing, and creating illustrations. She self-published *Harold and Louise: Troll Trouble* in high school. Her articles "Terrified of You" and "Four Eyes" have been accepted for publishing by *Outlook* and *Guide*. **July 5**

Iris L. Kitching enjoys creative endeavors, spoken-word poetry performances, and writing for children. She has worked at the General Conference of Seventh-day Adventists in Maryland, United States of America, for more than twenty years, first in Women's Ministries, and then in Presidential. She and her husband, Will, appreciate the joys of spending time with family and friends. **Feb. 21**

Kênia Kopitar is Brazilian but now lives in Florida, United States of America. She enjoys gardening, writing, reading, teaching music and piano, and taking care of animals. Her greatest desire is to meet God and her loved ones at Jesus' second coming. **Mar. 16**

Betty Kossick continues as a freelance writer of varied genres and as a journalist, author, and poet for both religious and secular publications. "I'm a blessed woman to serve my Lord and Friend, Jesus." She developed and edits *Front Porch Visits*, the newsletter for Florida Living Retirement Community. Much of her work appears on Google. Contact her at bkwrites4u@hotmail.com. **Feb. 27, Feb. 28**

Simea Kübler is a teacher at the Seventh-day Adventist school in Zurich, Switzerland. She teaches grades 1–3, and her favorite subject is Bible. She loves to learn and is looking forward to learning throughout eternity. **Oct. 23**

Mabel Kwei, a retired university and college lecturer, did missionary work in Africa for many years with her pastor husband and their three children. Now living in New Jersey, United States of America, she reads a lot and loves to paint, write, and spend time with little children. **Feb. 23**

Deidre Lanferman is a wife and mother of one child. She currently serves as an assistant Sabbath School superintendent at her local church, and she's a science teacher by profession. She enjoys reading, listening to music, and spending quality time with loved ones. **Nov. 17**

Maite Lavado lives in Madrid, Spain, with her American husband and their daughter. In addition to working full time, she is active with women's ministries in Spain, presents workshops around the country, and serves in her local congregation. For five years, she has been the director of her church's Pathfinder Club and has almost finished the requirements for Master Guide. She also enjoys studying psychology. **Mar. 2, June 25**

Wilma Kirk Lee, a licensed clinical social worker, currently directs the Center for Family Wholeness (CFW), located in Houston, Texas, United States of America. She serves with her pastor husband of five decades, W. S. Lee, as codirector of Family Ministries of the Southwest Region Conference of Seventh-day Adventists. She has a bachelor's degree in social work and a master's degree in social work. **Mar. 19, Mar. 20**

Loida Gulaja Lehmann spent ten years selling religious books in the Philippines before going to Germany and getting married. She and her husband are active church members and are both involved in radio, prison, and laypeople's ministries. Her hobbies are traveling, nature walks, writing, and photography. **Mar. 22**

Sally J. Linke has written stories for others since she was six years old: first, for her nephews and nieces, and later, writing for publications, medical grants, and manuals for her work environment. Her husband, John, is a retired helicopter pilot who has built his own Zenith airplane, which they fly to travel across the country to visit family from Ohio to Arizona. At the time of this writing, they reside in Norfolk, Nebraska, United States of America. **Dec. 19**

Sharon Long was born in Trinidad but lived most of her life in Canada. In 2015, she retired from the Government of Alberta after thirty-four years in child welfare. She does contract work for the Alberta College of Social Workers and is active at the West Edmonton Seventh-day Adventist Church. She is the mother of four, grandmother of six, and great-grandmother of two. She is passionate about people and is happiest when serving others. Every day above ground is a good day and a new opportunity. **Jan. 12, Aug. 10**

Rhodi Alers de López writes from Massachusetts, United States of America. Her ministry, ExpresSion Publishing Ministries, aims to inspire others to a closer relationship with Jesus. She's an author, singer, songwriter, and speaker, and she leads a prayer ministry. **Mar. 4**

Marcella Lynch is a home economics teacher, the author of *Cooking by the Book* (cookbook), and the host of a cooking show on 3ABN that ran for fifteen years. A member of the General Conference of Seventh-day Adventists Nutrition Council for twenty-five years, she presents Vegetarian Cooking Instructor courses across the country and hundreds of plant-based cooking classes. Retired now, she lives with her husband in Oregon, United States of America. They enjoy their nearby grandchildren. Marcella continues to be active teaching NEWSTART and cooking classes and supporting community health and wellness projects. **Oct. 2**

Nancy A. Mack is a blond American born in India to a missionary family. She attended college in the United States. She is married to Bill (also a missionary kid) and has raised their family in Maryland, United States of America. When they relocated to India to direct Adventist Child India, a donor-funded program for educating needy children, she became the third generation of Mattison missionaries to serve in India for more than half a century. Sponsoring a child is effortless at adventistchildindia.org. **Oct. 3**

Beverley Martin currently lives in California, United States of America, with her husband of thirty-five years. Together they have four adult children and one grandson. She attends the Lancaster Seventh-day Adventist Church and is currently serving as the Women's Ministries director for the Southern California Conference. She is a school principal and also a college professor. She loves the outdoors, cooking, and entertaining. Education is her passion, and she believes every child can learn if we decipher how they learn and teach to their uniqueness. **Oct. 9**

Gail Masondo is a wife, mother of two adult children (Shellie and Jonathan), women's and children's advocate, songwriter, chaplain, Life in Recovery coach, and international speaker. She authored *Now This Feels Like Home.* A New York native, she now resides in Johannesburg, South Africa, with her musician husband, Victor Sibusio Masondo. **May 28, May 29**

Deborah Matshaya writes from South Africa, where she is a teacher. She enjoys gospel music and has contributed many times to this devotional book series. **Feb. 3, May 5**

Mary H. Maxson, daughter of the King, wife, mother, and grandmother, is a retired associate pastor (Paradise, California). For forty-seven years, she ministered with her pastor husband, Ben, as an administrative church assistant, in women's ministries (Argentina and Uruguay), and as an editorial and administrative assistant with *Adventist Review* and Adventist World Radio. Mary served for more than seven years as the director of Women's Ministries for the North American Division of Seventh-day Adventists. She and Ben reside in Calhoun, Georgia, United States of America. **Jan. 1, Apr. 3**

Lorena Finis Mayer is a translator and writer who works as an international civil servant for a specialized agency of the United Nations. She lives in Bern, Switzerland, with her husband, Reto, and her cat, Angie. She writes monthly columns for a Christian magazine and enjoys making music in church. She added the line "cancer survivor" to her CV (curriculum vitae) and shares her story on the ByeBye Gecko channel on YouTube. **Oct. 25, Dec. 22**

Kathleen (Cooper) McEwan is the daughter of missionary parents, Charles and Virginia Cooper. When Kathleen was ten, the family moved to Canada. She was educated in Canada and the United States of America. Now Kathleen lives in the country near Ontario, Canada, with her husband, Roger, and two black cats—Ebony and Cinza. **Dec. 5**

Raschelle Mclean-Jones is an elementary teacher in Haines City, Florida, United States of America. She has two sons, Aaron and Josiah, who love basketball. She is married to a devoted, loving man, John Jones. She loves to cook, sing in the choir, and write. **Sept. 7**

Vicki Mellish was blessed to have been the daughter of a praying father. She lives in Caledon, Ontario, Canada, with her husband, nephew, and their dog, Samson. As a recently retired occupational therapist, she is now using her skills to make life easier and more fulfilling for her family. She enjoys connecting with family and friends, researching God's Word, and writing. **Sept. 5**

Annette Walwyn Michael writes from Saint Croix in the United States Virgin Islands. In her retirement, she enjoys spending time with her husband, a retired pastor, her adult children and grandchildren, and her Central Church family. **Jan. 19, Apr. 11**

Megan Michalenko, at the time of this writing, was a senior in high school, getting ready to graduate. She plans to pursue an elementary education major in college. She lives with her parents and sister in Colorado, United States of America. She has a passion for writing and loves playing the violin for church and her community. She has also enjoyed writing for her school newsletter and journalism class. **June 13**

Shushanna Mignott resides in Maryland, United States of America, and enjoys traveling, the beach, and a good cup of tea. She is the author of *Refocus and Thrive: A Devotional to Discover Your True Identity and Courageously Walk in Your Purpose.* **Nov. 11**

Madeleine E. Miyashiro was born in Minnesota and lives in Nebraska, United States of America. She is a freshman in high school with an untiring love for writing and music. Her father, the music director at Union College, has inspired her to be an oboist. Her mother has also been a major support. She is proud to be a member of the College View Church and a student at College View Academy. **May 13, Aug. 2**

Regina Nakanjako Mngumi resides in Tanzania with her husband and two sons. She works for a comprehensive community-based rehabilitation center as a training manager for health professionals. In her church, she is active as a Sabbath School superintendent. She enjoys growing tropical gardens and hiking. She especially likes reading devotionals, Spirit of Prophecy books, and Bible stories. **Dec. 27**

D. Reneé Mobley, PhD, is trained in clinical pastoral education and has owned a Christian counseling practice for more than ten years in Alabama, United States of America. A member of the National Christian Counselors Association, she trains and facilitates numerous workshops, seminars, and conferences. She is the mother of two adult women, mother-in-law to the greatest son-in-law in the world, and grandmother to three grand-dogs. **Aug. 28**

Susen Mattison Molé, born in India to missionary parents who worked in India for many years, has moved around the world with her husband and lived in many fun places: Italy; Spain; Okinawa, Japan; and Bahrain. They currently live in Nepal and work at the Seventh-day Adventist hospital, where they have been serving for the last six years. They have two wonderful adult daughters. She enjoys painting, hiking, and playing the cello. Serving God is a joy and a challenge. **Oct. 24**

Marcia Mollenkopf, a retired teacher, lives in Klamath Falls, Oregon, United States of America. She enjoys church involvement and has served in both adult and children's divisions. She loves to share God's Word. **Aug. 4**

Maureen H. Moncrieffe, EdD, MA, BSc, is Jamaican by birth but resides in the sunshine state of Florida, United States of America, with her husband, who recently retired from pastoral ministry. She is a retired reading specialist and kindergarten teacher whose passion is building strong reading skills in little ones. She also enjoys tending her flower and vegetable gardens. She and her husband of fifty years are blessed with five adult children and seven grandchildren. **Dec. 31**

Jane Wiggins Moore lives in Coalfield, Tennessee, United States of America, where she is the Community Services leader for her church and is active in their food ministry program, Hope for the Hungry. A retired registered nurse, she has two grown sons and delights in her granddaughter, Micah, and grandson, Andrew. She still mourns her beloved husband, John, who went to sleep in Jesus in 2001. **Jan. 2, May 1**

Lourdes E. Morales-Gudmundsson, PhD, recently retired as a university professor of Spanish language and literature and has been published widely in Seventh-day Adventist publications. Though living with her husband in California, United States of America, she has presented her seminar "I Forgive You, But . . . ," on three continents and in most of the United States. She can be reached at lmorales@lasierra.edu. **Mar. 24, June 24**

Lily Morales-Narváez lives in Texas, United States of America, and works for the Texas Adventist Book Center. She holds a bachelor's degree in psychology and has written articles for these women's devotional books and the *Adventist Review*. Active in her church, she is involved with personal ministries, "Build Your Ark," and preaching. She likes to sing, write, read, and decorate. Her greatest loves are her husband and family. **Feb. 26**

Lila Farrell Morgan, a widow, lives in a small town in the foothills of western North Carolina, United States of America. She loves her four adult children, five grandchildren, and three great-grandchildren. Reading, contemplating the Creator's handiwork in nature, researching different topics on the internet, baking, and table games are favorite pastimes. She looks for the positive in life and enjoys a good laugh. **Nov. 8**

Valerie Hamel Morikone lives in West Virginia, United States of America, and works at the Mountain View Conference office. She is the Communication director and conference clerk. A pianist and Sabbath School leader for the younger set, she enjoys reading, cooking, and doing activities with her academy sweetheart and husband, Daniel. They've been married for more than forty-six years. **Sept. 10**

Willietta Ann Morrow resides in Madison, Alabama, United States of America, with her husband, Dr. Lester Morrow, to whom she has been married for forty-three years. Together they have one daughter. Ann, as she is usually called, is a retired educator and writer. She is also a speaker on the South Central Conference of Seventh-day Adventist Women's Ministries Department's Morning Manna Prayer Line. **July 19**

Bonnie Moyers lives with her husband, Carl, and Milo, a ragdoll kitty, in Staunton, Virginia, United States of America. This freelance writer is a mother of two, a grandmother of three, and a musician for several area churches. **Nov. 24**

Esther Synthia Murali works as an honorary director for Women's Ministries in South Karnataka Section, Mysore, India. She is a physiotherapist by profession, but her passion is ministering with her pastor husband. She has a son, Ted, and enjoys playing guitar, painting, gardening, and photography. **Mar. 17, June 12**

Jannett Maurine Myrie, MSN, RN, is a medical missionary who finds joy and fulfillment in sharing the love of Jesus with everyone! She is the proud mother of Delroy Anthony Jr. She enjoys traveling, especially cruises; entertaining; reading; and just being still. She is ever so thankful to Jesus for loving her unconditionally and blessing her to trust the plans He has for her. **Nov. 22**

Ana Nadasan is Women's Ministries director in the South Transylvania Conference in the Romanian Union. She is married and active in the Teleac Seventh-day Adventist Church. She likes very much to pray, and her life is a life of prayer. She loves helping people in need and enjoys singing, reading, and cooking. **July 22**

Cecilia Nanni earned a degree in psychology, a master's degree in mediation and conflict resolution, and a master's degree in education, management mode. Currently, she works as volunteer coordinator in Central Asia. **Jan. 22, May 11**

Bienvisa Ladion Nebres, from the Philippines, teaches at Asia-Pacific International University in Thailand. She treasures the experience of having been able to work in Africa for two decades. A mother of three and grandmother of two, she likes poetry, church activities, traveling, and writing. **Aug. 20, Nov. 3**

Samantha Nelson is a pastor's wife who loves serving alongside her husband, Steve. She is also the CEO of The Hope of Survivors, a nonprofit organization dedicated to assisting victims of clergy sexual abuse and providing educational seminars to clergy of all faiths. She and Steve live in Wyoming, United States of America, and love traveling, hiking in the mountains, and enjoying the beauty of God's creation. **Mar. 29, Mar. 30**

Donna J. Norman of Silver Spring, Maryland, United States of America, has been a speech and language pathologist for the past sixteen years and works in an academic setting. She has served four years as the women's ministries leader and two years as the health ministries leader at Wheaton Seventh-day Adventist Church. Presently, she serves as a deaconess and a member of the family life ministry at Burnt Mills Seventh-day Adventist Church. Her favorite hobby is reading. **May 26**

Margaret Obiocha has been married to her husband, Fyneboy, for fifty years. They are now retired. She served her local church as Sabbath School teacher, deaconess, and treasurer. She and her husband are involved in church projects to help poor village churches in eastern Nigeria. She enjoys supervising her grandchildren with their schoolwork. **Feb. 17**

Elizabeth Versteegh Odiyar of Kelowna, British Columbia, Canada, has served God through church, Pathfinders, and mission trips. She has retired from managing the family chimney sweep business for thirty-three years. She is married to Hector. They have twin sons and a daughter—all married, all serving God—and four delightful grandchildren. **Aug. 26**

Pauline Gesare Okemwa is married to a pastor, and they have three grown children. She is a counselor by profession. She has earned a master of philosophy degree in public health, specializing in health promotion, and is currently pursuing a PhD in public health. She loves singing and listening to Christian music. She is grateful that God has blessed her with different talents and likes sharing her experiences to help other young women. She is a Kenyan from the western Kenya region (Kisii). **June 23, Nov. 26**

Monique Lombart De Oliveira is retired and lives in the United Kingdom. She is busy adapting *The Desire of Ages* into stories for children. She makes laminated religious bookmarks to insert in *Steps to Christ* books to give away. **Aug. 16**

Sharon Oster is a retired teacher assistant living in Evans, Colorado, United States of America, with her retired pastor husband. She enjoys automobile day trips in the nearby Rocky Mountains. She and her husband have three children and eight grandchildren. **Jan. 29, Aug. 8**

Hannele Ottschofski lives in Germany. She has written two books, *Das Hemd meines Vaters* (My father's shirt) and *Mit am Tisch* (Together at the table), and compiled several women's devotional books. She has four adult daughters and five grandchildren. **Aug. 12, Nov. 2**

Ofelia A. Pangan and her husband just came back from Hawaii, United States of America, where they ministered to the members of the Molokai and Lanai churches for a year and a half. They recently returned to California to be near their children and minister again to their grandchildren. **Jan. 20, Apr. 7**

Bonnie R. Parker resides in Yucaipa, California, United States of America, with her husband, Richard. She is a homemaker, former teacher, and office manager in her husband's dental office. She enjoys music, writing for her local church newsletter, and women's ministries. Her grown sons and their families, which includes six grandchildren, are a blessing. **Dec. 21**

Grace Paulson is working as a project manager for the South Pacific Division (Pacific) and lives in Cooranbong, Australia, with her family. She is interested in the agency (and voices) of biblical women. This interest is reflected in the thesis of her master of philosophy degree, which researched the contemporary rewriting of the Bible book of Esther in *Hadassah: One Night With the King*. Her research explored the portrayal of Esther, the main character. **Nov. 27**

Tricia (Wynn) Payne serves in the Lake Region Conference as the lead pastor of the Conant Gardens Seventh-day Adventist Church. She resides with her loving husband, Shawn, in the greater Detroit, Michigan, area, United States of America. **Jan. 13, Apr. 5**

Lori Peckham teaches English and communication at Union College in Lincoln, Nebraska, United States of America. She lives on a small lake with her husband, Kim, and teenage son, Reef. **July 15**

Premila Pedapudi is the administrative assistant for the Department of Women's Ministries at the General Conference of Seventh-day Adventists in Maryland, United States of America. She is married to Joseph Kelley and is mother to son, Praveen, and twin daughters, Serena and Selena (who are married to Samuel and Ebenesar)—all are a great support to her in her ministry. Her first grandson arrived in July 2019. She is passionate about women's ministries and loves to sing, read, teach, and preach. **Jan. 3, Jan. 4**

Kathy Pepper is a pastor's wife living in Pennsylvania, United States of America. She and her husband, Stewart, have a son, two daughters, a daughter-in-law, and a son-in-law as well as two lively and wonderful grandchildren. Her days are filled with babysitting the grandkids, working with her husband, and graphic designing, which she uses in their ministry. **Sept. 16, Dec. 11**

Sueli da Silva Pereira lives in Patos de Minas, Brazil, and works in the local city hall. She is married and has three children: Arthur, Eric, and Samuel. She likes to read, write, and study music. **Jan. 5, Apr. 9**

Sharon M. Pergerson is mother to two beautiful adult children who are her heart and joy. She is also an educator and writer who specializes in writing and developing Christ-centered resources. Her passion is always to bring out the richness, depth, and authenticity of the character of Christ in her writings. She lives in Texas, United States of America. **July 28, July 29**

Diane Pestes, author of *Prayer That Moves Mountains*, which was published by Pacific Press®, is an international speaker who resides in Oregon, United States of America. She is known for her commitment to Christ and her ability to memorize Scripture. She thinks exercise is relaxing and enjoys the grandeur of nature and traveling with her husband, Ron. **Apr. 17, July 11**

Margo Peterson writes from Eagan, Minnesota, United States of America. She is a special education teacher at an elementary school and also a tutor of reading and math. She has three children. She likes to speak of God's love to others by helping, listening, and praying. She enjoys spending time reading, traveling, walking, and being with her family. **Mar. 5, June 14**

Karen M. Phillips, writing from Omaha, Nebraska, United States of America, is happily married to her husband, John, and has four children and three grandchildren. Along with a full-time job as a human resources manager, she partners with John in their worldwide ministry, HeReturns. She is also a Bible teacher and the vice president of Communications for ASI Mid-America. Her passion is proclaiming the Lord's end-time message and being an instrument in saving souls. **Jan. 10, Apr. 12**

Prudence LaBeach Pollard, PhD, MPH, is the vice president for Research and Faculty Development, a professor of management, and the principal investigator for the Career Pathways Initiative at Oakwood University in Huntsville, Alabama, United States of America. She has authored the book *Raise a Leader (God's Way)* (available at AdventistBookCenter.com or as an e-book at adventist-ebooks.com). **Feb. 14**

Beatrice Tauber Prior, PsyD, is a clinical psychologist, author, speaker, and owner of Harborside Wellbeing in North Carolina, United States of America. She is a grateful mother of a delightful daughter and wonderful son. She is also a loving wife, sister, and friend. **Feb. 25, July 24**

Jessy Quilindo, originally from Seychelles, is currently the honorary Women's Ministries director of the Singapore Conference of Seventh-day Adventists. A clinical nurse by profession, she is studying counseling psychology to serve the women of her conference better. She is married to Steven, her husband of thirty years. They have two young-adult sons. She enjoys cooking, home decor, and gardening but finds her greatest reward in women's ministries. **July 10**

Katia Garcia Reinert, originally from Brazil, is an advanced practice family nurse practitioner practicing in Baltimore, Maryland, United States of America. She also serves as an associate director for the Health Ministries Department of the General Conference of Seventh-day Adventists. She enjoys spending time with her nephews and niece, bicycling, hiking, singing, and traveling the world on mission assignments. **Apr. 14**

Marli Elizete Ritter-Hein was born in the city of São Paulo, Brazil, married an Argentinean doctor more than forty years ago, and worked with him as a missionary in Nepal and now Paraguay. A mother of two young-adult sons, she is a teacher by profession, and she loves music that points to heaven. She also enjoys nature, flower arrangements, visiting family, interior decorating, and coordinating her church's music ministry. **Mar. 8**

Jenny Rivera lives and writes from Brisbane, Australia, where she is a registered nurse. She is an active member at the South Brisbane church, where she plays flute in the church orchestra, sings in the young-adult choir, and serves as a deaconess. She is also a proud auntie of six nieces and nephews. Every day she is overwhelmed at just how God blesses her life. She loves spending quality time with her family and friends, traveling, reading, and looking after her cockatiel, Luigi. **Nov. 1**

Taniesha K. Robertson-Brown, a contributor since 2013, is a teacher and author who writes from Pennsylvania, United States of America. She enjoys inspiring others through the written word and appreciates the support of her husband, Courtney, and the love of her children, Preston and Prescott. **Jan. 11, Apr. 4**

Charlotte (Swanson) Robinson has spent most of her life working and helping her husband raise three children. She has been published in *Our Little Friend, Primary Treasure, Guide,* and *Insight.* After living seventeen years with her parents near Ozark Academy, she moved to nearby Decatur, Arkansas, United States of America, when she married. She now lives on her late mother's property, where she lived as a child. **Oct. 7**

Terry Wilson Robinson lives in Hendersonville, North Carolina, United States of America, with her husband, Harry, who is an ordained minister. She enjoys working side by side with him in teaching Revelation Seminars. **Aug. 18**

Avis Mae Rodney writes from Guelph, Ontario, Canada. She is a retired justice of the peace who continues to work on a per diem basis. She is a mother and grandmother who enjoys gardening, writing, and her role as women's ministries leader for the Guelph Seventh-day Adventist Church. **Jan. 18, Apr. 10**

Dixil Lisbeth Rodriguez is an award-winning author, hospital chaplain, and writer living in California, United States of America, at the time of this writing. She holds two bachelor's degrees; a master's degree in English literature, with an emphasis in ethnic studies; a master of divinity degree, with a concentration in pastoral care and chaplaincy; and a doctorate in rhetoric, with concentrations in philosophy and linguistics. She works with humanitarian groups and participates in community projects. **Nov. 19**

Terry Roselmond-Moore lives in Dayton, Ohio, United States of America. She is a registered nurse and enjoys traveling, reading, and gardening. She is the mother of one daughter, Taryn. **Apr. 23**

Raylene McKenzie Ross is a labor and delivery nurse who lives in Jamaica and commutes to New Jersey, United States of America, for work. She is wife to Leroy Ross and mother to Zachary and Ricardo. As she writes this devotional, the world is in the middle of the COVID-19 pandemic, but she is able to work and is praying every day to be reunited with her family as soon as possible. **Oct. 20**

Robin Widmayer Sagel and her husband, David, live near Choctaw, Oklahoma, United States of America, and attend the Choctaw Seventh-day Adventist Church, where she is the Primary teacher. She works for the Midwest City Library. She loves reading, writing, baking, and spending time with her daughter Aprille's family, which includes her three beautiful granddaughters: McKenzie, Adelyn, and Keira. **Aug. 6**

Kollis Salmon-Fairweather resides in beautiful Central Florida, United States of America. She continues to enjoy Bible studies and witnessing. She plans to spend her remaining days working for the Master through outreach ministry. **Oct. 30**

Deborah Sanders lives in Alberta, Canada, with her husband, Ron, and her son, Sonny. In 1990, God blessed her with a successful writing and prayer outreach ministry—Dimensions of Love. In 2013, she selected the best stories and compiled a book of sacred memories titled *Saints-in-Training*, a book she hopes Sonny can use to continue his witness for Jesus. **Mar. 9, June 9**

Chipiliro Chonze Santhe is a new author writing from Malawi. A member of Lilongwe Central Seventh-day Adventist Church, Chipiliro is married to Richard and has a three-year-old daughter, Tinashe Gemma. A human resources professional working with UNICEF, she also loves to sing, listen to music, bake, and hike. **Nov. 10**

Christa White Schiffbauer lives in Florida, United States of America, with her husband, Dan. She has two adult children, Melissa and Michael. She has one cat and many fish. She loves to send cards of encouragement to people and enjoys scrapbooking and praising God in song. She has also recorded a CD of encouraging songs and hymns, titled *He Cares for You*. **July 12, Sept. 29**

Danijela Schubert lives in Sydney, Australia, where she works in the South Pacific Division, caring for women's ministries and women in pastoral ministry. Originally from Croatia, she lived, studied, and worked in France, the Philippines, Pakistan, Papua New Guinea, and Australia. She is happily married to Branimir. Together they have two grown sons. **Dec. 4**

Jennifer Jill Schwirzer, LPC, is a counselor and author residing in Orlando, Florida, United States of America, from where she directs Abide Counseling and runs a nonprofit ministry. She also hosts the television program *A Multitude of Counselors* on Three Angels Broadcasting Network. **May 24, July 4**

Shirley P. Scott is a woman who loves the Lord and the call He has on her life as a child of God, a wife, the mother of three amazing adult children, a grandmother of two beautiful princesses, a friend and confidant, a prayer intercessor, and a servant leader. She currently serves as the Southern Union Conference Women's Ministries director and the prayer coordinator for the South Central Conference. She has been married to Lionel, her husband and partner in ministry, for more than fifty-five years, and the couple resides in Huntsville, Alabama, United States of America. **June 28, Sept. 21**

Jodian Scott-Banton is a Jamaican currently residing in the Turks and Caicos Islands. She teaches at the Maranatha Academy. She is married to a very loving and supportive husband, David, and God has blessed them with two lovely daughters named Johanna and J'Lissa. **Nov. 7**

Omobonike Adeola Sessou is the Women's Ministries and Children's Ministries director at the West-Central Africa Division of Seventh-day Adventists in Abidjan, Côte d'Ivoire. She is married to Pastor Sessou, and they are blessed with three children. Her hobbies include teaching, counseling, making new friends, and visiting with people. **May 20, Aug. 3**

Victoria M. Shewbrooks lives and works in Bucks County, Pennsylvania, United States of America. She is an artist, illustrator, and photographer who shares God's love with others visually. She also enjoys keeping a journal of God's working in her life. **Aug. 11**

Bonita Joyner Shields currently serves as a general vice president for Ministries at the North American Division of the Seventh-day Adventist Church. She has worked for the church almost thirty-five years. A former associate pastor of the Spencerville Church in Silver Spring, Maryland, she enjoys reading, writing, Words With Friends, and culinary experimentation. She authored *Living in a Man's World: Lessons I've Learned (and Even Some I Haven't)*. She and her husband, Roy, have been married for almost thirty-seven years and live in Maryland, United States of America. **Dec. 18**

Sherry Taujale Shrestha and her husband, Prakash, live on a run-down acreage near Berrien Springs, Michigan, United States of America. They enjoy the farm critters and challenges their woodland home brings to them. Three grandsons are the light of their lives. **Aug. 15**

Esther Siceron-Reyna, MSW, lives in Massachusetts, United States of America, where she has her own mental health therapy practice. She attends the Nuevo Amanecer Seventh-day Adventist Church in Worcester, Massachusetts, and volunteers in both the Women's Ministries and Youth departments of her conference. An avid reader, she enjoys traveling, writing, singing, and serving the Lord. Her own ministry, God Doesn't Lie, mentors young people and helps churches organize conferences, workshops, and evangelistic campaigns. **Aug. 25, Nov. 12**

Rose Neff Sikora and her husband, Norman, live happily on their hobby farm in the beautiful mountains of North Carolina, United States of America. She is retired from a forty-five-year career as a registered nurse, and she volunteers at Park Ridge Health. She enjoys walking, writing, and helping others. She has one adult daughter, Julie, and three lovely grandchildren. She desires that her writing will bless others. **Oct. 14, Dec. 9**

Ella Louise Smith Simmons is a vice president at the General Conference of Seventh-day Adventist headquarters in Silver Spring, Maryland, United States of America. She is the first female to hold this position. A veteran educator, she has served as a provost, academic vice president, and professor in church and public sector universities. She is married to Nord, and they have two children, three grandchildren, and one great-grandson. **Sept. 26, Sept. 27**

Heather-Dawn Small is director of Women's Ministries at the General Conference of Seventh-day Adventists in Maryland, United States of America. She has been Children's Ministries and Women's Ministries director for the Caribbean Union Conference, located in Trinidad and Tobago. She is the wife of Pastor Joseph Small and the mother of Dalonne and Jerard. She loves air travel, reading, and scrapbooking. **Feb. 4, Sept. 1, Dec. 14**

Yvonne Curry Smallwood enjoys spending time with God, family, and friends along with reading, writing, and crocheting. When she is not writing, you can find her in a craft store purchasing yarn for the many crocheted items she creates and donates to local charities. Her articles and stories have appeared in several publications. **Sept. 14**

Debra Snyder was raised in Massachusetts but moved to Nebraska, United States of America, in 2012. She works as a medical biller and coder. Her greatest accomplishments are being a wife and mother. She enjoys writing and sharing the story of how God brought her together with her husband and how they came to Nebraska by God's providence. Both she and her husband are active in their local church and continue to watch for God's leading in their lives. **Aug. 22**

Jill Springer-Cato lives with her husband in the lovely Caribbean twin-island Republic of Trinidad and Tobago. She is the mother of two boys in their late teens. She is also a music minister who is totally involved in all aspects of church life, especially women's ministries, youth ministry, and communications. **Aug. 27**

Sylvia Sioux Stark lives in East Tennessee and is an artist who specializes in local scenes, landscapes, and flowers. She also tutors a special needs individual and loves feeding the wild critters that come to her door each evening for handouts. She has also been published in *Guide*. **July 14**

Lacey Stecker currently lives in Indiana, United States of America. She is studying communication at Union College in Lincoln, Nebraska. **July 13**

Ardis Dick Stenbakken edited these devotional books from her home in Colorado, United States of America, doing so after she retired as director of Women's Ministries at the General Conference of Seventh-day Adventists. She and her husband, Dick, love their two children and their spouses and four grandchildren. She is finding time once again to pursue some hobbies. **Jan. 28, Apr. 15, May 30**

Rita Kay Stevens is a church administrator's wife whose family recently moved to Olympia, Washington, United States of America. She has been working as a medical technologist in a hospital. Until their recent move from New Mexico, she was a liaison for Women's Ministries and sponsor for minister's wives in the Texico Conference for Seventh-day Adventists. She is the mother of two grown sons and is thankful for a daughter-in-law, grandson, and granddaughter. **Jan. 26, June 27**

Carolyn Rathbun Sutton is married to Jim and enjoys her role as a mother and grandmother. From Alabama, United States of America, where they live, she enjoyed editing this year's devotional book, the proceeds of which go to support higher education for women. She and Jim also serve as ambassadors for Adventist World Radio. Her interests include herb gardening, cooking, and digital ministry. **Feb. 22, June 15**

Evelyn Porteza Tabingo is a retired cardiac nurse living in Oceanside, California, United States of America. She and her husband, Henry, are from the Philippines and have served as missionaries to East Africa. She enjoys reading, writing, gardening, music, traveling, and spending time with family and her grandchildren. **Aug. 21, Nov. 4**

Arlene R. Taylor recently retired from health care after decades of working with Adventist Health facilities. Still living in the Napa Valley of Northern California, United States of America, she devotes her time and energy to brain-function research, writing, and speaking. **Mar. 13, June 16**

Edna Thomas Taylor is a conference Women's Ministries coordinator, former church women's ministry leader, and entrepreneur. She is the mother of Junia, Jamila, and Jamaal and the grandmother of Ammi, Najja, and Tyra. She writes from Tampa, Florida, United States of America. A musician, she also enjoys reading, writing, and working with our "legacies"—young women. **Dec. 23**

Rose Joseph Thomas, PhD, is the associate director for Elementary Education for the Southern Union of Seventh-day Adventists. She lives in the United States and is married to her best friend, Walden. She has two adult children: Samuel Joseph and Crystal Rose. She has a precious grandchild, Adrian, and her daughter-in-law, Rebekah, will give her a second grandchild soon. **Feb. 11, July 23**

Sharon M. Thomas is a retired public school teacher. She still enjoys working part time. Other interests include quilting, reading, walking, biking, and piano. She is always grateful for the omnipotent, omniscient, and omnipresent God of love whom we serve. **Dec. 13**

Stella Thomas is an administrative assistant at the General Conference of Seventh-day Adventists in Maryland, United States of America. She enjoys being with her grandson and twin granddaughters, and she has a passion to share God's love with the world. **May 18**

Bula Rose Haughton Thompson is a member of the Goshen Seventh-day Adventist Church in the West Jamaica Conference of Seventh-day Adventists. She has been married to Norman for twenty-one years. **Oct. 1**

Joey Norwood Tolbert lives in Ooltewah, Tennessee, United States of America, with her husband, Matthew, and their three-year-old daughter, Lela Joy. She works at Network 7 Media Center in Chattanooga and is an adjunct humanities teacher at Cleveland State Community College in Cleveland. She is a member of the musical group Message of Mercy and has also released three solo Christian music projects, which she coproduced with her husband. She enjoys being with her family, writing music, singing, and having tea time with her daughter. **Nov. 21**

Ella Tolliver has a PhD in education and is a retired college dean. She has authored one book, *Transformations*, and has published several articles. She lives in California with her husband of fifty-seven years. Together they have three adult children. She loves serving others, reading, traveling for pleasure and missionary service, and spending time with family and friends. **July 20**

Rebecca Turner belongs to several small groups and studies the Bible deeply. Her mission in life is encouraging her friends and family, particularly three tiny grandsons, to fall in love with Jesus. She is an editorial assistant at the General Conference Women's Ministries Department and lives with her husband, Charles, in Maryland, United States of America. **June 5, Dec. 24**

Ekele P. Ukegbu-Nwankwo, DMin, BCC, ND, is a Nigerian-born mother of four and a board-certified chaplain with a doctor of ministry degree in health care chaplaincy (Andrews University) and doctor of naturopathy (International Institute of Original Medicine in Virginia). She is trained in the counseling of singles, groups, and families. Her passion is to empower others for holistic, sustainable life transformation through the power of the Holy Spirit. Her newly published book, *Simple Solutions: A Trip Into Sustainable Well-Care*, is available on Amazon.com. She lives in Columbus, Ohio, United States of America. **Mar. 14, June 17**

Olga Valdivia is a published author and a passionate gardener who lives among the trees and birds surrounding a little house that is located in Idaho, United States of America. This is where she lives and makes a living with her husband. **July 21, Sept. 13**

Ellen Porteza Valenciano writes from Mugonero Adventist Hospital in Rwanda, where she works as a physician. She and her husband, Harville, have been missionaries to Zambia, South Sudan, and Kenya. She is actively involved in health and music ministries. She enjoys playing the piano and organ, traveling, and coin and stamp collecting. **Dec. 28**

Annette L. Vaughan is originally from Barbados. She currently resides in the Cayman Islands with her husband, Bentley. She recently retired from the teaching profession after a total of thirty-eight years of service in both countries. Among other hobbies, she enjoys traveling, writing, reading, and homemaking. She and her husband share their passion for music ministry with their local church in the Cayman Islands. **Nov. 18**

Donna J. Voth is retired and lives in Angwin, California, United States of America, with her husband, Al, and dog, Lola. She enjoys creative writing, travel, painting, and playing word games via computer with their daughter, Wendy, who lives in Lincoln, Nebraska. **Feb. 24, Aug. 24**

Cora A. Walker resides in Atlanta, Georgia, United States of America. She is a retired nurse, editor, and freelance writer. She enjoys reading, writing, sewing, swimming, classical music, traveling, and spending quality time with her family. **Feb. 5, May 15**

Diana L. Walters continues to work at the age of seventy-three with senior adults in a senior community, helping them remain active and involved. She and her husband also develop material to help people who are suffering from dementia to remember their faith. They live in Chattanooga, Tennessee, United States of America. **Nov. 15**

Anna May Radke Waters is a retired administrative assistant at Columbia Adventist Academy. She and her husband of sixty-six years enjoy living near their three daughters, four grandsons, and four great-grandchildren. They just wish the other members of the family were as close by. **Mar. 15, July 26**

Lyn Welk-Sandy lives in Adelaide, South Australia. She has worked as a grief counselor, spent many years as a pipe organist, and loves church music, choir work, and playing the hand chimes. She enjoys nature, photography, and caravanning around Outback Australia with her husband, Keith, and serving where needed. She is the mother of four, grandmother of nine, and great-grandmother of five. **Jan. 21, Apr. 13**

Avonda White-Krause is a wife, mother, grandmother, and great-grandmother to fifteen beloved offspring. She loves family, friends, going to church, reading, computers, gardening, and traveling. She is a retired special education teacher. **Oct. 28**

McKella O. Wiggins, from the land of many waters, Guyana, is a high school English teacher as well as a lay preacher. She enjoys reading, writing, spoken-word poetry, drama, and preaching, which she combines with her passion for youth ministry and evangelism to help inspire other young persons like herself to experience a closer relationship with Christ. **Oct. 26**

Charlotte Williams, a homemaker, lives with her husband in Belleville, Michigan, United States of America. She has four children and eight grandchildren. She loves to sew, sing in the choir, and work as a deaconess in her church. She also loves listening to Bible and missionary stories, traveling, and bowling. **Oct. 31**

Wendy Williams lives in Idaho, United States of America. Her favorite pastimes are writing, photography, traveling, hiking with her husband, and eating the world's supply of chocolate. **Mar. 21**

Rachel Williams-Smith is a wife, mother, writer, and speaker. She has a bachelor's degree in language arts, a master's degree in professional writing, and a doctorate in communication. She chairs the Department of Communication at Southern Adventist University in Collegedale, Tennessee, United States of America. She authored the book *Born Yesterday*, which was published by the Pacific Press® but to which she owns the copyright. **Jan. 17, Apr. 19**

Lynette Wilson recently retired from administrative assistant work in Bermuda. She is married to Trescot, and they have two adult children, Jerome (Lunette) and Amanda (Dwayne). They recently became grandparents. She is passionate about family and friends and loves shopping, baking, traveling, and sharing with strangers about the love of God. **Apr. 18**

Cyndi Woods is a mom of two and wife to a wonderful, God-fearing man for twenty years. She is a blogger and writer and has written articles for the Disability Network for over a year. Her heart is in ministry and leading others to know Jesus. She is also blind. Visit her on her blog at CyndiWoods.com. **Jan. 25**

Jeanne B. Woolsey currently serves as the church clerk at the Waynesville Seventh-day Adventist Church in Waynesville, Missouri, United States of America. Before retirement, her primary work was in health care positions. She enjoys writing. **July 30**

Siew Ghiang Yan is a Singaporean Seventh-day Adventist Christian who works as the in-home caregiver for her mother. The hawker center, an open-air complex where food is cooked and sold from vendor stalls, is her evangelism network. She loves to read and write and do indoor exercises. **May 16**